THE BRITISH

Avant-Garde Film

926 TO 1995

THE BRITISH
Avant-Garde Film
1926 TO 1995

AN ANTHOLOGY OF WRITINGS

EDITED BY MICHAEL O'PRAY

UNIVERSITY
UP *of* JL
LUTON PRESS

THE **ARTS COUNCIL** OF ENGLAND

British Library Cataloguing in Publication Data
A catalogue record for this page is available from the British Library

ISBN: 1 86020 004 4

Published by
John Libbey Media
Faculty of Humanities
University of Luton
75 Castle Street,
Luton, Bedfordshire LU1 3AJ
England

ACKNOWLEDGEMENTS

I would like to thank Will Bell at the Arts Council of England for not only his unstinting support but also for his patience and good humour in the face of a deadline-breaking editor. I'd also like to thank David Curtis for his support and his archives, Peter Gidal for his unfailing encouragement, and Nicky Hamlyn for talking through some of the issues with me. I'd also like to thank David Robinson for his permission to use Lindsay Anderson's essay on Jennings. Thanks also to Roma Gibson at the British Film Institute, Julia Knight and Professor Maggie Humm. As always I'm grateful to Judith Preece, Nikki Bainsfair and Jak Measure at the School of Art and Design Library, University of East London for their friendly assistance and hospitality. I'd also like to thank Gabrielle Dolan and Phil Davies for their friendship during the stitching together of the book, and Phil especially for his computer karma. My thanks to my colleague Gillian Elinor and her husband Jonathan for the generous use of their Welsh retreat. Most importantly, for my interest in and knowledge of British avant-garde film I must acknowledge a debt to AL Rees, Simon Field, Ian Christie, Malcolm Le Grice, Ray Durgnat, Tony Rayns, William Raban, Marilyn Halford, Jayne Parker, Chris Welsby, Archie Tait, Jayne Pilling, Paul Taylor, Tim Highsted, Michael Maziere, Moira Sweeney, Cordelia Swann and all the other British film-makers, writers, programmers and fanatics too innumerable to mention who I've had the pleasure and privilege to know over the years.
Of course, I must thank all the authors, notably the living, for their cooperation.
I'd like to thank the University of East London for sabbatical leave which made the editing of this book possible.
Finally I'd like to thank Sarah for her love.
Michael O'Pray
London, March 1996

Book designed by Design & Art, London
Printed in Hong Kong by Dah Hua Printing Press Co Ltd

Contents

Preface

In his introduction to the third ICA biennial of Independent Film and Video John Wyver contended that 'In the mid-1990s in Britain there is no independent film and video culture. None – at least of the kind so clearly identifiable 15 years ago, and none with any significant presence. No independent film avant-garde, no independent video art production'.[1] Attendant to that controversial statement is our concern that critical writing in this area is now all but non-existent. It is our contention that with its antecedent gone to ground it is not surprising that there is a paucity of contemporary writing on artists' film and video. Of course this hiatus mirrors the diversity of production practices and the shifting cultural arenas currently occupied by film and video-makers. However, criticism that was 'clearly identifiable 15 years ago' – through books, journals and magazines – failed to maintain its prominence and is now lost to a new generation of film and video artists. *The British Avant-Garde Film 1925 to 1995* – and its sister volume *Diverse Practices* (Ed. Julia Knight) – re-present that history, or rather present us with historical bricolage; critical fragments that give a sense of the concerns of the sectors. Our hope is that these two books – together with *A Directory of British Film and Video Artists* (Ed. David Curtis) – will highlight the rich practice of artists and independent production while outlining a history of critical thought that will help establish the foundations for new writing and comment.

This is the sixth volume in a series of books on the way the media has transformed our understanding of the arts. The first volume, *Picture This: media representations of visual art and artists* (Ed. Philip Hayward), deals with a range of topics, including the representation of visual art in popular cinema, and how broadcast television has revolutionised our relationship to culture and cultural practices. The second volume, *Culture, Technology and Creativity in the Late Twentieth Century* (Ed. Philip Hayward), addresses various aspects of how technology and culture inter-relate. Topics covered include digital technologies, computers and cyberspace. Volume three *Parallel Lines: media representations of dance* (Ed. Stephanie Jordan and Dave Allen) collects together accounts of how dance and dancing have been represented on public television in Britain. The book considers the role of dance in a variety of television practices including pop-videos, popular dance programmes, and experimental and contemporary dance. Volume four *Arts TV: A history of arts television in Britain* is the first general, systematic history of the various types or genres of arts programmes – review programmes, strand series, drama documentaries, artists profiles, etc. – and gives a chronological account of their evolution from 1936 to the 1990s. Volume five, *A Night in at the Opera: media representations of opera* (Ed. Jeremy Tambling), offers an arresting range of accounts of how the popular arts have represented this high art form written by specialists in music, media and popular culture. It raises issues which have bearings on the sociology of music and about its implications for television and video culture. Volume six *Diverse Practices* (Ed. Julia Knight) continues the interrogation of the creative use of film, video and broadcasting. Further planned volumes include a book on music and the media, volumes on drama and adapting the novel and a further volume on new technologies.

We would like to take this opportunity to thank Michael O'Pray for editing this book and the publishers John Libbey Media at the University of Luton who joined us in its production. We are grateful to them for the untiring and thoughtful way in which they have approached the task.

Finally, the views expressed herein are those of the authors and should not be taken as a statement of Arts Council of England policy.

Will Bell
Education Officer: Film, Video & Broadcasting
July 1996

1. John Wyver, *What you see Is What you Get,* London, ICA, 1995

MICHAEL O'PRAY

Introduction

DEFINITIONS

The cinema industry's ability to tell stories through moving images has meant that many aspects of our lives – politics, sex, religion, class, war, morality, fashion, death, birth and passion – have found their mesmeric projections on the 'silver screen'. But not all. The industrial 'dream machine' has never allowed 'unacceptable' subject-matter or 'innovative' form to jeopardise its prime concern – making money. But then its control has never been total. Since its beginnings, film has been used by artists, documentarists, scientists, advertisers, educators, politicians, pornographers and, before the arrival of video, by those wishing simply to preserve their own lives on film in 'home-movies'.

These by-ways of cinema remain largely unexplored. But artist's film which comprise the major part of avant-garde cinema, wherever it is found – in America, Germany, Austria, France, Spain, Italy, Holland, Poland – has often found its inspiration, its forms, its sensibility in these marginal practices. The animators Len Lye and Norman McLaren made work in the format of advertising; Jean Painlevé in France in the 1920s and 1930s made scientific film studies, famously of the sea-horse (*L'hippocampe* [1934]); Cavalcanti's classic innovative study of British coalmining *Coalface* (1935) was a documentary; Warhol's *Couch* (1964) enlists pornography to the cause of a fine art aesthetic and many of Derek Jarman's Super 8 films of the 1970s were 'home-movies'.

At its best then, avant-garde film has been a fluid, eclectic and irreverent concern. Unlike commercial cinema, the avant-garde does not have a stable mode of production, distribution or exhibition. It has been produced by the individual, by crews and by mechanical contraptions. It has been shown in galleries, backrooms, nightclubs, churches, discos and so on. It has been distributed by commercial companies, co-operatives, individuals and often not at all. Nor does it have any fixed aim – it has embraced and despised popularity; it has revelled in obscurity and obscurantism and at other times achieved an almost painful clarity. It has sought and scorned commercial success. It has built sets, made costumes, hired actors and it has simply pointed the camera outside the bedroom window and blindly shot. It has often lived dangerously, imaging sex, death, birth, politics and so forth in ways and at times that are traumatic. It is essentially a promiscuous activity.

In these ways it has more in common with the aspirations of the other visual arts in this century than with commercial cinema. In many of the major art movements of the century – cubism, dadaism, surrealism, pop art, conceptualism – there has been a similar impulse to steal and borrow from other forms, to explore environments outside that of the gallery, to confront and affront audiences. But, unlike avant-garde painting and sculpture, the film avant-garde never came to occupy the mainstream. It remained at the margins, forever overshadowed by the mainstream industry's products. But it is dangerous to identify avant-garde cinema too readily with the fine art camp, for it has borrowed from mainstream cinema itself as in the case of Joseph Cornell's *Rose Hobart* a film collage of B-movies and Andy Warhol's Factory 'superstar' system of the 1960s.

Though the presence of the term 'avant-garde' in this book's title will offend some of its contributors[1] and readers, especially in these postmodern times, I have resisted changing it; partly, by reason of the continued status of artists' film-making, and partly because no other notion covers quite the same broad range of film-making. The notion 'avant-garde', as the titles of many of the essays in the book testify, remained viable at least until the early 1980s at which point a pluralism took hold. If avant-gardism is associated with a 'high art' position, what some have seen as intrinsically elitist, then its 'death' in the late 1970s and early 1980s was part of a return to an engagement with popular culture, and an espousement of 'low art' so to speak. In this context the idea of the 'underground' re-emerged with its implication for an art that comes from 'below', from beneath the accepted culture, as opposed to leading from in front.

The parallel rise in the West of cinema and of modernism has meant that there has always been a relationship between the two quite different practices. In the early years of the century, cinema became rapidly a medium embedded in popular culture with a mass world-wide audience whilst modernist painting and sculpture addressed a small, if influential, minority. High art and low art seemed to follow their own paths largely indifferent to each other. Nevertheless from the beginning such artists as Picasso, Apollinaire, members of the Italian Futurist movement and others in the pre-First World War period were sympathetic to the 'vulgar' energy of this medium which seemed to express the modern – the city, cars, speed – as they also did.

There were two important moments of avant-gardism – one that stretched from the pre-World War I years of cubism and futurism to the late 1920s when the avant-gardes in the Soviet Union and Europe eventually collapsed; the other occurring from the 1960s to 1970s in North America and Europe. These were periods of intense activity and experimentation in sculpture, painting, photography, performance, theatre and film. Art movements proliferated – Cubism, Orphism, Constructivism, Futurism, Dada, Surrealism and later Conceptualism, Lettrisme, Minimalism, Super Realism, Fluxus, Land Art, Kinetic Art, Op Art and so on. In both periods, avant-garde ideas crossed over into the mainstream cinema. Oskar Fischinger's graphic animation turned up in Disney's cartoon studios; Eisenstein's montage and German expressionism surfaced in Hitchcock's early efforts and saturated the Hollywood Studios in the late 1930s and 40s; Dali designed for post-War Hitchcock and in the late 1960s Warhol's films influenced Hollywood's ideas of realism.

Like many art-historical categories, the notion of 'avant-garde film' is fuzzy at the edges. For example, the distinction between avant-garde cinema and art cinema is difficult to sustain. Eisenstein's films and German Expressionist cinema of the inter-war years are usually categorised as art cinema even though they enjoy avant-garde traits. Bunuel's *Un chien andalou* (1929) is usually incorporated into the avant-garde canon yet its maker was virulently opposed at the time to the avant-garde. Although this tells us probably more about surrealism than about the relationship between two kinds of cinema, yet it highlights the problem[2]. The historical and conceptual links between avant-garde and art cinema remain unexplored. In this book, I have not found a place for this debate except indirectly in Peter Wollen's essay on Jarman and Greenaway and in the discussions around the new black cinema of the 1980s. I have remained largely within the British avant-garde movement's own definition of itself.[3]

The avant-garde film tradition stems from two broad overlapping concerns. First, it is closely identified with modernism in painting, sculpture and music.[4] Many of its practitioners began their careers in art colleges where modernism had hegemony. Hence, film-makers were often responding through the medium of film to issues raised in painting and sculpture eg the autonomy and materiality of the art object, the contextualization of art and its process of

production and so forth. The second concern is encapsulated in the idea of the 'underground' with its connotations of social, sexual and political confrontation with established views, ideas and morals. In other words, for some film-makers in this area, subject-matter cannot be cut off from formal innovation. On the contrary, 'underground' film often perceives itself as emerging from sub-cultures to confront the dominant culture in a radical fashion. Formal innovation becomes a by-product of the 'underground' and not its *raison d'etre*.

A more institutional means of defining the area with respect to Britain is to see it as that mode of film-making centred around the London Film-makers' Co-operative (LFMC). To my knowledge, the LFMC is the only film organisation in which a film can be entirely made, screened and distributed within its walls. Its broad functions as workshop with printing, processing, equipment hire, and cinema and distribution library (one of the best in the world) makes it unique. After thirty years, it remains a place where young film-makers go to make and show their work. Its artisanal and artistic approach to cinema plus its ferociously democratic structure has helped it to survive wave after wave of factions and ideologies. Nearly all of the post-War film-makers and movements discussed in this volume have had connections, some strong others more tenuous, with the LFMC. Its comprehensive support for experimental film and its open-door attitude to film distribution are unique. Its monthly open screenings are almost perverse in cinema where closed doors are the norm. Its existence has been crucial in the history of avant-garde film-making in this country.

As I have already hinted, the category 'avant-garde' has been experienced as a burden by many film-makers. Like many artists they feel that art historians and critics are too quick and too keen to pigeon-hole them. Of course, this critical constriction is more likely felt once a practice has been established. At other times, such labels are useful in creating an identity for new views and attitudes. Interestingly Gidal, Le Grice, Curtis and Dwoskin never used the term 'avant-garde' in their book titles. Instead they incorporated other categories – 'structural film', 'abstract film', 'experimental film' and 'free cinema' respectively. Nevertheless, 'avant-garde' has stuck, one suspects largely as a means of distinguishing these films and their makers from other kinds of cinema.[5] For instance the term 'independent film' is associated mainly with a politically-based 'oppositional' practice. Whilst avant-garde film has not eschewed politics, it is distinct from this tradition. Sylvia Harvey[6], however, has traced the post-war British independent film movement back to the founding of the LFMC in 1966. The term 'experimental' is too much identified with a scientific approach to art current in the late 1960s and early 1970s.[7] The Arts Council committee[8] which has been responsible for much of the funding of this kind of film-making is called the

'Artists' Film and Video Committee' but this can suggest misleadingly that such films are made as a side-line by painters and sculptors[9] and not by artists dedicated to film. Other terms like 'underground film'[10] smacks too much of the American Beat-influenced aesthetic, adopted again in recent years by young film-makers connecting their films with a particular 'life-style'.

There have been very few books written on British avant-garde cinema. Malcolm Le Grice's book *Abstract Film and Beyond* (1977) is an account of formal film in Britain, with some reference to European film-makers like Kurt Kren and Peter Kulbelka and to American figures like Warhol and Michael Snow. It provides a historical contextualization of the British avant-garde between 1966 and 1975 around the concepts of duration and process. Peter Gidal's book *Structural Film Anthology* (1976) is a quite particular espousal of structural film, a species of Le Grice's formal film. For Le Grice, the formal is quite clearly the integrity of duration in film, while for Gidal structural film is more to do with filmic representation in relation to the spectator. Gidal's book celebrates British and European proponents of a film-making in which process and socio-political determinants operate to confront the cinematic institution. In the title of David Curtis's book *Experimental Cinema* (1971) we can witness a reflection of the times plus a desire to find a catch-all term that will encompass early 1920s abstract animation, Bunuel's surrealism, 1950s beat generation productions, 1950s and 1960s American West coast optical mysticism and hard-edged New York formalism. A broad history of the avant-garde, written as the British avant-garde was taking shape, it contains fairly limited references to the latter. Similarly, Steve Dwoskin's *Film Is... The International Free Cinema* published in 1975, was also a general history but told from a personal point of view. Peter Gidal's more recent publication *Materialist Film* brings his views up-to-date and covers British work of the 1980s from a younger generation of film-makers who had made their mark since the publication of his earlier book.

Dwoskin and Gidal arrived here independently from New York in the mid 1960s both immersed in the ideas and work of Andy Warhol and of the American avant-garde in painting, sculpture and music.[11] It is important to note that film-makers and not only influences came from abroad. In the early period, Len Lye arrived in England from New Zealand via Australia in 1926, keen to experience 1920s modernism at first hand. Similarly the Paris-based Alberto Cavalcanti was invited by John Grierson to join the GPO in 1934. Grierson, of course, was Scottish and when he set up the GPO Film Unit he had just returned from Chicago where he had studied communications media which had introduced him to the ideas of Walter Lippmann. Equally, the avant-garde film movement of the 1960s was primarily an international one, with the British centre in London, linking with those in

Germany, Austria, Holland, Italy, Yugoslavia, Poland and Hungary. Overshadowing this activity and acting as an ambivalent parental figure was America. New York was the unparalleled centre for post-war avant-garde art in the West displacing Paris's pre-war eminence. Much of the artistic energy, although by no means all, emanated from across the Atlantic in the mid-1960s. It was there that figures like Jonas Mekas, Paul Sharits, Andy Warhol[12] and others had inspired the setting up of the London Film-Makers' Co-operative in the mid 1960s. Interestingly, the most influential critic and historian of the British avant-garde in the 1970s was another American emigre, Deke Dusinberre.[13]

1920s AND 1930s

The early film avant-garde in this country appeared in the late 1920s and 1930s under the impact of international modernism. As early as 1926, the Bloomsbury group writer Virginia Woolf articulated a fascinating view of cinema that firmly identifies its potential in modernism.[14] She argues against popular cinema's easily attained realism too often propped up by literary ambitions. Her hints towards a cinema of abstract subjectivism in which indeterminate shapes could suggest emotions and fantasies, are astonishingly prescient:

> Anger is not merely rant and rhetoric, red faces and clenched fists. It is perhaps a
> black line wriggling upon a white sheet.[15]

Woolf's remark suggests a broader climate for the more 'abstract' film work of the 1930s found in Lye's GPO films and the writer Hilda Doolittle's (known as HD) lost film *Wingbeat* (1927). Given HD's known interest in Woolf's writings[16] she most likely read this essay when it was published in 1926.[17] Woolf's insights remain tantalisingly enigmatic reminiscent in ways of Walter Benjamin's stray remarks on cinema in the same period.[18]

The 1930s was an important period in film-making in this country. It witnessed the burgeoning documentary film movement and a political film-making strongly imbricated in the left-wing activity of the time. As we shall see, the film-makers and films comprising an avant-garde practice were dispersed among many different types of film practices, a point registered by Dusinberre who chose to describe an avant-garde 'attitude' as operating in this period, rather than a fully-fleshed practice as such.[19] For example, the animator Len Lye's[20] work was primarily in the form of advertisements for the GPO. Norman McLaren's[21] animation work embraced agit-prop, associated with the Scottish Communist Party, and also advertising work. On the other hand, the films involving H.D., Macpherson and others were

Berlin Horse – Malcolm LeGrice (1970)

privately funded and occupied an art-based avant-garde context. Humphrey Jennings worked for government agencies within the documentary framework until his early death on the Greek island of Poros in 1950.

The 1930s in Britain was a complex one in terms of developments in the visual and literary arts.[22] It also witnessed the British progressive intellectual class's involvement with film on an unparalleled scale. For example, the poet and literary critic William Empson referred to John Grierson's *Drifters* in his classic book *Some Versions of Pastoral*.[23] The young composer Benjamin Britten wrote music scores for Cavalcanti's *Coal Face* (1935) and Harry Watt's and Basil Wright's *Night Mail* (1936). The poet W. H. Auden wrote songs and poems for both these films. In 1936, the painter William Coldstream directed a GPO short *The Fairy of the Phone*. Some years earlier, in 1930, Kenneth Macpherson obtained the acting services of the famous Black American singer Paul Robeson for his experimental narrative film *Borderline* (1930).

The film experiments in the Soviet Union in the 1920s had a large impact as did other avant-garde work shown at the film societies in the late 1920s. The Soviet films influenced Grierson even if experimentalism for him was always at the dictate of social critique and communication. Through the auspices of the GPO Grierson was responsible for the outstanding films of the animators Len Lye and Norman McLaren during the 1930s, a body of the work which has entered the British avant-garde canon. Similarly, Grierson's invitation to Cavalcanti to join the GPO from Paris meant that educational films like *Coal Face* had innovatory qualities that lifted them into the domain of art. The film-maker Humphrey Jennings was never quite at home in the GPO. His relationship with Grierson was always strained. A painter and writer from an academic background at Cambridge where he was a contemporary and friend of the poet and critic William Empson, Jennings was also a committed surrealist, being a member of the organising committee of the Surrealist Exhibition held in London in 1935.

One of the key films of 1930s avant-garde was *Borderline*.[24] Long believed lost, it surfaced in the late 1970s. It was directed by Kenneth Macpherson, the writer Winifred Bryher and the poet HD[25] (under the name of Helga Dorn) who appeared in the film with Robeson, his wife Eslanda and Robert Herring. Macpherson made grand claims for the film – 'perhaps the only really "avant-garde" film ever made'. He was at the centre of the Pool group set up to make avant-garde work. Much of its small output is now lost. The involvement of the writers HD and Bryher is further evidence of the fascination of progressive intellectuals for film. As an experimental narrative film, *Borderline* interestingly balances the output of the 1930s period which in terms of innovation was dominated by social and political documentary, and animation. It is argued that the pressures of the 1930s in Britain were towards socialist pragmatics, thus providing the fertile grounds for documentary and commercially oriented animation. Perhaps more pertinent is the economics of the situation. It was Grierson's entrepreneurial and organisational qualities that sustained film-making in a climate of experimentation.

The 1930s saw the avant-garde film in all its guises slip virtually out of existence in this country (as it did elsewhere in Europe). The talents of the period were dispersed by other interests. The British avant-garde has a literary bias and HD and Bryher moved on to other things. The war too had its effects. Jennings, like others, joined the war effort by way of propaganda film. McLaren followed Grierson to Canada in 1941. Lye moved to America in 1944 to work for the March of Time newsreel series. Cavalcanti turned to directing feature films.

1950s

It was with the emergence of the Free Cinema movement in the 50s, with Jennings as one of the figures lauded by its leading spokesman Lindsay Anderson, that an alternative kind of cinema returned to British film culture. The Free Cinema[26] began as a Liberal-Left stance against popular cinema which Anderson and his associates believed ignored the poetry of film. Anderson cited Griffith, Renoir, de Sica, Ford and Jennings as the mark of cinema art[27].

Although Anderson together with 1930's documentarist Basil Wright helped to fund the American underground film-maker James Broughton's *The Pleasure Gardens* (1953)[28], the Free Cinema is not especially in the lineage of the 1930s avant-garde except in its espousal of Jennings. The latter's sensibility, formal dexterity and innovation placed him between the documentary movement of the 1930s and something much more radical in its use of memory, landscape and notions of Englishness. Gavin Lambert, Karel Reisz, Tony Richardson and Anderson formed the Free Cinema. The film journal *Sequence* between 1947 and 1952 served as a voicepiece for their ideas. Later between 1950 and 1958 *Sight and Sound* published many of their key articles especially Anderson's 'Stand Up! Stand Up!' (1956). Between 1956 and 1959, the group curated six programmes of films at the National Film Theatre which stand as much as anything for what they represented. The programmes included films by Georges Franju, Alain Tanner, Walerian Borowczyk, Francois Truffaut, Claude Chabrol, Michael Grigsby, Norman McLaren, Roman Polanski and of course work by

Anderson, Reisz, Richardson and Elizabeth Russell. At the core of the Free Cinema was the belief in film as personal expression and as a commentary on contemporary society. In many ways their aesthetic is closer to that of European art cinema than to any notion of avant-gardism. Nevertheless, in its early years when the members of the movement were making low-budget documentaries like Anderson's *O Dreamland* (1953) and Reisz's *We Are The Lambeth Boys* (1959), the Free Cinema did represent a connection between pre-War experimentation and that which was to erupt in the 1960s in Britain.

In many ways the poetic documentary films of Margaret Tait are close in spirit and time to the Free Cinema. More than Anderson and his associates who moved fairly quickly into mainstream cinema production, Tait bridges the 1950s and the avant-garde upsurge of the 1960s. She began making 16mm films in the early 1950s after studying at the Centro Sperimentale Cinematographia in Rome where she seems to have been influenced by the Neo-Realist movement with its emphasis on social cinema, poetics and authenticity. Her short poetic films found support eventually among the formal film-makers like Mike Leggett when she showed at the Bristol Independent film Festival in 1975. In the 1980s, as women's film burgeoned, she came even more to the centre. Her poetic documentary style connected with similar work by such artists as Tina Keane.[29]

THE 1960s

The 1960s heralded radical changes throughout British culture. Liberal reform in homosexuality, capital punishment, abortion and theatre censorship were to the fore. New ideas in pop music, photography, fashion and design signalled what was called the 'swinging sixties'. Radical art forms and politics permeated through drugs and notions of 'free love' formed what was known as the 'counter-culture'.[30] In reality there was much slippage between the two impulses. Controversy still surrounds histories of the decade[31]. Thatcher's comment in 1982 is typical of one view:

> We are reaping what was sown in the Sixties... fashionable theories and permissive claptrap set the scene for a society in which the old virtues of discipline and restraint were denigrated.[32]

Views on the period fluctuate according to ideologies. Even within its own radical art practices differences were quite strongly held. For example, performance artist Jeff Nuttall had fled by 1968 to the North of England (Bradford) to "get out of the psychedelic south where dope, vanity and commercial pop were already beginning to erode the so called alternative society"[33] The 'alternative society' was a rich amalgam of ideas, practices and institutions. It included photography, film, dance, theatre, poetry, painting, sculpture, happenings, events and performance. It was also enmeshed in various and often ambiguous ways with pop music, drugs and fashion. For some of the activists, it was this idea of a broad front in culture that signalled the possibility of revolutionary change. The students occupations in the late 1960s helped form the political framework of the 1970s. In the background was the American involvement in Vietnam. For example, one of Le Grice's earlier films was called *Spot the microdot or how to screw the CIA* (1969) and included found footage of what looked like American GI's in battle. With its air of paranoia, it perfectly reflects the mood of the period. The profound anti-Americanism of Le Grice and Gidal is not simply aesthetic but political, in reaction to America's military and cultural imperialism as it was experienced in the years between 1966 and 1975.

It must not be forgotten that there was a general air of experiment in the 1960s which extended to the film industry.[34] Nic Roeg and Donald Cammell made *Performance* in 1968. Released in 1970, its desultory narrative of sex, drugs and mysticism included an early example of the use of Super 8 footage. Made in the same year, Kubrick's *2001* was another film which attempted to stretch narrative conventions and to dazzle with its optical-printing special effects linked to drugs and quasi-mystical ideas. A third film released in 1968 was Lindsay Anderson's *If*, an allegory of institutions and a critique of the British class system through it fantasy-charged depiction of public-school life. Indebted to Jean Vigo, it testified to the radical impulses in British society in the late 1960s.

David Curtis' personal account of the early years of the British film avant-garde[35] traces its beginnings in Better Books among the poetry readings of "Ginsberg, Fainlight, Trocchi, Horowitz and the Liverpool poets"[36] and the performance work of Jeff Nuttall and DIAS (Destruction in Art Symposium) events of Gustav Metzger, Kurt Kren and John Latham. From what Curtis calls the 'chaos' of the period, the London Film-makers Co-operative was born in October 1966. Early film activity (or inspiration for such) was centred around Americans notably Steve Dwoskin, Harvey Matusow and Andy Meyer. Dwoskin remarks in 1967 that for 'financial reasons all my films have been shot in the States where CBS gave me the film. Over here, apart from the cost, Rank, for example, refused to process our stuff because we had no letterhead'.[37] In fact during the 1960s Dwoskin was one of the few avant-garde (or underground) film-makers active in Britain to be reviewed by the most influential art magazine of the period *Studio International*. Gidal (who appeared on the scene from America in July 1968) and Le Grice began writing for *Studio International* in

1971. The 1960s does not produce any real coverage of the new film-makers. This was for the reason that the avant-garde film movement only gathered real momentum from 1969 onward.

1970s

The early 1970s witnessed the consolidation of the British film avant-garde movement as formalist and political in stance. In 1972, the magazine *Art and Artists*[38] dedicated an issue to the new phenomenon, with pieces by Peter Gidal, Malcolm Le Grice, Annabel Nicolson and the critic Simon Field[39] In 1974 Gidal published the first version of his influential piece 'Definition and Theory of Structural/Materialist Film' in *Studio International*[40] which in the following year, published the most important collection of pieces on the movement. This special issue[41], edited by Richard Cork with help from Le Grice, contained not only Gidal's rework of his earlier Structural Materialist piece but also Peter Wollen's influential essay 'The Two Avant-Gardes'. Le Grice's and Gidal's determination to raise the profile of European avant-garde film was achieved here with the former writing on Kurt Kren. David Curtis provided a chronology of the movement. The German film-maker Birgit Hein covered her own country's and Austria's avant-garde film work. Peter Weibel also contributed an essay on the Austrian scene while Barbara Meter wrote on the Dutch film avant-garde, Dusinberre covered British 'expanded cinema', a practice which had been covered all too rarely.

The editorial to the 1975 *Studio International* was aimed at the critical neglect of the British avant-garde. Ironically, this is the year when Curtis remarks that more subsidy became available for the area. In the same year, the Co-op moved from Prince of Wales Crescent with a 'large grant for the re-equipment of its workshops'.[42] Le Grice also gathered a group around him in the early 1970s named Filmaktion; it comprised William Raban, Annabel Nicolson, Gill Eatherley, Mike Dunford, David Crosswaite and others. Their showing at Gallery House in 1973 revolved around expanded work that stressed the projection event and process. Curtis suggests that the earlier work of Le Grice with its 'high emotional and graphic content' owed much to the Arts Lab mixed-media aesthetic, which was pared down in the more film-dedicated and austere setting of the Robert Street co-op site.

If much has been made of the Le Grice/Gidal axis in the British Avant-Garde of the 1970s, it is instructive to see how different they were in many ways[43]. Unlike Le Grice who was deeply committed to expanded cinema, Gidal's own film trajectory, influenced by Warhol, rarely engaged with expanded work.[44] Its main concern was with the problems of representation of film qua film. Equally, their theoretical ideas are distinctive. Le Grice's formalism was firmly rooted in notions of duration[45]. From 1972 onwards, Gidal worked through his idea of a structural/materialist film-making which asserted itself against Abstract Expressionism and Minimalism in painting and music. It also had a complex notion of representation that was anti-illusionist and anti-formalist/abstract. Both artists shared the principle of anti-narrative and anti-illusion although Le Grice's multi-screen experiments like *After Manet: Le Dejeuner sur L'Herbe* (1975) and work like *Blackbird Descending* (1976/77) offered forms of narrative albeit subverted. On the other hand, Gidal's films in many ways were struggles with the image as representation, owing more to painting than any struggle with Hollywood suggested by Le Grice's *After Lumiere-l'arroseur arrose* (1974) a playful rework of an early classic film.

British avant-garde film also reflected traditional English art genres in the work of William Raban and Chris Welsby, who explored landscape using expanded-film techniques that had been evolved in Filmaktion. Welsby's use of devices for film-speed and structures developed into the use of documentation in *Estuary* (1980).[46] Both film makers explored multi-screen work that experimented with time-lapse in relation to the weather. Expanded work was celebrated at the Festival of Expanded Cinema at the ICA in 1976 when Curtis commented on the emergence of a young generation of expanded film-makers (what came to be called installation work) 'as if from nowhere', namely Steve Farrer, Nicky Hamlyn, Ron Haselden, Marilyn Halford, Rob Gawthrop, Lis Rhodes, Tony Hill, Guy Sherwin, Tony Sinden and Derek Jarman .[47]

At around the same time Laura Mulvey and Peter Wollen were embarking on film production with *Penthesilea* (1974) which Mulvey many years later linked with her feminist writings on the Amazon myth and Allen Jones's paintings.[48] Mulvey and Wollen were interested primarily in ideology itself, its specificity, whilst Gidal and Le Grice were largely concerned with the material mechanisms of the ideological apparatus. Subject-matter in Gidal seemed arbitrary and in Le Grice it was art historical. For Mulvey and Wollen the central issues were the structure of mythologizing, its position in mainstream culture and notions of modernism. In her article of 1978, Mulvey perusing the feminist film-making scene confirms its pluralism. She cites Annabel Nicolson's expanded work *Reel Time* (1973 using projector and sewing machine). While supportive of Nicolson's project, Mulvey asserts her own position in terms of the Vertov/Godard tradition argued by Wollen in 'The Two Avant-Gardes' and to that extent severs the possible links between the two strands. For Nicolson, there is a strong element of the feminist slogan 'the personal is political' and a

Fforest Bay – Chris Welsby (1973)

commitment to fine art practice with its strong tendency towards formal experimentation. The high art/low art distinction is most pervasive in these differences within the women's movement at this point.

Whatever the differences, the appearance of Lis Rhodes classic film *Light Reading* (1978) was an enormous breakthrough in terms of a feminist perspective within the British film avant-garde. It was in the late 1970s that women film-makers broke away from the London Film-makers' Co-op and set up their own organisation Circles in East London. The huge *Film as Film* exhibition at the Hayward in 1979 marked a publicly visible split in the avant-garde along gender lines when the women film-makers refused to show work and used the catalogue to make a statement of difference from what they saw as a male articulation of the history and practice of not only the avant-garde but importantly of women's film-making itself. Interestingly the dissenting women cited Maya Deren, Germaine Dulac and Alice Guy who represent by and large a poetic narrative cinema and not a formal one. Thus the political split was also an artistic one.

Rhodes's play with subjectivity through voice-over, narrativity (the visual site of a crime) and text in *Light Reading* remains a tour de force due not least for its energetic rhythms and razor-sharp editing. In a subtle way it is indebted to Deren for its poetics and sense of personal exploration whilst at the same time creating an ambiguous space for subjectivity. Rhodes had worked with Le Grice on his 'narrative' experiment *Blackbird Descending*, and perhaps shared in the general drift away from formal experimentation. At the same time Sally Potter broke through from the editing rooms of the London Film-makers Co-operative to art-house cinemas with her influential film *Thriller* (1979). This film's black and white deconstruction of an opera played with many elements – dance, opera, theory and acting itself. It was more aligned perhaps with Mulvey's own position at the time.[49] Mulvey and Wollen's *Riddles of the Sphinx* (1977) was an attempt by them to merge modernist forms with a narrative exploring feminism and psychoanalytical theory. A few years later, Wollen in interview sums up his feelings at the time:

> For me the problem is to find a way of working with narrative. There was a real
> polarisation in Britain around the issue of narrative – there was a strong anti-
> narrative streak in the Co-op and in the political documentary movement and as well
> as that a lot of the theory imported from France was strongly anti-narrative.[50]

Thus within a few years, the avant-garde and independent cinema of such as Potter and Mulvey/Wollen shared a significant development in visual language around women's issues.

What had been a relatively coherent movement to that point was never to be again.

There was an important attempt to bring together the disparate elements of 'independent' film-making into a loose alliance with the founding of the Independent Film-makers' Association (IFA) in 1974. Common ground was sought between avant-garde, women and political film-makers and their organisations in terms of a rejection of 'big capital', a determination to specify audiences and address them and a commitment to theory and critical practice.[51] The IFA's first conference in 1976 saw the conjoining, if somewhat uneasy, of such film-makers as Gidal, Wollen and political film groups like Cinema Action, Berwick Street Collective and Amber Films. In the long run, the interests of the independent film-makers gathered together in the IFA, especially around the latter's debates in the late 1970s on the new Channel 4, were not shared strongly by the avant-garde whose relationship to the new channel was a sceptical one. The political glue of the IFA was not enough it seems to keep the ferociously independent avant-garde within its fold.[52]

Towards the end of the decade there had been a number of shows dedicated to the British and European avant-garde film. In 1977 a large show was mounted at the Hayward Gallery[53] in London. Over fifty programmes were shown of international avant-garde film work. The programmes were wide-ranging including historical work and expanded film. The programme notes were written by a wide selection of film-makers, critics, historians and theorists including Tony Rayns, Simon Field, Ben Brewster, Annette Kuhn, Paul Marris, Ian Christie, Paul Overy and Paul Willemen. In the following year, Deke Dusinberre and David Curtis curated a touring exhibition *A Perspective on English Avant-Garde Film* for the Arts Council of Great Britain and British Council. It was inspired by the success of the Hayward Show and attempted to 'present and document the growing body of work which now constitutes a specifically English avant-garde tradition'[54]. In other words, it showcased the cinema that had developed in the ten years since the inception of the Film Co-op in 1966. The catalogue included writings by Gidal, Le Grice, Wollen, Dwoskin, Nicolson, Curtis and Dusinberre. Its nine programmes displayed the hegemony of the structural-formalist school with the exceptions of Stuart Brisley, David Larcher and Jeff Keen.

The explosion of what we can call avant-garde film-making, in the late 1970s and after, created different approaches and sensibilities. The political fragmentation in the post-1975 period, especially of the progressive Leftist culture of this country, led to film-making that was not simply governed by a formalist politics of film practice. The rise of the women's movement and the Black movement — to name the most cohesive programmes of action — led film-makers to explore different cultural reference points from those of the pioneers like Gidal and Le Grice.

1980s

The turn of the decade from the 1970s into the 1980s heralded profound sea changes in the avant-garde[55]. As already described, the impact of the women's movement in British culture in general, had its own effects on the avant-garde film community. The punk movement influenced British culture in ways that would only take hold in the 1980s. The climate – socially and politically – of the 1970s was in stark contrast to the 1960s. As Caroline Coon remarked recently:

> The years leading up to 1975 I remember as a time of dereliction, squatting, massed riot police protecting National Front rallies, IRA bombings, darkness and strange silence, like after an explosion … The Swinging Sixties party was over. People were reeling in shock.[56]

Similarly, a younger generation of film-makers made their mark by returning to an 'underground' notion of film practice and eschewing the formalist teachings of their teachers. Just as the make-shift no-budget world of punk music rejected the mega groups of the time, so the younger wave of film-makers rejected the relatively high production values of 16mm and returned to the no-budget 'amateur' gauge Super 8[57]. And similarly shock and outrage were back on the agenda.

The first wave of this movement was in the Super 8 films of Cerith Wyn Evans and John Maybury whose work was screened at the ICA in 1979 in a show dedicated to them and titled *A Certain Sensibility*. Wyn Evans was an ex-pupil of Gidal at the Royal College of Art, while Maybury came from a fine art department at North East London Polytechnic which was a hot bed of formalist avant-garde film under David Parsons. They were later joined by Michael Kostiff and Steve Chivers who was working at the Slade School of Art and had been taught by Le Grice and Raban at St Martins School of Art. Wyn Evans and Maybury were gay and their work showed the influence of Derek Jarman (Maybury as a young student had helped design *Jubilee*) who had been making Super 8 films throughout the 1970s in a style which was visually rich and sensuous and often used constructed and highly theatrical tableaux with (cassette taped) music over. This younger generation of film-makers was named the New Romantics.

Their response to the mainstream avant-garde was Oedipal. Since the 1960s many fine art departments had set up film and video units largely dominated by the ideas of the early movement and especially of their most vocal ideologists – Le Grice and Gidal. By the late

1970s and under the impact of the punk movement of 1976 and onward, students had different cultural references. Thatcher came into power in 1979 as the left drifted into a fatal period. The anarcho-Marxism of the first generation of film-makers was shunned by a generation cynical of political commitment or gestures of any sort. Aesthetically, the New Romantics responded more to the poetic imagism of Jack Smith, Ron Rice, Kenneth Anger, Maya Deren, Andy Warhol and Jean Cocteau than to any of the heroes of the formalist tradition. Their films were embedded in a subculture that embraced gay clubs, fashion and dance (the dancer Michael Clark appeared in some of the earlier films). Maybury stated that it was a return to an 'underground' film culture.

The work of the New Romantics and others inspired a huge interest in Super 8 film-making. A wave of Super 8 festivals flourished throughout Europe between 1984 and 1987. Leicester was the venue for the British International Super 8 Festivals. Organised by Lorraine Porter, they showed work from students, genuine amateurs and established film makers like Jarman and the German avant-gardist Klaus Wyborny. They were international with strong links with the younger super 8 film-makers in Germany, Holland and other mainly European countries. For a few years, the super 8 festivals seemed to replace the traditional avant-garde ones which had faded away in the late 1970s in this country. Based on a gauge and not on a particular kind of film-making, nevertheless their impulse was experimental dominated by a 'low budget' aesthetic (diaries, anarchic narratives). Their eclecticism and broad-mindedness was timely, drawing in artists who did not fit any traditional notion of film. Super 8 film was also much more tied to popular ideas – the use of pop music, street life and a general ransacking of film genres like gothic horror, road movies and so forth. The super 8 aesthetic began to have its effect on popular culture itself especially in television advertising.

Among film-makers like Nicky Hamlyn, Guy Sherwin, Michael Maziere and others who remained within the mainstream of the avant-garde more individual traits were coming to the fore. Hamlyn's work in the 1980s began to explore interiors in a way that was not formal but which expressed notions of subjectivity and sexuality even if in a quietest mode. Sherwin's ongoing *Short Film Series* (1976-) explored the sensuous nature of objects, light and the powers of film to create epiphanies of intense feeling. John Smith's films wittily played text and image against each other. Michael Maziere, who like Smith was an ex-student of Gidal, explored the material aspects of camera movement and framing but with exquisite colour and lighting effects.

The 1980s brought a new and fresh emphasis on social and sexual subversion and shock, far removed from formal experiment. The presence of often gay sexuality in the films of the New Romantics opened up the British avant-garde tradition, albeit in its new underground guise, to artifice, imagism and fantasy. This problematic space of sexuality was pushed forward by Jayne Parker whose film *I Dish* (1982) used narrative, Derenesque symbolism and sexuality in ways that developed even further Rhodes's earlier experiment.

The other major movement of the 1980s was that of the Black independent film-makers who almost singlehandedly raised the level of debate, dramatically posing questions of theory and of practice especially avant-garde film practice[58]. The two most influential film groups were the Sankofa Film and Video Collective and the Black Audio Film Collective. Interestingly, two of the major figures Kobena Mercer and Isaac Julien had been taught in Le Grice's film course at St Martins School of Art. It was with their work that a merging of avant-garde approaches with a political stance returned to British cinema.

Much debate has centred, justifiably, on the autonomy or otherwise of the black film movement and the problem of its being assimilated to a white modernist aesthetic and history. As in the gay and women's movement, the black movement's claim to an avant-garde position would rest on the reclaiming of an experience and history in filmic terms against mainstream ideologies and practices. As it was, avant-gardism was rejected by and large as a viable description of the position and strategies of these film-makers. Isaac Julien's *Territories* (1984) and Black Audio Film Collective's tape-slide *Signs of Empire* (1983) were key works in establishing a black experimental film-making practice in this country. The influence of British Black cinema was felt internationally, not only as a model for practice but also for its development of theoretical issues.

A form of internationalism was established at least at the level of influences, even if festivals were rare.[59] The international dimension of avant-garde work was largely sustained in the early 1980s by the Co-op's Distribution shows which showed the prior year's new work usually from all the major film countries and often including the recent work of Brakhage, Snow and others from abroad. In the mid 1980s the London Film Festival (under Derek Malcolm at the time) opened up to other venues and types of cinema including the Co-op and the ICA. In later years, the avant-garde programmes were actually shown at the National Film Theatre alongside the main programme. Part of the reason for the collapse of avant-garde film festivals no doubt was financial but also the notion of the experimental and avant-garde became so broad that such a festival would have demanded the articulation of a concept that seemed less and less possible to grasp. For example, Derek Jarman's own experimentalism in such films as *Imagining October* (1984), *The Angelic Conversation*

(1985) *The Last of England* (1987) and *The Garden* (1990) tested categorisation to the limits. These films fused politics and cultural critique with forms taken from avant-garde film as well as from art cinema. Their eclecticism fulfilled the postmodernist dream but in their political and sexual humanism they seemed old-fashioned. They were the films of someone from 1960's culture who by knight's moves had managed to escape pigeon-holing.

Other figures emerged in the 1980s who while associated with the London Film-maker's Co-operative worked in ways that engaged with the documentary tradition. Patrick Keiller was outstanding in this area and its solitary figure for some years. His incorporation of the British documentary tradition of Jennings, and the British B movies of the 50s with a brilliant surrealist narrative wit could be aligned with Julien, Maybury et al in their cultural critique. Like Wyn Evans, Keiller had also been taught by Gidal at the Royal College of Art. It is one of the great successes of the post 68 period that the efforts of Le Grice and others in setting up film and video departments within fine art courses at so many leading art colleges came to bear such enormous fruit in the 1980s. This turnover of film and video artists from the art colleges was supported by the Art Council of Great Britain's Film and Video Artists' Subcommittee which had been set up in 1977 and had funded production, exhibition and distributive efforts of film artists and their support systems eg festivals and distribution organisations.

Channel Four began broadcasting in 1982 with a brief to support innovative work. Rod Stoneman, a supporter of the avant-garde and especially its association with the IFA in the mid-1970s, in his role as a commissioning editor became another source of both funding and exhibition. The Channel also produced documentaries on various experimental film-makers (Jeff Keen, Margaret Tait and Malcolm Le Grice). The dream of bigger and broader audiences running into hundreds of thousands became a reality but scepticism and suspicion of the strictures of broadcast television were felt by some in the experimental community. In later years the BBC also joined in (through the Arts Council) by commissioning short pieces for BBC TV's Late Show. The British Film Institute Production Division also entered the fray with their 'New Director's' scheme which financed Patrick Keiller, Jayne Parker and Anna Thew. Many of these schemes revealed fairly close working relationships between the various institutions, with Channel Four negotiating access to the products of the Arts Council and BFI for broadcast. Channel Four often supplied part of the production funds for schemes like the Arts Council's 'Experimenta'.

If film flourished comparatively in the broadcast area, film magazines faded away during the same period. *Undercut* was set up in 1980 under the umbrella of the London Film-maker's

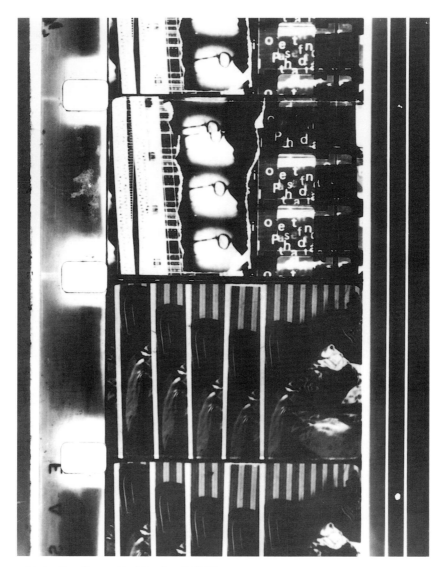

Light Reading – Lis Rhodes (1978)

Co-op although it was funded separately by the Arts Council. Its coverage was fairly broad — the gay film *Taxi Zum Klo* and Duras's *India Song* were reviewed alongside Le Grice and Gidal. *Framework* was also being regularly published in the early 1980s although it turned more and more towards Third World Cinema eventually becoming for a brief period a platform for the burgeoning British black film movement. *Screen* carried on as before with its interest in the avant-garde waning after the early 1980s. It did offer two key issues on the black film theorists and film-makers in the mid to late 1980s. By the end of the 1980s, *Undercut* and *Framework* had both ceased to publish faced with distribution problems, rising print costs and what seemed a lack of interest in the theoretical and critical aspects of film.

Two major shows of avant-garde film (and importantly video) work were organised in the mid 1980s. 'The New Pluralism' (curated by Tina Keane and myself) at the Tate Gallery in 1985 and 'The Elusive Sign: British Avant-Garde Film and Video 1977-1987' organised by the Arts Council of Great Britain and The British Council in 1987. It was curated by Tamara Krikorian, Catherine Lacey and myself and was conceived as a successor to the Perspectives touring show of 1978. Video art was included in both shows even if there was some awkwardness about these two quite distinctive traditions being mixed together. In retrospect, not enough emphasis was given to the difference between the two media's institutions, practices, discourses and histories. Although there was much more slippage in the 1980s between these two areas especially as film-makers under economic pressure and the presence of Channel Four showed film work on video and sometimes used the medium itself even if the aesthetic remained filmic. Scratch artists had absorbed film into their found-footage montages and some like George Barber had even explored film as narrative using video technology.

In the same period, there was an enormous growth in animation. Again the old barriers between avant-garde experimentation and an art cinema-like aesthetic were torn down. The relationship between animation and the commercial sector had historically been fairly strong. Len Lye's own practice at the GPO was not forgotten by animators working on music promos or television adverts. The arrival of the pop video, the rise in sophistication of television advertising which used many different kinds of animation, the explosion of special effects in mainstream cinema and perhaps the burgeoning computer area which gradually infiltrated the population at large could all be cited as general phenomena which created a climate of interest. In the area of experiment and innovation, animation seemed to respond to a desire for fantasy and a social critique which was not lodged in realism. The work of the Czech animator Jan Svankmajer was one of the great discoveries of the decade[60]. In his work surrealism, postmodern collage and political allegory went hand in hand, inspiring many film students. The films of the Brothers Quay working in this country, used similar devices to explore the darker aspects of mythology and an aesthetics of interior nightmares that had much resonance in the Thatcherite years. Others like Joanne Woodward, Simon Pummell, Vera Neubauer, Kayla Parker and David Anderson brought an imaginative energy to the experimental area and found an audience willing to take animation seriously. Especially interesting is the preponderance of women working in animation,[61] compared with other areas of film-making.

CONCLUSION

So this book of collected pieces witnesses many different ideas of avant-gardism or experimentalism. As one would expect, the films themselves and their makers were often sceptical, indifferent or outraged by these attempts to understand their work critically using such categories. Their work often tested the very concepts and ideas that quite quickly, even within the avant-garde, became rigid and orthodox. There is a clear sense of a series of usurpations, of palace coups, of reversals, leapfrogs, insolent confrontations between generations, groups and so on. Whether we decide to call these avant-garde, underground movements or whatever is in the end perhaps unimportant. Perhaps what remains most important is the process of trying to understand this history – its film works, its film-makers, its institutions and practices and its writings.

Research into British cinema has burgeoned over the past decade.[62] Hopefully, the present volume contributes to the picture slowly being assembled of that cinema. The anthology, by its nature, is not comprehensive, nor is it impartial. Much material could not be included either because of the restrictions of space, or because it was not appropriate, being perhaps too much tied to its time. The anthology has also resisted any serious attempt to cover the films themselves. There are too many and one of the aims was to provide some of the theories, polemics, aesthetics and histories and critical overviews of the tradition. The anthology is hopefully the starting point for further research and writings on the history of what can be called the British film avant-garde.

NOTES

1   See Peter Wollen's essay 'The Two Avant-Gardes' and notably, his more recent introductory essay in *Arrows of Desire: The Second ICA Biennial of Independent Film & Video*, Catalogue, ICA, London, 1992.

2   Nowadays these seem like antique arguments and debates to be left in the past where they belong. In the New Cinema that evolved around Jonas Mekas's magazine *Film Culture* in the early 1960s, John Cassavettes *Shadows* and films by the Beat generation were in many ways more like art-cinema in their aims and sensibility than was the work of Brakhage, Conner and Warhol.

3   Where film experimentation is concerned discussion of work like Roeg's *Performance*, Anderson's *If* and even Kubrick's *2001* would be necessary, but such an exploration of British cinema demands another book.

4   See Peter Wollen's recent essay on the link between painting and cinema especially in relation to R.B. Kitaj 'The Western and the Bather' *Sight and Sound* 'Art into Film' Supplement vol 4 no 7 July 1994.

5   For a discussion of the notion of 'avant-garde film' see John Hanhardt's 'The Medium Viewed: The American Avant-Garde Film' in *A History of the American Avant-Garde Cinema*, Catalogue, American Federation of Arts, New York, 1976 pp20-31 esp. David Curtis grapples with the notion in his essay 'The Artists Film/Avant Garde Film' for *Art inglesi oggi 1960-1976*, Catalogue British Council/Commune di Milano, Milan, 1976.

6   See Simon Blanchard & Sylvia Harvey 'The Post-War Independent Cinema – Structure and Organisation' in *British Cinema History* eds James Curran and Vincent Porter, Weidenfeld & Nicolson, London, 1983; also Sylvia Harvey 'The "Other Cinema" in Britain: Unfinished business in oppositional and independent film 1929-1984' in *All Our Yesterdays: 90 Years of British Cinema* ed Charles Barr, British Film Institute, London, 1986.

7   See for example Stephen Bann's *Experimental Painting* and David Curtis's *Experimental Film*.

8   Set up in 1972.

9   Barry Flanagan, Richard Long, Gilbert & George are among the British artists who made films in this period.

10 For example, Sitney's classic book *Visionary Film* on the American tradition quite justifiably, given its perameters, used the term 'avant-garde' in its subtitle, whilst Sheldon Renan's book which largely covered the 50s and early 1960s was titled *Underground Cinema*, again justifiably given its largely American bias. Le Grice used the notion of 'abstract' for the title of his book and Gidal has used 'Structural' and more recently 'Materialist' to denote quite specific aesthetic positions in this kind of film-making. The difficulty of finding an uncontroversial name for this

practice speaks volumes for its problems of definition. It should not of course be seen as necessarily a bad thing at all.

11 See *Structural Film Anthology* ed Peter Gidal, BFI, London, 1977.

12 See David Curtis 'A Tale of Two Co-ops' in *To Free the Cinema: Jonas Mekas & the New York Underground* ed David E James, Princeton University Press, Oxford, 1992.

13 But any art historical recovery of that period must now acknowledge a particular British tradition of radical art that came out of a home-grown Pop Art of the 1950s. For an account of this tradition which sadly neglects experimental film see *The Sixties Art Scene in London* David Mellor Barbican Art Gallery and Phaidon, London, 1993.

14 Virginia Woolf 'The Cinema' in *The Crowded Dance of Modern Life*, Selected Essays Volume 2, Penguin, 1993. On Woolf and modernism see Peter Wollen's 'Wild Hearts' *London Review of Books*, vol 17 no 7, 6th April 1995, pp28-31 and Ian Christie 'Has the Cinema a Career' *Times Literary Supplement* no 4833, November 17 1995.

15 Woolf ibid p 57.

16 See Shari Benstock *Women of the Left Bank Paris, 1900-1940*, Virago, 1987 pp318-320.

17 Woolf's essay was published in *Nation and Athenaeum* 3rd July 1926.

18 On the connection between Woolf and Benjamin see Rachel Bowlby's introduction to Woolf's *The Crowded Dance of Modern Life* op cit ppxxii-xxiii.

19 Deke Dusinberre 'The Avant-Garde Attitude in the Thirties' *British Cinema: Traditions of Independence* ed Don Macpherson, British Film Institute, 1980.

20 See *Len Lye* Catalogue, ed David Curtis, Animation Festival, Watershed, Bristol, 1987.

21 See *Norman McLaren* ed Lyndsay Gordon, Scottish Arts Council, 1977.

22 See *The Last Modern: A Life of Herbert Read*, James King, Weidenfeld & Nicolson, London, 1990.

23 See William Empson *Some Versions of Pastoral*, Chatto & Windus, 1935 pp8-9. The English aesthete Adrian Stokes refers to American documentary film-maker Robert Flaherty's 'Tabu' in *Tonight the Ballet* Faber and Faber, 1934.

24 On *Borderline* and HD's involvement especially see Rachel Blau Duplessis *H.D. The Career of That Struggle*, Harvester Press, Brighton,, 1986 pp56-59.

25 Writer Hilda Doolittle who also wrote on film for *Close Up* magazine.

26 On the Free Cinema see Alan Lovell's chapter in Alan Lovell & Jim Hillier *Studies in Documentary* Secker & Warburg, London 1972 pp133-172.

27 See Lindsay Anderson 'Stand up! Stand up!' *Sight and Sound* vol 26 no 2 Autumn 1956 pp63-9 and also his 'Get out and push!' in *Declaration* ed

Tom Maschler, MacGibbon & Kee, London, 1957.

28 See P. Adams Sitney op cit p86

29 Tina Keane filmed *Shadow of a Journey* in 1976 but it was only released in 1980 and reviewed by Peter Wollen and Tam Giles in *Undercut* no 1 March-April 1981.

30 Histories, often anecdotal, abound. For a sympathetic account see Robert Hewison's *Too Much Art and Society in the Sixties 1960-1975* Methuen 1986.

31 See Hewison ibid; Christopher Booker *The Neophiliacs: A Study of the Revolution in English Life in the Fifties and Sixties*, Collins, London, 1969; Arthur Marwick *Culture in Britain since 1945*, Blackwell, Oxford, 1991; Derek Jarman *Dancing Ledge*, Quartet, London, 1984.

32 Quoted in Marwick op cit p73

33 *Performance Art: Memoirs*, vol 1 Jeff Nuttall, John Calder, London, 1979 p72

34 See my essay 'The British Avant-Garde and Art Cinema from the 1970s to the 1990s' in *Dissolving Views: Key Issues in British Cinema* ed Andrew Higson, Cassell, forthcoming, 1996; and Andrew Higson 'A diversity of film practices: renewing British cinema in the 1970s' in Bart Moore-Gilbert ed *The Arts in the 1970s: Cultural Closure?* Routledge, London 1994.

35 David Curtis 'English Avant-Garde Film: An Early Chronology' *A Perspective on English Avant-Garde Film*, Arts Council of Great Britain/British Council Catalogue, 1978 pp9-18

36 ibid p9

37 Quoted in Kevin Gough-Yates 'A Underground move trip' *Studio International* November 1967 vol 174 no 894 p185

38 *Art and Artists* December 1972 vol 7 no 9 issue no 81.

39 Field had been writing for the magazine for some years although largely on artists like Michael Snow, Meredith Monk, Warhol. His main and almost only piece on British work was on David Larcher's *Mare's Tail*. He eventually established the film magazine *Afterimage*.

40 *Studio International* February 1974 vol 187 no 963

41 *Studio International* November/December 1975 vol 190 no 978

42 *Perspective* op cit p18

43 On some theoretical differences see my 'Framing Snow' *Afterimage* no 11 Winter 1982/3

44 Gidal's book on Warhol was published in 1971. *Andy Warhol: Films and Painting* Studio Vista 1971, reprinted by Da Capo Press 1991.

45 See my 'framing' Snow in Afterimage or sit for a discussion of Gidal, Le Grice's and Heath's views on Michael Snow encapsulating different brands of 'structuralism' at work in the 1970s

46 See *Chris Welsby Films/Photographs/Writings* ed David Curtis, Arts

Council of Great Britain, London, ud

47 Reviewed by Curtis in *Studio International* March/April 1976 vol 191 no 980 pp209-212.

48 Laura Mulvey *Visual and Other Pleasures* Macmillan, London, 1989 pix

49 I remember a screening of this film at the LFMC shortly after its release after which Mulvey held a seminar which included several members of the *Undercut* editorial collective.

50 'Crystal Gazing: an interview with Laura Mulvey and Peter Wollen' *Framework* issue 19 1982 p19.

51 See Harvey op cit pp237-43.

52 The relationship between the avant-garde and its organisation the LFMC and the IFA in this period remains to be unravelled.

53 *Perspectives on British Avant-Garde Film*, Hayward Gallery, London, March/April 1977.

54 Deke Dusinberre's introduction to *A Perspective on English Avant-Garde Film* Arts Council of Great Britain/British Council, London, 1978 p7

55 For a snapshot view of the British film avant-garde in the early 1980s see my article 'In the Trenches' *Undercut* no 10/11 Winter 1983.

56 Caroline Coon 'The Summer of Hate' *Independent on Sunday* Review 6th August 1995, p16.

57 See Nicky Hamlyn 'Recent English Super 8 at B2 Gallery' *Undercut* nos 10/11 Winter 1983.

58 See *Screen* vol 29 no 4 Autumn especially Introduction by Isaac Julien and Kobena Mercer; Coco Fusco 'Fantasies of Oppositionality – Reflections on Recent Conferences in Boston and New York'; Judith Williamson 'Two Kinds of Otherness – Black Film and the Avant-Garde'; *Black Film British Cinema* ICA Documents 7, London 1988; *Undercut* No 17 on Cultural Identities Spring 1988.

59 The animation festivals regularly incorporated such animators as Fischinger, Lye, Breer, Svankmajer, Norstein, Brothers Quay and so forth under the direction of Irene Kotlarz and through the writings and curatorial efforts of Jayne Pilling at the BFI, and Keith Griffith's production company Koninck.

60 On Svankmajer see *Dark Alchemy: The Films of Jan Svankmajer*, ed Peter Hames, Flicks Books, 1995.

61 See Jayne Pilling ed *Women and Animation: A Compendium* British Film Institute, London, 1992.

62 For example, *British Cinema History* eds James Curran & Vincent Porter, Weidenfeld & Nicolson, 1983; *All Our Yesterdays: 90 Years of British Cinema* ed Charles Barr, British Film Institute, 1986; *Realism and Tinsel Cinema and Society in Britain 1939-48* Robert Murphy, Routledge, 1989; *Dissolving Views: Key Issues in British Cinema* ed Andrew Higson, Cassell, 1996.

October – Eisenstein

1920s and 1930s

The Cinema

First Published in *Arts*, June 1926. This
version published in *The Captain's Deathbed
and Other Essays* Virginia Woolf, 1950

People say that the savage no longer exists in us, that we are at the fag-end of civilization, that everything has been said already, and that it is too late to be ambitious. But these philosophers have presumably forgotten the movies. They have never seen the savages of the twentieth century watching the pictures. They have never sat themselves in front of the screen and thought how, for all the clothes on their backs and the carpets at their feet, no great distance separates them from those bright-eyed, naked men who knocked two bars of iron together and heard in that clangour a foretaste of the music of Mozart.

The bars in this case, of course, are so highly wrought and so covered over with accretions of alien matter that it is extremely difficult to hear anything distinctly. All is hubble-bubble, swarm, and chaos. We are peering over the edge of a cauldron in which fragments of all shapes and savours seem to simmer; now and again some vast form heaves itself up, and seems about to haul itself out of chaos. Yet, at first sight, the art of the cinema seems simple, even stupid. There is the King shaking hands with a football team; there is Sir Thomas Lipton's yacht; there is Jack Horner winning the Grand National. The eye licks it all up instantaneously, and the brain, agreeably titillated, settles down to watch things happening without bestirring itself to think. For the ordinary eye, the English unaesthetic eye, is a simple mechanism, which takes care that the body does not fall down coal-holes, provides the brain with toys and sweetmeats to keep it quiet, and can be trusted to go on behaving like a competent nursemaid until the brain comes to the conclusion that it is time to wake up. What is its surprise, then, to be roused suddenly in the midst of its agreeable somnolence and asked for help? The eye is in difficulties. The eye wants help. The eye says to the brain, 'Something is happening which I do not in the least understand. You are needed.' Together they look at the King, the boat, the horse, and the brain sees at once that they have taken on a quality which does not belong to the simple photograph of real life. They have become not more beautiful, in the sense in which pictures are beautiful, but shall we call it (our vocabulary is miserably insufficient) more real, or real with a different reality from that which we perceive in daily life? We behold them as they are when we are not there. We see life as it is when we have no part in it. As we gaze we seem to be removed from the pettiness of actual existence. The horse will not knock us down. The King will not grasp our hands. The wave will not wet our feet. From this point of vantage, as we watch the antics of our kind, we have time to feel pity and amusement, to generalize, to endow one man with the attributes of the race. Watching the boat sail and the wave break, we have time to open our minds wide to beauty and register on top of it the queer sensation – this beauty will continue, and this beauty will flourish whether we behold it or not. Further, all this happened ten years ago, we are told. We are beholding a world which has gone beneath the waves. Brides are emerging from the abbey – they are now mothers; ushers are ardent – they are now silent; mothers are tearful; guests are joyful; this has been won and that has been lost, and it is over and done with. The war sprung its chasm at the feet of all this innocence and ignorance, but it was thus that we danced and pirouetted, toiled and desired, thus that the sun shone and the clouds scudded up to the very end.

But the picture-makers seem dissatisfied with such obvious sources of interest as the passage of time and the suggestiveness of reality. They despise the flight of gulls, ships on the Thames, the Prince of Wales, the Mile End Road, Piccadilly Circus. They want to be improving, altering, making an art of their own – naturally, for so much seems to be within their scope. So many arts seemed to stand by ready to offer their help. For example, there was literature. All the famous novels of the world, with their well-known characters, and their famous scenes, only asked, it seemed, to be put on the films. What could be easier and simpler? The cinema fell upon its prey with immense rapacity, and to this moment largely subsists upon the body of its unfortunate victim. But the results are disastrous to both. The alliance is unnatural. Eye and brain are torn asunder ruthlessly as they try vainly to work in couples. The eye says: 'Here is Anna Karenina.' A voluptuous lady in black velvet wearing pearls comes before us. But the brain says: 'That is no more Anna Karenina than it is Queen Victoria.' For the brain knows Anna almost entirely by the inside of her mind – her charm, her passion, her despair. All the emphasis is laid by the cinema upon her teeth, her pearls, and her velvet. Then 'Anna falls in love with Vronsky' – that is to say, the lady in black velvet falls into the arms of a gentleman in uniform, and they kiss with enormous succulence, great deliberation, and infinite gesticulation on a sofa in an extremely well-appointed library, while a gardener incidentally mows the lawn. So we lurch and lumber through the most famous novels of the world. So we spell them out in words of one syllable written, too, in the scrawl of an illiterate schoolboy. A kiss is love. A broken cup is jealousy. A grin is happiness. Death is a hearse. None of these things has the least connection with the novel that Tolstoy wrote, and it is only when we give up trying to connect the pictures with the book that we guess from some accidental scene – like the gardener mowing the lawn – what the cinema might do if it were left to its own devices.

But what, then, are its devices? If it ceased to be a parasite, how would it walk erect? At present it is only from hints that one can frame any conjecture. For instance, at a performance of Dr Caligari the other day, a shadow shaped like a tadpole suddenly appeared at one corner of the screen. It swelled to an immense size, quivered, bulged, and sank back again into nonentity. For a moment it seemed to embody some monstrous, diseased imagination of the lunatic's brain. For a moment it seemed as if thought could be conveyed by shape more effectively than by words. The monstrous, quivering tadpole seemed to be fear itself, and not the statement, 'I am afraid.' In fact, the shadow was accidental, and the effect unintentional. But if a shadow at a certain moment can suggest so much more than the actual gestures and words of men and women in a state of fear, it seems plain that the cinema has within its grasp innumerable symbols for emotions that have so far failed to find expression. Terror has, besides its ordinary forms, the shape of a tadpole; it burgeons, bulges, quivers, disappears. Anger is not merely rant and rhetoric, red faces and clenched fists. It is perhaps a black line wriggling upon a white sheet. Anna and Vronsky need no longer scowl and grimace. They have at their command – but what? Is there, we ask, some secret language which we feel and see, but never speak, and, if so, could this be made visible to the eye? Is there any characteristic which thought possesses that can be rendered visible without the help of words? It has speed and lowness; dart-like directness and vaporous circumlocution. But it has also, especially in moments of emotion, the picture-making power, the need to lift its burden to another bearer; to let an image run side by side along with it. The likeness of the thought is, for some reason, more beautiful, more comprehensible, more available than the thought itself. As everybody knows, in Shakespeare the most complex ideas form chains of images through which we mount, changing and turning, until we reach the light of day. But, obviously, the images of a poet are not to be cast in bronze, or traced by pencil. They are compact of a thousand suggestions of which the visual is only the most obvious or the uppermost. Even the simplest image; 'My luve's like a red, red rose, that's newly sprung in June,' presents us with impressions of moisture and warmth and the glow of crimson and the softness of petals inextricably mixed and strung upon the lilt of a rhythm which is itself the voice of the passion and hesitation of the lover. All this, which is accessible to words, and to words alone, the cinema must avoid.

Yet if so much of our thinking and feeling is connected with seeing, some residue of visual emotion which is of no use either to painter or to poet may still await the cinema. That such symbols will be quite unlike the real objects which we see before us seems highly probable. Something abstract, something which moves with controlled and conscious art, something which calls for the very slightest help from words or music to make itself intelligible, yet justly uses them subserviently – of such movements and abstractions the films may, in time to come, be composed. Then, indeed, when some new symbol for expressing thought is found, the film-maker has enormous riches at his command. The exactitude of reality and its surprising power of suggestion are to be had for the asking. Annas and Vronskys – there they are in the flesh. If into this reality, he could breathe emotion, could animate the perfect form with thought, then his booty could be hauled in hand over hand. Then, as smoke pours from Vesuvius, we should be able to see thought in its wildness, in its beauty, in its oddity, pouring from men with their elbows on a table; from women with their little handbags slipping to the floor. We should see these emotions mingling together and affecting each other.

We should see violent changes of emotion produced by their collision. The most fantastic contrasts could be flashed before us with a speed which the writer can only toil after in vain; the dream architecture of arches and battlements, of cascades falling and fountains rising, which sometimes visits us in sleep or shapes itself in half-darkened rooms, could be realized before our waking eyes. No fantasy could be too far-fetched or insubstantial. The past could be unrolled, distances annihilated, and the gulfs which dislocate novels (when, for instance, Tolstoy has to pass from Levin to Anna, and in so doing jars his story and wrenches and arrests our sympathies) could, by the sameness of the background, by the repetition of some scene, be smoothed away.

How all this is to be attempted, much less achieved, no one at the moment can tell us. We get intimations only in the chaos of the streets, perhaps, when some momentary assembly of colour, sound, movement suggests that here is a scene waiting a new art to be transfixed. And sometimes at the cinema, in the midst of its immense dexterity and enormous technical proficiency, the curtain parts and we behold, far off, some unknown and unexpected beauty. But it is for a moment only. For a strange thing has happened - while all the other arts were born naked, this, the youngest, has been born fully clothed. It can say everything before it has anything to say. It is as if the savage tribe, instead of finding two bars of iron to play with, had found, scattering the seashore, fiddles, flutes, saxophones, trumpets, grand pianos by Erard and Bechstein, and had begun with incredible energy, but without knowing a note of music, to hammer and thump upon them all at the same time.

ROBERT FAIRTHORNE

The Principles of the Film

The Principles of the Film
First published in *Film* no1 Spring 1933

Although artistic beliefs demand that knowledge of theory should be unconscious, it is a pity that both practical and theoretical workers should demonstrate this faith in print. The practical man of the film world has the same contempt for film theory as the village blacksmith has for theoretical metallurgy. Both know they can turn out better work than the theorists, and both prove the uselessness of theories by brandishing their own.

Some conflict between practical and theoretical tendencies is essential for sound achievement, but in the cinema the conflict is partly due to the fact that neither theorist nor applicant seem to know what a theory is, and what it can, or cannot do. Another cause of trouble is the general belief that film theory began and ended with Kuleshoff's attack on the principles of construction. To prevent better brains wasting time by upsetting the already unstable Kuleshoffian Aunt Sally, this article attempts to sum up the development of film theory to the present day.

There is a qualitative difference between the film of today, and the film of, say, twelve years ago, quite apart from the presence of sound. This is not due to any change in the themes, which remain one or other of the immortal three, nor to technical advances affecting technique. The only two technical developments worthy of notice, apart from the invention of photographic cinematography, are the camera truck (first used in Swedish films in about 1918, but too generally adopted after the success of Dupont's *Vaudeville*), and the addition of sound. The former had the more profound influence on the nature of films, for it helped to distinguish a film from the stage and the lantern lecture.

The film of today differs from the film of yesterday in the theoretical principles of its construction, and this difference is greater than that caused by the coming of sound. The film of the past was a photographed stage play. It would have remained so – the public found it adequate – but for the fact that films have to be made. The actual making of a film, as opposed to its inception demands intelligence and technical ability, which implies, in spite of contemporary social mythology, some artistic qualifications. Thus it comes about that, though mostly the film industry exists by doing well what is not worth doing at all, the theory of film construction possesses a certain narrow and thumby thoroughness.

The number of formulated theories is in excess of the number of theorists, but the principles affecting general practice have been evolved from them and from experiment – or fashion. In practice they work fairly adequately but, owing to their fundamental unsoundness, they can only be applied to immediate problems. Like all machine-shop theories, they are almost useless for prediction or for other than routine problems. Their effect is natural, for the problem of film construction has been attacked before investigating the formal properties of the material. In fact the material has never even been described.

Until recently a film was made by placing the camera in the front row of the stalls, and then presenting to the audience a potted version of the camera's evening out. The film was a two-dimensional monochromatic version of the stage, sometimes enlivened by camera tricks. Well done it was terribly boring, but at its worst was excellent entertainment, till shackled by dialogue.

Dramatic episodes, linked by redundant and sometimes explanatory lettering, were the basis of the film till well after the War. They would be still, frozen stiffer by acoustic technique, if the technicians had not unconsciously evolved a new conception. It is worth noting that progress comes first in the short film, generally the 'comic', where experiments are looked at as legitimate eccentricity. This is particularly noticeable at the moment.

The credit for the new conception cannot be given to any one man. It was actually articulated by Kuleshoff, in 1920. The principle was simple and obvious, but ran athwart the idea of the film as a theatrical record with elaborate settings. In it the strips of film, or rather, the visual impressions resulting therefrom were the material only. They had only visual significance. The image of an elephant walking down the street was an image of an elephant walking down the street, nothing more. Intellectual significance, ever the most direct, was formed by the relations of an image to the other images forming the film; like the letters of a word, they had significance in combination not deducible from their separate meanings. The making of a film was supposed to begin, after the photography, with the cutting and editing. It was the subjection of the camera by the Sickle. Eisenstein added the Hammer later.

In Kuleshoff's view the recording of incident was a preliminary, the film incident being synthetized from the records as sentences are from words. Some of his demonstrations were crude but amusing, and may be unfamiliar to the uninitiated. In one he created the impression of a moving woman by consecutive presentation of close-ups of the arms, legs, head, and body of different women, photographed at different times and in different places. In another, a shot was made of an actor looking at something off the screen. This was placed in three parts of the film where it was followed by shots of a plate of food, a dead man, and a woman respectively. Although the actor had the same neutral expression on his face in all three shots, the audience was impressed by his acting, or so the story goes. Thus 'stars' are made.

The virtue of this theory of construction was that it recognized the film as depending more on the interaction of its parts than on the content of the parts themselves. This merit was, and is still, obscured by lack of clear thought in its exposition. As usual, the implicit assumption was made that the film consists of strips of celluloid. It was also implied that a visual event was altered only in duration by shortening its celluloid equivalent, as if a man were only altered in height by having his head cut off.

None of these errors alter the truth of the importance of ordinal relations, and the lack of importance of the camera as such, but these were the errors which were hailed as the basis of the theory. Their cruder manifestations, unlike those of the theatrical film, were not amusing. In the more esoteric circle appeared films so crammed with irrelevant shots, giving alleged significance by contrast or comparison, that there was some suspicion that they were put in to make it more difficult. Though there is no *a priori* objection to shots in negative or upside down, they require some justification.

In Dziga Vertov's *The Man with the Movie Camera* the cameraman himself is shown at work, a scene as factitious as anything in a *spielfilm.* This part of the theory, the Kino-Eye, can never be carried into practice, for 'real' material is inevitably manipulated by the very process of obtaining it. Which side of the lens the manipulation takes place is a matter of indifference.

Because of the increasing importance of the documentary film, it is as well to clear up the error in Vertov's dichotomy. The clue lies in the fact that a 'real photograph' has no more significance than an artist's picture to an audience *having no previous acquaintance with the photographic process.* 'Actuality' is not a fundamental property, but a relation between film and audience of precisely the same order as slow motion, which demands previous knowledge of natural motion to give its peculiar effect.

The value of Vertov's work does not lie in his theory of the Kino-Eye, but in his theory of the assembly of film. Having no control over the secondary visual characteristics of the material he collected, he was forced to make the interaction of the content of the film events more powerful than their appearance. This was done by impressing a more or less temporal metric on the film, to echo, emphasize, or run contrapuntal to the intellectual relations. The principle was used by Eisenstein in *Ten Days that Shook the World* (*October*), and for the first time with sound, to which the method is peculiarly applicable, in Milestone's *All Quiet on the Western Front.*

When the metrical construction was over-applied it destroyed itself. It is possible to inflict on the film temporal relations so complicated that they can only be ascertained by measuring up the celluloid with a footrule, but they are not necessarily rhythms. Also the visual content must be considered. Film rhythm is spatial as well as temporal, and the duration of a shot and its visual content interact on each other. In fact, the duration of the film events can only be controlled before they are made. Understanding would be helped by some term implying both *pattern* and *rhythm.*

From such considerations Eisenstein arrived at his idea of Overtonal Montage. The theory, as stated by the originator, is somewhat complex. So complex, indeed, that one suspects it of being an explanation rather than a tool. This may be so, but does not affect the value of the theory, which is considerable, or its truth, which is at least partial.

Briefly, Eisenstein recognizes a hierarchy of methods of assembly. These will be referred to as montage methods, with the understanding that the montage is not to be confused with film splicing. Each montage operates on the results of the last in such a way as to co-ordinate the significances of the action with the visual qualities of the images. Going up the series the significances concerned become more diffuse, and the coordinated visual qualities intrinsic rather than predominant. It is worth noting that the visual, not the pictorial qualities, are those considered. The film image cannot possess pictorial qualities as commonly understood, for it has both duration and direction in time. It is a visual event, not a picture – not even a moving picture.

Kuleshoff's synthesis of a woman is an example of the lowest order of montage. The order and predominant characteristics of the events were combined to achieve the immediate purpose of the film, the representation of a woman. The next step is to combine the result of the last so as to fit the durations into the dramatic action. *This is Metric Montage.* Above this is formed the metric of the metric, or rhythm, which combines the significance of the action with the motions in the ordered film images. Above the rhythmic lies the tonal montage, of which a purely spatial example is the deliberate use of 'camera angle'. We are now free of any superstition that the film can be made at the cutting desk. The final stage is what Eisenstein calls Overtonal Montage, the analogy being with the musical theories of Scriabin and Debussy. In it the screen images are treated as psychical stimuli having no individual significance, only their integrated effect being subjected to the process of montage. The direct action of the film is carried by the dominant qualities of the images, while the significance and appeal are conveyed by the summation of diffuse qualities below the level of awareness. In much the same way a printer uses different type faces, whose distinctive appearance is due to the summation of minute differences separately unnoticed by the reader. There is a verbal parallel in the methods of James Joyce.

Concentration on the more diffuse qualities of film components, rather than on the still fundamental primary qualities of action and duration, has led to a very great apparent simplification of the rhythmic structure. At its best, the rhythmic construction could give a flavour of Bach to the film, at its worst it produced a kinetic patchwork. Only in an abstract film should the structure overshadow the content.

Though the pragmatic correctness of overtonal montage is a matter of experience, and though it seems to be a necessary consequence of the properties of film material, the greatest objection to it, as used by Eisenstein, is that it is frankly hypnotic. If the hypnosis is unsuccessful there is an emotional dislike to the film. Thus *The General Line,* which dealt with the unemotional and almost politically neutral subject of collective farming, caused greater commotion in this country than frankly revolutionary films like *The End of St. Petersburg.* Possibly this is only a defect of present day Soviet mentality, or is intrinsic in the nature of the purpose for which such films are made. The method certainly seems to attract propagandists of all countries and creeds.

Since the statement of Overtonal Montage, theory has remained inarticulate though there is evidence of the growth of a purely practical and implicit understanding of film material. The coming of sound led to a number of wild statements, by courtesy, theoretical. They are not worth comment, or the trouble of looking them up, as they made no attempt to analyse the nature of the visual-acoustic. Although a visual event combined with an acoustic event is something more than the sum of the two, the formal qualities of the combination can be understood from study of the formal properties of the components and the nature of the cross relations between them. The mildly mathematical will see the analogy with complex numbers. The comparative structural simplicity of acoustic events makes them most suitable for controlled use in the higher orders of the Eisenstein montage hierarchy.

On the constructive side film theory of today is useful without being theoretical. The few feeble attempts at fundamental analysis are too ludicrous for criticism. The absurdity of 'motion composition' implies that there is no distinction between the beginning and end of a film event, and theories that cannot see anything odd in a film run backwards. should be rejected at sight.

A worse fault in practice, is the lack of research into available material. The range of the film is all visual and acoustic experience. Even visual experience is by no means confined to the representational. This article is visual experience, if nothing else, but it is not representational. Possible visual material ranges from the abstract pattern event (a somewhat ideal conception) having sharp visual and diffuse intellectual significances, to the verbal typographic events, having sharp intellectual and diffuse visual significances. The classification of visual and acoustic material can be left, in the manner of text books, as an exercise for the reader. No distinction can be made between 'documentary' and 'studio' shots in a fundamental classification, for the distinction depends on a relation between film and audience.

The only film theorist to use non-representational methods was *Felix the Cat.* His habit of interchanging typographical symbols with reality was probably a manifestation of the scientific and the economic spirit of the age.

In conclusion, a prediction. In about eight years stereoscopy, variable screen openings, colour, and the like, will have ruined film achievement by finding the practical men of the cinema influenced by *fashion* instead of *understanding.* A small, but dreadful, example is the current fashion in scene changing. There are two conventions – the Sternbergian sleepy sickness mix, and the British geometrical wipe of the duster. Apparently the employers of these methods are so blind to the basic principles of the cinema film that they fail to realise the transition from one scene to another to be a separate scene in itself.

Borderline – Kenneth Macpherson (1930)

ROLAND COSANDEY

On Borderline

First published in *Afterimage* no 12
Autumn 1985

'I want to arrange that people making films, and experimenting in all sorts of ways shall be able to see what others are doing in the same way.'
K. Macpherson, *Close Up*, vol 1, no 1, July 1927, p. 15

A vast retrospective of avant-garde films from the end of the silent era was held in Lausanne in 1979 to mark the fiftieth anniversary of the first International Congress of Independent Cinema. The Lausanne show was a striking tribute to the original event – reproducing even the confusion of the 1929 Congress – which took place in Madame de Mandrot's Château de La Sarraz, in the small town of the same name, some 15 miles from Lausanne near the Jura.

Organised by the Swiss Cinémathèque for the annual convention of the International Federation of Film Archives (FIAF), the retrospective adopted a deliberately celebratory attitude rather than pursuing the rigorously analytical approach which prevailed at the famous FIAF convention – devoted to primitive cinema, 1900-1906 – held in Brighton the preceding year.

This choice can be easily explained by the continued existence of attitudes, values, prejudices even, which date back to the early years of avant-garde cinema and which paradoxically coincide with the event which would put an end to those years: the arrival and ascendance of sound film. In addition, the legitimisation of film as an art and the original inspiration behind the cinémathèque itself are so closely linked to the 'independent' activity of that period that its inheritors are naturally inclined towards both acknowledgement and revival. The presence of film-makers like Joris Ivens, Henri Storck, Jean Painlevé and Ivor Montagu at screenings of their earliest efforts, which were sometimes made more than fifty years before, added to the spirit of celebration. As did the participation of people such as a protagonist like Jean Mitry or the eye-witness Alberto Satoris, and the knowledge that somewhere between Montreux and Geneva, even if unable to attend, were Bryher (co-editor of *Close Up*), Freddy Chevalley (Geneva correspondent for *Close Up*), and Arnold Kohler (founder of the Geneva Cine-club in 1927), could only nourish the cult of a tradition whose trajectory is marked by several attempts at galvanisation: the second (and last) International Congress of Independent Cinema (Brussels, November 1930); Cinema Today (Basle, August/September 1945); the first Festival of the Cinema of Tomorrow (Antibes, 1950); and even the project for an international Cinémathèque of experimental documentary and avant-garde film launched by Ado Kyrou and Serge Goldfayn's ephemeral periodical *L'Age du cinéma* (no 16, 1952).

When, at the end of the Lausanne retrospective, Jean-Luc Godard – that paragon of the film 'artist' – was asked to comment out loud on the (true) History of cinema in front of an assembly of rather reticent archivists, his presence clearly underscored the impression that a symbolic torch was being passed.

A missed opportunity for 'research'? Certainly not. The possibility of questioning the people involved during that period and, above all, the direct and overwhelming confrontation with the total mass of films offered an extraordinary opportunity to make discoveries and verifications.

The sheer abundance of the programme forced one to admit, in the first place, the extent to which the notion of avant-garde cinema was and remains fuzzy. From amateur film to the first works of a future professional, the film clubs promoted everything that was produced outside the norms of the production/distribution system of the day.

This independence, this marginality, this difference – we now know the fate of all these terms – are affirmed at every level. And if the accent is traditionally placed on aesthetic distinctions, nevertheless one should not forget the peculiar production conditions of this wilful independence. Economically, production depended on private resources (personal wealth, inheritance or patronage), occasionally on a commission for a documentary or – more rarely – political film. Production was undertaken by a small team of friends, often unpaid, contemporaries from the generation of 1895-1910. There was a constant recourse to the use of exteriors, and the interior scenes were done in improvised studios or in an unused corner of an industry studio set, at least up until the advent of sound.

The equipment might have been just a 35mm clockwork camera with a 25 metre magazine and a maximum shot-length of six metres (13 seconds, at 24fps). But professional cameras were also used, such as the Parvo Debrie 35mm/120 metres (used by Jean Vigo and Boris

Kaufman for *A propos de Nice* (1929), and sold by Vigo, along with five lenses, to Henri Storck and Mannus Franken for the sum of 20,000 francs in 1931 – cf. *Centrofilm*, no. 18-19, Feb/March 1961, Turin, special *Jean Vigo* issue), or the Eclair 'Caméclair', used for fiction films. These were tripod cameras, 'already very sophisticated and highly complicated... which allowed for special trick effects - fades, masks, filters, distorting lenses, variable speeds, reverse shooting, single framing, etc... ' (Henri Storck, in a letter to the author, Brussels, 21 May 1981). Finally, the circulation of prints was extremely brisk, thanks to several specialised cinemas and to the cine-clubs (which often had film-makers sitting on their committees). Distribution was conducted on a European scale, forming a veritable network (which deserves serious study) stretching from Paris to Brussels, Ghent, Ostende, Amsterdam, Berlin, Stuttgart, London, Barcelona, Geneva, and as far as the United States.

The Lausanne retrospective of 1979 – which remains the largest of its kind to date – confirmed the perennial 'classics' of the avant-garde: the films of Richter, Buñuel, Vigo, Ivens, whose status as classics dates in fact from the time of their initial appearance. It also demonstrated the need for an historiographical approach which would not 'innocently' restore the diverse and contradictory values united under the term 'avant-garde' (see Francois Albéra in Buache (ed.), *Cinéma indépendant...* vol. 2). Lastly, the retrospective also revealed curious silences due to particular circumstances of critical reception and distribution, of which the main 'victims' were the Belgian Charles Dekeukeleire (in his early period *Combat de boxe* (1927), *Histoire de détective* (1929), and especially *Impatience* (1928)) as well as the Englishman Kenneth Macpherson and his friends gathered under the 'Pool' banner.

By way of simple inventory, I would also add two other recently re-surfaced titles which should not be overlooked in any historical picture of the international avant-garde: *Limit*, by the Brazilian Mário Peixoto (1931) and *A Page of Madness* (1926) by the Japanese Teinosuke Kinugasa.

However, this list merits a moment's reflection – the importance assigned to these films is completely theoretical. On the historical level, none of them had much of an impact on the international European scene which represented the real testing ground for their reception: *A Page of Madness* was immediately excluded by its geographical isolation (but could have been part of the movement if Kinugasa hadn't decided to come to Europe with *Crossroads* (1928), thought to be more commercial!); the distribution of *Limit* outside Brazil is difficult to assess, but it must have been extremely limited; lastly, *Borderline* had only a fleeting public existence.

This raises one of the tasks essential to a renewed historiography of avant-garde cinema: the systematic study – following in the footsteps of the research already devoted to the Soviet silent cinema – of the circulation and critical reception of films commonly categorised as avant-garde.

2

> '...the hope of the cinema lies with the amateur.'
> K. Macpherson, *Close Up*, vol 1, no 1, July 1927, p.14

The activity of Kenneth Macpherson and the more or less fixed group united under the Pool banner – Winifred Bryher, Robert Herring, H.D. (Hilda Doolittle), Dorothy Richardson, Oswell Blakeston – is exemplary in all respects. For no other group managed to create this unique and concentrated combination of all (or almost all) the various forms which constituted the international network of European avant-garde cinema between 1925 and 1933. Founded by Macpherson and his wife, Bryher, Pool was initially a publishing house which followed the model established by Robert MacAlmon, who was one of the most important publishers of American writers in France and the first husband of Winifred Bryher (the couple separated in 1926). Pool published several volumes of prose by Bryher and Macpherson, an essay by Hanns Sachs against the death penalty, three monographs on cinema, and a film review, *Close Up*, which joined the still-young tradition of literary 'little magazines'. In addition, Pool undertook the production of films, an activity equally dependent on private financing. In all probability, the publishing and film production activities were subsidised – as was the construction in 1930 of a modern house in the international style – by Bryher's family fortune. Her father, Sir John Reeves Ellerman, an English ship owner of German origin, was one of the richest men in England (he died in 1933).

Close Up, published between July 1927 and December 1933, represented the critical and promotional pole of Pool's activities. Publication was assured with admirable regularity by a minimal team; the consistently high aesthetic quality of the magazine culminated in a larger and more ambitious format in March 1931. Editorial duties were shared in order to cover the whole field.

Macpherson, the editor-in-chief, generally contributed articles defining the role of the director, discussing the intellectual and material conditions of independent film production, and defending the integrity of cinema and its right to be considered an art.

Bryher, an impassioned pragmatist, promoted the activities of spectators' organisations, denounced the censorship of the films of Stroheim, Pabst, and Metzner, as well as of Soviet films, and insisted that the cinema be used in school not only as an educational tool but also as an autonomous branch of culture. In 1929, after exhaustive screenings in Berlin, she wrote a monograph on Soviet cinema, *Film Problems of Soviet Russia*, a remarkable introduction to an area of production which only two years earlier had been totally unknown.

Robert Herring and Oswell Blakeston also contributed introductory articles on production techniques which were soon published in expanded form by Pool, in a volume entitled *Through a Yellow Glass* (1928).

H.D. and Dorothy Richardson also discussed specific films, but were above all concerned with questions of the individual perception and reception of cinema, which they raised in texts ranging in style from prose poems to subjective essays.

This division of labour is highly schematic and obviously allowed for other tasks to be assumed at times by various members of the basic group or by the international correspondents who supplied a fundamental part of the editorial content from Berlin (Andor Kraszna-Krausz), New York (H.A. Potamkin), Hollywood (Clifford Howard), Geneva (Freddy Chevalley), Moscow (P. Attasheva), and Vienna (Trude Weiss).

Close Up, was published in English, but included occasional contributions in French, such as Freddy Chevalley's Geneva letter. The Macphersons edited the magazine from their Swiss home (Montreux-Territet until 1931, then Burier in the canton of Vaud) and from London, working mainly by correspondence.

Though the Pool group appeared neither among Madame Mandrot's guests at La Sarraz for the International Congress of Independent Cinema, nor at the regular screening of the Geneva cine-club, their magazine was nevertheless read by a growing number of the 'happy few'. The print-run went from 500 in 1927 to 1,000 in the first half of 1928 and reached – if Bryher's memoirs are to be believed (and I haven't received any evidence to the contrary) – 5000 copies in 1933.

Compared to its rare European counterparts, *Close Up* was characterised by a close and permanent relationship with Great Britain, by its early support for film-makers like Abram Room, G.W. Pabst, and Eisenstein (one of his earliest essays was published in May 1929), by its stress on the importance of the educational sphere, by its staunch position against the censor, and by its links to psychoanalysis as developed by Hanns Sach (1881-1947), a disciple of Freud who established himself in Berlin as a teaching analyst and co-editor of the review *Imago.* (On this last aspect, as well as on the determining role played by the women

writers H.D., Dorothy Richardson, and Bryher herself, see the pioneering research by Anne Friedberg, cited in the bibliography below.)

I should also like to stress the geographical specificity of Pool. The Swiss Alps and the Lake Geneva basin were long familiar to the Ellermans. Bryher's father engaged in mountain climbing in the area before 1900, and Bryher moved with her mother to Montreux-Territet in 1922. In 1932 she moved into 'Kenwin', the modern villa she had built for Macpherson and herself at Burier, facing Lake Geneva and Mount Grammont, where she continued to live until her death in 1983. The villa was designed by Hermann Henselmann, a Berlin architect and influenced by Le Corbusier, and was situated about ten kilometres from the famous Petite Maison. Le Corbusier described the location of the Petite Maison as follows: 'geography confirms the choice of the site – just twenty minutes away is a station where all the express trains stop, interconnecting Milan, Zurich, Amsterdam, Paris, London, Geneva, Marseille... (*Une petite maison, 1923* Editions d'architecture, Zurich 1981, p.8). When in a hurry, Bryher would go to Geneva and take the plane. Whatever reasons the Macphersons had for installing themselves on the Vaud Riviera – familial, financial, or aesthetic – their geographical position translated into a unique location at the heart of the rather diffused avant-garde movement of those years.

Of the cardinal roles that a group like Pool could have theoretically played – the production and promotion of its own films, critical analysis, and the exhibition/distribution of films made in a similar spirit – only the last was never undertaken by the Macphersons. They created neither a cine-club nor an independent distribution system, even though they supported both ideas.

The promotion of their own films remained remarkably discreet. *Close Up* published several photographs with brief captions for two apparently completed films – *Wing Beat* (1927) and *Monkey's Moon* (1929) – but it is probable that neither was ever shown publicly. Nor were the editorial efforts of the magazine really mobilised on behalf of *Borderline*: just thirty photographs, all published in 1930, plus an editorial by the director defending the film after its unsuccessful London opening ('As Is', *Close Up*, vol 7, no 5, November 1930, pp.293-298), approximately ten lines on the film by Oswell Blakeston (*Close Up*, vol 7, no 6, December 1930, pp. 409-410, 411, 412), and a few adverts for the film in 1931...

On the level of critical activity, on the other hand, the magazine greatly benefited from its geographical eccentricity. For Switzerland, which produced no films and thus had no need for protectionist measures, was perhaps the European country best furnished with films – at least until the arrival of sound which cut the market into two distinct linguistic zones, French and German. And the canton of Vaud apparently exercised a remarkably liberal censorship policy. More than anywhere else, a large part of international film production in commercial distribution was accessible, either in Montreux, Lausanne, or Geneva. When this 'open market for the world', as Bryher called it, began to shrink, *Close Up* was obliged to compensate for the scarcity of material by increasing the number of foreign contributors and by reducing the number of issues per year, two measures which were announced by the magazine in December 1930.

The publication would thus retain its privileged situation which allowed it to be present on all 'fronts' while remaining on the fringes of the large urban centres. This position was particularly productive in so far as the editors were only moderately interested in theory, usually preferring to stress practical considerations arising from the call for a fairly broad consensus.

Other contemporary publications which evoked the same international scope – such as *La Revue du cinéma* (Paris, 1928- 1931), or periodicals linked to the communist left, like *Film und Volk* (Berlin, 1928-1930), *Arbeiterbühne und film* (Berlin, 1930-31), *Experimental Cinema* (New York, 1930-34), *Nuestro Cinema* (Spain, 1932-35) – were however much more determined by a centripetal perspective, in terms of geography or ideology. The centrifugal cosmopolitanism of *Close U*p makes it perhaps the purest expression of the free circulation – of works, of models and of people - that constituted the movement of this avant-garde.

3

'One point that might be made for the cheap camera is that it *is* free from those
means whereby one achieves "effects", thus delivering us from temptation.'
K. Macpherson, *Close Up*, vol 2, no 6, June 1982, p.9

'I have said that *Borderline* has many faults. How idiotic to pretend that it has not.
Traversing new ground, it had all the rawness of a pioneer. But pioneer it was. And I
have said to my critics, in ten years' time, the "obscurity" of which they complain
will be plain as punch. And I think it will take ten years for them to recognise it.'
K. Macpherson, *Close Up*, vol 7, no 5, November 1930, pp.294-295.

And what of Pool films, in the context of cinematic production mentioned earlier? Or, more precisely, of Macpherson's films (it seems that Oswell Blakeston produced a few films under the Pool aegis, but I haven't been able to trace them). Not wanting to construct hypotheses on scant fragments, there's only one film about which one can speak with any assurance:

Borderline. Made in 1930, it's the only film (to my knowledge) for which the original negative and a print from the period still exist, and is also the only one for which supporting texts and contemporary accounts are available.

The critical fate of *Borderline* turned out to be as sad as its timing was unfortunate. Planned as early as spring 1929, shot the following spring and finished in June, this 60-minute film (at 24 fps) is one of the few feature-length avant-garde productions. But, unlike *L'Age d'or* (1930) and *Sang d'un poète* (1930), it had neither sound nor dialogue, and very swiftly appeared obsolete at a time when silent film was permanently on its way out. The break was experienced by many, including Macpherson, as especially violent since it came when everything seemed to be just beginning. Hadn't Eisenstein recently declared '…cinematography is for the first time availing itself of the experience of literature for the purpose of working out *its own language, its own speech, its own vocabulary, its own imagery…* The new period for cinema attacks the question *from within* – along the line of the methodology of purely cinematographic *expressiveness*.' (*Close Up* vol 4, May 1929, p. 1 1, italics in the original)? Now the entire basis of his argument seemed devastated by the sound of words, and, what is more, words without the power of metaphor.

The arrival of the 'talkies' nevertheless had no direct influence on the critical reception of the film. Three types of reaction can be distinguished, from the enthusiasm of a few convinced critics to the more numerous expressions of disbelief, to the most common judgement of all: the well-tried tactic of dissociation. *Borderline* was praised for its photographic beauty (the combination of the ambiguous notion of 'photogénie' and panchromatic film stock), on the other hand insisting on the fact that the narrative demanded a taste and judgement far above the ordinary for it to be understood in all its complexity. The reaction of the British press was so negative that Macpherson abandoned his usual reserve and defended the film in an editorial in *Close Up*. In an argument typical of his position, Macpherson reminds the reader that *Borderline* is a pioneering experimental film, 'perhaps the only really "avant-garde" film ever made'. Whilst he recognises the film's faults, he claims that it is precisely these faults which the critics approved or even praised, at the same time ignoring or panning those aspects which Macpherson considered successful. The 'obscurity' of which the critics complained represented, according to Macpherson, a desire to translate the chaotic complexity of life into film, it was the result of an aesthetic plan which would only be fully recognised ten years hence.

Where does *Borderline*'s 'unreadability' – which some considered the film's crippling weakness and others the film's major success – really come from? The determination of the critics to locate a narrative within the flux of images offered up to their wisdom suggests part of the answer.

The film offers several easily graspable reference points. The characters are endowed with clear dramatic personalities, and the first intertitles carefully identify each by name: *Pete?/Astrid on the phone!/You must go back to Pete and leave Thorne/Adah is his girl, isn't she - not yours?* (These four intertitles occur during the first ten minutes. The film contains twenty-six titles in all, twenty three of which carry direct dialogue: note the importance of speech and the extreme economy of use.)

The characters can be described: there's Pete, a black man associated with images of solidity, of frankness, and of nature – water, mountains, sky. And there's Adah, a mulatto who briefly returns to him, leaving her lover, Thorne, a young white man who is weak-willed, alcoholic, with thin-skinned and 'thorny' reactions. There's Astrid, Thorne's companion, an ageing white woman who is jealous, monopolising, hysterical and who wants to reclaim her friend at all costs and who will 'accidentally' die, killed by the knife which she brandishes threateningly at Thorne.

The in-between world of a bistro, sketched around these two couples, is shaken by their interaction. The bistro is inhabited by a few middle class clients and a somewhat extravagant trio comprised of the barmaid, the bar's owner, and the pianist. And finally, intruding from the outside, is a puritanical and racist old lady whose inflammatory comments incite the authorities to expel the negroes.

The place? Nowhere geographically specific, no spot on the map, just a place composed of an ensemble of traits signifying 'somewhere provincial', stifling tradition, western parochialism, a social context engendering neurosis and racism: the interior of the bistro, the small room where Pete is staying, the briefly traversed streets of the village, the lonely station. In short, all the elements of a *Kammerspiel*, with a few escapes from the 'huis-clos', the closed rooms of bistro and hotel (Pete and Adah's happy promenade in the hills, Thorne's reverie in a peaceful springtime landscape), plus an anti-racist theme which was recognised to be innovatory for the cinema.

But *Borderline* can't be reduced to this sort of approach, which would presuppose dramatic and psychological conventions devoid of surprise and would stem from a wish to bring the experience of the film back on to more familiar territory. For Macpherson elaborates, in fact, a narrativity completely determined by the movement of emotional states, on the level of acting as well as on the level of narration. The acting is subordinated to an extreme physical expressivity, the body being used as an unconscious indicator of emotions and at the same time the most appropriate way of communicating them to us. It would even appear that the film-maker occasionally varied the shooting speed when an acceleration or deceleration of the body might assume an expressive function. The succession of shots, in turn, was dictated by a subjective logic whose associative principles don't lead to the construction of the unified spatio-temporal universe of realist montage. The appearance of places, faces and landscapes, although contained within a chronological framework, corresponds largely to a sort of interior call on the part of one of the characters, summoning them there at that moment.

Borderline's gamble was to never use the distinctive signs of passage from an exterior state, serving as referent, to the interior states – fantasy, reminiscence, vision, dream. And with good reason: the 'subjective use of inference' which Macpherson claims as the original contribution of his editing doesn't lend itself to visualising the imagery *and* reality, not even a reality filtered by the refracting prism of a subjective consciousness. Certain isolated images in fact refer directly to the vision of a particular character (the superimpositions function like this) but in general it is subjectivity which guides the narration; a subjectivism, one might say, which constitutes an absolutely objective system.

Which is what allowed the film-maker, thanks to the psychoanalytic context, to have claimed a true realism, that is to say of life itself, not an opposition to the conventional realism in cinema which ruled the day. This also allowed him, at the same time, to offer his film as the aesthetic product of his own interior vision.

This approach links Macpherson to those directors who manipulate, to the artists of a plastic 'language' of cinema, to the makers of films as discourse 'on' things rather than discourse 'made up' of things. Which explains the issue of a network of repetitions, of indexical or even symbolic value, in the decor (a picture pinned to the wall showing two cocks squaring off, a stuffed seagull, and a witch's doll associated with Astrid), in the form of objects handled unconsciously until the moment of action (the knife which will kill Astrid), or the leitmotiv of the hand, designed to communicate the values attached to each of the characters and to represent certain dramatic moments.

Though the film-maker manages to avoid certain temptations of technique, about which he warns other film-makers aspiring to expressivity (see the epigraph above), he nevertheless indulges in a type of overstatement which, in my opinion, destabilises the formal rigour of his project and occasionally gives the film the air of an exercise in style. In this case, it's a question of changes in the register of the editing to introduce two virtuoso pieces into the flow of the narrative (a dance sequence rendered by rapid impressionist editing and a kaleidoscopic montage of images of nature), as well as of the typological dissonance between the three groups of characters who appear in the story: the two couples, the bistro trio, and the customers.

The 'passion to express' to which I'm tempted to attribute these characteristics (without being able to discern what part they played in the mixed critical reception at the time) is moreover perfectly consistent with the wish to experiment and the attendant 'risks' of heterogeneity, and with the 'dilettantism' to which Macpherson professed.

4

> 'Mr. Kenneth Macpherson is himself, you might say, a borderline among the young
> cinema directors. He is not at all allied with the ultra-modern abstract school of
> rhomboid and curve and cross-beam of tooth pick or coal shovel.'
> H.D., *Borderline. A Pool Film with Paul Robeson*, 1930, p.7.

To conclude, let us consider the title of Macpherson's film. The anonymous pamphlet – authored by H.D., no doubt, to present *Borderline* to the anglo-saxon film-going intelligentsia – opens with a chapter delineating the metaphorical meanings of 'borderline'. The term refers to the indefiniteness of the place of action, to the precarious social and psychic identity of the two white protagonists, Thorne and Astrid (played by H.D. herself), and to the situation of the black couple as victims of racial prejudice. The author extends this interpretation beyond the film itself. Marginality thus defines and valorises not only every aspect of the work of creation (including the film-maker's special stance even within the avant-garde), but also the quality of its inspiration, linked not so much to England as to a more ancient celtic source. The wilful amateurism of film-maker and actors is both a sign of marginality and a guarantee of authenticity. And finally, a distinction on the level of content: *Borderline*'s approach to racism has nothing to do with a political position, but represents above all the act of an artist attentive to the problems of being human.

I should point out that the psychoanalytic use of the term 'borderline' (*Grenzfall* a 'limit case') is of recent origin and would pertain only to an anachronistically modern interpretation of the film. The semantic scope of *Grenze* was never meant by Freud to cover an analytic concept, and was used by him in its common meaning. On the level of hidden sources for *Borderline*, the most interesting instance of the word appears in the last chapter of *The Psychopathology of Everyday Life*, not because of the term itself, but because of the context in which it is found. In fact, this volume – whose aesthetic impact is known to have been extensive – might shed light on certain aspects of the script, the acting, and the editing of Macpherson's film.

Returning to the multiple distinctions in H.D.'s article, one should probably take into account that some of them were designed, for purely tactical reasons, for the small cultivated public of English film enthusiasts. What remains particularly interesting now is the way in which the pamphlet describes, with rare clarity, one of the 'programmes' by which an avant-garde film-maker/auteur was defined at that time. In one of the final chapters, H.D. significantly juxtaposes the Renaissance and the modernity of the cinema. With a rhetorical sweep of which Abel Gance would have approved, she describes Macpherson as a new Leonardo Da Vinci, working simultaneously in all the arts and crafts of cinema, breathing life into the inert machine... .

Transcendence of the artist and an extreme sophistication of the work: *Borderline* is probably one of the most emblematic productions of the independent/avant-garde cinema at the end of the silent era, one which at any rate demonstrates most clearly its founding principle of 'difference'.

Translated from the French by Deke Dusinberre.

APPENDICES

1. Credits for *Borderline*

    Original title cards appearing at the beginning of the print:

    1. BORDERLINE
    2. A Pool Film
    3. Featuring Paul Robeson
    4. Written and Directed by Kenneth Macpherson
    5. In the cast:

Pete, a negro	Paul Robeson
Adah, a negro woman	Eslanda Robeson
Astrid	Helga Doorn
Thorne, her husband	Gavin Arthur
The barmaid	Charlotte Arthur
The old lady	Blanche Lewin

COMMENTS:

Certain information is not included in the credits: the role of the bistro owner was played by Winifred Bryher, that of the pianist by Robert Herring. Helga Doorn was a pseudonym for Hilda Doolittle.

The Robesons' participation in the film is not recounted in any of the biographies of Paul Robeson which I have been able to consult.

Finally, who are Charlotte and Gavin Arthur, and Blanche Lewin? Perhaps they were members of the considerable English community established in the area around Montreux – any further information on them would be welcome.

John Macpherson, the director's father and a portrait painter, worked on the lighting. The few extras who appeared in the bistro (a waiter, three customers) and in an exterior scene (an old lady and a little boy) were probably makeshift actors, the three customers having been obviously chosen for their 'type', according to a typology similar to that of the Soviets and of the cinematic Neue Sachlichkeit (Pabst, Metzner).

The role of 'husband' accredited to Thorne is explicit only in the title. This was probably a gesture in the direction of the censor, a gesture which resulted in the British Board of Film Censors granting a certificate – as seen on the sixth titlecard, date illegible – authorising the projection of the film for 'Adult Audiences'.

Kenneth Macpherson wrote the script which, according to H.D. (in the promotional pamphlet, 1930, cited in the bibliography), was a shot-by-shot text containing 910 shots illustrated by roughly a thousand drawings in pencil and ink. I have not been able to uncover this script. Macpherson was also responsible for the cinematography and editing.

The shooting very probably took place in April and May of 1930. The following outdoor locations were used: Lutry, Montreux-Territet (Maison Riant Château), the area around Caux, and different spots on the Rhône plain (the Aigle station, the Pissevache Falls, the bridge and near the castle of St Maurice.

The interiors, comprising three different rooms and the bistro, were shot in Lutry in an unused hall converted into a studio. All of the locations were within a 25km radius of Montreux-Territet, where the Macphersons were then living.

The camera was a Debrie 35mm Model L, for which Macpherson had a range of six lenses. The film was shot on panchromatic stock – which had been recently introduced on the market – for the advantages it offered in terms of lighting and spectral range. It is also possible that certain shots were filmed with a Bell and Howell Eyemo. According to Bryher (*The Heart to Artemis*, 1962, p.264) the film cost 2000 dollars.

2. Screenings

An initial cross-check suggests the following tour of *Borderline* among the non commercial venues:

13 October 1930	London, Academy Cinema.
27 November	Brussels, Palais des Beaux-Arts, during the Second International Congress of Independent Cinema.
Late February 1931	Barcelona, Studio Cinaes.
March 1931	Neuchâtel, a screening organised by the Ciné-club of Neuchâtel or by the Independent Cinema League, at an unknown venue.
25 April 1932	Berlin, Rote Mühle.
4 & 11 May	Berlin, Kamera, screenings organised by the Deutsche Liga für unabhängigen Film.

Borderline was screened in Glasgow and in Holland (by the Filmliga) prior to March 1931, and in New York after that date.

3. Prints

Rediscovered by chance in 1983 in the canton of Vaud, the original edited negative (35mm), with English intertitles, is now at the Swiss Cinémathèque in Lausanne. The negative seems to have come from a German laboratory, as indicated at one spot on the leader ('Fabrikation Weltvertrieb und Verleih/Bilton-film Aktien, Gesellschaft Berlin Friedrichstrasse 13').

I haven't studied the negative, but worked from the 35mm print struck from it by the Swiss Cinémathèque (six reels, 1802m., ref. 84A 185).

A 35mm print is also to be found at Eastman House, Rochester (New York). It probably dates from the period (1930); I haven't been able to compare the two copies.

4. Stills

Images from *Borderline* appeared in the following issues of *Close Up*: May 1930 (three photos, including the cover illustration), June (six), July (four, including cover), August (two), October (six), November (six, including cover and three production stills).

It is interesting to note that *Borderline* was not included in the collections of avant-garde film stills of other magazines and occasional books of the period. An exhaustive search has not yet been undertaken, but *Close Up* would seem to be the only publisher of *Borderline* photos, and then only during the year 1930. After that date, the magazine referred to the existence of the film only in the form of a few unillustrated adverts.

The promotional pamphlet, *Borderline, A Pool Film with Paul Robeson* (1930), distributed in England, contains twelve images and a montage of photos on the cover.

In terms of images, the subsequent invisibility of the film matched its disappearance until the publication of *Cinéma Indépendent...* (Buache (ed.), vol. 2, 1980) which printed twelve frame enlargements, and with the appearance of the German version of this article, illustrated by a series of thirty two frame enlargements (Roland Cosandey, 'Borderline, Spuren des Avant garde um 1930'. *Bild für Bild*, Cinema, Zurich, 1984). See also Anne Friedberg 'Approaching Borderline', *Millenium Film Journal*, no 7-8-9, Fall 1980.

5. Macpherson Filmography
Description of the other films by Macpherson remains problematic. All were shot in the Montreux area. *Wing Beat*, shot in early 1927 with Robert Herring and H.D. as actors, seems to have been completed. Two photos were printed in *Close Up*, vol. l, no. 1, July 1927.

Foothills, which dates from 1928-29, was described as a 'full length five reel film' (approximated 60 minutes at 24 fps). Several critics apparently saw it in private projection, but it was never publicly screened by Macpherson, who considered it inadequate. Some of the *Borderline* team worked on *Foothills*: Bryher, Robert Herring, H.D., Blanche Lewin. *Close Up* published four stills in July 1929 and Macpherson described the shooting in a lead article which appeared in the amateur cine magazine edited by Andor Kraszna-Krausz ('Statt Laien: Kenner!', *Film für alle*, 1929, probably issued in December).

Monkey's Moon, shot in the summer of 1929, was described as 'A document of commercial lenghts (sic) of Macpherson's two pet Douracouli Monkeys'. The title appeared on the list of avant-garde films distributed world wide by the Paris firm Studio Film, as of December 1929. Four stills were published in *Close Up*, vol 5, no. l, July 1929, with a fifth photo on the cover. And yet another still – the last trace of the film – appeared in the final issue of the year, vol 5 no 6, December 1929.

After *Borderline*, Macpherson filmed several stages of the construction of the villa commissioned by the Macphersons from the young Berlin architect Hermann Henselmann. These sequences were shot in 1931 on the construction site at Burier, bordering Lake Geneva, several kilometres from Montreux-Territet. Two photos of the villa appeared in *Close Up* vol. 8, no 3, September 1931.

Roughly thirty minutes of fragments, very probably rushes and out-takes, edited together by Anne Friedberg in an attempt at reconstruction, are preserved at the Museum of Modern Art, New York (16mm reversal, three reels). As far as I know, these are the only remaining traces of *Wing Beat, Foothills,* and the sequences of the Villa 'Kenwin' (from the first syllables of Kenneth and Winifred).

6. Bibliography

A

Close Up, July, 1927 - December, 1933. Monthly until December, 1930 (42 nos. vols 1-7); quarterly from March, 1931 until December, 1933 (12 nos. vols 8-10). Published by Pool, Montreux and London. Reprinted by Arno Press, New York, 1971, complete (including the advertising pages), with index.

B

Oswell Blakeston, *Through a Yellow Glass*, Pool, London, 1928.

Oswell Blakeston, *Books, Booklets and Relics*, Catalogue of Haringey Libraries exhibition, London, 1980.

Bryher, (pseud. of Annie Winifred Ellerman), *Film Problems of Soviet Russia*, Pool, Territet, 1929.

Bryher, *The Heart to Artemis. A Writer's Memoirs,* Harcourt, Brace and World, New York, 1962. English edition: Collins, London, 1963.

Guy Collomb, Roland Cosandey, "Ces quatre perches fichées sur les pentes de la colline. La Maison Kenwin sise à Burier", *Repères* (Lausanne), n° 12, automne 1985, pp. 54-76.

Eric Elliott, *Anatomy of Motion Picture Art*, Pool, Territet, 1928.

H.D. (Hilda Doolittle), *Borderline. A Pool Film with Paul Robeson*, Mercury Press, London, 1930. 39 pages, illustrated.

H.D., *Tribute to Freud*, Pantheon Books, New York, 1956. Reprinted by Carcanet Press, Oxford, 1971.

Hermann Henselmann, *Drei Reisen nach Berlin*, Henschel Verlag, Kunst und Gesellschaft, Berlin, 1981.

A. Kossowsky, *Taschenbuch des Kameramannes (für Lehr – und Nachschlagezwecke)*, Verlag Max Mattison, Berlin, 1928.

Kenneth Macpherson, 'Statt Laien: Kenner!', *Film für alle*, no 12, 1928.

Kenneth Macpherson, 'As Is', *Close Up*, vol 2, no 6, June 1928, and vol. 7, no 5, November 1930.

Mercurius (pseud. of James Burford), 'Film Structure and the Work of Close Up', *Architectural Review*, vol 68, 1930.

L. Saalschutz, 'The Film in its Relation to the Unconscious', *Close Up*, vol 5, no 1, July 1929.

Hanns Sachs, *Psychoanalyse, Rätsel des Unbewussten*, Lichtbild-Bühne, Berlin, 1926.

Freddy Buache (ed), *Cinéma Indépèndant et d'avant-garde à la fin du muet*, Travelling/Documents Cinémathèque Suisse, no 55, Summer 1979 and no 56-57, Spring, 1980.

Deke Dusinberre, 'The Avant-Garde Attitude in the Thirties', in Don Macpherson (ed), *British Cinema. Traditions of Independence*. British Film Institute, London, 1980.

Anne Friedberg, 'Approaching Borderline', *Millenium Film Journal*, no 7-8-9, Fall, 1980.

Anne Friedberg, 'Fragments de Films Pool 1927-1929' in Buache(ed), *Cinéma indépendant...*, vol 2, 1980.

Anne Friedberg, 'And myself have learned to use small projector', on H.D., Woman, History, Recognition. *Wide Angle Conference*, Athens, Ohio, 25 April, 1981.

Anne Friedberg, *The Film Journal Close Up: Writing About Cinema*, (1927-1933), Doctoral thesis presented at University of New York, 1983, (which the author was unable to consult for this study).

Stéphane Link, *La Villa Macpherson*, Ecole Polytechnique Fédérale de Lausanne, 1983. Unpublished

Barry Salt, *Film Style and Technology: History and Analysis*, Starword, London, 1983.

Borderline

7. Acknowledgements

    This article, part of ongoing research, owes a great deal to the help and considerateness of Anne Friedberg (New York), Henri Storck (Brussels), Ian Christie (London), to whom I express my gratitude.

    I would also like to thank the following institutions for placing their facilities at my disposition: The Swiss Cinémathèque (Lausanne), The Arsenal Library (Paris), Film Study Center (Museum of Modern Art, New York), the Beinecke Library (Yale University, New Haven).

8. Photo Credits

    Swiss Cinémathèque, Lausanne/National Film Archive, London.

NOTES

This text is a reprint from *Afterimage*, 12, Autumn 1985, pp. 66-84 and it has been very slightly revised. The translation from the French is due to Deke Dusinberre.

The study was first published in German: "*Borderline* – Spuren der Avant-garde um 1930", *cinema* (Zurich), Vuille-Mondada).

The French original version was issued in 1988: "Autour de Borderline", *Les Cahiers de la Cinémathèque* (Perpignan), n°49, 1988, pp. 51-65, 32 ill. With additional unpublished appendices.

Coalface – Cavalcanti (1935)

DEKE DUSINBERRE

The Avant-Garde Attitude

IN THE THIRTIES

First published in *Traditions of
Independence: British Cinema in the Thirties*
ed Don Macpherson, British Film Institue,
London, 1980

In the autumn of 1966, in the midst of that period of prolific art activity in London, a telegram was composed for (though never despatched to) Jonas Mekas in New York, advising him of the imminent arrival of the London Film-Makers' Co-operative. And in the short lifetime of the London Co-op, this telegram has achieved almost mythic status: it finds its way into every history of the English avant-garde scene, and a reproduction of the telegram still graces – despite several changes of location and personnel – the office of the Co-op. Part of the charm of the telegram resides in its formulation:

> *London Film-Makers Coop about to be legally established stop purpose to shoot shoot
> shoot shoot shoot stop never stop no bread no place to lay our heads no matter just mind
> if you want to make money stop if you like Bryan Forbes stop if you read sight and sound
> stop if you want to make films I mean films come all you need is eyes in the beginning
> stop gen from 94 Charing Cross Road W.C.2 parturition finished screams begin stop.*

It is generally considered to be – as the text itself implies – the birth certificate of the Film-Makers' Co-op and the avant-garde film movement it spawned, and therefore the telegram retains an insistent fascination for those who draw their identity from it. Like personal birth certificates, like very first photographs, there it *is,* irrefutable proof of one's existence, of one's formal entrance into history.

The validity of this document has never been challenged; that is to say, Britain claimed no avant-garde cinema prior to 1966. Hence it is with an eerie sensation – almost a shudder on recognition of an earlier incarnation – that one begins to unearth unmistakable traces of a coherent and productive avant-garde film practice in London in the Thirties. Of course, the work of Len Lye has long been acknowledged, as has the magazine *Close Up;* but these two incidents were never recognised as corresponding to a 'movement' or an identifiable corpus of work – they remained peripheral to the over-determining influence of the documentary movement fostered by John Grierson.

The term 'avant-garde' is intended toward those films (and that film criticism) which seek an alliance with modernism in the other arts, which demand a consistent interrogation of the medium; they challenge the industry not only on the levels of content and of production/distribution/exhibition, but also on the level of the aesthetic/representational postulates on which the industry's commerce is based. In the Thirties, the characteristic ambiguity of the term was amplified, since 'the avant-garde' was manifest only through an institution of criticism (not, as in the Sixties, through an institution of production/distribution/exhibition). The avant-garde was thus really an attitude formulated by a series of film periodicals, an attitude which comprehended a disparate body of film-making practice. This in turn devolved on an intricate relationship between the avant-garde attitude and films produced by the documentary movement, the political newsreel movement, and even certain commercial (advertising) films. The common relationship existed on the level of a shared progressive aspiration, an aspiration which varied in degree and goal (from reformist to revolutionary) as well as in strategy but which nevertheless lent, at times, a spirit of unity among those who anticipated a progressive intervention from the cinema.

Indeed, the entire history of film could be written in the light of the progressive aspiration and its frustration. Annette Michelson has observed that '…a certain euphoria enveloped the early film-making and theory. For there was, ultimately, a real sense in which the revolutionary aspirations of the modernist movement in literature and the arts, on the one hand, and of a Marxist or Utopian tradition, on the other, could converge in the hopes and promises, as yet undefined, of the new medium.'[1] When those hopes were squashed by the pressures of capitalist society, those who retained revolutionary fervour had to adopt a position of opposition rather than one of enthusiastic participation. The first reaction came with the first real consolidation of the industry: the avant-garde of the Twenties, capped by the combined aesthetic and political goals of the surrealist movement. And, until the production and financial changes wrought by the introduction of sound technology eventually polarised the situation, the emerging counter-cinema was able to contain contradictory versions of the progressive vision within a pluralist perspective. It is this pluralist perspective which yielded an avant-garde movement best characterised as an 'attitude' – as distinct from a specific aesthetic style or a specific production situation – which in turn leads to a certain ambiguity as to which films adhere to that avant-garde attitude.*

The initial focal point for avant-garde film activity in Britain was the film review *Close Up,* which commenced publication in July 1927 under the editorship of Kenneth Macpherson and Bryher. Edited from London and from Switzerland, *Close Up* immediately acquired an international reputation and, in conjunction with the exhibition work of the Film Society, established London as the site of an intellectual approach to film form. Writing of the intellectual film enthusiasts at the close of the silent film era Richard Griffith says: 'Their leadership came mainly from Britain, which, though it had produced few films and no good ones, seems to have been a fertile field for the ideal of cinema perfectionism.'[2] If its opposition to the dominant industry could be construed as 'perfectionism', *Close Up's* eclectic endorsement of alternatives to that industry embodied an ambivalent attitude which remained characteristic into the first half of the subsequent decade. This ambivalence is expressed in Macpherson's introductory editorial where he asserted that 'really good art IS commercial' and expressed the wish that the film industry would awaken to the possibilities of the medium; but he felt it was more important to consider 'the film for the film's sake', conceding that 'the hope of the cinema lies with the amateur'.[3] *Close Up's* cultural sympathies with the avant-garde are suggested by its publication of contributions from people such as the imagist poet H.D. (who often wrote reviews and criticism and occasional poems), Gertrude Stein (who contributed a short story, *Mrs. Emerson)* and Man Ray (who published some photographs and a short piece on his film work). H.D.'s poem for the first issue, titled *Projector,* evokes the utopian expectations of the silent cinema which anticipate similar aspirations on the part of the 1960s' 'underground'. Hailing the power of the projector, she describes how it arrives:

in a new blaze of splendour
calls the host to reassemble
and to readjust
all severings
and differings of thought,
all strife and strident bickering
and rest...[4]

Close Up concentrated its film criticism on assaults on Hollywood 'mediocrity' and support for UFA and Soviet 'art' films, occasionally covering what it described as 'cine-poems' as well as documenting the work of the well-known French surrealists and the less-organised activities of independents such as the Belgian Charles Dekeukeleire and major individual

*Further ambiguity is engendered by the incompleteness of the research for this article. At the time of writing too few of the films have been unearthed and too little of the documentation examined; my observations and apparent conclusions thus remain intellectually obstetric (D.D.).

figures such as Eggeling, Richter, Ruttmann and Lye. It also noted the formation of avant-garde production groups like Neofilms in Paris (under Cavalcanti) and Excentric Films in America (Herman Weinberg and Robert van Rosen).

The magazine similarly encouraged the production of cine-poems and other independent films in Britain. Pool Films sponsored H.D.'s attempt to make the 'first free verse film poem', *Wing Beat,* in 1927 (Pool Publishers produced *Close Up).* After two initial announcements of the work as 'in progress', *Close Up* was silent on the project; the lack of any trace of the film today or of any mention or review of it at the time have led me to assume that it was never completed. However, Oswell Blakeston – a film-maker and critic associated with *Close Up* – recollected in a recent interview[5] that the film was in fact finished and that *Close Up's* silence was due to an obscure embarrassment, either between H.D. and Macpherson or over the film itself. At any rate, no other record of the film's completion or screening has yet come to light. Blakeston himself made *I Do Like to be Beside the Seaside* (1927?), acted by H.D. and others, as something of a spoof on the pretentiousness of 'intellectual' film criticism. Described by a contemporary reviewer as '… a brilliant and amusing commentary on the technical devices of many well-known producers of films' (Dulac, Man Ray, Leni, Dreyer and Eisenstein are subsequently cited), it was contrived around 'an airy thread of story' involving a typist.[6] Blakeston advises that the only print of the film was destroyed by fire during the Second World War. Blakeston, who was to become one of the main apologists for an avant-garde attitude in the Thirties, also worked closely with the photographer Francis Bruguière. The two made *Light Rhythms,* an abstract film, in 1930. 'Pure' in conception, the 5-minute film represents a radical statement in film aesthetics, '…in which the material consisted of static designs in cut paper over which various intensities of light were moved. The appeal of the film lay in the changing light values, which were revealed by the cut paper patterns.'[7] A look at the graphic 'score' detailing the light movements reveals five sections or 'movements', each with six sequences. The symmetry and dynamism evoke the patterned structures of Eggeling or perhaps Richter, while stills suggest a more complex surface of light and shadow than is offered in either *Diagonal Symphony* or the *Rhythmus* series.[8] In addition, the musical score, by Jack Ellit, who was later to work with Len Lye (on *Tusalava* and at the GPO), was composed to enhance the sensation of progression and permutation.

If, in 1930, *Light Rhythms* and *Tusalava*[9] represented one pole of independent activity – that most comfortable with the epithet 'avant-garde' – that pole was nevertheless linked to other poles representing the progressive aspiration for the cinema. Two important developments – the political crisis in exhibition forced by film censorship and the aesthetic crisis in production following the advent of sound – cut across the independent sector and illustrate aspects of unity and difference.

The alignment of forces over the censorship issue suggests that association with specific film groups is not a sufficient guide to political position. Huntly Carter, in *New Spirit in the Cinema,* surveyed the positions as they were drawn in 1929-30, mobilised by the London County Council's recalcitrance in granting private exhibition permits for Soviet 'propaganda' films *(Potemkin, End of St. Petersburg, Storm over Asia)* to those groups formed expressly to circumvent the public censor. Carter writes: 'The combination of forces thus brought about for the purpose of making war on censorship, and obtaining a free hand in the importation and exhibition of 'artistic' and social pictures and the reduction or abolition of Custom duties, is a very unusual one. It is a strangely variegated legion... broadly speaking it falls into three divisions answering to those of the three present political ones: Right, Centre, and Left.' Carter lists the Film Society as 'Right', the Masses Stage and Film Guild as 'Centre', and the Federation of Workers' Film Societies as 'Left'. The Masses S. F. Guild is appropriately labelled 'Centre' due to its support by many members of government and the established theatrical profession, with Fenner Brockway as the President and six other MPs on its 25-member Advisory Council. The Film Society is labelled 'Right' apparently because of its aim (according to Carter) 'to act as a body supplementary and useful to the commercial film world in introducing to its study the work of talented new-comers and experimenters who might later contribute to its progress', and because its Council is compromised of 'The Honourable Ivor Montagu' (much is made of his parentage) as well as Iris Barry, Sidney L. Bernstein, Frank Dobson, Edmund Dulac, E. A. McKnight-Kauffer and W. C. Mycroft, and because of its association with *Close Up,* whose objects are 'in some respects similar to that of the Film Society'. (Macpherson is singled out as the editor and Blakeston as a principal contributor.[11]) Carter's 'Left' – the FOWFS – paradoxically has a Provisional Council which includes Montagu, Macpherson and Blakeston along with Harry Pollitt, W. Gallacher, Monica Ewer, Henry Dobb and G. P. Wells. Carter adds that although he is not sure that the Masses S.F. Guild is represented formally on the Council of the FOWFS, 'I think I am right in saying that it is affiliated with the FOWFS'. Carter then attempts to dismiss the paradox that is raised by his schematic divisions by subdividing the Federation into a 'Right', 'Right Centre', 'Centre', and 'Left'. Thus Carter misses the significance of the obvious conclusion that, on issues such as the political censorship of films, political distinctions were blurred, *even on an institutional level.* Macpherson and Blakeston had dubious credentials as political activists, but their commitment to a progressive role for the cinema merited their inclusion on the Council of the FOWFS.

Carter does point to an important difference between the groups, exemplified by the fact that the Film Society had an easy time with the censor by minimising the political aspect of the films in question. He cites a grievance raised by the *Daily Worker* of 9 January 1930:

'The Censors have allowed the film *New Babylon* to be shown to The Film Society, but the Workers' Film Society is refused permission to screen it… Why is The Film Society permitted to exhibit these films at one of the largest West End cinemas, and workers' societies are not? It is not hard to say why. The Film Society and *Close Up* clique have always done their best to convey the impression that they are obsessed far more with technique than with social content.'[12] This useful observation leads Carter to make an obtuse conclusion that, 'Indeed it is doubtful whether the leaders and members of these two groups have any knowledge of sociology and the transformation which present-day society is undergoing. The game is quite plainly to promote the idea that the moving picture must be detached from actuality and infuse it with a new aesthetic having nothing whatever to do with actual fact or a life-centred society.'[13] Thus Carter dismisses the likes of Blakeston, Macpherson and the Honourable Ivor Montagu.

The complex interdependence of progressive attitudes informed the production situation as well as the exhibition situation, and the production situation was of course further complicated at this point by the introduction of sound technology. At this juncture, Macpherson mounted an ambitious feature-length production titled *Borderline.* Incorporating a socially progressive theme into a 'psychoanalytic drama' (Bryher and H.D. collaborated on the film and both later were to be analysed by Freud), the film explored the social and sexual tension generated by the shifting passions of an interracial foursome (black Americans Paul Robeson and Eslanda Goode Robeson played starring roles) which found itself in a small European town. The film was silent and, as is obvious from an illustrated review in *The Architectural Review,*[14] camera angle and mobility were exploited in the best silent technique for expressive purposes. A relatively disinterested description of the film was written some time later by Peter Noble from the perspective of *The Negro in Films.* His slightly condescending tone is balanced by his admiration for the thematic ambitions of the film and for Macpherson's 'delicate' handling of those themes.[15] The film was apparently not well received by the press, as Macpherson was compelled to defend it in the pages of *Close Up* after the film had its run, and it vanished from sight. Whatever the reasons for its disappearance,* an irresistible conjecture is that part of its problem lay in its non-specificity: not radical enough in form to adopt a marginal avant-garde status; not, as a silent film released in the summer of 1930, accessible enough to reach the mainstream. I would guess that it looked rather stylised and perhaps sadly 'rear-guard', certainly not qualities sought by those who consider themselves avant-garde.

It is now a cliché to attribute the 'decline' of the international avant-garde during the

---

*a print of the film is still in existence and may be acquired for preservation by the National Film Archive (Ed.).

Thirties to the crippling effect of the added production costs of sound technology. Like most clichés, it offers a crude truth which masks a more subtle understanding of the issue. Silence itself was not considered a virtue (as would become the case in many avant-garde films of the Sixties and Seventies), as even the 'silent' avant-garde productions of the Twenties were invariably presented with musical accompaniment, but the 'talking picture' did frustrate one of the original aspirations of the silent cinema to formulate an 'international language'. Avant-garde critics welcomed sound, albeit warily, as yet another tool for creative production. From the modernist perspective it offered another level of control over the signifying relationship between image and sound and, as a progressive intervention, suggested new modes of formulating the internationalism promised by silent movies. Thus they railed against simple talkies as reactionary theatre, and lauded 'true sound pictures' which treated sound-image in a problematic vein. Blakeston, writing in 1931, cites as examples of 'the most intelligent contemporary use of sound' Fischinger's 'sound abstracts' (images derived from sound), Buñuel's *L'Age d'Or* (visual-aural counterpoint), and the *Secrets of Nature* science series (image motivated by word/text).[16] A few years later, in an article titled *Enslaved by Sound,* avant-garde film-maker Andrew Buchanan continued to complain of the turgidity of 'dialogue films' and admired documentaries for remaining 'sound films' in which '… dialogue is practically ignored, and the sound track is kept at bay… It is this freedom from microphones which enables documentary producers to create the maximum of movement, nothing hampering the picture, either during shooting or in the cutting room.'[17] Hence the advent of sound initially reinforced the pluralist attitude toward progressive counter-cinema in so far as it endorsed all practices aligned against the commercial talkie. The crisis it fomented within the avant-garde (which subsequently had a polarising effect throughout independent cinema) resulted not simply from the threat to the existence of avant-garde production through oligopolistic control of sound technology, but from a concomitant threat to the role and *identity* assumed by avant-garde film-making: silent avant-garde films were suddenly rear-guard, the cutting edge of their vanguard formal practice blunted and the films rendered effete. Silent films no longer represented the wave of the future, and that constituted a serious challenge to the avant-garde attitude. As private production became less feasible, many film-makers looked toward marginal industrial or advertising film-making or to state-sponsored production units, all of which, from the pluralist perspective of the time, retained at least the possibility of working within the avant-garde ambience, if in somewhat compromised circumstances.

Whatever the ultimate reasons for *Borderline's* lack of success, Pool Films made no more ventures into film production.[18] *Close Up's* spirit seems to have followed the stream of European directors who were drawn to Hollywood's studio attractions in the early Thirties.

The magazine retained a Hollywood correspondent and became more sympathetic to the industry, finally folding towards the end of 1933.

Its role as 'voice of the avant-garde' had already been usurped earlier in that year when, in the spring of 1933, B. Vivian Braun published *Film.* With the next issue, the quarterly became *Film Art* and continued publication, somewhat irregularly, until 1937. While under Braun's direction, *Film Art's* masthead proclaimed itself as the 'international review of advance-guard cinema'. The magazine's tenure is perhaps most notable for its efforts to co-ordinate production and exhibition with the criticism it offered. Braun, like Macpherson, understood that critical intervention was only part of his role in the avant-garde and he completed several films, one of which, *Beyond This Open Road,* was screened by the Film Society in November 1934. Made with Irene Nicholson, then an assistant editor of *Film Art,* it was 'symphonic treatment of the open air'. The programme notes to the Film Society performance offer a laconic description of the production: 'This silent film was made in thirteen days and shot with a hand camera. The director was given waste material amounting in all to 1,500 feet, out of which in the final cutting emerged 1,000 feet of completed picture.'[19] The production is credited to the 'Film Art Group' which announced itself at that point as the 'First Cinema Unit for the production of Specialist Films' and eighteen months later listed five films for distribution, of which three were credited to Braun, including *Beyond This Open Road* distributed in a sound version. Additional films were made under the magazine's aegis, such as Nicholson's *Ephemeral,* a seven minute 'film poem of light and passing time', and a mathematically abstract film by Robert Fairthorne and Brian Salt designed to demonstrate visually the equation of its title, $X+X=O$ (distributed in 9.5, 16 and 35mm versions), and so on. Most impressive, perhaps, is the fact that *Film Art* almost immediately launched a 'Cinema Art Course' offering practical and correspondence courses in film-making, devising parallel courses for those with and those without access to 16mm equipment. It apparently became quite popular: the notice which re-advertised the course claimed that the first session 'met with enormous success – many persons having to be refused admission', and maintained correspondents in America, Germany, Ireland and England.[20] The need for systematic film-making courses grounded in aesthetic theory was perhaps partially inspired to combat the 'amateurishness' of the 'cine clubs'. Writing in the first issue of *Film,* Judith Todd refers to the function of 'Exhibiting Film Societies' as distinct from the film-making 'Cine Clubs': 'They should realise that they [Exhibiting Film Societies] are at present fulfilling two functions: that of shewing [sic] films and that of understanding cinema. The latter, to which far too little attention has been given, is the active side and implies far more than shewing films; it must, of course, include making them, which is at present largely left to the cine clubs.' Whom she proceeds to dismiss: 'From examples of their work one would say that they exist, and will exist, chiefly as a means of using up film. Hence their name, as they start from the apparatus end, and are good customers of the makers of and dealers in cinematograph apparatus. The 16mm camera in the right hands is no toy. The pity is that the Film Societies, in concentrating on the exhibiting side, have not made more use of it for inexpensive experimental work.'[21]

Film Art was not to ignore the importance of exhibition, however. In 1923, Robert Herring complained in *Close Up* that 'London has no *salle d'avant-garde.* There is no place in London where good pictures can be regularly seen... It is absurd and maddening to go on cooing over the cinema when, in England, one is ignorant of Dulac, Dreyer, Epstein, Gance even...'[22] The same year did see the Avenue Pavilion Theatre in Shaftesbury Avenue dedicate itself to showing 'art' and 'absolute' (i.e. abstract) film. Although still very much a commercial venture, it did offer opportunities for public exhibition of non-commercial work. Blakeston recalls that the Avenue Pavilion, enthusiastically supported by *Close Up* and for a time the venue for Film Society screenings, was supportive of his work *(Light Rhythms* ran there) and was consistently willing to programme his and others' short films. The Avenue Pavilion sustained its policy for only a few years, but in the pilot issue of his periodical Braun could allude to two London cinemas [The Academy and The Everyman?] which were at least sympathetic to non-commercial films. In the same editorial he declared that '*Film is* not going to devote a certain amount of incidental space to good cinema, but is going to be entirely devoted to the film as an art. We shall seek a film-form, and attempt to solve the problems which prevent a realisation of that film-form.'[23]

Good to his word, issue two of *Film Art* proudly announced the opening of the Forum Cinema in Villiers Street as 'London's Advance-Guard Cinema'. The Forum's organisers were M. Hatzfeld, B. Vivian Braun and Irene Nicholson. A year later Braun could list 'London's four worthwhile cinemas: the Forum, Villiers Street, the Curzon, Mayfair, the Academy, Oxford Street, and the Everyman, Hampstead.'[24] Despite its supportive image, the screening record of the Film Society was not particularly good. From 1925-1939 the only *British* avant-garde films it programmed were *Light Rhythms* (1930), *Beyond This Open Road (1934) X+X=0* (1936), and four films by Lye: *Tusalava* (1929), *Kaleidoscope* (1935), *Birth of a Robot* (1936) and *N. or N. W.* (1937). In fact, the Film Society's selection of British films was habitually confined to scientific films, sporting films, or documentaries.[25] Exhibition opportunities for London's avant-garde film-makers seem to have been at least as good through commercial cinemas as through the various film societies.

The concerted efforts of those involved in *Film Art* to produce, distribute, exhibit and criticise avant-garde film were impressive, but their impact was almost certainly weakened as a result of internal dissensions. Following a nine-month hiatus after issue five of *Film Art,* number six appeared with Nicholson and John C. Moore as editors and Braun presumably banished. The masthead dispensed with references to 'advance-guard cinema' and described itself as 'An Independent Quarterly devoted to The Serious Film'. The magazine did not change drastically in either style or content (articles on abstract film, on photography by Blakeston, etc, continued to appear), but it took a swipe at the 'advance-guard' six months later on the appearance of the rival *New Cinema:* 'The *avant-garde* film movement died in France many years ago, and *New Cinema* has only just realised it.'[26] *New Cinema* was edited by... B. Vivian Braun. It incorporated the familiar slogan of 'An International Review of Advance-Guard Cinema' and added, for those with any remaining doubt, that *New Cinema* was the 'Only Cinema Review in the World *Solely* Devoted to Art in Cinema'. *Film Art's* snide forecast of a single-issue publication for *New Cinema* turned out to be accurate, despite *New Cinema's* promising beginning with articles by Blakeston and Herman Weinberg and Robert Fairthorne (regular contributors to *Film Art)* and a particularly good one by Moholy-Nagy, all of which were quite theoretical in tone. Confusingly, however, the British films that were covered in the review section are uncompromisingly commercial: Paramount's *The Scoundrel* and *The Crusaders** and Hitchcock's *Thirty-Nine Steps* for Gaumont-British, etc.

Film Art carried on for another year, during which Nicholson and Brian Montagu left for Trinidad to make a film for the *Trinidad Guardian* about 'the varied life of Trinidad, its industries... and its cosmopolitan population', production stills from which graced the final issues. It is unclear whether the film was ever completed.

Film Art and *New Cinema* had sustained the avant-garde attitude (during a decade of limited avant-garde production) within the progressive aspiration as inaugurated by *Close Up* and the activities of the late Twenties. This attitude constituted itself as a vaguely progressive political line and a specific formal radicalism as the best strategy to combat the hegemony of the film industry. A manifesto published in the third issue of *Film Art* distills many of the ideas which informed that attitude. The language and visual style of the manifesto invoke those of Dziga Vertov, and in tone it attains the stridency of a political manifesto; yet its priorities remain clearly aesthetic: 'To analyse the potentialities and solve the aesthetic problems of cinema art' is listed first and 'to encourage the use of the cinema as social reformer...' is listed last.[27] Those, uncynically, were its priorities. The manifesto even asserts that *Film Art* would remain 'as non-political as possible', for example, but also that articles would be printed as received, 'except when space demanded cutting'. That is to say, while *Film Art* (Vivian Braun) could be identified with left wing politics, it affirmed the liberal

*The Scoundrel by Hecht and MacArthur; *The Crusaders* by DeMille (Ed.).

pluralist tendency of the avant-garde to avoid an explicit political line, defining its role as one of open access to those with political ideas related to the cinema; hence it published articles on political film, by Herbert Marshall, then in the Soviet Union, and an anti-fascist article by John Sydney titled *Films and Internationalism,* etc. Braun himself would write that: 'The newsreel's (one might say the cinema's) two greatest tasks are: (1) the prevention of international war via the promotion of international understanding... and (2) the putting before the public facts concerning the conditions under which those persons some call 'workers' (others, more aptly, 'slaves of capitalism') live.'[28] Typically, Braun subsequently feels obligated to qualify that position: 'Our [i.e., *Film Art's]* interest in films is judging them first and foremost as art...'[29]

The attitude of openness, encouraging contact and co-operation ('Always in contact with our readers. CONTACT. And co-operation. Two essentials.'[30]) extended to an eclecticism regarding the production situation and stylistic tendencies of all non-industrial cinema. Thus the avant-garde attitude treated sympathetically the early GPO Film Unit and advertising films. For instance, Irene Nicholson reviewed Basil Wright's *Liner Cruising South* in 1933: 'If a little of it is ordinary it is the fault of the super producers... But the photography has a fine feeling for surface textures and the opening and closing sequences are pure poetry.'[31] Braun meanwhile described Wright's *Cargo from Jamaica* as an 'exquisitely photographed, beautifully mounted essay', noting Wright's 'eye for sculptural beauty'.[32] In addition to the vocabulary used (poetic, painterly, sculptural) these comments are characteristic in that they are highly selective, stressing certain qualities or points in the film and understating less attractive aspects of such commercial/institutional commissions. Hence a relatively brief sequence in Arthur Elton's *Aero-Engine* could be hailed as follows: 'For pure visual thrill, and impressionistic beauty, and cinematic value, the sequence of the aeroplane's first flight is unsurpassed. This sequence is a film in itself, and at that one of the finest that has ever come from England.'[33] This selective encouragement of certain sequences paralleled the celebration of individual film-makers as the bastion against industrial production-line anonymity. The avant-garde ambience thus sought to include not only those who financed and executed their work entirely alone, but also those who had chosen a slightly different production route. Nicholson would laud Paul Rotha's documentary *Contact* because it was 'a film directed, mounted and photographed by one man, an artist...'[34] Similarly, Wright is described as exemplary 'because he is, with Arthur Elton, and one or two others, one of the few men in England making real films which he writes, directs, AND EDITS.'[35] Since the best strategy for the formal radicalisation sought by the avant-garde seemed to lie in selective encouragement of those production aspects which permitted formal experimentation, it developed the 'selective pluralism' in which certain advertising films and documentaries were recruited as part of the avant-garde project (particularly those which experimented with sound/image signification). As early as 1931 Bruguière and Blakeston made a short advertising film, an entirely abstract film again involving the movement of light and shapes which eventually delivered a lettered message: 'Empire Buyers are Empire Builders.'[36] Blakeston defended the advertising efficacy of such an approach with the comment that through such abstraction 'the screen [was] used as the ultimate nerve end'. He also optimistically assessed the creative and economic potential for film-makers: '… an experimental approach can only be found in the new possibility of the advertising film. Indeed, the advertising film provides an economic basis for all pioneer work at the moment.'[37]

The search for an economic base for their work actually led pioneers, who had previously relied on private patronage, in three directions: the fringe of the industry, the advertising film, and state funding. Apparently several of the avant-garde film-makers tried stints at the studios (Blakeston among them) but only Andrew Buchanan appears to have had some success. Buchanan produced a fortnightly 'cinemagazine' (first known as *Ideal Cinemagazine,* then as *The Gaumont-British Magazine)* which ran as a support to commercial features. The flexible format of the magazine permitted some degree of experimentation and Buchanan directed sequences which explored dance and movement through experimental montage, which he theoretically justified in the pages of periodicals like *Film Art* and *Cinema Quarterly.*[38] Similarly, despite Blakeston's claims for advertising work, only a few European animators managed to support themselves in this manner, George Pal being the only one to work in England for any period. However, the term 'advertising work' included the commercially sponsored films like Lye's *Birth of a Robot* and Wright's *Liner Cruising South,* which were designed not so much to sell a specific product as to sell a corporate image (arts patronage eventually becoming part of that image). Though this type of work provided only occasional support for avant-garde film-makers in the Thirties, it did lead in the direction of the more substantial state patronage, for selling the corporate image was often coincident with selling the state image. And, indisputably, the most significant new economic base for pioneer film work was the one provided by state patronage in the form of the Empire Marketing Board and GPO Film Units headed by John Grierson.

The history of the Film Unit is sufficiently well documented to obviate the need for further discussion here, except in so far as the Film Unit influenced the notion of an avant-garde practice. As mentioned above, the avant-garde apologists perceived state patronage as a potential ally. By stressing the 'poetic moment' in otherwise unadmirable (to the avant-garde) films and by emphasising individual control over specific projects (even where control may have been ambiguous[39]), the avant-garde critics intervened in a clearly contradictory production situation in hopes of tipping the balance their way. This means that in the mid-Thirties the productions of the Film Unit were often perceived as within the avant-garde ambience. This suggests that documentary and promotional films should be re-analysed for evidence of their contribution to a modernist interrogation of the medium and, more importantly, that to the financial security and progressive connotations of working within the Film Unit should be added the attraction of enhanced *artistic* possibilities. Thus Len Lye and Norman McLaren no longer pose a serious contradiction within the history of the Film Unit, and the attraction of the Unit for young artists such as the painters Coldstream and Jennings, the composers Ellit and Britten, and the poet Auden, becomes not only understandable but, given the progressive aspirations still associated with the medium, almost inevitable.

But the demands of state sponsorship (as well as commercial sponsorship, of course) inflected the films away from those values of incisive formal experiment and complete individual control. Although freed from the requirement to yield profit, Grierson considered mass exhibition and mass comprehension a palpable goal. Wright gently formulates the contradiction: 'The price to be paid for the privilege of aesthetic experiment was therefore the discipline of public service.' But Grierson was known to expect firm discipline. He is reputed to have introduced the young McLaren to the Film Unit with the following admonition: 'What you will learn here is discipline. You have enough imagination, you need not worry about that. But you are going to get disciplined.'[40] In addition, Grierson's conception of the propaganda role for the Film Unit militated against the ambiguous or problematic formulation of ideas accruing to aesthetic innovation, and the documentary movement increasingly adopted a 'realist' aesthetic. Finally, state control could impose more direct forms of censorship as well: one of McLaren's finest GPO films, *Love on the Wing,* an animated fantasy about a new airmail service, was suppressed by the minister responsible for the GPO, who found its linear transmogrifications 'too erotic and too Freudian'.[42] These factors frustrated the avant-garde spirit, and after the demise of *Film Art* in 1937 there was no voice to assert the avant-garde attitude within the contradictions of state patronage.

State sponsorship also inflects history. The state tends to preserve (when it does so at all) its own films, not other films by those working occasionally for the state, much less those by Bruguière, Blakeston, Fairthorne, Salt, Buchanan, Macpherson, Braun, Nicholson, etc, who worked completely outside of the state apparatus. If those films were (or prove to be) extant, no doubt a different history, one with a space for a distinct avant-garde ambience, would emerge. Yet there are other factors which suggest themselves as contributory reasons for the absence of any 'history' of the avant-garde in the Thirties. It is striking that none of the relatively established visual artists in Britain had any regard for the cinema, and none explored its visual possibilities. In Paris, artists such as Leger, Duchamp, Man Ray (not to mention the surrealist celebration of cinema) elevated its status and imbued those avant-garde productions with an immediate historical value, a value which increases not just through film history, but also through the increasing art historical value of these artists' other work. It is impossible to assert that Robert Fairthorne and Brian Salt's abstract film $X+X=0$ is any less interesting or successful than, say, Man Ray's *Emak Bakia;* but it is obvious that Fairthorne and Salt's anonymity works against the film ever being found and, if rediscovered, equitably evaluated. It is equally difficult to ascertain why London-raised artists ignored the progressive aspiration of the cinema. One can only allude to the presence of a general anti-modernist trend within the milieu that professed modernism in terms of a hesitation, a reluctance to assume the logical extensions of that position or to relate it to film; so that a group of important young artists who named themselves 'Unit One' – Barbara Hepworth, Ben Nicholson, Henry Moore, Edward Wadsworth, Paul Nash, Frances Hodgkins and Edward Burra – restricted their call for modernism to the most traditional of arts. Nash asserted that 'Unit One may be said to stand for the expression of a truly contemporary spirit, for that which is recognised as peculiarly *of today* in painting, sculpture, and architecture'.[43] In relation to 'modern' art, cinema was doomed not even to a marginal role, but to a non-existent one. (Consequently, attempts to integrate cinema as a modern art were not notably successful.) *The Architectural Review* did cover avant-garde film for a period, but ceased to do so in 1935. *Cinema Quarterly,* founded in 1933, initially drew on an eclectic list of contributors which included the art historian Herbert Read (ironically, the author of the article on Unit One), the poet Hugh MacDiarmid and the designer McKnight Kauffer (who did the cover) as well as Blakeston, Braun, Buchanan and Fairthorne. But *Cinema Quarterly* shifted its commitment to realist documentary in a trajectory which describes the rise of the Film Unit and the decline of the avant-garde. It is paradoxical that consistent support for the cinema as a radical visual art came from literary directions. Macpherson, Bryher, Herring, Nicholson all had literary connections and careers, and it is their efforts to promote the avant-garde through literary periodicals which dictate this sketchy history.

And yet there is a further reason for the sketchiness of this history: the very a-historicism of the avant-garde attitude. That attitude stressed the newness, the nowness, of the work being done (cf. the crisis provoked by technological supersession of sound). It stressed *action.* This is evident not only in *Film Art's* manifesto but also in Blakeston's recollection of the period; it was not the films but their immediate impact which was crucial. Blakeston resists the idea of restoring and institutionalising the films made during that period but adds: 'If you could capture the *impact* of those films and put it in a museum, that would be ok...' He claims that he simply wanted 'to do something quick and magic'. Such an attitude was reinscribed in the mid Sixties in London when the founders of the Film-Makers' Co-operative drafted their telegram affirming that **all you need is eyes in the beginning**. Not to be confused with an *aloofness* from history, this almost infantile fascination is necessary to sustain that level of commitment to a marginalised and as yet powerless mode of representation and expression. And such an a-historical fascination condemns one to (rewards one with) eternal rebirth.

NOTES

1   Michelson, *New Forms In Film* (Exhibition catalogue), Montreux 1974, p. 10.

2   Griffith (with Paul Rotha), *The Film Till Now,* London, 1967, p. 416.

3   Macpherson, *Close Up,* no. 1, July 1926, p. 46.

4   H.D., 'Projector' in *Close Up,* no. I, p. 46.

5   Subsequent unattributed quotations are from an interview between Blakeston and this author in December 1977.

6   Mercurius, 'The Pipes of Pan' in *The Architectural Review,* vol. 67, p. 341. Mercurius was James Burford, a friend of Blakeston's who, with his brother Robert Burford, was also associated with *Close Up.* Blakeston later assumed J. Burford's role as regular film critic for *The Architectural Review.*

7   Rotha, *The Film Till Now,* p. 342n. Rotha admired the film.

8   Mercurius, 'Light and Movement' in *The Architectural Review,* vol. 67, pp.154 155.

9   For a description of the films of Lye see, for example, David Curtis, *Experimental Film,* London, 1971.

10   Huntly Carter, *New Spirit in the Cinema,* London, 1930, p. 285

11   *Ibid,* p. 286.

12   *Ibid,* p. 290.

13   *Ibid,* p. 290.

14   Mercurius, 'Art, Fact and Abstraction' in *The Architectural Review,* vol. 68, p. 258.

15   Noble*, The Negro in Films,* New York, 1970, p. 144.

16   Blakeston, 'Film Enquiry – *3'* in *The Architectural Review,* vol .70, p. 47.

17   Andrew Buchanan, 'Enslaved by Sound' in *Film Art,* no. 2, p. 54.

18   Apart from H.D.'s *Wing Beat,* Pool also sponsored Macpherson's first film, *Monkey's Moon.* I surmise, although I have no evidence, that much of the money behind Pool Films and Pool Publishers came from Bryher, whose given

name was Annie Winifred Ellerman, of the Ellerman shipping firm.

19 Programme note, The Film Society, 25 November 1934.

20 *Film Art,* no. 4, pp. 4 and 86.

21 *Film,* no. 1, pp. 12-13. The relationship of the avant-garde to the burgeoning
    amateur film movement of the Thirties remains ambiguous. Although
    encouraging amateur production, avant-garde apologists were dismissive of the
    amateurs' attempts to ape the industry. Some of this was perhaps due to an
    élitist attitude, some of it perhaps to a reasonable defence of different criteria.
    See, for example, Ralph Bond, 'The Amateur Convention' in *Close Up,* vol. 5,
    no. 6, pp. 479-483.

22 Herring, *Close Up,* May 1928, p. 56.

23 *Film,* no. 1, p. 3.

24 *Film Art,* no. 5, p. 31

25 Film Society programme notes. In fact, through its eclectic programming the
    Film Society reinforced the pluralist aspect of independent cinema during
    this period.

26 *Film Art,* no. 8, p. 39.

27 *Film Art,* no. 3, p. 9

28 *Film Art,* no. 4. p- 55

29 *Ibid,* p. 55.

30 *Film Art*, no. 3, p. 4.

31 *Film Art*, no. 2, p. 53

32 *Ibid,* p. 53

33 *Ibid,* p. 53

34 *Ibid,* p. 52

35 *Ibid,* p. 50

36 *Commercial Art*, no. 10, p. 65 (illus, p. 68)

37 *The Architectural Review,* vol. 69, p. 137

38 See, for example, *Film Art,* no. 2, p. 63, and *Cinema Quarterly,* vol. 1, p. 165

39 See Annette Kuhn 'British Documentary in the 1930's and "Independence":
    Recontextualising a Film Movement' in *Traditions of Independence: British
    Cinema in the Thirties* ed. Don Macpherson, British Film Institute, London,
    1980, p. 24.

40 *Norman McLaren,* catalogue by Scottish Arts Council, Edinburgh, 1977, p. 11

41 See Kuhn op cit

42 *McLaren,* p. 13

43 Herbert Read, 'Unit One' in *The Architectural Review,* vol. 74, p. 126

APPENDIX: PROVISIONAL LIST OF ENGLISH
AVANT-GARDE FILMMAKERS

Below is a list of the names of those principally identified with the avant-garde in London in the 1930s, followed by titles and, where films are obscure (or not extant), a reference to a description or mention of the film. Although the argument of this article is that the avant-garde attitude during this period was a pluralist one (selectively encompassing, for example, the work of the film units or certain aspects of commercial productions), this list is limited to those film-makers who worked exclusively within the avant-garde ambience and therefore have been completely overlooked by conventional film history (Lye and McLaren excepted, of course). Any additional information on film-makers (their whereabouts) or prints (ditto) would be greatly appreciated.

Oswell Blakeston: *I Do Like to be Beside the Seaside* (1927) – *The Architectural Review,* vol. 67, p. 341.

Light Rhythms (with Bruguière, 1930) – *The Architectural Review,* vol. 67, p. 154.

Empire Buyers are Empire Builders (with Bruguière, 1931) – *Commercial Art,* vol. 10, p. 65 and *The Architectural Review, vol.* 69, p. 137.

Guy Branch: *Punch and Judy* (1936?) – *New Cinema,* no. 1, p. 31.

B. Vivian Braun: *Exhilaration* (1933 ?) – *Film Art,* no. 1, p. 18.

Beyond the Open Road (with Irene Nicholson, 1934), also known as *Beyond This Open Road* – *Film Art,* no. 5, p.33.

Terrific Adventure (1936?) – *New Cinema,* no. 1, p. 31.

Rustic London (1936?) – *New Cinema,* no. 1, p. 31.

Francis Bruguière: *Light Rhythms* (with Blakeston, 1930);

Empire Buyers are Empire Builders (with Blakeston, 1931);

The Way (?) – *Film Art*, no. 10, p. 24

Andrew Buchanan: Produced fortnightly (sometimes weekly) 'cinemagazines', including the following sequences –

Machine (1933?) – *Film Art,* no. 2, p. 63.

Time (1933?) – *Film Art,* no. 2. p. 63.

Chess-Bored – *Film Art*, no. 5, p. 38.

Dance Flaws – *Cinema Quarterly*, vol. 1, p. 165

Robert Fairthorne: *X+X=O* (with Salt, 1936)—*Film Art,* no. 9, p. 18.

H.D.: *Wing Beat* (completed ? 1927).

Brian Desmond Hurst: *The Tell Tale Heart* (1933?)—*Film Art,* no. 1, p. 28.

Len Lye: *Tusalava* (1928); A *Colour Box* (1935); *Kaleidoscope* (1935); *The Birth of* A *Robot* (1936); *Rainbow Dance* (1936);
Trade Tattoo (1937); N *or NW* (1937); *Colour Flight* (1938); *Lambeth Walk* (1939); *When the Pie was Open* (1939-40).

Norman McLaren: Untitled (1933); *Seven till Five* (1933);
Camera Makes Whoopee (1935); *Colour Cocktail* (1935);
Five Untitled Shorts (1935);
Hell Unltd. (with Helen Biggar, 1936); *Book Bargain* (1937); *News For the Navy* (1937); *Many A Pickle* (1937-38);
Love on the Wing (1938); *The Obedient Flame* (1939).

Kenneth Macpherson: *Monkey's Moon* (1928?);
Borderline (1930) – *The Architectural Review,* vol. 68, p. 258.

Brian Montagu: Trinidad film (with Nicholson, completed?) – *Film Art,* no.7, p.8; no.9, p.23; no. 10, p.9.

Irene Nicholson: *Ephemeral* (1934)—*Film Art,* no. 5, p. 42; Trinidad film (with Montagu, see above).

Brian Salt: $X+X=O$ (with Fairthorne, 1936).

POSTSCRIPT

This article, completed some time ago, is ageing rapidly. Some of the films I described as lost have already come to light. A print of *Borderline* is in the collection at Eastman House in Rochester, New York, and fragments of *Wing Beat* have recently been deposited in the Museum of Modern Art, New York. The latter surfaced through the timely efforts of Mrs. Perdita Schaffner (H. D.'s daughter) and Anne Friedberg (in connection with her research on her doctoral thesis for the Cinema Studies Department of New York University). I have not yet had the opportunity to see the films, and thus have decided to let this article stand unaltered.

However, I would like to make one correction. In a brief illuminating discussion with Friedberg, she asserted that *Wing Beat* was primarily Macpherson's film, despite my inclination to credit it to H. D. and in spite of the discovery of the fragments within H. D.'s estate (the film is described in

Close Up simply as 'a Pool film'; H. D. is identified as the star). After a quick review of the meagre documentation currently available to me, I am inclined to agree with Friedberg that although the film relied on the contributions from H. D. and Bryher, it was probably the inspiration of Macpherson, and should be credited either to him or to the Pool group as a whole.

Deke Dusinberre, July 1979

Interregnum

Fires Were Started – Humphrey Jennings (1943)

LINDSAY ANDERSON

Only Connect

SOME ASPECTS OF THE WORK
OF HUMPHREY JENNINGS

First published in *Sight and Sound*
April-June, 1954

It is difficult to write anything but personally about the films of Humphrey Jennings. This is not of course to say that a full and documented account of his work in the cinema would not be of the greatest interest: anyone who undertook such a study would certainly merit our gratitude. But the sources are diffuse. Friends and colleagues would have to be sought out and questioned; poems and paintings tracked down; and, above all, the close texture of the films themselves would have to be exhaustively examined. My aim must be more modest, merely hoping to stimulate by offering some quite personal reactions, and by trying to explain why I think these pictures are so good.

Jennings's films are all documentaries, all made firmly within the framework of the British documentary movement. This fact ought not to strike a chill, for surely 'the creative interpretation of actuality' should suggest an exciting, endlessly intriguing use of the cinema; and yet it must be admitted that the overtones of the term are not immediately attractive. Indeed it comes as something of a surprise to learn that this unique and fascinating artist was from the beginning of his career in films an inside member of Grierson's GPO Unit (with which he first worked in 1934), and made all his best films as official, sponsored propaganda during the second world war. His subjects were thus, at least on the surface, the common ones; yet his manner of expression was always individual, and became more and more so. It was a style that bore the closest possible relationship to his theme – to that aspect of his subjects which his particular vision caused him consistently to stress. It was, that is to say, a poetic style. In fact it might reasonably be contended that Humphrey Jennings is the only real poet the British cinema has yet produced.

II

He started directing films in 1939 (we may leave out of account an insignificant experiment in 1935, in collaboration with Len Lye); and the date is significant, for it was the war that fertilised his talent and created the conditions in which his best work was produced. Watching one of Jennings's early pictures, *Speaking from America,* which was made to explain the workings of the transatlantic radio-telephone system, one would hardly suspect the personal qualities that characterise the pictures he was making only a short while later. There seems to have been more evidence of these in *Spare Time,* a film on the use of leisure among industrial workers: a mordant sequence of a carnival procession, drab and shoddy, in a Northern city aroused the wrath of more orthodox documentarians, and Basil Wright has mentioned other scenes, more sympathetically shot: 'the pigeon-fancier, the "lurcher-loving-collier" and the choir rehearsal are all important clues to Humphrey's development'. Certainly such an affectionate response to simple pleasures is more characteristic of Jennings's later work than any emphasis of satire.

If there had been no war, though, could that development ever have taken place? Humphrey Jennings was never happy with narrowly propagandist subjects, any more than he was with the technical exposition of *Speaking from America.* But in wartime people become important, and observation of them is regarded in itself as a justifiable subject for filming, without any more specific 'selling angle' than their sturdiness of spirit. Happily, this was the right subject for Jennings. With Cavalcanti, Harry Watt and Pat Jackson he made *The First Days,* a picture of life on the home front in the early months of the war. On his own, he then directed *Spring Offensive,* about farming and the new development of agricultural land in the Eastern counties; in 1940 he worked again with Harry Watt on *London Can Take It,* another picture of the home front; and in 1941, with *Heart of Britain,* he showed something of the way in which the people of Northern industrial Britain were meeting the challenge of war.

These films did their jobs well, and social historians of the future will find in them much that makes vivid the atmosphere and manners of their period. Ordinary people are sharply glimpsed in them, and the ordinary sounds that were part of the fabric of their lives reinforce the glimpses and sometimes comment on them: a lorry-load of youthful conscripts speeds down the road in blessed ignorance of the future, as a jaunty singer gives out 'We're going to hang out our washing on the Siegfried line'. In the films which Jennings made in collaboration, it is risky, of course, to draw attention too certainly to any particular feature as being his: yet here and there are images and effects which unmistakably betray his sensibility. Immense women knitting furiously for the troops; a couple of cockney mothers commenting to each other on the quietness of the streets now that the children have gone; the King and Queen unostentatiously shown inspecting the air raid damage in their own back garden. *Spring Offensive* is less sure in its touch, rather awkward in its staged conversations and rather over-elaborate in its images; *Heart of Britain* plainly offered a subject that Jennings found more congenial. Again the sense of human contact is direct: a steel-worker discussing his ARP duty with his mate, a sturdy matron of the WVS looking straight at us through the camera as she touchingly describes her pride at being able to help the rescue workers, if only by serving cups of tea. And along with these plain, spontaneous encounters come telling shots of landscape and background, amplifying and reinforcing. A style, in fact, is being hammered out in these films; a style based on a peculiar intimacy of observation, a fascination with the commonplace thing or person that is significant precisely because it is commonplace, and with the whole pattern that can emerge when such commonplace, significant things and people are fitted together in the right order.

Although it is evident that the imagination at work in all these early pictures is instinctively a cinematic one, in none of them does one feel that the imagination is working with absolute freedom. All the films are accompanied by commentaries, in some cases crudely propagandist, in others serviceable and decent enough; but almost consistently these off-screen words clog and impede the progress of the picture. The images are so justly chosen, and so explicitly assembled, that there is nothing for the commentator to say. The effect — particularly if we have Jennings's later achievements in mind — is cramped. The material is there, the elements are assembled; but the fusion does not take place that alone can create the poetic whole that is greater than the sum of its parts. And then comes the last sequence of *Heart of Britain.* The Huddersfield Choral Society rises before Malcolm Sargent, and the homely, buxom housewives, the black-coated workers, and the men from the mills burst into the Hallelujah Chorus. The sound of their singing continues, and we see landscapes and noble buildings, and then a factory where bombers are being built. Back and forth go these contrasting, conjunctive images, until the music broadens out to its conclusion, the roar of engines joins in, and the bombers take off. The sequence is not a long one, and there are unfortunate intrusions from the commentator, but the effect is extraordinary, and the implications obvious. Jennings has found his style.

III

Words for Battle, Listen to Britain, Fires Were Started, A Diary for Timothy. To the Jennings enthusiast these titles have a ring which makes it a pleasure simply to speak them, or to set them down in writing; for these are the films in which, between 1941 and 1945, we can see that completely individual style developing from tentative discovery and experiment to mature certainty. They are all films of Britain at war, and yet their feeling is never, or almost never, warlike. They are committed to the war – for all his sensibility there does not seem to have been anything of the pacifist about Jennings – but their real inspiration is pride, an unaggressive pride in the courage and doggedness of ordinary British people. Kathleen Raine, a friend of Jennings and his contemporary at Cambridge, has written: 'What counted for Humphrey was the expression, by certain people, of the ever-growing spirit of man; and, in particular, of the spirit of England'. It is easy to see how the atmosphere of the country at war could stimulate and inspire an artist so bent. For it is at such a time that the spirit of a country becomes manifest, the sense of tradition and community sharpened as (alas) it rarely is in time of peace. 'He sought therefore for a public imagery, a public poetry.' In a country at war we are all members one of another, in a sense that is obvious to the least spiritually-minded.

'Only connect'. It is surely no coincidence that Jennings chose for his writer on *A Diary for Timothy* the wise and kindly humanist who had placed that epigraph on the title page of his best novel. The phrase at any rate is apt to describe not merely the film on which Jennings worked with E.M.Forster, but this whole series of pictures which he made during the war. He had a mind that delighted in simile and the unexpected relationship. ('It was he', wrote Grierson, 'who discovered the Louis Quinze properties of a Lyons' swiss roll'.) On a deeper level, he loved to link one event with another, the past with the present, person to person. Thus the theme of *Words for Battle* is the interpretation of great poems of the past through events of the present – a somewhat artificial idea, though brilliantly executed. It is perhaps significant, though, that the film springs to a new kind of life altogether in its last sequence, as the words of Lincoln at Gettysburg are followed by the clatter of tanks driving into Parliament Square past the Lincoln statue: the sound of the tanks merges in turn into the grand music of Handel, and suddenly the camera is following a succession of men and women in uniform, striding along the pavement cheery and casual, endowed by the music, by the urgent rhythm of the cutting, and by the solemnity of what has gone before (to which we feel they are heirs) with an astonishing and breathtaking dignity, a mortal splendour.

As if taking its cue from the success of this wonderful passage, *Listen to Britain* dispenses with commentary altogether. Here the subject is simply the sights and sounds of wartime Britain over a period of some twenty-four hours. To people who have not seen the film it is difficult to describe its fascination – something quite apart from its purely nostalgic appeal to anyone who lived through those years in this country. The picture is a stylistic triumph (Jennings shared the credit with his editor, Stewart McAllister), a succession of marvellously

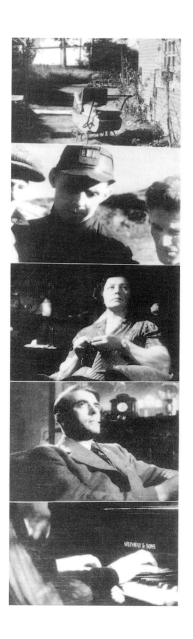

A Diary for Timothy (1945)

evocative images freely linked by contrasting and complementary sounds; and yet it is not for its quality of form that one remembers it most warmly, but for the continuous sensitivity of its human regard. It is a fresh and loving eye that Jennings turns on to those Canadian soldiers, singing to an accordion to while away a long train journey; or on to that jolly factory girl singing 'Yes my Darling Daughter' at her machine; or on to the crowded floor of the Blackpool Tower Ballroom; or the beautiful, sad-faced woman who is singing 'The Ash Grove' at an ambulance station piano. Emotion in fact (it is something one often forgets) can be conveyed as unmistakably through the working of a film camera as by the manipulation of pen or paint brush. To Jennings this was a transfigured landscape, and he recorded its transfiguration on film.

The latter two of these four films, *Fires Were Started* and *A Diary for Timothy,* are more ambitious in conception: the second runs for about forty minutes, and the first is a full-length 'feature-documentary'. One's opinion as to which of them is Jennings's masterpiece is likely to vary according to which of them one has most recently seen. *Fires Were Started* (made in 1943) is a story of one particular unit of the National Fire Service during one particular day and night in the middle of the London blitz: in the morning the men leave their homes and civil occupations, their taxi-cabs, newspaper shops, advertising agencies, to start their tour of duty; a new recruit arrives and is shown the ropes; warning comes in that a heavy attack is expected; night falls and the alarms begin to wail; the unit is called out to action at a riverside warehouse, where fire threatens an ammunition ship drawn up at the wharf; the fire is mastered; a man is lost; the ship sails with the morning tide. In outline it is the simplest of pictures; in treatment it is of the greatest subtlety, richly poetic in feeling, intense with tenderness and admiration for the unassuming heroes whom it honours. Yet it is not merely the members of the unit who are given this depth and dignity of treatment. Somehow every character we see, however briefly, is made to stand out sharply and memorably in his or her own right: the brisk and cheery girl who arrives with the dawn on the site of the fire to serve tea to the men from her mobile canteen; a girl in the control room forced under her desk by a near-miss, and apologising down the telephone which she still holds in her hand as she picks herself up; two isolated aircraft-spotters watching the flames of London miles away through the darkness. No other British film made during the war, documentary or feature, achieved such a continuous and poignant truthfulness, or treated the subject of men at war with such a sense of its incidental glories and its essential tragedy.

The idea of connection, by contrast and juxtaposition, is always present in *Fires Were Started* – never more powerfully than in the beautiful closing sequence, where the fireman's sad little funeral is intercut against the ammunition ship moving off down the river – but its general movement necessarily conforms to the basis of narrative. *A Diary for Timothy,* on the other hand, is constructed entirely to a pattern of relationships and contrasts, endlessly varying, yet each one contributing to the rounded poetic statement of the whole. It is a picture of the last year of the war, as it was lived through by people in Britain; at the start a baby, Timothy, is born, and it is to him that the film is addressed. Four representative characters are picked out (if we except Tim himself and his mother, to both of whom we periodically return): an engine driver, a farmer, a Welsh miner and a wounded fighter pilot. But the story is by no means restricted to scenes involving these; with dazzling virtuosity, linking detail to detail by continuously striking associations of image, sound, music and comment, the film ranges freely over the life of the nation, connecting and connecting. National tragedies and personal tragedies, individual happinesses and particular beauties are woven together in a design of the utmost complexity: the miner is injured in a fall at the coal face, the fighter pilot gets better and goes back to his unit, the Arnhem strike fails, Myra Hess plays Beethoven at the National Gallery, bombs fall over Germany, and Tim yawns in his cot.

Such an apparently haphazard selection of details could mean nothing or everything. Some idea of the poetic method by which Jennings gave the whole picture its continual sense of emotion and significance may perhaps be given by the sequence analysed and illustrated here, but of course only the film can really speak for itself. The difficulty of writing about such a film, of disengaging in the memory the particular images and sounds (sounds moreover which are constantly overlapping and mixing with each other) from the overall design has been remarked on by Dilys Powell:

'It is the general impression which remains; only with an effort do you separate the part from the whole… the communication is always through a multitude of tiny impressions, none in isolation particularly memorable.' Only with the last point would one disagree. *A Diary for Timothy* is so tensely constructed, its progression is so swift and compulsive, its associations and implications so multifarious, that it is almost impossible, at least for the first few viewings, to catch and hold on to particular impressions. Yet the impressions themselves are rarely unmemorable, not merely for their splendid pictorial quality, but for the intimate and loving observation of people, the devoted concentration on the gestures and expressions, the details of dress or behaviour that distinguish each unique human being from another. Not least among the virtues that distinguish Jennings from almost all British film-makers is his respect for personality, his freedom from the inhibitions of class-consciousness, his inability to patronise or merely to use the people in his films. Jennings's people are ends in themselves.

I V

Other films were made by Jennings during the war, and more after it, up to his tragic death in 1950; but I have chosen to concentrate on what I feel to be his best work, most valuable to us. He had his theme, which was Britain; and nothing else could stir him to quite the same response. With more conventional subjects – *The Story of Lili Marlene, A Defeated People, The Cumberland Story* – he was obviously unhappy, and, despite his brilliance at capturing the drama of real life, the staged sequences in these films do not suggest that he would have been at ease in the direction of features. *The Silent Village* – his reconstruction of the story of Lidice in a Welsh mining village – bears this out; for all the fond simplicity with which he sets his scene, the necessary sense of conflict and suffering is missed in his over-refined, under-dramatised treatment of the essential situation. It may be maintained that Jennings's peacetime return to the theme of Britain (*The Dim Little Island* in 1949, and *Family Portrait* in 1950) produced work that can stand beside his wartime achievement, and certainly neither of these two beautifully finished films is to be dismissed. But they lack passion.

By temperament Jennings was an intellectual artist, perhaps too intellectual for the cinema. (It is interesting to find Miss Raine reporting that, 'Julian Trevelyan used to say that Humphrey's intellect was too brilliant for a painter.') It needed the hot blast of war to warm him to passion, to quicken his symbols to emotional as well as intellectual significance. His symbols in *Family Portrait* – the Long Man of Wilmington, Beachy Head, the mythical horse of Newmarket – what do they really mean to us? Exquisitely presented though it is, the England of those films is nearer the 'This England' of the pre-war beer advertisements and Mr Castleton Knight's coronation film than to the murky and undecided realities of today. For reality, his wartime films stand alone; and they are sufficient achievement. They will last because they are true to their time, and because the depth of feeling in them can never fail to communicate itself. They will speak for us to posterity, saying: 'This is what it was like. This is what we were like – the best of us'.

POSTSCRIPT

October 1981

Since 'Only Connect' was published in *Sight and Sound* in 1954, I have written several times about Humphrey Jennings. One always hopes – without too much presumption – that one is helping to keep the work alive. Yet as the years pass, these films, which should be familiar to every schoolboy and girl in the country, seem to be seen and known by fewer people. As far as I know, BBC Television, which in recent years has shown films like *The Foreman Went to France, Angels One Five, The Way to the Stars* etc., has practically never shown a film by Humphrey Jennings in its entirety.* (They commissioned Robert Vas to make a film about him but the result was, as usual with Robert's films, as much about Robert himself as about Jennings. And the extracts from Jennings's work could surely not mean a great deal to people who were not already familiar with it.) Recently, perched on a camera crane waiting for clouds to pass, I asked the crew how many of them had heard of Humphrey Jennings. One had. But he could not remember the name of any of his films.

So I am happy that Riverside Studios are mounting this exhibition; that this book is being prepared; and that 'Only Connect' has been chosen for reprinting. Although it was written nearly thirty years ago, it still reflects pretty faithfully what I feel. I got into trouble when it was first published, for saying that Jennings was 'the only real poet the British cinema has yet produced'. Lady Elton was particularly annoyed – though, with the exception of Basil Wright, I cannot see that the British documentary movement produced any other director who could be called a poet. But then (again with the exception of Basil) I don't think the British documentarists ever really approved of Jennings; certainly they never expressed any enthusiasm for his work until it was too late. The Griersonian tradition – into which Jennings only fitted uneasily – was always more preachy and sociological than it was either political or poetic.

One aspect of Humphrey Jennings's work I would have to be stricter about if I were writing today: its last phase. My allusion in this piece to *Dim Little Island* and *Family Portrait* is pussy-footing and unilluminating. Of course there is distinctive and distinguished compositional style to these films. But in the end they *can* be dismissed. In fact they must be. They demonstrate only too sadly how the traditionalist spirit was unable to adjust itself to the changed circumstances of Britain after the war. By the time Jennings made *Family Portrait* for the 1951 Festival of Britain, the 'family' could only be a sentimental fiction, inhabiting a Britain dedicated to the status quo. I don't know whether Jennings thought of himself as a 'Leftist' in the old Mass Observation days. Traditionalism, after all, does not always have to be equated with Conservatism. But somehow by the end of the war, Jennings's traditionalism had lost any touch of the radical: *Spare Time* (which is a beautiful, sharp, bitter-sweet and touching picture) is infinitely more alive than his academic *Family Portrait.* He found himself invoking great names of the past (Darwin, Newton, Faraday and Watt) in an attempt to exorcise the demons of the present. Even the fantasy of Empire persists ('The crack of the village bat is heard on Australian plains...'). The symbol at the end of the film is the mace of Authority, and its last image is a preposterous procession of ancient and bewigged dignitaries. The Past is no longer an inspiration: it is a refuge.

But of course whether Humphrey Jennings was able to find the inspiration in peace that he had in war does not matter. That particular problem has been ours rather than his for some time now: and we can hardly claim to have solved it much better. There remain his precious handful of films. They may not seem directly dedicated to our dilemmas; but they can still stir and inspire us with their imaginative and moral impulse, they are still alive (for those who have eyes to see and ears to hear) with that mysterious oracular power which is the magic property of art. The poetry survives.

Listen to Britain was shown on BBC in 1946.

Listen to Britain

1960s and 1970s

FIVE EVENINGS OF
FILM, PERFORMANCE
SOUND. MAY 14 → 18
AT THE LONDON FILMKERS
COOP ISA PRINCE OF WALES
CRESCENT NW3.
SHOWS START 5.00
ENTRANCE 30P   BE THERE

DAVID CURTIS

English Avant-Garde Film

AN EARLY CHRONOLOGY

First published in *Studio International*,
November/December 1975

This account of the English avant-garde is little more than a practical list of who showed what and when – its justification, if any, being that it may give some sense of the chaos of events and influences out of which grew what is now recognisable as a strongly motivated (if heterogeneous) movement.

As a participant in that movement, my own activity as a film programmer at the Drury Lane and Robert Street Arts Laboratories, London, was prompted by the belief that a strong English cinema could be stimulated into existence by exposure to the best international work available, 'international' for the first few years of this chronology being virtually synonymous with 'American'. Yet the evidence gathered by Deke Dusinberre for his (unpublished) thesis on the English avant-garde, and my own experience in reconstructing this history, both strongly suggest that the extent to which American work has been a catalyst to English production tends to be greatly overestimated. On the contrary, the trends that seem to have endured are precisely those that sprang from original and distinctly English impulses – in most cases before the film-makers concerned had any direct experience of New American Cinema.

This is particularly true of the film-makers involved in the earliest phase of English film-making, Jeff Keen, Malcolm Le Grice and Scotty (Anthony Scott). In one respect, however, none of them could claim to have come to film in complete ignorance or innocence, for as artists already at work during the period of English painting's infatuation with the New York school and American Pop, they must without exception, and with whatever reaction, have been aware of the accounts of Warhol's film activities that were reaching even the Sunday colour magazines by the mid-sixties. But significantly none of the three I've mentioned would appear to have attended the sole exhibition of New American Cinema held in England before 1968, P. Adams Sitney's week-long series of programmes at the Institute of Contemporary Art, Dover Street in 1964.[1]

As a painter at the Slade School of Art, already more than politely interested in film, my own reaction to Sitney's show is probably symptomatic. Somehow I heard that an event was taking place at the London School of Film Technique in Charlotte Street. Having got there I sensed a feeling antipathy to whatever was going on, and decided not to stay. I missed the only complete screening of Warhol's *Sleep* ever held in England. To me the year 1964 was the year of Johns and Rauschenberg at the Whitechapel Art Gallery, as '65 was the year of Noland and Louis at the Kasmin Gallery. But by '66 the Sunday magazines had done their work: I *knew* about Warhol, and was even prepared to go to New York to try and see what he was on about. How far a distant knowledge of Warhol's approach to film could itself provoke serious consideration of the medium by English artists is a question that can't be answered; that the English point of departure bore little relation to Warhol's is indisputable.

What follows, then is a skeletal diary of events from 1966 onwards, with the bias, inaccuracies and omissions inevitable in any account based upon one person's notes and records.

August '66. To New York. I fail to see Warhol in any shape or form, but have my fill of the New York school and Kandinsky. Accompanying Losey's *The Servant* at the Bleecker is Bruce Conner's *A Movie*, which appears as a revelation. Instantly the Russians are put in perspective. Montage can involve Pop Art's taken imagery (Vertov knew that, I later discovered). More important, film is simply a material-to-be-used as in any other art. At the Cinematheque, – Jacobs' and Smith's *Blond Cobra*, the apparent lack of organisation is mystifying (but I took copious notes); Breer's *Eyewash*, which I read as a *stand*, an affirmation of film's right to differ from frame to frame; jokey films by Nelson and the Kuchar brothers; and Brakhage's *Loving* which sinks from memory without a trace.

September '66. Back in London, I start frequenting Better Books. The weekly underground film screenings there are part of an extraordinary rich series of events arranged by the poet Bob Cobbing: the first Peoples' Shows in environments by Jeff Nuttall, Nutall's own performances, the DIAS events (Metzger, Kren, Latham), readings by Ginsberg, Fainlight, Trocchi, Horowitz and the Liverpool Poets. In this context film is a curiously second-hand experience, encumbered by the need to black out the shop, the projector's noise and stray light, and the lack of the presence of an author. What it gains is a sense of belonging to a wider cultural movement; a homogeneity that diminishes in direct proportion to the emergence of the film co-op's separate identity.

The repertory shared by Cobbing's screenings, the Co-op's first screenings, the famous *International Times* (*IT*) launching party, the 'Spontaneous Festival of Underground Film' at the Cochrane Theatre (organised by *IT* and the 2-week-old-co-op), reveals an astonishingly catholic interpretation of the word 'underground'. The film-makers represented are worth listing; of Anger (*Fireworks, Scorpio Rising*), Kren, Conner, Keen, Dwoskin, (James) Whitney, Emshwiller (*Relativity*), Balch/Burroughs (*Towers Open Fire*), Goldman; American work from the forties and fifties by Breer, Brakhage (*Shadow Garden* period), Deren, Broughton, Hirsch, Harris, Tourtelot, (all residue in Europe from the 1949 and '58 Knokke Festivals); and Hugo (*Gondola Eye*), Pike, the animators Kuri and Sens, Bartell, and Richard Bartlett. That we, the co-op, actually went out of our way to purchase works by the last six mentioned is a measure of our collective ignorance at the time.

The common denominator shared by the films we watched, and one to which we already attached great importance, was their emanation from a single imagination.

13 October '66. The London Film-makers' co-op announces its formation and intention to 'shoot, shoot, shoot' in a telegram to Jonas Mekas.[2]

This act of combined optimism and loyalty is inspired by the presence of Harvey Matusow, Steve Dwoskin and Andy Meyer, three New Yorkers with films to their names now resident in London. (Meyer's *Match Girl* film gives us our first movie-image of Warhol's silver factory). Significantly, Keen, Le Grice and Scotty are not members, but the notion of film-making as an activity within the co-op is established. Dwoskin, Mayer, Hartog, Cobbing and Matusow are photographed for *Town* as 'some of London's most active underground film-makers' – not one of them has shot a foot of film in England.[3] But the popular notion is not entirely false. By late spring '67 Matusow, Dwoskin, Latham, Stacy Waddy, Roland Lewis, Les Philby and Paul Francis are all ostensibly at work on film; the critic Ray Durgnat is secretly shooting; even I am showing loops and scissors-and-tape collages (very sub Conner) at the 'underground's' UFO Club.

American visitors to the co-op and UFO during '66 and '67 included Bill Vehr with his Jack Smith-like *Avocado* and *Brothel*, and Warren Sonbert. Sonbert shows his juvenilia *Where Did Our Love Go?*, *Amphetamine*, *Hall of Mirrors*, part psychodrama, part diary, part adoption (in parentheses) of Hollywood Cliché. More important, he appeared as a walking demonstration of the intuitive use of camera we later saw in the work of Mekas, Brooks and Brakhage; he shot wherever he went, always with an unerring sense of purpose and with an ability to bypass the appalling responsibilities of setting up a shot. Nobody worked like that in England, is shown at the UFO Club, burdened with awe-inspiring tales of perversion and prosecution. (Our first reference work – Alpert and Knight's 'Survey of the underground avant-garde' in *Playboy* – has just hit the stands.) That Smith's concepts of editing, framing and the organisation of 'action' on the screen constituted a radical innovation was immediately apparent, heightened if anything by recent exposure to the altogether 'tamer' Vehr. But our enthusiasm was expressed almost entirely in terms of *Flaming Creature's* subversive content, the degree to which it defied the accepted aesthetic and moral codes of cinema. It was acclaimed as evidence of one man's cerebral and sexual emancipation; that it was also ravishingly beautiful to look at (even reactionarily so, I've recently heard said) largely evaded us.

September/October '67. Better Books is forced to close. The Drury Lane Arts Lab opens with Peter Goldman's *Echoes of Silence* – a disastrous flop. In the shift between the two locations our audience undergoes a subtle change. The student and ex-student informed art-public who formed the clientele at Better Books are outnumbered in Drury Lane by a younger, music-oriented audience, brought together by *IT* and *UFO*, and to them the *underground* film rightly belongs. Since the Arts Lab is open six days a week, the cinema schedule is filled out with camp and classic feature films, open screenings and a once-a-week co-op show. When the co-op screenings ended, the proportion of underground movies remains the same, increasing with the arrival of further film-makers. The two major additions to our repertory in '67/68 (both via commercial distributors) were Warhol's 2-screen *Chelsea Girls* and Anger's *The Inauguration of the Pleasure Dome*, both of which were received as drug culture movies and attracted capacity audiences. In the mounting hysteria the Living Theatre came to London, Warhol appeared and announced his intention to show all future work at the London Pavilion (an ambition ironically fulfilled some years later by Morrissey), and Antonioni, Tynan, Pinter and Princess Margaret commanded performances of *Flaming Creatures*. More significantly, the first phase of co-op film-making ended with the showing of Lewis's *Short Film*, Waddy's *3 Pig Poems* and Latham's *Speak* and *Talk*. Of the original group only Dwoskin was to continue making films.[4]

December '67/January '68. *Exprmntl 4* at Knokke. Cobbing, Collins (co-op secretary), Dwoskin, Hartog, Latham, Haynes (Arts Lab) and I are the only English underground personae present; Latham and Dwoskin the only film-makers. Latham's *Speak* is acclaimed by the French critics; Dwoskin wins the Solvay Prize; but the festival is dominated by Gregory Markopoulos and two new figures, Mike Snow and Paul Sharits. (Kren is conspicuous by his absence), Markopoulos impresses through sheer force of technique; his ability to keep his static, meticulously lit tableaux alive through bursts of cross-cutting; his synthesis and condensation of the codes of narrative cinema. Of the work of Sharits and Snow, the most radical feature seemed to be one already implicit in Markopoulos, a realisation that the New American Cinema, contrary to our previous conviction, was not exclusively concerned with psychodrama and aesthetic subversion. Here were two didactic but distinctly constructive speculations about possible forms in cinema. Almost incidentally they seemed to share a respect for colour as an autonomous element in film, and a concern for the integrity of the materials involved, that wrongly or rightly allowed us to construct analogies with contemporary painting. From Europe the films of Werner Nekes and Dore O were the clearest evidence of any possible parallel development. (Markopoulos visited London in June, Snow in August/September, Sharits not till September 1970).

Spring '68. Malcom Le Grice comes to the Drury Lane Arts Lab sometime in January or February to show me his film *Castle 1* (dating from 1966). Le Grice's only previous contact with the co-op group had been at a screening arranged by Durgnat at the ICA in Dover Street in the autumn of '67. The only film that impressed him there was the one Kren film show, significantly one of the Kren/Brus 'actions'. ('Significantly', in terms of the state of English film culture – since it was the 'sensational' Kren that tended to get shown: the Kren/Brus, Kren/Muehl actions of '64/65, and the *Eating, Drinking, Pissing, Shitting Film* of '67, which we rightly took to be a masterful piece of associative montage.) The formal strengths of works like *Trees in Spring* (Made in 1960) and *TV* made in '67, were often passed over as secondary to the more controversial work.

Le Grice's film appeared to be an arbitrary selection of found footage plus occasional shots of a light bulb, assembled according to some predetermined (if random) formula, permutated *ad infinitum*. It seemed purposeful and yet entirely mad. But my Arts Lab colleague Jack Moore admired it (as he admired anything outrageous), and we scheduled it to run under Le Grice's pseudonym Mihima Maas (M. Mouse), some weeks later. On that occasion the film's meaning became somewhat clearer. Beside the screen Malcolm hung a real light bulb that flashed on and off at regular intervals, flooding the screen and cinema with light, and totally obliterating the projected image. The light bulb and mechanism were borrowed from an earlier painting, but their new role, as described by Le Grice in a programme note of exemplary simplicity, appeared to be much more appropriate: 'The awareness of the audience is returned to the actual situation (viewing a film) by reference to the bulb and the perceptual problems which its flashing creates.'

Spring '68. Scotty makes his appearance and threatens to make his Meaningless Movies a permanent installation at the Arts Lab. His *Longest Most Meaningless Movie in the World* was begun late in '67, but he refers in his co-op catalogue entry to having spent four years 'getting together a 25 min 8mm film called *Our Honeymoon Winter Sports Atomic Bomb Explosion*'. The construction of his *Longest Most...* is of archetypal simplicity: it consists indiscriminately of any 35mm footage contributed, fragments of features, rejected re-takes of a single shot, repeated commercials that vary only in colour density or the degree to which they are scratched, the result being as he puts it 'a maximum amount of variety of content in a maximum amount of footage.' Defensively surrounded by statements of purpose that invariable stress the frivolous, the 'film' provides a radical if throw-away critique of commercial cinema practice simply by disregarding every known law of continuity; paradoxically giving its audience a responsibility to 'build their own experience' that in many ways parallels later avant-garde concerns.

Late February '68. Le Grice takes me to see works by his students at the Young Contemporaries (which has included film for the first time), including Fred Drummond's animation and re-freezing of Muybridge (*Photo Film Based on Muybridge*) and Roger Ackling's *Boot Film*.

April '68. Hartog and I arrange for P. Adams Sitney and his New American Cinema Exhibition to tour 12 universities in England prior to his week of programmes at the National Film Theatre. The programmes at the NFT are a broader and more detailed survey of New American Cinema (NAC) than any mounted before or since, corresponding in scope to Sheldon Renan's book (*An Introduction to the American Underground Film*) which had just become available in England in the American paperback edition. (Our second reference work!) Breer, Brakhage, Jacobs, Baillie, Kubelka, Markopoulos, Mekas, Rice, Harry Smith, Jack Smith, Sonbert, and Warhol (*Inner & Outer Space* and *Eat*) are all substantially represented, many for the first time. But the two-year delay between the putting together of the show in New York and its arrival in England means that no work by Sharits or Snow is included (excepting Sharits' embryonic *Sears Catalogue* etc in the *Fluxus Anthology*) and only Landow's enigmatic *Bardo Follies* and the related works of Kubelka represent the as yet unlabelled structuralist group. England's own emerging structuralists, Le Grice, Du Cane, and the shortly-to-arrive Peter Gidal continue to develop largely under their own steam.

Two years later I read Sitney's account of his English tour in *Film Culture*: 'the university tour of England was considerably less successful than I had anticipated... The sponsors sometimes had only a vague or more often wrong notion of what they were showing. In one university, Essex... a claque managed to disturb the entire performance with incessant noise and wisecracks'.

The state of knowledge in the provinces was hardly to be surprised at, given the repertory of films available to us and the dearth of informed critical writing. The three issues of *Cinim*, the co-op's own magazine, had included co-op news, a passionate credo by Hartog and an article on Dwoskin by Durgnat, but otherwise devoted most of their space to Godard and the aesthetics of the Nouvelle Vague. *IT* published supplements for the 'Spontaneous

Festival' of '66 and for Sitney's tour itself (the latter composed mainly of reprints from *Film Culture*) and printed a list of 'films available ' compiled in early '67 and my long report on Knokke. But none of the established film magazines devoted even occasional space to the underground till after 1970. Sitney's tour itself was a catalyst to the publication of a series of new film magazines at Oxford, Cambridge and Essex, all devoted to discussion of new forms in film (but destined to share – as Dusinberre points out in his thesis – an addiction to NAC that largely precluded coverage of European developments). The appearance of these magazines was part of a wider provincial response to Sitney's tour, which taken together represent the one real instance of direct American intervention in this chronology. From their experience of Sitney's programmes one can date the sustained interest in the underground avant-garde film shared by Rayns (already making film) DuCane and Hammond in Cambridge, (Philip) Drummond, Cawkwell and Harding at Oxford (founders of the 8mm Co-op there and the Oxford New Cinema Club), and the critic/activists Sainsbury and Field at Essex. (That the last two should have been nominally part of Sitney's noisy audience is one of life's better attempt at irony). For these then, the point of departure at least was American; specifically the romantic American tradition of Brakhage, Anger, Baillie and Markopoulos.

The location of Sitney's London shows at the NFT, rather than at the Arts Lab or elsewhere on underground territory, was itself an indication of another change that was taking place at this time: the further separation of film from the rest of avant-garde and underground culture in England. Its temporary alliance with the NFT audience was, as it still is on such occasions, tenuous, but its claim to be a legitimate branch of cinema, rather than a deviant form of theatre/painting/poetry was becoming increasingly manifest. And through becoming *cinema* it finally lost the interest of the English art-going public. The spirit of Better Books was decidedly dead. None of this concerned us at the time. The prospects for film seemed unlimited.

July '68. Mike Dunford, a student introduced by Le Grice, shows at the Arts Lab. His films are simple and logical. They record single events and changes (a girl walking on and off screen, a slow lap dissolve) through the most economic means possible; he accepts accident – the lab's return of a stray reel with his own – and includes it; he borrows ideas like painting on film without apology. More important, he seems to have begun film-making without feeling the need to make an extreme stand (of the Le Grice/Scotty variety), the implication being an encouraging one – that film-making is perhaps not so unnatural to the English psyche after all.

July '68. Peter Gidal arrives in England, shows works at the Arts Lab and immediately joins the co-op.

August '68. Jeff Keen puts on his first expanded show at the Arts Lab. (He has shown two-screen works before here and at Better Books). Juxtaposition with Sitney's NAC programmes provokes some English/American comparisons. Essentially a collagist, Keen's basic technique since his first films of the early sixties has involved overlapping layers of taken movie imagery (often from TV), drawn and painted animation, pixillation of cut-outs, and single-frame 'live-action'. His imagery is that of Pop Art, old advertisements, single words and phrases, cartoon strip pictures, plus 'real' and re-created personae from the Hollywood B Picture. The technical parallels with Vanderbeek and early Breer are self-evident, as his fascination with Hollywood parallels that of Anger, Warhol, Jack Smith and others; but the particular obsession with Maria Montez shared by Keen and Jack Smith (and, by adoption Warhol), allows a direct contrast of English and New York sensibilities. To Keen, Montez is a personification of the success of the Hollywood star system, a triumphant creation of a mythic image of womanhood. But the power of her image is curtailed by the extent to which she is simply part of a larger iconography that Keen maintains in a constant state of flux (the overlapping images), her influence seldom lasting longer than the length of one shot (or pose in performance) before becoming submerged in the flow and inevitably displaced. To Smith she represents the total artifice of Hollywood, and as played by a man, she exists as a double-edged parody of femaleness, the homosexual implications being an essential element in the larger strategy of subversion.

September '68. Mike Snow is in London to show *Wavelength, New York Eye and Ear Control,* and films by Joyce Wieland. Tonino Debernardi from Italy shows his *Il Mostro Verde* and a version of *Dei* for 6 screens at the Arts Lab. The multiple superimpositions and tableaux are like those we've seen in Ron Rice, but further multiplication through 6 projectors emphasises the leisure of his approach. He lacks the precariousness and anarchy of Rice but gives instead a vision of almost classic (orthodox/traditional – in the best sense of the word) beauty. He seems happily rooted in the great tradition of Italian fresco painting.

October '68. Steve Dwoskin and I go the Munich for the first European film-makers' meeting. Seeing the Heins' *Rohfilm* there I'm startled by how close it is to being a portrait of the aggression in Le Grice's early movies. Both Le Grice and the Heins seems to have made their first approach to film through violent attacks upon illusion, the viewing experience, the conventional language and art of film, and in the Heins' case upon the actual materials of film itself. This seems a uniquely European equivalent of the New York 'subversion of Hollywood' tactic of Rice, Smith and Warhol. (Again none of this occurs to me at the time – but I tell Le Grice of his spiritual brothers on returning to London.)

The Munich meeting was arranged by the Heins as a follow-up to Sitney and Shirley Clarke's suggestion, at the Knokke, that a European co-op ('Europ') be formed. Nothing of substance resulted. Practical proposals that secretaries be appointed and minor bureaucracies set up were countered by the pure poetry of the Italian delegation's insistence that a co-op meant equal division of work amongst all participants – no sleeping partners and no paid executives. Germany, taking the opposite view, revealed the existence of a selective commercial promotional outlet, PAP (Progressive Art Productions!), in addition to its three regional co-ops.

In London, after a long struggle over the more pragmatic issue of financial viability, the co-op had decided to employ a paid secretary, and simultaneously achieved the major coup of securing the greater part of Sitney's travelling collection for its library. (The latter event being not totally unconnected with our choice of Carla Liss of the New York Cinematheque as secretary). These acquisitions greatly advanced the co-op's impact upon the college and film-society circuit. The Federation of Film Societies began to include co-op films in its annual viewing sessions and the Central Booking Agency (run by the BFI) began to include them (or some of them at least) in its annually published lists. But a greater repertory of titles and a wider circulation, though they improved the co-op's turnover, can't be credited with the origination of any further film-makers. Almost all the film-makers who surfaced during the next two yeas did so as a result of meeting existing film-makers, either in teaching situations or through the newly important film coop workshops. During early '68 the Drury Lane Arts Lab had attempted to establish a film-making group based on the rudimentary workshops and equipment-sharing co-op organised by Le Grice, Ben Yahya (an London School of Film Technique student) and a number of professionals and amateurs. But the only (and incomplete) achievement of the group was a collective record of the Grosvenor Square demonstration of that year (partly sold to the BBC and partly impounded by the lab responsible for colour processing). Subsequently the beautifully Heath Robinson developing and printing equipment, designed and largely built by Le Grice, was moved from the Arts Lab to his home in Harrow, where the stalwarts who continued to use it increasingly tended to be his own students from Goldsmith's and St Martin's. Fred Drummond, Gill Eatherley, Annabel Nicolson and William Raban were amongst those who later emerged from the group.

November '68. Withdrawal from the Drury Lane Arts Lab. During the year before the second Arts Lab opened in Robert Street, the co-op's office moves from Covent Garden to Ladbroke Grove, and Carla Liss organises occasional shows at the newly independent 'Electric Cinema' there.

February '69. Alfredo Leonardi shows an Italian programme at the Electric, only notable for his own lyrical *Book of the Saints of Eternal Rome*.

March '69. The first Hamburg Filmschau is organised by the co-op there. Despite these signs of activity in Europe, the programmes I put together for Derek Hill's New Cinema Club are still exclusively of New American Cinema.

August/September '69. The co-op organises two weeks of programmes at the Edinburgh Festival; again predominantly of NAC works, but Gidal, Hartog, Scotty, Drummond, Larcher and Le Grice are represented. Bill Moritz, in Edinburgh, shows a programme of West Coast movies including new works by the Whitneys (which send Le Grice off into the Elysian Fields of computer-assisted film-making – the original subject of his recent book)[5] and David Lourie's *Project One*, which introduces the notion of re-filming from the screen to the English experience.

September '69. PAP mount a show with the art dealers Gimpel Fils at the ICA. Gimpel's announce that they're to sell films as art works from now on (but nothing further is heard of the venture). The Heins come to show *Reproductions* and meet Malcolm for the first time. (Immediate rapport). Other works in the show include Markopoulos's *Political Portraits*, new works by Kren, and Brakhage's *Scenes from Under Childhood Pt 1* – the first 'new' Brakhage seen in England.

4 October '69. The New Arts Lab opens in Robert Street with David Larcher's *Mare's Tail*. Like Kren, Le Grice and Scotty, Larcher made his first films in virtual isolation (as he still does), but unlike them he came to film already an accomplished photographer. (A photo-essay shot in New York in '66 for *Image* magazine includes a portrait of Andy Warhol projecting his light-show at the DOM theatre – but no reference to film-making work there per se.) His first film, *KO*, was made while he was at the RCA in '67/8, and *Mare's Tail* contains some sections shot at that time that bear the distinct RCA-student stamp. But elsewhere the amount of local interest he is able to concentrate upon the screen/image through distortion, scratching and painting on the emulsion and so on is unlike the work of any other English film-maker. (Dunford's one exercise in the Brakhage idiom, *Weeds*, and the work of Larcher's own 'students' Gary Woods and Jonathan Langren are the only possible parallels that come to mind). Brakhage is the obvious root-source of both the technique and the epic-form of *Mare's Tail* (its attempt to bring birth, life and death together with the elements in one great construction), but as an epic it is ultimately flawed by the insistence of some of its constituent parts upon being read as such.

5 October '69. In America to gather book material. Learn at second hand from Sitney of new works by Sharits, Snow and Jacobs in the notorious structuralist vein (now so-named), but fail to see any. For the book I have to rely on the distant memory of Knokke.[6] See

French twenties avant-garde works and Crockwell at MOMA; early West Coast works (Harrington, Whitneys, Belson) courtesy of Moritz in Los Angeles. Revelations: the 8mm movies of Saul Levine which further convince me of O'Neill and Belson.

21 October '69. Mike Weaver's *Concrete Film* series at the NFT. Fischinger's work en masse, but minus his two most important works, *Leibesspiel* and *Radio Dynamics*.

November '69. The last programme I arrange for the New Cinema Club is also the first to consist entirely of European work (films by Le Grice, Drummond, Keen and Barucello). Also Warhol's *Hedy* (under the title *The Shopper*), the most complexly structured of the Warhol films shown to date. Through the efforts of distributor Jimmy Vaughan, a spate of Warhol films is about to flood over London. In January '70, we open *Lonesome Cowboys* at the Robert Street Arts Lab, the Open Space Theatre simultaneously premières *Flesh*, and we follow with *Bike Boy* and *My Hustler* runs at the RCA and NFT early in '71. But Warhol, key figure in the development of the American avant-garde film, appears too late to have any such impact in England. The innovations in these late Warhol movies that most appeal to the English film-makers are his use of the so-called strobe-cut – the flash frames and blips caused by in-camera editing during sync-sound shooting, and his denial of the space-time continuum within a single extended (frequently 45 minute) take. (Particularly evident in both *Hedy* and *My Hustler*.) Interesting thought these innovations were, they were all distinctly outside the range of technical possibility for most film-makers in England at that time. The two film-makers most indebted to Warhol, Dwoskin and Gidal, both made their contact with him in America during the early sixties, and absorbed what they did before these later concerns were evident. Dwoskin's debt to Warhol is, interestingly, precisely that feature of his work that makes him unique on the English scene – his obsession with 'actors' and the precarious area that exists between 'acting' and self-revelation on the screen. Gidal (at work on his book on Warhol during 1970) was exclusively concerned with the formal innovation in Warhol's early work: the 'straying' focus and zoom, 'arbitrary' pans and the mismatch of camera and projection speeds. To the extent that these early concerns were transmitted to English film-makers, they were transmitted as already codified by Gidal.

But more influential at this time than the knowledge of any one film-maker was the co-op's acquisition of its own professional developing and printing equipment. At the Robert Street opening party, Le Grice's persuasiveness and Victor Herbert's hatred of indecision came together to produce £3,000 worth of equipment for the co-op's workshops. by the end of a year of operation (that is by spring '71) the value of these tools could be measured in the number of co-op film-makers with substantial programmes of work to their names: Ewens, Crosswaite, Hammond, Leggett, Botham, Pound. But more significantly than the mere boost to production that this equipment represented, was the freedom it gave film-makers to work within a new area of aesthetic decision-making. The loops and straying images of Le Grice's *Little Dog*... proved to be the beginning of a whole genre of English film-making. Nicolson's *Slides*, Eartherley's *Hand Grenade*, Botham's *Eiffel Trifle*, Crosswaite's *Film No. 1* and '*A*' *Film*, Drummond's *Maja Replicate*, Dunford's *Part Time Virgin*, Leggett's *Shepherd's Bush*, Le Grice's own *How to Screw the CIA* series, various films by Pound – all involve major intervention by the artist during the printing stage. The following co-op catalogue entry almost caricatures by understatement an approach to film-making that is now unique to England: 'The first half of the film is made by running 8 mm colour positive through the co-op printer and the second half is the re-print original and the stuff that went wrong'. (The 12 year old Stephen Morrow describing his film – *Sprocket Holes*).

At face value it might represent an abandonment of responsibility for the work (in some cases perhaps it does), but implicit in the English situation is a belief in the value of a dialogue between 'original' and 'print', and the possibility of discovery in the printing that the results of accident can be interesting and worth pursuing. A whole new level of informal and structured response has been opened up in the previously mechanical field of 'reproduction'. The comparative formality of American structural work may well be the result of the artist's limitation to operating decisions involving camera, splicer and *direct* reproduction. Such examples as there are of American interest in a literal re-reading of filmed images (notably Ken Jacobs' *Tom Tom*...) result from projection and re-filming from the screen – a procedure engaging the artist's response to a decidedly different set of stimuli and circumstances.

January '70. Larry Kardish shows a programme of new American work at the NFT and elsewhere including Noren's *Kodak Ghost Poems* and James Herbert's *Porch Glider*, two diary-form films of a kind still unparalleled in England (with the exception perhaps of Larcher).

April '70. Dore O and Werner Nekes show films at Robert Street; Rosa Von Prauenheim and Werner Schroeter at the Goethe Institute.

May '70. Robert Street screening policy begins to recover from a plethora of Warhol, and re-establishes the pattern that lasts till its closure (and the building's demolition) a year later. Given the number of native film-makers and the size of the co-op's collection of NAC, it was possible at Robert Street to run programmes devoted to the avant-garde and underground 2 or 3 times a week. The remainder of the 4 day-a-week (often 3 shows a night) schedule we filled with series devoted to new narrative; the shorts produced by Resnais, Godard, Marker, Franju and co., the use of colour in film, student films, expanded performances, and a long series on the changing definition of 'experimental' as reflected in the Knokke-Le Zoute Festivals from the forties onwards. The model we distantly tried to emulate was that of the recently opened Anthology Film Archives in New York, in that we tried to establish our image as that of a cinema devoted to one branch of film, where current work could be shown in the context of the history from which it had emerged. In this we were restricted by the continuing inaccessibility of whole areas of historical material, but we did succeed in establishing that a new English movement had come into existence.

September '70. The first International Underground Film Festival is held at the NFT, organised by the Robert Street Arts Lab, the co-op, the Other Cinema and other independent film distributors, with the purpose of bringing together film-makers and films from the international scene. Deliberately unselective (but restricted by our inability to pay full travelling expenses to those with furthest to travel), the Festival was nonetheless important as an occasion on which European and American film-makers were able to show each other the kind of work they were producing. (That there was indeed any European work was news to many Americans). Included from America were Mekas's *Diaries*, *Notes and Sketches*, new films by Baillie, Conner, Frampton, Snow and Sonbert, and what to many was a first viewing of any work by Sharits; and from Europe, new films by Kren, the Heins, Nekes and O, Winkelman's *Heinrich Veil*, Sistiaga's extraordinary 35mm Cinemascope sprayed animation, and of course Muehl's *Sodoma* and chicken killing 'action'. Published to coincide with the Festival, *Afterimage* issue 2 (edited by Field and Sainsbury) is devoted entirely to the avant-garde film, the first English magazine to make such a commitment (though only one of the films discussed is English).

Spring '71. The Robert Street building is demolished; the co-op re-housed in Prince of Wales Crescent, sets about rebuilding its workshops and constructing its own cinema. The NFT in the meantime allows us to follow the Festival with a weekly series, 'Development of the New Cinema', which shows English and international work but heretically includes features by Hanoun and others. This series initiated a continuing policy at the NFT of allowing occasional seasons devoted to the avant-garde. (Gidal arranges 'English Independent Cinema' in '72 and 'Films from the LFM Co-op' in '73, both exclusively of English work; and a second International Festival happens in 1973).

September '71. The co-op cinema opens under Gidal's direction with once-weekly showing of international work in the co-op's collection, concentrating on new acquisitions and increasingly on new English work *per se*. The year '71/2 saw Gidal and DuCane enjoying the unprecedented luxury of being able to precede each new programme of films shown at the co-op with a critical review in *Time Out*, plus occasional bonus features on individual film-

makers. This brief honeymoon with the media possibly did more to establish a popular appreciation of the concerns of avant-garde cinema than any other single event. It is more than just coincidence that the belated beginnings of a recognition by the BFI and Arts Council of their responsibilities in this field originate precisely during this period.

November '71. In his final involvement with the computer film, Le Grice announces a series of programmes displaying the 'historic background and current situation in Abstract, Concrete and Cybernetic (Computer-based) Cinema'. As part of the unrealised series Vanderbeek and John Witney show full retrospect at the US Embassy...

In its first draft (written in late 1975) this chronology petered out with the end of Robert Street; partly because this was the point at which I ceased all but a sporadic involvement in events, and partly because the remainder seemed relatively recent history. Its striking, in 1978, how much of the most significant history would seem to have been excluded by that decision.

In the chronology I mentioned the importance of the Co-op's printing equipment as an aid to a particularly English aesthetic quest, but stopped short of acknowledging the particular character of the work at camera and processor stage associated with the Co-op group at Prince of Wales Crescent – the activity described by Dusinberre as *Structural Asceticism*. It was this development that at last allowed one to say with some certainty how and why English structural work differed from its American counterpart. With hindsight its easy to suggest that the message should have been clear in Le Grice's *Castle 1* more and Gidal's *Hall*, but the 60s inclined one to attribute the particular qualities of the films to a perverse disregard for clarity; to sheer bloody-mindedness. Dusinberre discusses structural asceticism elsewhere in this catalogue; I must admit that for me its rigor is inextricable from the physical deprivations of the Prince of Wales Crescent building, a period when the Co-op was extremely active but at a financial all-time low. The Co-op's will to survive (largely held together by Le Grice and Gidal) seems essential to these films. If as I suggested earlier, it was Gidal's excellent publicity machine that engaged the Arts Council and the BFIs' attention during this period, it was perhaps lucky that it was this relatively difficult work that first they encountered – everything thereafter would be downhill by comparison.

Equally striking in its absence from the chronology is any proper recognition of the development of expanded cinema. In both 1969 and 1970 the Co-op's shows at the Edinburgh Festival had included multiscreen presentations, much of this early work revolving round Le Grice and his determined focus on aspects of 'pre production' and the parameters of the projection event. But again one can sense a change in emphasis between the work of the group that collected round him (Drummond, Crosswaite, Eatherley,

Nicolson and Raban) during the Robert Street period – which was still prepared to explore imagery with a high emotional and graphic content – and the later more austere works at Prince of Wales crescent. Again the question of context has some relevance here. At Robert Street the Arts Lab philosophy of 'mix all the arts!' meant that film was produced in an environment that might contain performances by Brisley, Schneemann, any of the current fringe theatre groups, Jim Ballard's *Crashed Cars* exhibition and so on' 'hot' imagery abounded. The gulf between Brisley's *Albeit Macht Frei* or Schneeman's *Viet Flakes* and say Drummond's 2 screen *Maja Replicate* or Hammond's *High Stepping* is not so enormous.

For a year or more, Le Grice, Nicolson, Raban and co performed together under the group name of *Filmaktion*, showing at Gallery House in March '73 (in a post-script to Rosetta Brooks' 'Survey of the Avant-Garde in Britain' of Oct '72), at the Walker Art Gallery in Liverpool and at the Festival of Independent Avant-Garde film at the ICA and NFT in September of '73. This grouping would seem to have been of considerable value to those involved, since each emerged with a much enhanced sense of individuality as a film-maker. Ironically, the next two year marked something of a low point for Expanded Cinema (except for Nicholson and Anthony McCall), but just as people began to discuss its demise, the ICA Festival of Expanded cinema in January 1976 proved that not only were all the old school still very much alive, but a whole new generation had emerged as if from nowhere. Farrer, Fearns, Garratt, Gawthrop, Halford, Hamlyn, Haselden, Hill, Rhodes, Sherwin, Sinden are but a few of the many artists who showed significant work at this time. 'As if from nowhere' is misleading: like the new film-makers of the Robert Street period most of this influx came from art schools – students and teachers – most having established on at least tangential relationship with the film-makers' co-op (and this remains the pattern today). With them they brought a diversification of strategies and concerns – some of them strikingly informal by comparison with those of the Filmaktion group. Yet the focus on 'film as material' persisted. It as if the field of study were being divided amongst the film-makers allowing each to investigate a particular area in depth; the 'live' reproduction of (and dialogue with) illusion in Halford; the exact correspondence of image and sound in Rhodes/Kerr; the recreation through still photographs of move-photographic space in Haselden and so on. Things left implicit in earlier expanded work were becoming *explicit* subjects in their own rights.

Interestingly this diversification narrowed the gap between the work associated with the co-op group and that of the significant number of artists from other media who from time to time have strayed into film. Rosetta Brooks' 'Survey...' in 1972 had attempted a reconciliation between the 'artist' and 'film/video' film-makers if simply by exhibiting then together – but the gesture, though it may have generated a more catholic response form the

exhibition public, failed to result in any extensive cross-fertilisation. The work being done by many of the 'film-makers' (Gidal, du Cane, Hall, Leggett, Pound & co) emphatically denied the validity of the kind of subject matter and conventional film-language of the work of many of the artists (Latham, Breakwell, Stevens and co). But perhaps some middle ground *did* exist in the single-event films of Lundbery and McCall. Both showed straightforward records of fire-sculptures in 1972, but Lundberg's later steam pieces (of which *Noumenon* is a record) like McCall's development of light-sculptures using film and projector as his medium (*Line Describing a Cone* etc), brought them closer to the phenomenological investigation of the apparatus of cinematography and projection (light-beams, lenses, photosensitive material and so on) so beloved of the mid 70s conception of expanded cinema.

The lull in expanded cinema activity round 1974/5 conveniently coincides with the exhibition of 'Avant-garde British Landscape Films' at the Tate Gallery (March '75), an event which highlights yet another area given less than proper recognition in the chronology. This was also Dusinberre's first appearance as critic and impresario, and, as I *did* comment in the original draft, one of the first occasions on which films were accompanied by a critical analysis rather than the film-makers' own writings. (European avant-garde film-makers have a long, and on the whole honorable tradition of having to be their own best critics.) In his notes for the exhibition Dusinberre commented on the link between the kind of measured progress through the landscape found in many landscape films (Renny Croft's *Attermire* is a good example) and the photographs of the English artists Richard Long, Hamish Fulton and John Hilliard; and here perhaps some cross-fertilisation did take place. Dusinberre's discusses the landscape film at some length elsewhere in this catalogue; perhaps its greatest relevance in this context is the reminder it represented that alternatives existed to the materialists (anti-illusionist) school. That some form of synthesis even is possible is illustrated by William Raban's ability to move back and forth between both areas.

One final but important influence on events has been the recent growth of subsidy available to the avant-garde film-maker. The Co-op's move from Prince of Wales Crescent in 1975 was for the first time accompanied by a large grant for the re-equipment of its workshops: since 1973 all the major avant garde film festivals and exhibitions and many individual performances have been at least in part grant-aided, and most film-makers themselves have been the recipients of individual 'work' grants. As Leggett and Gidal remark in their statements in this catalogue – this development must inevitably influence the work produced; subsidy will be writ large in the films – as lack of it was (for most anyway) at Prince of Wales Crescent. My own viewpoint on all this is hopelessly compromised – I now work for one of the main funding bodies – but I would hazard that to date the influence has not been entirely detrimental. Certainly the lack of state subsidy in most European countries has frustrated the growth of the international avant garde movement that we confidently predicted in the late '60s. A choice between private and public patronage doesn't exist in England – simply the question 'what kind of state patronage?' The continuing health of the English avant garde must rest in the answer that film-makers give to this question – and on their ability to make their collective voice heard. To that end the role of the Film-makers Co-op, the Independent Film-Makers Association and other such film-makers organisations remain of crucial importance.

NOTES

1 Jeff Keen in fact *did* attend and saw Ken Jacob's *Blonde Cobra*.
2 Published, but never sent!
3 Dwoskin and Hartog correct me, they *had*, but few feet!
4 And Latham, intermittently.
5 *Abstract Film & Beyond* Studio Vista 1977.
6 The results may be seen in *Experimental Cinema* Studio Vista 1971.

Alone – Steve Dwoskin (1966)

STEVE DWOSKIN

Film Is

Extract from Steve Dwoskin *Film Is*,
Peter Owen, 1975

BRITAIN

Of the many film-makers' co-operatives that began to spring up in Europe the London one was the first. It began in October 1966 before the New American Exposition toured Europe, in a room at the back of the Better Books bookshop in Charing Cross Road. It grew out of a very different situation from that surrounding the New York or Canyon Cinema Co-operatives, for there were hardly any indigenous films or film-makers about at the time. It began rather from an interest in film, with the support of only a handful of film-makers, many of them Americans, and apparently with the optimistic hope that film-makers would suddenly emerge from secret hiding-places. Very few in fact appeared. The London Co-operative was clearly a premature venture, but it none the less continued, with many ups and downs, showing the few films that were available plus more from abroad.

It is important to realize that the British environment has never been conducive to the practice of the visual arts, including film. It is one of a prevailing literalness, of classification, of systematizing, a maze of labels, endless compartments and rigid class structures. To have any sense of achievement or recognition in Britain one must always reach some intellectually definable position. The undefinable and the unclassifiable must remain introspective secrets. This is important, because artistic self-expression has nothing to do with definable positions but works in a world of ambiguities and abstractions. If we look at Britain's visual history, we find few highly personal, individual and non literal painters (the outstanding exception is Turner); similarly Britain has produced very few memorable exponents of that most abstract of the arts, musical composition, whereas in literature and science she has excelled.

The visual arts have chiefly developed in two directions: towards the so-called decorative arts, involving surface embellishment and patterns (which are now giving way to mechanical solutions and computer ideology); and towards story-telling, satire, documentation and allegory, in the tradition of Hogarth. In terms of film, the second of these *genres* is the backbone of the British documentary – the predominant form of film-making in the country and the basis of the Free Cinema group in the 'fifties. It is noticeable that attempts at other forms of visual expression, especially more personal ones, tend to be copied from elsewhere. A good example is Pop Art, which originated in the United States as a dynamic personal response to a way of life; in Britain it tended to become narrative and highly picturesque.

The London Film-makers' Co-operative began as one of the many liberating influences that hit Britain in the mid-'sixties, along with the Beatles, the miniskirt and 'swinging London'. It was a time when the Vietnam War brought in many young Americans; when first Pop Art then Op Art came to the Whitechapel, the Royal College, then everywhere. Plastic. The Albert Hall poetry Wholly Communion. The Beats, the hippies, the Provos. Marijuana. Underground press and the Anti-University. The new generation that came of age no longer knew or cared about the Battle of Britain. It opened up and each little group soared like roman candles. The light burnt and died because there was nowhere to go; the old rules still held sway and Swinging London merely rocked the boat a bit. But the ground had been prepared for new values.

In 1966 attempts were being made to make London an all-night city like New York. Among the first of these was the UFO Club, which opened in a mirror-lined Irish dance-hall in Tottenham Court Road (later to be used for the Open Space Theatre) and stayed open all night. Pop groups played, such as the Pink Floyd; there were light-shows and films; people dressed in anything and everything you could imagine. Much of the idea for the UFO Club developed from earlier events in Notting Hill Gate, in and round the London Free School and the week-long First Notting Hill Festival (1966), during which one night was given over to underground films. The patriarch of such events was John ('Hoppy') Hopkins. This was also the time when London's first underground newspaper, *International Times* (*IT*) began. (Like other underground publications it was the victim of constant police harassment.)

The UFO Club continued to thrive and its example was followed by the Middle Earth Club. Under UFO influence three vast and memorable twenty-four-hour film/light/pop/sound events came into being, one at the Roundhouse, to celebrate the first issue of *IT,* the second, called the *Technicolour Dream,* at Alexandra Palace, the third, called *Christmas on Earth Revisited,* at Olympia. These events also attracted a large number of film companies, mostly Italian, who wanted to use the 'with-it' London scene as their back-drop. (Examples are Antonioni with *Blow Up* and Godard with *One Plus One* – later called *Sympathy for the Devil.*) The Roundhouse (a converted railway roundhouse) became a film-set for many other productions and later housed happenings and festivals plus more orthodox shows (such as Tony Richardson's *Hamlet*) and the Living Theater. When the UFO Club was chased out of its dance-hall it went straight over to the Roundhouse.

Both the UFO Club and Middle Earth eventually sank into oblivion, but this period also saw the opening of the first Arts Laboratory (Arts Lab), in Drury Lane in 1967. The Arts Lab concept, fostered by Jim Haynes, involved a place where new ideas and attitudes in art could flourish. The Arts Lab contained a theatre (for live drama and musical performances), an art gallery, a bookshop, a cinema and a television room and also tried running a restaurant, though without success. Meanwhile the back room of Better Books was still a centre for poetry readings, 'happenings' and small-scale performances, including the much-talked-of International Destruction in Art Symposium. It was also a central meeting-place, as was another bookshop called Indica Books.

The London Film-makers' Co-operative, still based at Better Books, ran weekly film shows to increasingly large audiences. At this early stage it also managed to put on a week-long Spontaneous Film Festival at the Jeanetta Cochrane Theatre, building up its programme from the few new independent films available in London, plus some seldom-seen films by earlier independent film-makers, which were dug out from layers of dust in the libraries of private distributors and the British Film Institute. But the days of the Co-op's life at Better Books were numbered. The shop's manager, concrete poet Bob Cobbing, who was also secretary of the Co-operative, was told by the owners to remove the Co-operative and its films, along with any books, prose or poetry dealing with controversial subjects such as drugs. The Co-operative had to go into temporary exile, though it managed to continue its distribution and was held together by the few remaining committee members.

The Arts Lab in Drury Lane now formed its own group of film-makers, which fragmented the Co-operative effort. Eventually a difference of approach caused a split within the Arts Lab itself, forcing one group out. This latter group formed a New Arts Lab (known as the Institute for Research in Art and Technology), where the Co-operative finally had an office, plus film-processing and editing facilities. The original Arts Lab closed soon after that. By the end of 1969 the Co-operative's film library had grown to about two hundred films, though the bulk of them were from the New American Cinema. In the early stages, only a few British-based film-makers supported the Co-operative. Apart from myself, among the first were Jeff Keen, John Latham, and Simon Hartog, who were later joined by David

Larcher, Peter Gidal, Malcolm Le Grice, Fred Drummond and Mike Dunford.

Younger people were gradually becoming more aware of this type of film and a whole new attitude towards the cinema was emerging. By the beginning of the 'seventies the Co-operative had also begun to build and operate its own processing laboratory, which was essential for experimental and economic reasons. As we have seen, it also built up editing facilities to complement the processing. The existence of this equipment brought in many 'interested' film-makers. The Co-operative had by this point already brought out three issues of its magazine *Cinim,* originally under the editorship of Philip Crick and later under Simon Hartog.

Many of the Co-operative's American films came with Carla Liss, who took on the job of its full-time paid secretary. The presence of a full-time person increased distribution, improved co-ordination of films and activities, and provided a sort of core for the organization. The lack of a core had been the main weakness of the Co-operative, and has remained one of its main weaknesses. Not only had it been formed without a strong body of film-makers or a central figurehead – as Jonas Mekas was for the American Co-operative – it also failed to cement a strong social bond between members. At least half the people involved were after all not film-makers themselves, but were merely interested or involved with films in another capacity, perhaps as writers or poets. Personality differences were often extreme, even among the film-makers, so social communication and exchange was slim, and functioned, if at all, in small cliques. Emotionally the Co-operative never formed a whole, though its members had the same intellectual approach. Co-ordination and co-operation were often difficult, and unfortunately remained so. This is perhaps endemic to all such activities and groups, but it certainly has a retarding effect. It is also within this social and co-operative gap that the hustlers and spoilers begin to move. Yet distribution did continue and film shows did occur, at least in universities, film clubs and societies and in the increasing number of Arts Labs throughout the country. Thus the ideas, interest and possibilities inherent in the new cinema became an effective reality in a country that had previously been starved of such stimuli.

In Britain anyone who wants to make a film independently runs into even more frustration than in other countries. Any Briton who has managed to get away from the oppressive classification (professional, amateur and so on) and from the social conditioning that regards success as greatness and failure as an incurable disease is also confronted with an economic problem; aliens living in Britain are of course exempt from all but the latter consideration – they have other hang-ups. Personal economics are the primary concern. Film is expensive anywhere, and when the general cost of living becomes greater than one's earning power it is even more expensive; but in Britain the government imposes an additional 50 per cent tax on such material. Exemption from this tax can be acquired only by a 'professional business', not by the independent artist/film-maker. Film-processing laboratories, being expensive and geared to professional, bulk users, have little sympathy for the small user and experimenter. They also act in Britain as censors, because the authorities invoke fear of reprisals against them if they do not (and any censorship, especially based on fear, is confused and dangerous). Lab censorship does not take into account the context in which the images are used, or even consider whether the images will be used at all in the finished film, but is based on the appearance of the isolated image (a single frame of the film).

One of the greatest restrictions on film-making in Britain (for after all economic and censorship problems exist in most countries) is the cataloguing of attitudes and actions that is due in large part to educational conditioning. The Establishment's attitude towards film-making is well expressed in this statement from a proposal to establish a National Film School: '…in our view great emphasis will have to be placed on practice training and acquiring a high level of knowledge of all the numerous technical aspects of film-making so as to equip the successful candidates ultimately to take their place as practical film-makers within the industry.' The report further considers that: 'Although film-making may derive some sustenance from its association with visual arts and design, it seems to us self-evident that the visual arts are in themselves quite different from film-making, both as an art and as a craft… The drama undoubtedly has close links, in some ways closer links than that of the visual arts, with the art of film-making.' This attitude is the product of the accustomed commercial tradition in the film industry, but it is peripheral to the art of film as a whole. To teach this as the major and, in a sense, the only aspect of film is to control the general public's view of what film is and should be.

In an environment that establishes singular and narrow definitions, such definitions become the direction towards which the interested turn, and the sole criterion of success. For many people this might seem a satisfactory arrangement, but if any creative form is to develop its potential it must be allowed the broadest possible arena for discovery. This means the widest definition, not the narrowest, and it applies to all the arts, not just to film. Yet emphasis is constantly placed on definition, on the need to have a place within society (such as a job).

It is in this basic situation that young people must grow up. Those who want to become film-makers are taught that these definitions exist, and find it difficult later on to consider any other possibility. Luckily, a few people in Britain have managed to break free of such bonds. Social difficulties in Britain, especially since the Industrial Revolution, have produced not only a survival problem but a strong environmental influence. Most people experience other people, their struggles, living conditions and attitudes within a technical environment, rather than trees, mountains and landscape. Thus when independent films are made they tend to express and reflect this environment. This has given Britain its predisposition towards the documentary style of film-making.

If we consider the physical landscape of England (as opposed to Scotland or Wales) the visible impression is one of moderation: of subtle rather than dramatic change; of repetition and of closeness. This landscape is lit generally by a diffused, mellow and almost shadowless light (though there is some sunshine!). The roads are small and winding; the views offer little sense of scale. This induces a feeling for pattern (decorative design), which basically involves surface treatment and textures without any strong central points or dynamics. Hence the British supremacy, for example, in textile and typographic design, with such visual movements as the one originated by William Morris. Combined with the ordered landscape, the reduced sense of scale and the technical facility, a concern with details and pieces emerges that shies away from direct self-contained gestures.

The mock paternity of 'socialized' governments, combined with social and economic classifications, is another constricting force. Legislation to provide for the arts involves a number of narrow and inflexible definitions, yet since support is provided, it creates a feeling of dependency on the government. In their mock-paternal attitudes the various governments have given people the feeling that the arts will always be granted provision and support, as will education in the arts. Almost every county in Britain supports at least one art-school at the higher-education level, and in London alone there are almost as many specialized art colleges (as opposed to those that are part of universities) as in the whole of the United States. But this abundance of art and design education has tended to make most of these schools function on the level of middle-class 'finishing' schools, or else as purely functional training establishments. Most of them are state-supported, with fees paid by county councils, which encourages many people to expect continuous and regular financial support for their activities in the arts. The government also maintains its sense of patronage through such a body as the Arts Council, which deploys sums of money for art exhibitions, theatre groups, literary journals and the like. But the deployment of money is dependent on strict definitions of art activities. In regard to film, the Arts Council will provide money only for films made about an artist (such as Richard Hamilton) or by a qualified artist (a graduate practising painting or sculpture) as an extension of his work. Film as an art form is not considered as art in this context, and all other applications concerning films are referred to the British Film Institute.

The British Film Institute (BFI), which also embraces the National Film Archive and the National Film Theatre, was one of the first of its kind in the world. It represents a well-ordered, nationalized way of administering, preserving, showing and making films and providing the public with information about films (library, stills collection, publications, lectures). It also works in conjunction with the Federation of Film Societies. But the Institutes definition of film has primarily been determined by the commercial concept, as reflected in the proposals for a National Film School. It has cinema, not only through its activities but through its widely read, subsidized journal *Sight and Sound,* and it neglects newer forms of independent and personal cinema. The way in which the BFI runs its London Film Festival is another example of this attitude. It has been so closed to the new cinema that even staunch traditionalists have become bored. The National Film Theatre has certainly managed to show a great range of classical and traditional cinema, much of which would not otherwise have been seen, but this has been at the expense of the newer cinema and the film archive has shown virtually no interest at all in acquiring new avant-garde films. It is worth mentioning here that though there are also two film schools in the London area – the Royal College of Art's Film and Television School and the London School of Film Technique – both of these institutions have upheld the concept of film as a commercial activity.

The BFI has also maintained the British Film Institute Production Board; which was formed to aid the production of new films by young people. Ironically, the Production Board was originally called 'The Experimental Film Fund', yet one of its criteria for providing funds to young film-makers was that they must present a script, though more recently this requirement has been diminished. One submitted a script but was refused help because she had no previous experience in directing (though she had made 8mm films); she was told however that her application would be considered if she could find an acceptably experienced director to make the film for her. On the other hand, the Production Board (with the BBC) sunk good money in producing such an embarrassingly poor film as *Herostratus* (poor even by commercial standards) and followed this up with a bleak propaganda campaign to promote it as one of Britain's major achievements in experimental film. The Board also produced a film called *The Park* and sent it to the Fourth International Experimental Film Festival as a representative example of a British short film. A rather dry and unsympathetic story of an old man seeing his favourite park change, it was booed more than any other film at the festival. (To be fair, the Board has produced the occasional good film, such as Anthony Stern's *San Francisco* and My *Childhood* by Bill Douglas.)

Within this narrow establishment interest in the new cinema began to be apparent by 1970. A surprisingly large number of small magazines and independent film groups, clubs and distributors began to appear. Not many felt any sympathy for the Co-operative, or for the co-operative ideal; many, in fact, thought of it as a specialized film-distribution organization, dealing solely in a fixed style of film-making. But this sudden growth did show that the traditional view of the cinema in Britain was changing.

Three groups, The Tattooist, Cinema Action and The Other Cinema were among the most important. The Other Cinema stated that 'its aim is to provide a system of film distribution and exhibition which will function as an alternative to the existing methods of distribution which repeatedly prove themselves unable to handle the numerous independently made films for which there is clearly an audience'. It grew out of an invited meeting held at the Institute of Contemporary Arts (ICA) to establish a 'parallel' cinema and an alternative distribution circuit. This had become necessary because much major cinema distribution is run by monopolies that own cinemas, control the types of film made and make their own films for their own circuit. For example, the drab *Look at Life* series is made by Rank for themselves. A weak anti-monopoly action was taken by the government against Rank, and this did make the company agree to give up thirteen weeks each year to other short films. So Rank's own films run for only thirty-nine weeks a year instead of fifty-two. No other change took place.

The idea voiced at the original 'parallel' cinema meeting was, in principle, similar to that of the co-operatives: to establish a distribution circuit by which any money received could be fed into making new films. The difference was that the group would gather the money collectively and would thereby be able to act as a production company. In other words, the group would support the production of films, whereas in the co-operatives a percentage of the money earned by each film goes to the individual film-maker. One view expressed at this parallel cinema meeting was that if a film was to earn enough money to support the production fund it must have considerable public appeal. Films were therefore to be generally feature-film length (around the 90-minute mark).

Other groups beside The Other Cinema now began to distribute films, with names such as PolitKino, Newsreel and Cineindependent, while various individuals acquired a few films and the smaller commercial film distributors also began to buy many independent films. (An important point to mention here is that in these early stages only a small number of the films acquired were by British film-makers. For example, the first films handled by Andi Engel's PolitKino were by the German film-maker Jean-Marie Straub and included his *Chronik der Anna Magdalena Bach* (Chronicle of Anna Magdalena Bach, 1967) though he did also acquire *Events,* by the British film-maker John Llewellyn.) The increased interest in the New Cinema is also exemplified by such successes as the New Cinema Club and the

Trying To Kiss The Moon – Steve Dwoskin (1994)

Electric Cinema Club. The New Cinema Club, formed by Derek Hill, grew out of his Short Film Service, which functioned as an agency to place films with distributors and other buyers. Hill began to show feature films as well as short films under the club banner in order to create an interest in such material. He showed them in hired cinemas and as interest increased expanded his repertoire. The Electric Cinema Club became a great success after acquiring the old Imperial Cinema in Notting Hill. It ran late-night shows and showed a large variety of films, from classics to 'underground'. It had fuller houses than many commercial cinemas, though we must not forget that it was in Notting Hill, which has a younger and more cosmopolitan population than many other areas.

Interest did not emerge solely in London, but was awakened in many centres throughout the country. The Film Co-operative's distribution to universities and film societies was constant and widespread. Requests for lecturers with the films were also regularly received. A New Cinema Club and an 8mm Film Co-operative opened in Oxford, another in Southend, while film shows began to take place in Liverpool, Brighton, Birmingham, Cambridge, Portsmouth and Edinburgh, among other places. In London, places like the ICA, the Arts Lab and The Place increased audience awareness by allowing much of the new, independent cinema to be shown. But probably one of the most striking signs of interest in film was the rapid increase in film publications. Books on all aspects of the film poured out from numerous publishers and one, Lorrimer Books, was virtually founded on scripts of well-known films, which it continues to publish today. The number of big and small magazines being issued seemed by 1970 to be greater than in any other country. They ranged from the glossy, commercial film magazines like *Sight and Sound, Films and Filming, Continental Film Review* and *Film* to semi-glossy independent journals like *Cinim, Movie, Cinema, Cinemantics, Independent Cinema, Fiba, AfterImage* and *Cinema Rising,* plus numerous university magazines, while commercial art and 'underground' journals also gave a good deal of space to the newer cinema.

Yet however much *interest* in film had increased at this point, a corresponding increase in new indigenous films and film-makers was not so apparent. One recurring feature of all these various interested groups and publications has been the activity of non-film-makers. In the early Film-makers' Co-operative half the active members were not film-makers but critics, journalists, writers and the like, and so it was with many of the newer activities. As their interest tended to be verbal and intellectual, this meant, to some extent, that concern for film depended more on theory, politics, documentation and technique. The innate (or latent) recording and propaganda attributes of the film medium make it an available and tempting means of communication for people who think in journalistic terms. Whereas painting, poetry, music, sculpture and so on rely on conveying more abstract and subjective matter, film can also act as a recording system for literal and objective imagery strung together like sentences. In this way it is related to the journalist's method of describing within a literal and verbal structure. Thus those with verbally descriptive ideas would turn first to film (or television) as the most immediate way of visualizing them. Similarly, since film's whole physical existence is dependent on machinery, optics, light and chemistry, people whose interests are with such technicalities also find themselves at home with it. It is in these two general areas that many of the newer, independent film-makers were working by 1970, not only in Britain but in most other countries. These directions explain in part the early absence of film-makers from the London Film-makers' Co-operative. Some potential and existing film-makers assumed that it was concerned only with films that they considered to be 'poetic' or 'art' films. They did not understand or want to understand that the co-operative idea merely involved co-operation between film-makers making any kind of film outside the established commercial system. The journalistic film-makers were not in sympathy with the so-called 'art' film-makers, while for others 'art' had nothing to do with films – all these definitions are of course a *'grande illusion'*. Some came but went away again because, in the early stages, the co-operative could not provide them with equipment. When it announced that it now had processing and editing equipment many interested 'film-makers' did turn up. (Of course, a large number of film-makers do genuinely prefer to be part of the established film industry.)

One wonders if all this lack of co-operation and the formation of different groups (even within the Co-operative), plus the existence of so many different independent film journals, are not symptoms of megalomania. To quote from the Tattooist group:

> The terrible problem in England is that there are large numbers of talented people who have lived for years in total isolation, and vicious competition with each other. They believe that nobody understands them, that everybody is warping against them. And by now they've built up an almost classic tradition in British films – so that their isolation speaks more loudly than their borrowed politics.

The journalistic attitude we have been discussing fitted the growing involvement in politics, the use of film as a direct political weapon. Much of the political direction, particularly in Britain and on the Continent of Europe, involved an increasing swing to the left, with a strong Marxist line against existing capitalist/imperialistic systems in Europe and America, with special emphasis on American domination and the Vietnam War. Other activities were aimed against the capitalist, 'bourgeois' film industry itself, which was alleged to put forward a false reality in order to uphold its own consumer ideologies, and to work as a closed capitalist system for making money. The more extreme political attitudes of the Left have seen the cinema as the art of the masses, and in these terms transform films into an active means of revolution rather than mere entertainment. The camera then becomes a gun, and the cinema must be a guerilla cinema.

PETER WOLLEN

The Two
Avant-Gardes

First published in *Studio International*,
November/December 1975

Film history has developed unevenly, so that in Europe today there are two distinct avant-gardes. The first can be identified loosely with the Co-op movement. The second would include film-makers such as Godard, Straub and Huillet, Hanoun, Jancso. Naturally there are points of contact between these two groups and common characteristics, but they also differ quite sharply in many respects: aesthetic assumptions, institutional framework, type of financial support, type of critical backing, historical and cultural origin. There are other film-makers too who do not fit neatly into either camp, and films which fall somewhere in between or simply somewhere else – Jackie Raynal's *Deux Fois,* for instance – but in general the distinction holds good.

At the extreme, each would tend to deny the others the status of avant-garde at all. Books like Steve Dwoskin's *Film Is* or David Curtis's *Experimental Film*[1] do not discuss the crucial post-1968 work of Godard and Gorin, for example. And supporters of Godard – and Godard himself – have often denounced the 'Co-op avant-garde' as hopelessly involved with the established bourgeois art world and its values. The reasons for dismissal are often quite beside the point and misplaced. By no means all the directors (to use a word taboo in the other camp) in one group work with narrative in 35mm, as you might sometimes imagine – Godard has worked in 16mm for years and recently with video (to open up another hornet's nest). Conversely, many Co-op film-makers are well aware of political issues and see themselves in some sense as militant. (Not that political militancy in itself is any guarantee of being avant-garde.)

The position is complicated too by the fact that in North America there is only one avant-garde, centred on the various Co-ops. There are no obvious equivalents of Godard or Straub-

Huillet, although their influence can occasionally be seen – in Jon Jost's *Speaking Directly* for example. Moreover, American critics and theorists of the avant-garde have long tended to overlook their European counterparts or see them as derivative. The Europeans – and perhaps particularly the English – then tend to react by stressing their own credentials, making claims to have occupied the same ground as the Americans earlier or independently. From outside, the quarrel often looks of secondary importance. After all, no-one denies that the capital of narrative fiction 35mm film-making is Hollywood, however innovative European directors, such as Antonioni or Fellini or Truffaut may be. In the same way, New York is clearly the capital of the Co-op movement. Consequently, from New York, Godard looks much more distinctively European than Kren or Le Grice, a fact which simply reflects the realities of power in the art world, to which the Co-op movement is closely tied. Indeed, there is a sense in which avant-garde Co-op film-making in Europe is closer to New York than Californian film-making is, and the leading New York critics and tastemakers – Sitney, Michelson – are not appreciated in San Francisco any more than they are in London.

It seems to me much more important to try and understand what unites and separates Godard and Straub-Huillet on the one hand, and, say, Gidal and Wyborny on the other hand, than what unites and separates Europe and North America within the Co-op ambit. Moreover, I think the absence of any avant-garde of the Godard type in North America could ultimately prove a severe limitation on the development of the New American Cinema itself, narrowing its horizons and tying it unnecessarily closely to the future of the other visual arts, condemning it to a secondary status within the art world. Close relationship with 'art' – painting, post-painting – is both a strength and a weakness.

To understand further the split which has developed within the avant-garde it is necessary to go back into history. A similar split can be seen in the twenties. On the one hand films were being made by Léger-Murphy, Picabia-Clair, Eggeling, Richter, Man Ray, Moholy-Nagy and others – many of them discussed in Standish Lawder's recent book on *The Cubist Cinema*[2] – that were attempts to extend the scope of painting, to move outside the confines of the canvas, to introduce the dimension of time, to use light directly as well as colour, and so on. On the other hand, there were the Russian directors, whose films were clearly avant-garde but in a different sense: Eisenstein's *Strike,* Dovzhenko's *Zvenigora,* Vertov's *Man with the Movie Camera.* It was only at the very end of the decade that there was any real contact between the two groups – when Lissitzky (whose ideas about the electro-mechanical spectacle and admiration for Eggeling put him clearly in the 'painters' group) first met Vertov to discuss the Stuttgart *Film und Foto* exhibition,[3] and when Eisenstein met Richter on his first trip out of the Soviet Union and went with him to the conference at Le Sarraz, which turned out to mark the end rather than the beginning of an epoch.

As today, part of the difference lies in the backgrounds of the people involved. One group came from painting. The other from theatre (Eisenstein), and futurist sound-poetry (Vertov) – Dovzhenko, in fact, had trained as a painter but deliberately gave it up, leaving all his painting materials behind him in Kharkov when he set off for Odessa and the film studios, seeking a complete break with his past. And, of course, there are premonitory links between these different currents of the twenties and those of recent years – Godard and Gorin carried out their collaboration under the name of the Dziga Vertov group; Van Doesburg, in 1929, already anticipated many of the ideas of 'expanded cinema', realized decades later: 'The spectator space will become part of the film space. The separation of 'projection surface' is abolished. The spectator will no longer observe the film, like a theatrical presentation, but will participate in it optically and acoustically.'[4]

Painting, I think it can be argued, played the leading role in the development of modernism in the other arts. The break, the *coupure* – to use the Althusserian terminology – the shift of terrain that marked the substitution of one paradigm or problematic for another, the beginning of modernism, the work of the historic avant-garde, was a break that took place in painting pre-eminently, with the discoveries of Cubism. It is not hard to show how painting affected the other arts, how early Cubism had a decisive impact on Gertrude Stein and Ezra Pound, for example, in literature, and later on William Carlos Williams, Apollinaire, Marinetti, Mayakovsky, Khlebnikov – all were influenced at a crucial point by their encounter with Cubism. The innovations of Picasso, and Braque, were seen as having an implication beyond the history of painting itself. They were intuitively felt, I think, very early on, to represent a critical semiotic shift, a changed concept and practice of sign and signification, which we can now see to have been the opening-up of a space, a disjunction between signifier and signified and a change of emphasis from the problem of signified and reference, the classic problem of realism, to that of signifier and signified within the sign itself.[5]

When we look at the development of painting after the Cubist breakthrough, however, we see a constant trend towards an apparently even more radical development: the suppression of the signified altogether, an art of pure signifiers detached from meaning as much as from reference, from *Sinn* as much as from *Bedeutung*. This tendency towards abstraction could be justified in various ways – a transcendental signified could be postulated, in symbolist or spiritualist terms, a meaning located in the *Uberwelt* of pure ideas; a theory of formalism, of art as pure design, could be proposed; the work of art could be defended in terms of objecthood, pure presence; it could be explained as a solution to a problem, often set by the relationship between a signifier – a form of expression, in Hjelmslev's phrase – and its physical, material support (the matter or substance of expression).[6]

Literature, on the other hand, tended to fall back into forms of writing in which the signified clearly remained dominant. Modernism could be interpreted in terms of the expansion of subject-matter, new narrative techniques (stream of consciousness) or play on the paradoxes of meaning and reference (Pirandellism). It is significant, for instance, that so many of the most radical experiments, such as attempts at sound poetry, were the work of artists or writers working closely with painters: Arp, Schwitters, Van Doesburg among them. In theatre the most radical developments were invariably associated with changes in set design and costume, including the use of masks: Meyerhold's Constructivist theatre in the Soviet Union, Schlemmer's Bauhaus theatre, Artaud. In this context, it should be added, Brecht appears as little more than a moderate.

Cinema is, of course, a form of art employing more than one channel, more than one sensory medium, and uses a multiplicity of different types of code. It has affinities with almost all the other arts. Music and verbal language, as well as natural or artificial noise, can form elements of the sound-track. Theatre and dance can be elements of the pro-filmic event, placed in front of the camera to be photographed. Editing can be used to develop narrative or to produce a 'visual rhythm' by analogy with music. Film itself can be painted or paintings can be animated. Light can be used as a medium, and through projection a third dimension can be introduced, to produce a kind of mobile light sculpture. Cinema too has its own 'specifically cinematic'[7] codes and materials, associated with the various phases of film production.

As a result of this variety and multiplicity, ideas have fed into film-making from a variety of sources in the other arts. One powerful influence has come from painting, bringing with it a tendency to abstraction – pure light or colour; and non-figurative design – or deformation of conventional photographic imagery, involving prismatic fragmentation and splintering, the use of filters or stippled glass, mirror-shots, extreme and microscopic close-ups, bizarre angles, negative images, all of which are to be found in twenties films. Editing tended to follow principles of association (related to poetry or dream) or analogies with music – shots of fixed length, repetition and variation, attempts at synthetic effects, theories of counterpoint.

But this influence, and the films associated with it, are marked as much by what they excluded as what they included. Primarily of course verbal language was missing and also narrative. During the silent period, the absence of language was not foregrounded; it seemed a natural quality of film, but in retrospect its significance can be seen. Language is still excluded from an enormous number of avant-garde films, which are shown either silent or with electronic or other musical tracks. Again, there are real technical and financial reasons for this, but these practical disincentives coincide with an aesthetic itself founded on concepts of visual form and visual problems that exclude verbal language from their field, and may be actively hostile to it. This is part of the legacy of the Renaissance that has survived the modernist break almost unchallenged, except in isolated instances – Lissitzky, Duchamp, Picabia and, extremely important, recent conceptualist work.

There is one further important point that must be made about the development of film in relation to art history. Film-makers at a certain point became dissatisfied with the search simply for 'kinetic solutions to pictorial problems',[8] as in the films of Man Ray and Moholy-Nagy, and began to concentrate on what they saw as specifically cinematic problems. Structural film-making over the last decade has thus represented a displacement of concerns from the art world to the film world rather than an extension. This way of thinking about art has remained one that film-makers have in common with painters and other visual artists, but an effort has been made to insist on the ontological autonomy of film. Thus, for instance, Gidal's work has foregrounded and been in a sense 'about' focus; Le Grice's work has foregrounded and been in a sense 'about' printing or projection. The tendency of painting to concentrate on its own sphere of materials and signification, to be self-reflexive, has been translated into specifically cinematic terms and concerns, though here again 'specifically cinematic' is taken to mean primarily the picture-track.

Thus the impact of avant-garde ideas from the world of visual arts has ended up pushing film-makers into a position of extreme 'purism' or 'essentialism'. Ironically, anti-illusionist, anti-realist film has ended up sharing many preoccupations in common with its worst enemies. A theorist like André Bazin, for instance, committed to realism and representationalism, based his commitment on an argument about cinematic ontology and essence that he saw in the photographic reproduction of the natural world. We now have, so to speak, both an extroverted and an introverted ontology of film, one seeking the soul of cinema in the nature of the pro-filmic event, the other in the nature of the cinematic process, the cone of light or the grain of silver. The frontier reached by this avant-garde has been an ever-narrowing preoccupation with pure film, with film 'about' film, a dissolution of signification into objecthood or tautology.[9] I should add, perhaps, that this tendency is even more marked in the United States than in Europe.

Where does the other avant-garde stand? Here, as one would expect, the tendency goes in the opposite direction. The Soviet directors of the twenties, though they saw themselves in some sense as avant-garde, were also preoccupied with the problem of realism. For the most part they remained within the bounds of narrative cinema. The most clearly avant-garde passages and episodes in Eisenstein's films (experiments in intellectual montage) remain passages and episodes, which appear as interpolations within an otherwise homogeneous and classical narrative. There is no doubt that the dramaturgy is modernist rather than traditional – the crowd as hero, typage, *guignol* – but these are not features that can be attributed to a break with rather than a renovation of classical theatre. They are modes of achieving a heightened emotional effect or presenting an idea with unexpected vividness or force.

In Eisenstein's work the signified – content in the conventional sense – is always dominant and, of course, he went so far as to dismiss Vertov's *Man with the Movie Camera* as 'formalist jack-straws and unmotivated camera mischief,'[10] contrasting its use of slow motion with Epstein's *La Chute de la Maison Usher,* in which, according to Eisenstein, it is used to heighten emotional pressure, to achieve an effect in terms of a desired content or goal. Vertov's film was, of course, a milestone for the avant-garde and it is a sign of its richness that it can be seen as a precursor both of *cinema-verité* and of structural film, though also, evidently, a sign of its ambiguity, of its uncertainty caught between an ideology of photographic realism and one of formal innovation and experiment.

In broad terms, what we find with the Soviet film-makers is a recognition that a new type of content, a new realm of signifieds, demands formal innovation, on the level of the signifier, for its expression. Thus Eisenstein wanted to translate the dialectical materialism of his world-view from an approach to subject-matter to an approach to form, through a theory of montage that was itself dialectical. The aesthetic was still content-based, it saw signifiers primarily as means of expression, but at the same time it demanded a radical transformation of those means. It was an aesthetic that had much in common with the avant-garde positions of, say, Léger or Man Ray, but which also kept a distance, a distance of which the fear of formalism is symptomatic. It is as if they felt that once the signifier was freed from bondage to the signified, it was certain to celebrate by doing away with its old master altogether in a fit of irresponsible ultra-leftism and utopianism. As we have seen, this was not so far wrong.

The case of Godard, working forty years or so later, is slightly different. In Godard's post-1968 films we glimpse something of an alternative route between contentism and formalism, a recognition that it is possible to work within the space opened up by the disjunction and dislocation of signifier and signified. Clearly Godard was influenced by Eisenstein's theory of dialectical montage, but he develops it in a much more radical way. In the last resort, for Eisenstein, conflict occurred primarily between the successive signifieds of images. Although he recognizes a form of dialectical montage in the suprematist paintings of Malevich, he himself remains within the confines of 'naturalism'. (Interestingly enough, he identifies a middle road between naturalism and abstraction, which he relates, somewhat surprisingly, to Balla and 'primitive Italian futurism')[11] Godard takes the idea of formal conflict and struggle and translates it into a concept of conflict, not between the content of images, but between different codes and between signifier and signified.

Thus, in *Le Gai Savoir,* which he began shooting before the events of May 1968, but completed after, Godard tries programatically to 'return to zero', to de-compose and then re-compose sounds and images. For Godard, conflict becomes not simply collision through juxtaposition, as in Eisenstein's model, but an act of negativity, a splitting apart of an apparently natural unity, a disjunction. Godard's view of bourgeois communication is one of a discourse gaining its power from its apparent naturalness, the impression of necessity that seems to bind a signifier to a signified, a sound to an image, in order to provide a convincing representation of the world. He wants not simply to represent an alternative 'world' or alternative 'world-view', but to investigate the whole process of signification out of which a world-view or an ideology is constructed. *Le Gai Savoir* ends with the following words on the soundtrack: 'This film has not wished to, could not wish to explain the cinema or even constitute its object, but more modestly, to offer a few effective means for arriving there. This is not the film that must be made, but it shows how, if one is to make a film, one must necessarily follow some of the paths travelled here.'[12] In other words, the film deliberately suspends 'meaning', avoids any teleology or finality, in the interests of a destruction and re-assembly, a re-combination of the order of the sign as an experiment in the dissolution of old meanings and the generation of new ones from the semiotic process itself.

Put another way, *Le Gai Savoir* is not a film with a meaning, something to say about the world, nor is it a film 'about' film (which, after all, is simply a limited part of the world of interest in itself to film-makers and film-students) but a film about the possibility of meaning itself, of generating new types of meaning. The array of sign-systems at work in the cinema are thus brought into a new kind of relationship with each other and with the world. Nor, of course, is Godard indifferent to what types of new meaning are produced. Although his work is open-ended, it does not offer itself simply for a delirium of interpretation, as though meaning could be read in at will by the spectator. Signifieds are neither fixed, or fixed as far as possible, as they are in conventional cinema, nor are they freed from any constraint, as though the end of a content- dominated art meant the end of any control over content.

In a sense, Godard's work goes back to the original breaking point at which the modern avant-garde began – neither realist or expressionist, on the one hand, nor abstractionist, on the other. In the same way, the *Demoiselles d'Avignon* is neither realist, expressionist or abstractionist. It dislocates signifier from signified, asserting – as such a dislocation must –

the primacy of the first, without in any way dissolving the second. It is not a portrait group or a study of nudes in the representational tradition, but on the other hand, to see it simply as an investigation of painterly or formal problems or possibilities is to forget its original title, *Le Bordel Philosophique.* The same could be said, of course, about *The Large Glass.* The battle between realism/illusion/'literature' in art, and abstraction/reflexiveness/Greenberg-modernism, is not so simple or all-encompassing as it may sometimes seem.

There are two other topics that should be mentioned here. The first is politics. As I suggested above, it is often too easily asserted that one avant-garde is 'political' and the other is not. Peter Gidal, for example, defends his films on grounds that clearly imply a political position. And the supporters of Godard and Straub Huillet, by distinguishing their films from those of Karmitz or Pontecorvo, are constantly forced to assert that being 'political' is not in itself enough, that there must be a break with bourgeois norms of diegesis, subversion and deconstruction of codes – a line of argument which, unless it is thought through carefully or stopped arbitrarily at some safe point, leads inevitably straight into the positions of the other avant-garde. Nonetheless, in discussing Godard, the fact that his films deal explicitly with political issues and ideas is obviously important. He does not wish to cut himself off from the political Marxist culture in which he has steeped himself from before 1968 and increasingly since. This culture, moreover, is one of books and verbal language. The important point, though, is that a film like *Le Gai Savoir* – unlike some later work of Godard, as he fell under Brecht's influence – is not simply didactic or expository, but presents the language of Marxism itself, a deliberately chosen language, as itself problematic.

Politics – the influence and presence of Marxist writing – has been an obvious force of impetus and strength for Godard, but it also relates to another question – that of audience. On the whole, the Co-op avant-garde, happy though it would no doubt be to find a mass audience, is reconciled to its minority status. The consciously political film-maker, on the other hand, is often uneasy about this. The representatives of Marxist culture are on the whole aesthetically conservative and avant-gardism is damned as élitism. Godard, as is well-known, defended himself against this charge by citing Mao's dictum about the three types of struggle and placing his own work in film under the banner of scientific experiment, rather than class struggle, an instance in which theoretical work could be justified and take precedence over political work, in the short term at least. Yet it is also clear that it was pressure to rediscover a mass, popular audience which led to the artistic regroupment of *Tout Va Bien,* which abandons avant-gardism for a stylized didacticism, set within a classical realist frame, though with some Eisensteinian interpolations.

The second topic is that of 'intertextuality', to use Julia Kristeva's terminology.[13] One of the main characteristics of modernism, once the priority of immediate reference to the real world had been disputed, was the play of allusion within and between texts. Quotation, for instance, plays a crucial role in the *Demoiselles d'Avignon* and, indeed, in *The Large Glass.* In avant-garde writing it is only necessary to think of Pound and Joyce. Again, the effect is to break up the homogeneity of the work, to open up spaces between different texts and types of discourses. Godard has used the same strategy, not only on the sound-track where whole passages from books are recited, but also on the picture-track, as in the quotations from Hollywood western and the *cinema novo* in *Vent d'Est.* Similarly, the films of Straub-Huillet are almost all 'layered' like a palimpsest – in this case, the space between texts is not only semantic but historical too, the different textual strata being the residues of different epochs and cultures.

It is significant perhaps that the latest films of Malcolm Le Grice have a similar quality of intertextuality in their quotation of Lumière and *Le Déjeuner sur l'Herbe.* The Lumière film is especially interesting – in comparison with, for example, Bill Brand's re-make of Lumière's destruction-of-a-wall film.[14] It is not simply a series of optical re-combinations, like cinematic anagrams, but an investigation into narration itself, which by counterposing different narrative tones, so to speak, neither dissolves nor repeats Lumière's simple story, *L'Arroseur Arroseé,* but foregrounds the process of narration itself. And this, as we have seen, is semiotically very different from foregrounding the process of projection. The way into narrative cinema is surely not forbidden to the avant-garde film-maker, any more than the way into verbal language.[15]

Cinema, I have stressed earlier, is a multiple system – the search for the specifically cinematic can be deceptively purist and reductive. For most people, after all, cinema is unthinkable without words and stories. To recognize this fact is by no means to accept a conventional Hollywood-oriented (or Bergman/Antonioni/Bunuel-oriented) attitude to the cinema and the place of stories and words within it. It is perhaps the idea, so strongly rooted by now, that film is a visual art that has brought about a blockage. Yet this idea is obviously a half-truth at best. The danger that threatens is that the introduction of words and stories – of signifieds – will simply bring back illusionism or representationalism in full flood. Clearly this fear is the converse of Eisenstein's anxiety about 'unmotivated camera mischief'. There are good reasons for these fears, but surely they can be overcome.

I have tried to show how the two avant-gardes we find in Europe originated and what it is that holds them apart. To go further, I would have to discuss as well the institutional and economic framework in which film-makers find themselves. The basis of the Co-op movement, as has often been pointed out, lies in artisanal production, with film-makers who do as much as possible themselves at every stage of the film-making process. If there are performers involved they are usually few, generally friends of the film-maker, often other film-makers. The other avant-garde has its roots much more in the commercial system, and even when filming in 16mm Godard would use stars known in the commercial cinema. The difference is not simply one of budgets – Dwoskin or Wyborny have made films for TV as well as Godard, and Dwoskin's are clearly much more conventional, yet they are almost automatically assigned different cultural places. It is much more one of the film-makers' frame of reference, the places from which they come and the culture to which they relate.

The facts of uneven development mean too that it would be utopian to hope for a simple convergence of the two avant-gardes. The most revolutionary work, both of Godard and of Straub-Huillet, was done in 1968 – *Le Gai Savoir* and *The Bridegroom, the Comedienne and the Pimp.* In comparison *Tout Va Bien* and *Moses and Aaron* are a step backwards. Godard works increasingly in isolation, cut off from any real collective work or movement. In *Le Gai Savoir,* Juliet Berto says towards the end that half the shots are missing from the film, and Jean-Pierre Léaud replies that they will be shot by other film-makers: Bertolucci, Straub, Glauber-Rocha. We can see now how wrong Godard was in some of his judgements – the shots missing from his film could be supplied by the other avant-garde – and it is not clear that he has ever realized this.

Nonetheless, though a simple convergence is very unlikely, it is crucial that the two avant-gardes should be confronted and juxtaposed. History in the arts goes on, as Viktor Shklovsky long ago pointed out, by knight's moves. During the first decade of this century, when the historic avant-garde embarked on its path, the years of the *coupure,* the cinema was still in its infancy, scarcely out of the fairground and the nickelodeon, certainly not yet the Seventh Art. For this reason – and for others, including economic reasons – the avant-garde made itself felt late in the cinema and it is still very marginal, in comparison with painting or music or even writing. Yet in a way, the cinema offers more opportunities than any other art – the cross-fertilization, so striking a feature of those early decades, the reciprocal interlocking and input between painting, writing, music, theatre, could take place within the field of cinema itself. This is not a plea for a great harmony, a synesthetic *gesamtkunstwerk* in the Wagnerian sense. But cinema, because it is a multiple system, could develop and elaborate the semiotic shifts that marked the origins of the avant-garde in a uniquely complex way, a dialectical montage within and between a complex of codes. At least, writing now as a film-maker, that is the fantasy I like to entertain.

NOTES

1 Stephen Dwoskin, *Film Is ...*, London, 1975. David Curtis, *Experimental Cinema*, London, 1971.

2 Standish Lawder, *The Cubist Cinema*, New York, 1975.

3 See Sophie Lissitzky-Kuppers, *El Lissitzky*, London, 1968.

4 Theo Van Doesburg, 'Film as Pure Form', *Form*, Summer 1966, translated by Standish Lawder from *Die Form*, 15 May 1929.

5 See Victor Burgin, 'Photographic Practice and Art Theory', *Studio International*, July/August 1975.

6 See Roland Barthes, *Elements of Semiology*, London, 1967.

7 Christian Metz, *Language and Cinema*, The Hague, 1974.

8 Barbara Rose, 'The Films of Man Ray and Moholy-Nagy', *Artforum*, September, 1971.

9 See 'Ontology and Materialism in Film', pp. 189-207 below.

10 Sergei Eisenstein, 'The Cinematographic Principle and the Ideogram', *Film Form*, New York, 1949.

11 Eisenstein, 'A Dialectic Approach to Film Form', in *Film Form*.

12 Jean-Luc Godard, *Le Gai Savoir*, Paris, 1969. The script, 'mot-à-mot' d'un film encore trop réviso', was published by the Union des Ecrivains formed during May 1968.

13 Julia Kristeva, *Semeiotike*, Paris, 1969.

14 See Ian Christie, 'Time and Motion Studies: Structural Cinema and the Work of Bill Brand', *Studio International*, June 1974.

15 The British landscape film-makers often use a new type of narrativity, in which both film-maker and 'nature' as causal agent play the role of protagonist. A pro-filmic event, which is a conventional signified ('landscape'), intervenes actively in the process of filming, determining operations on the 'specifically cinematic' codes.

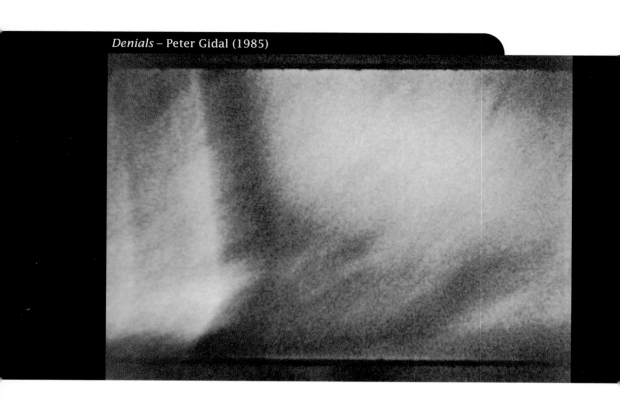

PETER GIDAL

Theory and Definition

OF STRUCTURAL/MATERIALIST FILM

First published in this version in
Structural Film Anthology, ed Peter Gidal,
British Film Institute, London, 1976

Structural/Materialist film attempts to be non-illusionist. The process of the film's making deals with devices that result in demystification ot attempted demystification of the film process. But by 'deals with' I do not mean 'represents'. In other words, such films do not document various film procedures, which would place them in the same category as films which transparently document a narrative, a set of actions, etc. Documentation, through usage of the film medium as transparent, invisible, is exactly the same when the object being documented is some 'real event', some 'film procedure', some 'story', etc. An avant-garde film defined by its development towards increased materialism and materialist function does not *represent*, or *document*, anything. The film produces certain relations between segments, between what the camera is aimed at and the way that 'image' is presented. The dialectic of the film is established in that space of tension between materialist flatness, grain, light, movement, and the supposed reality that is represented. Consequently a continual attempt to destroy the illusion is necessary. In Structural/Materialist film, the in/film (not in/frame) and film/viewer material relations, and the relations of the film's structure, are primary to any representational content. The structuring aspects and the attempt to decipher the structure and anticipate/recorrect it, to clarify and analyse the production-process of the specific image at any specific moment, are the root concern of Structural/Materialist film. The specific construct of each specific film is not the relevant point; one must beware not to let the construct, the shape, take the place of the 'story' in narrative film. Then one would merely be substituting one hierachy for another within the same system, a formalism for what is traditionally called content. This is an absolutely crucial point.[1]

DEVICES

Through usage of specific filmic devices such as repetition within duration one is forced to attempt to decipher both the film's material and the film's construct, and to decipher the precise transformations that each co/incide/nce of cinematic techniques produces. The attempt is primary to any specific shape, otherwise the discovery of shape (fetishising shape or system) may become the theme, in fact, the narrative of the film. This is a crucial distinction for a (dialectically) materialist definition of structural film. That is why Structural/Materialist film in fact demands an orientation of definition completely in opposition to the generally used vague notions concerning 'Structural Film'.

PRODUCTION

Each film is a record (not a representation, not a reproduction) of its own making. Production of relations (shot to shot, shot to image, grain to image, image dissolution to grain, etc.) is a basic function which is in direct opposition to *re*production of relations. Elsewhere in this essay I shall try to elucidate further this problematic of production versus reproduction. Suffice it to say here that it is the core of meaning which differentiates illusionist from anti-illusionist film. When one states that each film is a record of its own making, this refers to shooting, editing, printing stages, or seperations of these, dealt with specifically. Such film militates against dominant (narrative) cinema. Thus viewing such a film is at once viewing a film and viewing the 'coming into presence' of the film, i.e. the system of consciousness that produces the work, that is produced by and in it.

REPRESENTED 'CONTENT'

There is this representational 'reality' one is aiming the camera at. This remains true even if for example the representational content is pared down to the filmstrip itself being pulled through the printer. In fact this isn't necessarily a paring down at all. The Structural/Materialist film must minimise the content in its overpowering, imagistically seductive sense, in an attempt to get through this miasmic area of 'experience' and proceed with film as film. Devices such as loops or seeming loops, as well as a whole series of technical possibilities, can, carefully constructed to operate in the correct manner, serve to veer the point of contact with the film past internal content. The content thus serves as a function upon which, time and time again, a film-maker works to bring forth the filmic event.[2]

The usage of the word *content* so far has been within the common usage, i.e. representational content. In fact, the real content is the form, form become content. Form is meant as formal operation, not as composition. Also, form must be distinguished from style, otherwise it serves merely in its reactionary sense to mean formal*ism*, such as: this formal usage (e.g. Welles) versus that (e.g. Sternberg).

FILM AS MATERIAL

The assertion of film as material is, in fact, predicated upon representation, in as much as 'pure' empty acetate running through the projector gate without image (for example) merely sets off another level of abstract (or non-abstract) associations. Those associations, when instigated by such a device, are no more materialist or nonillusionist than any other associations. Thus the film event is by no means, through such a usage, necessarily demystified. 'Empty screen' is no less significatory than 'carefree happy smile'.[3] There are myriad possibilities for co/optation and integration of filmic procedures into the repertoire of meaning.

THE VIEWER

The mental activation of the viewer is necessary for the procedure of the film's existence. Each film is not only structural but also structuring. This is extremely important as each moment of film reality is not an atomistic, separate entity but rather a moment in a relativistic generative system in which one can't *simply* break down the experience into elements. The viewer is forming an equal and possibly more or less opposite 'film' in her/his head, constantly anticipating, correcting, re-correcting, – constantly intervening in the arena of confrontation with the given reality, i.e. the isolated chosen area of each film's work, of each film's production.

DOMINANT CINEMA

In dominant cinema, a film sets up characters (however superficially deep their melodramas) and through identification and various reversals, climaxes, complications (usually in the same order) one aligns oneself unconciously with one or more characters. These internal connections between viewer and viewed are based on systems of identification which demand primarily a passive audience, a passive viewer, one who is *involved* in the meaning that word has taken on within film-journalese, i.e. to be not involved, to get swept along through persuasive emotive devices employed by the film director. This system of cinematic functioning categorically rules out any dialectic. It is a cinematic functioning, it should be added analogous on the part of the film director to that of the viewer, not to mention the producer, who is not a producer, who has no little investment in the staking out of the economics of such repression. What some of the more self-defined 'left-wing' directors would rationalise in terms of dialectic are merely cover-ups for identification, selling the same old wares, *viz* Antonioni and the much less talented Bertolucci, Pasolini, Losey, not to mention committed right-wing directors. Thus, if a character is somewhat more complex, or if the acting is of a higher order, or if the lightning cameraman does most of the work, then the director rationalises the work which would seem to imply that he is as taken in by the phantasy as the viewer. Whether he is or not (there are few shes in such a position) is in fact irrelevant. The ideological position is the same.

DIALECTIC

There is a distinct difference between what can be termed *the ambiguousness of an identification process*[4] and a *dialectic functioning*. Ambiguousness posits each individual viewer (or reader, listener, etc.) as subject: the subject, that is, who forms *the* interpretation. One becomes posited, formed, constituted, in fact, as the subject of the self-expression and self-representation through the mediation of a repressive ideological structure. That ideological structure is in this case narrative cinema, part of which is the process of identification. Ambiguousness aligns itself as a concept (and therefore as a reality) with the concept of freedom and individualism. The two latter concepts are extremely rigidified in late capitalism. The individual also thus becomes posited as static, as essence, as ideal (or referring to the possibility of such). The individual becomes posited as unitary, 'free' view, centred in deep perspective space away from the screen, and invisibly solidified, ever-present. Our whole formation towards, and in, filmic enterprises, is dominated by such ideological strangleholds.

IDENTIFICATION

The commercial cinema could not do without the mechanism of identification.[5] It is the cinema of consumption, in which the viewer is of necessity not a producer,[6] of ideas, of knowledge. Capitalist consumption reifies not only the structures of the economic base but also the constructs of abstraction. Concepts, then, do not produce concepts; they become, instead, ensconced as static 'ideas' which function to maintain the ideological class war and its invisibility, the state apparatus in all its fields.

The mechanism of identification demands a passive audience, a passive mental posture in the face of a life unlived, a series of representations, a phantasy identified with for the sake of 90 minutes' illusion. And that 'phantasy' is often not *even* the (insipid) utopian romance of 'what should be' (Marcuse's justification for Goethe's poems) nor the so-called 'intervention' in bourgeois morality that at moments *may* be approached in de Sade, Lautréamont, Sacher-Masoch (never without intensely counterproductive repressions and paranoiac violence stimulating and appeasing the bourgeois' tastes and tolerances).

Identification is inseparable from the procedures of narrative, though not totally covered by it. The problematic centres on the question as to whether narrative is inherently authoritarian, manipulatory and mystificatory, or not. The fact that it requires identificatory procedures and a lack of distanciation to function, and the fact that its only possible functioning is at an illusionistic level, indicates that the problematic has a clear resolution. In that sense, it is more of a problem than a problematic. The ramifications of the crucial question are very limited. Narrative is an illusionistic procedure, manipulatory, mystificatory, repressive. The repression is that of space, the distance between the viewer and the object, a repression of real space in favour of the illusionist space. The repression is, equally importantly, of the in-film spaces, those perfectly constructed continuities. The repression is also that of time. The implied lengths of time suffer compressions formed by certain technical devices which operate in a codified manner, under specific laws, to repress (material) film time.

NARRATIVE AND DECONSTRUCTION

A further point on narrative: while the deconstruction of narrative as an academic exercise is not of vital import, it would be in any case a useful function towards expropriating the ownership of the codes of narrativity. Which means that the meanings formed by certain filmic operations could be analysed and no more be the privileged possession of the owners of the means of production; in this case, the means of production of meaning in film. Thus deconstruction exercises, in their limited way, are not irrelevant as sociological insight into certain filmic operations. Deconstruction exercises, maintained filmically (i.e. on film, in film) are direct translations from the written into film, and are thus filmically reactionary, though illustrative of certain ideas *about* film. The re-translation back into language (words) would seem to negate the necessity of narrative-deconstruction being undertaken on, or in, film, rather than in writing. This has now dawned, perhaps, on the overzealous graduates who wish to make statements about certain usages of narrative.

Apart from work in deconstruction, there is also that filmwork which is interpreted as deconstruction, works which have as their basic project an overhauling (not a criticising and not a smashing) of narrative, such as the pseudo-narratives of Robbe-Grillet's appalling films, or Straub's post- (and sometimes pre-) Brechtian exercises in distanciation and reflection. (Even here the Brecht of the theatre is mistaken for the Brechtian theoriser.)[7] Other examples are Dreyer's purist set pieces of dramatics, straightforward identificatory narratives, the identification merely shifted from the psychological/emotional to the psychological/rationalistic. The identification into the narrative is through the thoughts, the ideas about the actions, the decisions, the *ratio*, instead of the melodramatic unthought motivations of characters propelled by unthought 'fear', 'desire', etc. as in most other films. A study is urgently needed on the theme of narrative versus non-narrative form and on the inadequacy of the mechanistic deconstruction approach which ends up illustrating rather than being, which ends up static, time denying, posited as exemplary rather than relative, contradictory, motored into filmic, durational transformation through dialectic procedures.

ART MOVEMENTS

Two art movements had their special effects on the current avant garde, Structural/Materialist film, and on those structural films which are working in that direction. The art movemnts were: the aesthetics of Abstract-Expressionism (though not necessarily the imagist results) and Minimalism (to include such work as Stella's).[8] A major problem erupts here: that of making visible the procedure, presenting such as opposed to using it. Throughout this essay, virtually every problem centres on the opposition between usage and presentation, incorporating versus foregrounding, etc. There exists also the problem of the 'sensitive' artist, ever-present *in* the final object, which can be one end the means to which is an art which may record its own making. But the other end, and the division must be carefully analysed and researched with each case in question, is that of an art which is *not* an imagist creation, a decorative object (narrative or otherwise) separated from its means of production without a trace left. If the final work magically represses the procedures which in fact are there in the making, then that work is not a materialist work. This is a crucial point as to usage versus presentation. And in each work many factors are operating which produce either an over-determination of the usage (i.e. repression) of the procedures, *or* an over-determination of the presentedness of the procedures.

Jacques Derrida has clarified what in fact is at stake in a work, in the procedure of constituting a work. His definition of *differance* (with an 'a') is useful precisely because it clarifies an aspect of work which previously was latent but not brought to speech, not adequately theorised, and which therefore always fell back into the ideology of illusionism and unseen subject (the artist).

> We shall designate by the term *differance* the movement by which language or any code, any system of reference in general, becomes historically constituted as a fabric of differences ... *Differance* is what makes the movement of signification possible only if each element that is said to be 'present', appearing on the stage of presence, is related to something other than itself but retains the mark of a past element and already lets itself be hollowed out by the mark of its relation to a future element. This trace relates no less to what is called the future than to what is called the past, and it constitutes what is called the present by this very relation to what it is not, to what it absolutely is not; that is, not even to a past or a future considered as a modified present ... We ordinarily say that a sign is put in place of the thing itself, the present thing – 'thing' holding here for the sense as well as the referent. Signs represent the present in its absence; they take the place of the present. When we cannot take hold of or show the thing, let us say the present, the being present, when the present does not present itself, *then* we signify, we go through the detour of signs. (J. Derrida, in *Speech and Phenomena*, 'Differance')

The aesthetics of Abstract-Expressionism in fact could produce an imagist object which never separated itself from individualist psychological origins, whereas the 'same' aesthetic base could function in certain works as production itself *presented*, distanced. Such presentation of production functions in certain drawings of targets by Jasper Johns (for example), distancing the object as object, as created text, towards which the various marks added to each other, negating, erasing, produce further elaborations towards an as yet unfulfilled total surface.[9] (*Total* is used in the sense of at some point coming to a stop.) The essential locus is again the question of psychological orientation, that is, *identification*, whether into the 'fantastic' or the 'real' or the 'surreal', in opposition to stated notions of *distancing*. But it must be clarified that the distancing is *not* from some *wholly elaborated* fantastic, real or surreal, from which a distance is created. Rather, the text itself is elaborated and constituted in such a way that the whole work process of reading the marks necessitates a reading of differences and a dialecticisation of the material procedures which produce the marking one is confronted with. The subject of the work is not the invisible artist symbolically inferred through the work's presence, but rather the whole foregrounded fabric of the complex system of markings itself.

What Frank Stella may have verbalised correctly (see footnote[8]) did not prevent his work from becoming exactly the Abstract-Expressionist problem, the whole conglomeration of feelings, associations, seductions, representations which an imagist work demands no matter how 'process'-orientated the production process itself was. Similarly the process of making a Welles or Fassbinder film is not in an adequate way the product. This is the root of the whole problem I am trying to get at. Some of Stella's early works could escape this Abstract-Expressionist route, just as many of Johns' and Giacometti's works fail to avoid or solve that problem. Process as general definition is in fact vacuous. This vacuous definition is nevertheless filled, ideologically rigidified, in such a way that few works escape through the gap left, and those works are a conjuncture (happenstance or not) of a whole range of incidents and factors, co/incide/nces which enable this escape from the co/opting 'process'-definition (and concreteness). This 'escape' is not a displacement (which would therefore create a misunderstanding, or a theoretical gap, elsewhere) or a suppression, but an adequate solution of questions correctly posed in terms of materialist practice and theoretical embodiment.

That does not mean the artist consciously verbalised the degrees and factors which had significance in the creation of the object that finds its way out, escaping the recuperative pseudo-freedom of the epithet 'process'. Stella's good intentions count for little, and vice versa for Klee's often naturalistic, representational, evolutionist notions, radically countermanded by those works which form a conjuncture of structural dissociation, pared down 'simplicity' in terms of imagery and internal relations, formalised colour schemes and other factors, to realise (produce) works which function in a non-naturalised, textual presentedness. Non-naturalisation means specifically that the works don't fit into the category of naturalness, whether this naturalness refers to the image-content (i.e. naturalness of the representation) or to what is natural *for painting*, what is allowable, what does not necessitate a reading but rather falls blindly into parameters of meaning consciously or unconsciously predefined.

READING DURATION

A materialist reading at one with the inscription of the work (which *is* the work) is enabled or forced; Klee's usage, in these cases, of the virtually unloaded or nearly empty signifier

(Foucault cites them as 'completely empty signifiers') is possibly the dominant factor in the adequate presentation of materialist art practice in works such as *Alter Klang, Doppelzelt*, etc.[10] Signifiers approaching emptiness means merely (!) that the image taken does not have a ready associative analogue, is not a given symbol or metaphor or allegory; that which is signified by the signifier, that which is conjured up by the image given, is something formed by past connections but at a very low key, not a determining or over-determining presence, merely a not highly charged moment of meaning. Thus, although this example is oversimplified, the edge of a leaf seen for a moment only, or only seen (in a film, for instance) slightly related to other equally insignificant signifiers (within a context which allows them to operate as insignificant), does not necessarily lead to associations stronger than 'leaf' or 'another leaf quite similar' or a nonemotional grasp of 'room, leaf' without existential *angst,* doubt, a sense of lonely fragility, etc. And that low-level signifier in momentary interplay with other low-level signifiers foregrounds a possibly materialist play of differences which don't have an overriding hierarchy of meaning, which don't determine the ideological reading, which don't lead into heavy associative symbolic realms. The actual relations between images, the handling, the appearance, the 'how it is', etc., takes precedence over any of the 'associative' or 'internal' meanings. Thus is presented the arbitrariness of meaning imbibed in, for example, such an image-moment of a leaf. The unnaturalness, ungivenness, of any possible meaning is posited. Such practice thereby counters precisely the ideological usages which are dominant; the usages which *give meaning* to images, things, signs, etc., meanings which are then posited as natural, as inherent. The whole idealist system is opposed by a materialist practice of the production of meaning, of the arbitrariness of the signifier. (Meaning is *made.)* And for this concept, this thought, the semiotic notions of signifier/signified are of tremendous import.

In film, duration as material piece of time is the basic unit.

> Does a painting come into existence all at once? No, it's built up piece by piece, not different from a house. When a point becomes movement and line, it takes up time. Similarly, when a line pulls itself out into a plane. And the same when a fiat plane becomes a three dimensionai enclosure. And the viewer, does he (she) respond to the work as a whole? Often yes, unfortunately.
> (Paul Klee, *Schöpferische Konfession*)

I am not positing direct cause and effect, or even direct analogue, between painting and film. Similarly, the effect, more specifically, of Abstract-Expressionism and Minimalism on Structural/Materialist film is not direct.

The problematic of reading duration when viewing a painting was important to Klee and others.

Actual duration can only exist in film, in terms of the approximation towards a 1:1 relation between work and viewer (production time and 'reading' time). Vertov's *Man With a Movie Camera,* Eisenstein's *Strike,* Lumière's films, form a core of basic work in this field of research, the anti-illusionist project. As to Structural music, Bach's preludes and fugues relate strongly to some of the work of Terry Riley. Steve Reich's *Stick Piece,* etc. More specific to film: more often than not, 'real' time is utilised in the Structural/Materialist film, in clearly defined segments or in the film as a whole, thus breaking from illusionistic time (substructured in codes of narrativity). The closing of the gap in space between viewer and viewed, and between the representation in one shot and another, is a basic repressive illusionist device. The implication of an unseen splice to integrate two shots also elides the function of editing, the function of producing, from material segments, a new complex relation. Instead, there is a seeming natural flow established, which suppresses all procedures of the editing stages. The concept of integration rather than disruption is predicated on a repression of the material relations specific to the film process, and this of course is not unconnected with the violence done to (eradicate) the adequate *presentation* of material relations in the spheres of ideology, the image, plastic representation, narrative mimesis, etc. Attempted in Structural/Materialist film is a non-hierarchical, cool, separate unfolding of a perceptual activity. That perceptual activity is *not* to be understood as relegating the primary function to the individual perceiver, who of course is embedded in ideological structures/strictures. The problematics of perception as a concept have yet to be satisfactorily delineated. Still, film is a perceptual activity (amongst other things) and without perception and the relations attendant upon that process there is no film practice (or in any case not one that is non-idealistic, not one that is not mechanistically materialist).

DISTANCE

Through the attempted non-hierarchical, cool, separate unfolding a distance(ing) is sought. This distance reinforces (rather than denies) the dialectic interaction of viewer with each film moment, which is necessary if it is not to pass into passiveness and needlessness. This interaction on the physical level and on the level of critical praxis is obvious. The real time element demands such a consciousness and will. I can here only hint at the deeper problematic within which the 'real time' 1:1 relation between viewer and viewed is located.

ASPECTS OF TIME

(1) 'Real time', that is, time present as it is for the film-maker, denoted not connoted, at the

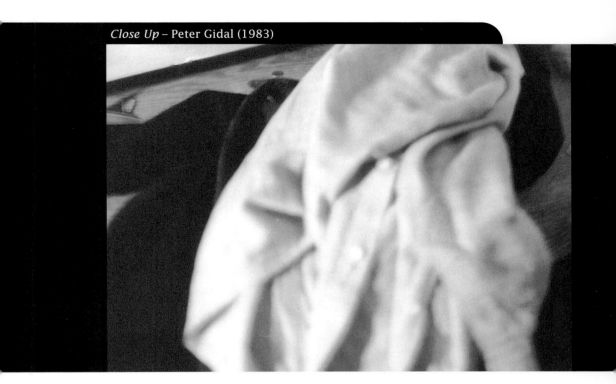

Close Up – Peter Gidal (1983)

stage of shooting, editing, printing, projecting, and interrelations of these. Commonly, 'real time' is presented in single takes or film segments utilised for their actual duration (often after many viewings they separate themselves as such). (2) There is illusionistic time, time made to seem what it is not, such as in conventional and (it must be said) in much Eisensteinian editing. E.g., cut from 10.15 p.m. London interior – the lovers kiss – to midnight near the lake, husband and wife murder each other (long shot), either implying a linear thread of events with time compressed, or a simultaneity with time compressed. (3) The third 'example' is that of post-Newtonian, Einsteinian time. There is here no absolute value other than that of the interaction of film moment and viewer. This relativistic time may but does not necessarily connect with 'real time'. The notion of 'real time' on its own fails to take account precisely of this relativistic nature of time, the absence of some universal clock, though for lack of a more precise definition 'real time' did serve its purpose apropos for example much of Warhol's filmwork (interrupted by splices and leader-fogging).

REFLEXIVENESS

Another matter which the investigation of Structural/Materialist film brings forth is the bearing it has on reflexiveness, which is inculcated by a film through certain procedures. Reflexiveness, self-reflexiveness or auto-reflexiveness, is a condition of self-consciousness which invigorates the procedure of filmic analysis *during* the film viewing event. Thus it is not merely a matter of reflec*ti*on, or thinking, broadly taken. Reflexiveness, as a concept, can serve a meaning counterproductive to the direction Structural/Materialist film would give it.[11] It can, for example, serve as a decoy, an alibi, the opening up of individual interpretation. Such simulacra turn the ideological thrust of an issue towards radically reactionary paths, and bring one's work to a point where each conceptual entity must be clearly defined in order not to move down a blind alley. Without such rigour, one finds the illusionist, narrative, identificatory individualist mode of cinema is re-presented, re-instated without a battle, and the wearying struggle to define clearly and precisely is taken up again at the moment of least vigilance. A weak link in one's analysis of idealist, anti-materialist practices can turn a whole body of work (in film, for example) to uselessness in countering a forthcoming film's radically *retrograde* practice.

A film practice in which one watches oneself watching is reflexive; the act of self-perception, of consciousness *per se,* becomes one of the basic contexts of one's confrontation with work. The process of the production of *film-making,* and the filmic practice of film-viewing *as production,* become interlinked. 'Reflection' does ideological combat with self-consciousness, reflexiveness. To operate thus is to break the dichotomy between feeling and thinking; or rather to break the illusion of their necessary separation and the illusion of their automatic oneness. The filmic enterprise, if such, presents consciousness of film to the self. The radical rejection of the *representation* of consciousness is a main concept.

Film cannot adequately represent consciousness any more than it adequately represents meaning; all film is invisibly encumbered by mystificatory systems and interventions which are distortions, repressions, selections, etc. That a film is not a window to life, to a set of meanings, to a pure state of image/meaning, ought to be self-evident. Thus the documenting of an act of film-making is as illusionist a practice as the documenting of a narrative action (fiction). And consciousness is as encumbered by the illusionist devices of cinema, if one is attempting to document 'it', as anything else. Filmic reflexiveness is the presentation of consciousness to the self, consciousness of the way one deals with the material operations; filmic reflexiveness is forced through cinema's materialist operations of filmic practice.[12]

Self-consciousness, and consciousness *per se,* must in no way imply consciousness as deflecting on to a mythical subject; it must in no way imply transcendence or transcendent subjectivity; it does not set itself up in opposition to real relations, i.e. consciousness as knowledge in opposition to material relations as knowledge. One can see it in schematic 'T' form, the horizontal being the work upon which functions operate (the film plane), the vertical being 'consciousness', the line to the recipient as his/her necessary mode of inculcated dialectic operation.

TECHNIQUE

Access to involvement with technique is the formidable basis of all art which poses questions seriously, and which moves forward to new stages of development, the working through of contradiction in its practice. Thus technical innovation is itself ideologically conditioned; in many cases innovations and conceptual entities were not thought through inside a culture, though the apparatus and the actual scientific discoveries were already present. Or 'one crucial element' would wait 200 years to be discovered. The lag between the possibilities for innovatory technical practices (such as camera and photographic printing) and the realisation of such practice (two centuries later)[13] is an ideological one. At the same time, when a new technical practice becomes operative, it bears directly on aesthetic practice (whether it produces that aesthetic practice or is produced by it is a complex matter).

Technique, which is often categorised as separate from aesthetic issues, is in fact inseparable; mass reproduction of photography had considerable influence on the aesthetic possibilities of the mass reproduction of photography, and vice versa. It seems virtually a circular argument, which makes it all the more uncanny that it is so often belied. The aesthetics of silkscreening as it is practised by a Warhol has a not insubstantial relation to the technical fact of silkscreening *and* to the techniques made possible by certain *inventions* and their utilisation at a certain period. In film, the flattening out of space is possible through various devices of camera and this is an involvement with technique that is unavoidably present as the aesthetic basis of the work. In film, also, slow motion is a technical *invention,* inseparable from analytic work on representation. Thus involvement with technique refers to two phenomena: (1) *inventions* which make possible, fulfill, technical needs (and those technical needs are inseparable from the aesthetic which produces them and which they produce); (2) aesthetic *usage,* inseparable from technical possibilities.

THEORY AND PRACTICE

An important problem is the question of continuing and broadening advanced practice without elaborating distinct theory. The filmwork itself is an ideological practice, and in some cases a theoretical practice. Film theory, if such exists, takes the form of written retrospective history which can function as a basis for its own practice (theoretical practice) and/or for the practice of film-making as it correlates to the theoretical embodied in it. (How it is how it is what it is.) Much formulation taking place at the moment deals with retrograde work but this may be a step towards being equipped to deal adequately with Structural/Materialist film. Adequate work is indeed necessary in film-making and writing 'on' film. A semiotics that is right-wing is not the only one I can envisage, though little else is at the moment forthcoming. One can cite, in support of the above assertion, the lamentably reactionary symbolic interpretation by Roland Barthes of a series of Eisenstein stills.* Such a position needs to be combatted, but so too does Foucault's superb Marxist/Althusserian *interpretation* of, for example, Magritte's retrograde picture-puzzle-gimmicks. What we are stuck with is often advanced theoretical formulation, critically adapted to work which does not warrant it. This results in a *reading into* the work. For such a critical operation, the most reactionary work will suffice because, after all, one can project one's 'personal' wishful thinking into virtually any film. Partaking of the primal scene and 'work on the signifier' seem to be the dominant current malpractices.

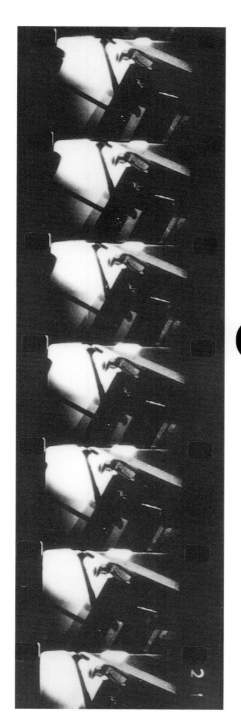

Room Film 1973 – Peter Gidal (1973)

Left to itself, a spontaneous (technical) practice produces only the 'theory' it needs as a means to produce the ends assigned to it; this 'theory' is never more than the reflection of this end, uncriticized, unknown, in its means of realization; that is, it is a by-product of the reflection of the technical practice's end on its means. A 'theory' which does not question the end whose by-product it is remains a prisoner of this end and of the realities which have imposed it as an end. Examples of this are many of the branches of psychology, of sociology, and of Politics, of Economics, of Art, etc...
Louis Althusser, *For Marx*

We have, among English advanced film-makers, work which utilises traditional, transparent documentary film-making in an unthought manner, under the guise of Structural/Materialist operation. The use, for example, of black leader cut into a film to be the image of the time when the camera motor was not running is a mystification of the most dangerous sort. That mystification can devise routes back to the apparent point of departure. One then ends up, through this repressive re-routing, at a stage prior to that of the anti-illusionist project. In fact, these mis-routings can lead further back, to the original point of aggression, the stimulus to one's film practice in the first place, i.e. the 'straight' documentary against which the anti-illusionist film is working. In this example, black leader posits a direct representation of time, which in fact it is not. It posits a direct representation of an action, 'camera motor turned off', which it is not. Thus it is a representation which does not present itself. It posits itself as an image of something other than itself, which in fact it is not. It posits a gap between two 'realities', i.e. the preceding shot and the following shot, thus attempting to annihilate its *presence* (thus representing and repressing at the same time). Unquestioned in the above operation is the signifying area as well: no investigation, let alone intervention, is undertaken apropos that area. Thus the use of black leader as posited in my example instantiates an illusionist operation which is then covered, or masked.

The demarcations must be drawn all the more strictly when dealing with such work precisely because the rearguard revision it performs is seemingly not obvious. That some films do not in any way posit such rearguard work, though their makers cannot fully articulate their filmic method and practice, is in no way a contradiction in terms. The question of (artistic) intention comes up here, and whether or not that intention can be said to exist precisely by its presence in the work. More often than not, the nonverbalisation of intention is not a sign of the nontranslatability of the specific film practice into words, but rather a mere absence of *correct* verbalisation, which does not deny in those cases the 'absolute' translatability into words of intention. In some few cases, indeed, this is not the case. The root of this question is the mechanistic, simplistic notion that without speech there is no production. It is obvious, nevertheless, that those intentions which are articulated are often not what is in fact operating as inscription in (and of) the work. It is the work one deals with; slight shifts in words, like slight shifts in filmwork operations, can radically alter the position and meaning. These slight shifts, which are in fact major shifts, exist in that untranslatability between the maker's intention as thought in speech, the maker's intention as unthought in speech though capable of being verbalised, the maker's intention as unthought *at all,* the maker's intention as untranslatable into speech, though thought ('I know what I want to do, i.e. in advance and having gone through decision-making processes, but I don't know why, i.e. can't say why') etc.

Anglo/American Structural and Structural/Materialist fiim has so far failed to attract any attempt at theory. Advanced – mainly French – theory (not necessarily concerning film directly) is either not capable of dealing with film or posits retrograde illusionist, post-Bazinian manifestations of film. With the (at best) nearly total demise of New American Cinema,[14] mainly through its resurgent romanticism or (worst) its continued operation as pseudo-narrative investigations, there remain the few English (plus one Canadian and one Austrian) Structural/Materialist film-makers, who are working to a great extent without the beginnings of a theoretical/historical approach. Consequently, in most cases (at best) these films open up contradictions between theory (not necessarily of film) and the practice of film-making as it embodies theory, i.e. *is theoretical.* That these contradictions are opened up by films which are largely 'unconsciously thought' on the part of the film-makers is another problem.

As to the theoretical practice of film theory, nothing at all seems to have been begun. The derivative material published in *Screen* is merely importation from at most three Paris sources; though at moments useful it is not directed correctly, is not made to interact with avant-garde film practice in this country (or any other). Operating in a vacuum as far as avant-garde cinema is concerned, it finds itself not coincidentally aligned with dominant cinema, with no production capacity of its own. British avant-garde film since 1966 has not been studied; nor the works of the European avant-garde experimental film of the late 1950s and the 1960s. Witness to this lack of knowledge is the following extract from the absurd 'dialogue' which *Screen* conducted with Laura Mulvey and Peter Wollen (no fault of theirs):

Screen: Nevertheless, the importance of language and the way it is used in your film is very different from the kind of irrational, mystic overtones of the Anglo/Saxon avant-gardes, such as Sharits, Wieland, Frampton, and so on. I see your film as closer to a materialist conception of language such as e.g. modern French theories of writing.

Wollen: That's an absolutely false characterization of those films. For instance, Hollis Frampton's *Zorns Lemma* (1971) is based on mathematical transformations in relation to the alphabet...

Screen: Which again comes out of mysticism and Kabbala.

Wollen: But by that token Kabbalism is also very strong, e.g. in Robbe-Grillet. I would say Kabbalism runs very strongly through all that French thought. You can see how, for instance, Jabès and Jewish thought feeds into Derrida. There is a very strong streak of Kabbalism in *Tel Quel*... I see *Zorns Lemma* on the Straub side of the interface rather than the Brakhage side, though it does have a neoplatonist aspect concerning light.

Screen: Maybe we should talk about that some other time.

(Screen, Autumn 1974)

More unfortunately *Screen*'s interviewers wrote an introduction ending with the following statement: 'The interview with Peter Wollen and Laura Mulvey can be described as polemical in the sense that the ideas discussed in it as well as the film itself *(Penthesilea)* may appear totally aberrant when seen in the context of British film culture at the present time.' Apart from the coy, non-normative use of the word 'aberrant', the statement unmasks the complete repression by *Screen*'s editors of the film culture *as it exists.*[15]

CONCLUSION

Structural/Materialist films are at once object and procedure. Some are clearly, blatantly of a whole, others work as obvious fragments, non-beginning-non-end film. Both rely upon an aesthetic that tries to create didactic works (learning not teaching, i.e. operational productions not reproductive representations). At the same time there is attempted avoidance of empiricism, and the mystic romanticism of higher sensibility individualism. This romantic base of much American Structural film has been elucidated by P. A. Sitney. Visionary film-making is precisely the post-Blakean mire that Structural/Materialism confronts, whether this confrontation is articulated or not. 'Unconsciously thought' processes define themselves in practice. One must go on after Warhol, not revert to a re-invigorated pre-Warholian stance; one ought to be, by now, tired of *expressing* the same old thing... 'trying to express when there is nothing to *express*'. To ignore the ideological function of Sitney's exegesis of a 'new romantic affirmation in recoiling against the tremendously crucial aesthetic attack that Warhol made' is precisely to be embedded in dominant ideology as located in the specific area being discussed: film. *(Film Culture,* Spring 1972, P. A. Sitney.)

The ideological direction of Sitney's arguments is not mentioned here as part of my criticism, since it coincides with the ideological weight of the works he discusses and therefore he becomes in fact the most adequate spokesman for and exegete of the films he deals with, with notable exceptions. (I shall also not attempt to elucidate the dominant ideology here in specific terms.) Structural film became merely another aesthetic mode, another formalism, in fact, with a vague set of rules and self-definitions yet without important function or meaning outside its mere differentiation *per se* from previous modes. I see Structural/Materialist film of course within a materialist function if it is to operate usefully. *Some* such works of Structural/ Materialist film are the following: *Little Dog For Roger, Yes No Maybe Maybe Not, Spot the Microdot* (Malcolm LeGrice); *Wavelength, Back and Forth, Central Region* (Michael Snow); *Trees in Autumn, TV, Szondi Test, Auf der Pfaueninsel* (Kurt Kren); *Diagonal* (William Raban); *Adebar, Schwechater* (Peter Kubelka); *Process Red, Zorns Lemma* (Hollis Frampton); the problematic *Erlanger Program. Window Box* (Roger Hammond); *Deck* (Gill Eatherley); *Film No. 1, 'A' Film, Man With a Movie Camera* (David Crosswaite); *Word Movie, 3* min. section *Razor* in *Fluxus* (Paul Sharits); my own *Clouds, Hall, Room Film 1973; Green Cut Gate* (Fred Drummond).

To make distinctions between works is a matter of clearly contextualising the problematic, and each work's operation within it. Each work must be brought forth to clarity from the multilayered inscriptions that it *is*. Using the term Structural/Materialist is dangerous as well, since it refers to Structural Film. Equal emphasis must be put on the Materialist 'half' of the term (and a dialectical materialism, not a mechanistic materialism, is necessary). The term Structural Film took as basic assumption the contexts of merely three or four works and evolved a thesis from them, works not all of more than minor importance. Perhaps the same can be said at this juncture of my definition of Structural/Materialist film. The 'theory' was meant for more than parochial definition of these (above) works.

One creates a work. One also creates, in varying degrees, a negation of past work, of historically constituted bases for tradition. The Structural/ Materialist film and production of meaning in film is the production of *film* itself, in its (thought or 'unthought') theoreticalness and (thought or 'unthought') ideological intervention. To intervene *crucially* in film practice, the 'unthought' must be brought to knowledge, thought. The set of relations between film practice, theoretical practice, and film as theory, can then be brought forth to operate in clarity.

NOTES

1   The concept of structure's importance, vis à vis that of representational content, led to the notion of shape taking precedence and confused the issue nearly irreparably. Slight shifts become major theoretical interventions which change the locus of meaning of the work being produced, and the axis along which it operates in time. This is not mere obsessive Talmudic or French academic preoccupation. Althusser's concept of the absolutely essential importance of the correct usage of the word bears remembering; the correct formulation is necessary to close the gap between advanced theoretical practice and the dominance of idealist speech. (Louis Althusser, *Reading Capital,* London, 1970.)

2   By the word film-maker, though, I do not mean to imply that the producer (film-maker) is inserted as mythical figure, as shadow symbol of the 'real', as mirror. Anonymity is indeed a prerequisite; but a superficial anonymity brought into a false existence through such things as 'coldness' – heavy atmospheric intervention – functions precisely as the opposite of its supposed intention. Anonymity must in fact be created through transformation, dialectically posited into the filmic event itself. That is, anonymity must be the result, at a specific instance; it too must be produced rather than illustrated or obliquely 'given' in a poetical sense.

3   This is so because of: associativeness, symbolic reading, integration into the diegesis, subsumation to the dominant illusory system posited, displacement to a mere different level of phantasy-acceptance, poetic shock supportive of the primary story, etc. The signifier and the signified as arbitrary, as artifice, and as less than primary, is the area in which production of 'meaning' must take place. Meaning at this stage must be seen to clearly obtain to Structural/Materialist reading. Yet by collaborating in the current usage of the term *reading* I separate myself from the bourgeois oppression of the dominance of the word while acknowledging its hegemony.

4   In the Japanese theatre, an actor holding a mask in front of his/her face, so that the audience can see the 'real' face behind, is for all that no less identificatory, no less co/optable into the narrative structure and diegetic linearity. The grasping of this example is crucial to the basis for the whole theoreticisation of the problem of narrative. So far all essays on narrative and narrative deconstruction have been mechanistic, derivative of dominant cinema's needs, in inverted form, with no break (epistemological or otherwise). The same goes for all attempts at narrative-deconstructive cinema. It is in order to point to the fact that illustration of a thesis (of deconstruction, or otherwise) in (on) film denies duration, the basic cinematic structure. *Illustration mystifies real filmic relations*; the basic project is thus illusionism, not deconstruction of representational codes, the latter being recuperated as the narrative is constituted.

The latter statement should not be seen to imply naiveté on my part as to the frequent occurrence of so-called non-narrative film which in fact sets up an imagist illusionism, a set of ideological codifications equally manipulatory, undialectical, identificatory. The system of identification into the imagist code relies heavily on the usage of the imaginary referent, that which is referred to transparently, wherein the medium is not produced as opaque. This system of identification also relies heavily on the repression of the production of the signifier-as-arbitrary, that is, as the strictly ideologically posited coherence artificially manufactured between signifier and signified. As long as these relations are not studied and made to produce work, the illusionist project is not one step further out of its miasmic repressed state.

I must add: when stating that in identification real relations are mystified, I in no way refer to real *relations* in a positivist or empiricist manner.

'For objective dialectics the absolute is also to be found in the relative. The unity, the coincidence, identity, resultant force, of opposites, is conditional. temporary, transitory, and relative.' Lenin, On Dialectics, in *Materialism and Empirio-Criticism*.

'Feeling like a voyeur watching Warhol's pornographic *Couch* is precisely *not* to be in the position of a voyeur. It is precisely the *stare* (and the seeming stare of *Wavelength*) that works to counter the identificatory process, though it does not of necessity smash it. And the word *subvert* has become too clichéd and ambiguous to be used effectively in this context. The ineffable stare presents the medium's presence, though positing a deep space centrepoint out from the screen, across from the objects of the film. particularly in *13 Most Beautiful Women* and parts of *Chelsea Girls*.' (London College of Printing Notes on Film, Peter Gidal, 1971.)

5   Aristotelian catharsis is inseparable from identification and the purging (whether this is a pseudo, i.e. unreal, concept or not) is inextricably bound to the latter's operations.

6   In reference to my own work, Michael Snow implies such a constant production rather than consumption. The example is apt because often what seems like (and is, in fact) an untheorised position is of the order of a theoretical supposition. Snow's words: '... your film *(Room Film 1973)* had to be worked at. I felt as if it were made by my father, as if it were made by a blind man. I felt that searching tentative quality, that quality of trying to see.' (Michael Snow, Sept. 1973, London.) This attempt at verbalisation, loose as it is, in fact is stating theoretically, beneath the surface, an aesthetic necessitating dialectic attempts at image arrestation, the necessity for production rather than consumption. 'Sometimes the repeating shots would be clear, sometimes one couldn't tell if it was continuous.' The constitution of the work, coming from the material relations of the work, but not mechanistically positioning (i.e. illustrating) itself tautologically, is at the base of the meaning of Snow's statement. Similarly, what seems an aesthete's formalist delight in light in Jonas Mekas' (*Village Voice,* 10 February 1975 and 29 October 1973) and to some

extent Lucy Fischer's pieces on my film are really attempts to articulate verbally a problematic of the constitution of the filmic image, opaquely through the agency of light; thus the whole problematic of image-constitution *through* something, a representation as a constitution rather than as a given, 'captured' transparently. This theoretically important difference is thus elucidated beneath the idealist mask which filmprose in fact mostly is. Fischer is more analytical and less poetic than Mekas. I quote only the former, the quote most apt to be diversionary *without meaning to be so.* 'The rest of the film proceeds with an examination *of* a room and the way that light illumin*ates* the objects *within it'* (Lucy Fischer, *Soho Weekly News,* 16 January 1975, italics mine.)

According to Lawrence Van Gelder in the *New York Times* (17 January 1975), 'It *(Room Film 1973) is* a murky, granular *journey around* a room, *broken* by occasional *incursions* of light' (italics mine). The ideological concept of journey, a man's journey through a *given* universe, is somehow at the base of the writings on *Room Film 1973.* It is as if all film were (and I suspect this to be the case) still recuperated as some form of masked or not-so-masked documentary rather than a filmic articulation and constituting presence, a filmic production precisely in its operations on the level of the *problematics* of procedure and representation. That the pseudo-documentary is *the* unspoken gap in current film knowledge, in terms of theory, practice and theoretical practice, I have hinted at elsewhere ('Un Cinéma Matérialiste Structural', *L'Art Vivant,* Février 1975, pp. 16-17, as well as *Studio International,* March 1975, '5th Knokke Experimental Film Festival').

7   As to Brecht, there are some illuminating comments from his writings. 'Science isn't so free of superstition. Where knowledge doesn't suffice, faith produces itself, and that is always superstition… our lyricists didn't lose their voice because of the book *Capital* but in the face of Capital itself.' 'If Realism *isn't* defined purely formalistically (that which in the 90's was considered Realism, in the realm of the bourgeois novel) then much can be said against techniques like montage, interior monologue, or distancing (*Verfremdung*), only not from the point of view of Realism!… as a technical means, the interior monologue (of Joyce) was rejected; one called it formalist. I never understood the reasoning. Just because Tolstoy would have done it differently isn't a reason to reject the way Joyce does it. The objections were constructed so superficially that one got the impression that if Joyce had put the same monologue (Molly Bloom's final one) in the psychoanalytical session, everything would have been all right.' 'Realist, that means consciously influenced by reality, and consciously influencing reality… the techniques of Joyce and Döblin are not simply waste products; if one eliminates their influence, instead of modifying it, one ends up merely with the influence of the epigones, such as the Hemingways. The works of Joyce and Döblin betray, in the largest sense, the world-historical contradictions into which the forces of production have fallen vis à vis the relations of production. In the works, productive forces are represented to a

certain degree. Socialist writers particularly can learn valuable, highly developed technical means *(Elemente)* from these documents of hopelessness *(Ausweglosigkeit). They* see the way out.' 'Perhaps our readers might just *not* feel that they've been given the *key* to events when they, seduced by many wiles *(Künste)* merely take part in *(beteiligen)* the soulful emotions of the heroes.' Bertolt Brecht, *Über den Realismus,* 1938-1940, Suhrkamp Gesammelte Werke (my translation).

Brecht also, of course, wavered from the above views more often than not; though he fought against the formalist notions of Realism which the social(ist) realists conveniently sidetracked, he also wrote often of a 'Realism directly from the standpoint of a class, unfolding the ruling viewpoints as the viewpoints of the ruling, and... representing reality, the way it is' *(die Realität wiedergeben)*. Brecht's usage of the word representation, of modification, will not be questioned at this point. Correct class position and representation were linked for B.B. For certain film-makers currently working, this is not only *not* a necessary link, it is a vital weak link. The whole platform between two ideological camps within film production rests, finally, on this opposition; it is the overdetermining aspect. The anti-illusionist project is determined, or not, at this juncture.

8. Stella's emotional and critical reaction at this time against what he considered rhetorical in the Abstract-Expressionist posture was more marked than the gradual mutation of his style suggests. "I think I had been badly affected by what could be called the romance of Abstract-Expressionism", Stella recalls, "particularly as it filtered out to places like Princeton and around the country, which was the idea of the artist as a terrifically sensitive, everchanging, ever-ambitious person – particularly as described in magazines like *Art News* and *Arts,* which I read religiously. It began to be kind of obvious and... terrible, and you began to see through it... I began to feel very strongly about finding a way that wasn't so wrapped up in the hullabaloo, or a way of working that you couldn't write about... something that was stable, in a sense, something that wasn't constantly a record of your sensitivity, a record of flux." *(Frank Stella,* by William Rubin, MOMA, New York.)

"I always get into arguments," he reported, "with people who want to retain the 'old values' in painting – the 'humanistic' values that they always find on the canvas. If you pin them down, they always end up asserting that there is something there besides the paint on the canvas. My painting is based on the fact that only what can be seen is there... If the painting were lean enough, accurate enough, or right enough, you would just be able to look at it. All I want anyone to get out of my paintings, and all I ever get out of them, is the fact that you can see the whole idea without any confusion... What you see is what you see." (Ibid.) I quote the above with full awareness that the statements broaden the parameters and raise as many confusions as they attempt to close up, yet in relation to the problematical, humanistic, ideology of process, Stella was more aware than most. And this his painting at its best is also clear on.

9 Michel Foucault in 'On the Subversion of Knowledge', in the interviews with Gilles Deleuze and Paulo Caruso, is particularly illuminating. (Hanser paperback).

10 For a beginning though also insufficient piece of work on the above mentioned, see my *Beckett & Others & Art: A System (Studio International,* November 1974, pp 183-187).

11 Reflexiveness can be as much a diversionary tactic from the anti-illusionist project, as anything. Similarly, the concept of subversion. i.e. subverting the codes, subverting the meaning, is merely a rationalised annexation of precisely those codes and meanings, with attendant guilt contributing the enormous libidinous energy necessary for this repressive operation. The bourgeois academic cine-semiotician's simplistic usage of psychoanalysis is a ruse.

12 The *self* posited here is situated in its self-alienation/distanciation, though this still refers to the concept, which must be fought, of self as centre (distanced though it be), self as unitary. This psychological centering of the self must be nullified in order to even begin to set up a concept of a dialectically posited distanciated self. Merely to drop the usage of a word such as *self* does not fulfil the requirement of redefining the word. And the redefining must be done so that *self is* understood, not to be a unitary centre of knowledge, an 'I' through which the world is. For the *'I'* does not form the world. Consciousness does not form the world. Material relations form the 'I'. The self is merely a clinical word for a cipher.

13 Thomas Neumann, *Sozialgeschichte der Photographie,* Luchterhand 1966.

14 The reactionary basis of most American film-making has only been clarified recently, and this through only the beginnings of analyses which work upon the mystificatory and individualist aesthetics (ethics) of that movement. The English problematic, as I've stated, is a pseudo-documentary production which does not question itself. (See 'On Mike Dunford's *Still Life With Pear'* in '5th Knokke Experimental Film Festival' in *Studio International,* March 1975, p. 138.) 'The European film-makers certainly made a much stronger impression though without the presence of clearly established masters. But that's a way of thinking which many of the Europeans reject... It's difficult to pin down, but one senses an attitude towards film-making not as the production of certain great works but as an on-going motive of artistic work... European film-makers are wary of the structure and ideology which might create the conditions for cultural imperialism in the area of film-making. They are, therefore, involved in a redefinition of the nature and function of film-making that differs from those of the Americans who are making their way gradually toward the centre of our own culture.' P. A. Sitney, talking with Annette Michelson, 'A Conversation on Knokke and the Independent Film-maker', *Artforum*, May 1975. The spectre of romantic illusionism and mystique of the individual artist is the

reactionary concept of artist as god, artist as magician, artist as purveyor of beauty, artist as fascist.

(a) *The Film-maker.* The film-maker makes the film. It is a source of constant frustration that the illusion is so rigidly upheld that the film-maker produces not (only) the film but him/herself in it. Reception of the film ought to be productive, relational, not consumptive of the invisibly visible artist's character/persona. Even if Peter Gidal films dark rooms what does it say about me except what it says about itself, i.e. handheld consistency and repetitiveness presents procedures on to 'subject matter', dehierarchicalising it, presenting its arbitrariness as against an essentialness; meaning is (ideologically) produced, not innate. Not a centreframe steadyfocus annexation; constitution/deconstruction, deconstruction/constitution of image through lightness blackness, and annihilation as well through extremes of such... The film-maker is specifically not produced in the film, if the film operates on a materialist anti-illusionist level, functioning as a practice – film not literature, dealing *with* illusionism, not inside it. Films that end up being adequate documentaries about the artist (subject's) concerns transparently posit themselves against anti-illusionist cinema.

(b) *Illusion.* A constant illusionist/anti-illusionist procedural operation is not the same as a positing of illusion and questioning its 'reality' in the 'next' shot. True deconstruction (for which the term is not usable) is simultaneous with construction and vice versa.

(c) *Narrative.* Narrative is indeed a strategic category in the investigation of illusion-systems, systems of representation, in the process of representation; but *filmically* this study involves suspension of disbelief. It is this aspect, which is a central base for the whole narrativity-investigation, which is most consistently repressed. This repression over-determines the whole 'study' of the codes of narrativity, and exposes its essentially reactionary state.

15 I thank Peter Wollen for having brought the issue up in the first place in the interview. I must add that my diatribe is not meant to imply that I subscribe either to Mulvey/Wollen's film or to their views.

I would be untruthful if I did not admit to a wish to have the Journal of the Society for Education in Film and Television deal seriously with current film practice, avant-garde film. The editors do, after all, attempt a Marxist film theory; and, yes, important translations have been published. But anger seems justified when *Screen*'s policies and writings are not just ignoring and ignorant, so far, of current film practice in Britain, but in fact extremely aggressive towards it: by innuendo, omission, condescension and concentration on the narrative cinema, thus to some degree sustaining its dominance, at least theoretically. Actual *power* over the cinema-goer none of us has at this stage. It would have been useful in the past if there had been some critical work done; the film-makers also would have found themselves reflecting on their practice to a greater degree. Which can't be bad.

POSTSCRIPT

I have elaborated, clarified and corrected certain formulations since 1974 when this essay was written. I refer to the following: *Further Footnotes*, London Filmmakers' Co-operative paper, seminar on Practice/Theory, February 1976; *The Anti-Narrative*, Edinburgh Avant-Garde Film Conference, July 1976; letter on Ontology, *Screen*, Summer 1976; exchange on *Theory and Definition of Structural/Materialist Film*, *Afterimage* No. 8, London 1978 (written September 1976); *Technology/Ideology in/through/and Avant Garde Film*, in *The Cinematic Apparatus*, (eds.) de Lauretis & Heath, St Martins Press, New York, 1978.

P.G. January 1978

POSTSCRIPT

No changes have been made to the text although one couldn't pretend not, occasionally, to have been tempted.

P.G. Paris, January 1996

STEPHEN HEATH

Repetition Time

NOTES AROUND 'STRUCTURAL/MATERIALIST FILM'

First published in *Wide Angle*, vol 2 no1 1977

The term 'materialist' in the expression 'structural/materialist film' used to characterize a certain development of work in avant-garde independent film-making[1] has to be understood away from any simple reference to the physical materiality of film. 'Materialist' stresses process, a film in its process of production of images, sounds, times, meanings, the transformations effected on the basis of the specific properties of film in the relation of a viewing and listening situation. It is that situation which is, finally, the point of 'structural/materialist film', its fundamental operation, the *experience* of film, and the experience *of film.*

Any film is the fact of a process, whether it be *Hall* (Gidal, 1968) or Welles's *Touch of Evil.* The practice of 'structural/ materialist film' is defined in the *presentation* of a film's process, 'the presentation of the material construction of film'; process, construction are displayed reflexively, not displaced uniformly into the pattern of a narrative, bound up for the stable subject-centred image.

Important to presentation of process is an attention to temporality (time is 'film's primary dimension'), duration ('how long something lasts'). It is usual in this connection to begin by adducing the exposition of the possible one-to-one relationship between shooting time and reading time, equivalence between the duration of the event recorded and the duration of the film representation of that event; a film such as *Couch* (Warhol, 1964) providing a stock example, with its takes the length of single rolls of film that are then joined together in sequence, this giving 'a 'shallow' time which permits a credible relationship between the time of interior action and the physical experience of the film as a material presentation... Warhol's most significant innovation'. That quotation is from Le Grice, for whom durational equivalence often seems to be something of a primary ethic of film-making, in the light of which Snow's *Wavelength* (1967), for instance, can be found seriously wanting: 'One-to-one relationship between the projection duration and the shooting duration is lost through breaks in the shooting not made clear in the form of the film. By utilizing a contrived continuity to parallel the implied time of its narrative, the film is in some ways a retrograde step in cinematic form.' Durational equivalence, however, is itself a turning back in cinema's history (accepting for a moment the idea of a progressive development), right back to the practice of the films screened by Lumière in the Grand Café; which is to say that it is not necessarily the realization of the physical experience of the film as a material presentation: on the contrary, it can function perfectly well, as with the historical reception of the Lumière films, as a foundation of the supreme illusion of the real, the actual 'before one's eyes', the vision of 'nature caught in the act' (the excited comment of one of the first spectators). So that, in fact, much more is at stake in 'structural/materialist film', in the films themselves: Le Grice's own *White Field Duration* (1973), for example, aiming to establish the length of projection time as a material experience by exposing the viewer to a white screen, or Snow's *One Second in Montreal* (1969), a film which Le Grice praises and which holds still images for increasing and decreasing periods of time, patterning durational experience of the film for the viewer.

Any film works with time and duration; Indeed, narrative cinema classically depends on the systematic exploitation of a multiplicity of times: the time of the narrative action but equally the time of the elaboration of the narrative, which brings into play a whole number of figures, rhymes, movements that cut across the film in differing rhythms, shifting the spectator in their relations. Simply, the exploitation is systematic, in final time with the elaborated narrative, the achievement of that (so the film 'goes quickly'); the multiplicity is constantly tied down to the narrative which gives purpose and direction to the film, is its principle of homogeneity. Nor is narrative the only mode of binding time. Consider Bruce Baillie's *All My Life* (1966): the single-shot three-minute pan – sky, hedge, flowers – traces a duration which is held in time with the song on the sound-track, the song closing camera movement, colour, screen duration into the unity of its time and significance. The contrary practice of 'structural/materialist film' is to break given terms of unity, to explore the heterogeneity of film in process. Snow's *Standard Time* (1967), for instance, cites one reference (one standard) for time on the sound-track, a morning radio broadcast, another on the image-track, an extremely elliptical human presence which conventionally serves as the centre for the elision of the process of film production, and then works over an eight-minute duration of film with an unbound series of pans and tilts that ceaselessly pose the question of viewing time.

The disunity, the disjunction, of 'structural/materialist film' is, exactly, the spectator. What is intended, what the practice addresses, is not a spectator as unified subject, timed by a narrative action, making the relations the film makes to be made, coming in the pleasure of the mastery of those relations, of the positioned view they offer, but a spectator, a spectating activity, at the limit of any fixed subjectivity, materially inconstant, dispersed in process, beyond the accommodation of reality and pleasure principles. 'Boredom' is a word which is sometimes assumed by the film-makers with regard to their films, the boredom which is the loss of the imaginary unity of the subject-ego and the very grain of drive against that coherent fiction, the boredom which Barthes sees close to *jouissance* ('it is *jouissance* seen from the shores of pleasure'[2]).

A specific strategy for the tension of duration set up by 'structural/materialist film' is that of repetition, at its simplest in the use of 'loops'. Gidal's work, for instance, has made particular and complex use of repetition: *Hall* with its pattern of long-to-medium-to-close shot movements from the view of the hall into the various objects seen at its far end, then repeated over again; *Room Film 1973* (1973) with its five second units each shown twice in succession; *Condition of Illusion* (1975) with its repetition of the camera's mobile angling focusing course over the surfaces of a room.

In Freud, repetition can go two ways, comes round with both a 'positive' and a 'negative' inflection. The compulsion to repeat is a way of remembering, resistant, symptomatic, difficult, that the analysis needs to shift towards a different engagement of the patient to its meaning, rendering the repetition *'useful'*. Thinking outside the analytic situation, Freud also ascribes to repetition a pleasure of remembering which he illustrates interestingly by reference to rhyme in poetry, the coherence of a formal organization that maps out paths of recognition, of the known. Repetition is in function with the binding – *Bindung* – that Freud describes as co-extensive with the unity of the ego, the maintenance of relatively constant forms within which the free flow of energy is channelled and so contained. As against all of which, or more precisely going along with all of which, repetition is also and increasingly recognized by Freud as the very type of the resistance characteristic of the unconscious, a compulsion that can be rendered useful but that is first and foremost a threat to ego coherence, as the very essence of drive, tending beyond the pleasure principle to absolute discharge, to the total dispersal of unity; Lacan talks of 'the more radical diversity constituted by repetition in itself'.[3]

The economy of repetition in classic narrative cinema is an economy of maintenance, towards a definite unity of the spectator as subject; systems of repetition are tightly established but on the line of a narrative action that holds the repetitions as a term of its coherence and advances with them, across them, its sense of difference, of change, of the new. The practice of 'structural/materialist film' is another economy; the spectator is confronted with a repetition that is 'in itself', not subsumed by a narrative and its coherence, that is literal, not caught up in the rhymes that habitually serve to figure out the narrative film. The spectator is produced by the film as subject in process, in the process of demonstration of the film, with the repetition an intensification of that process, the production of a certain freedom or randomness of energy, of no one memory: in *Condition of Illusion,* the return of an impossible openness of the film as object of desire, flashes of memories, this statuette, this rapid zoom in and out, this white surface, this pulling of focus, a network in which the vision of the I, the ego, is no longer confirmed as the master view. Literal repetition is the radical new that *jouissance* demands; Lacan again; 'Everything which varies, modulates in repetition is only an alienation of its meaning.'[4]

Perhaps paradoxically at first consideration, the strategy of repetition in 'structural/ materialist film' breaks identification. In *Condition of Illusion,* which involves the instability of possibilities of recognition (speed of camera movement, use of focus, proximity, angle, etc., leaving only a few objects and places in the room identifiable according to the norms of photographic reproduction), the repetition suggests a possibility of 'catching up', 'making sure', 'verifying' which in fact remains unexploitable, ineffective (one never sees 'more'), resistant in the very literalness of the repetition (no variation, modulation, no 'new angle'). In *Hall* something of the reverse procedure arrives, via the repetition, at something of the same kind of break: extremely stable, normally reproduced objects are given clear from the beginning, the editing moreover reducing the distance from which they are seen, cutting in to show and detail them, repetition then undercutting their simple identification; the second time round, the bowl of fruit cannot be seen as a bowl of fruit, must be seen as an image in a film process, detached from any unproblematic illusion of presence, as a production in the film, a mark of the presence of that.

Discussion of identification in film, of course, is not habitually concerned with this identifying of (objects, what is shown) but rather with identifying into (the film's narrative movement), identifying with (the characters of the narrative, 'the people in the film'). 'Structural/materialist film' works counter to these appropriations, by the elimination of narrative action and agents *(Condition of Illusion),* by their extreme marginalization as a kind of legibly illegible disjunct (Gidal's *Silent Partner,* 1977, with its fragments of noise of conversation, glimpse of legs, person whistling on the soundtrack, very title), by their derisively obvious quotation (as sometimes in Snow's films, *Wavelength* or *Back and Forth,* 1968-9), by their strictly measured delimitation for the demonstration of the film process (the picnic in Le Grice's multi-projection *After Manet,* 1975, or the repeated phone ringing incident in *Blackbird Descending,* 1977, picnic and incident given as functions in transformation, notions such as 'record' and 'actuality' displaced from the reproduction of life to the production of film reality). The spectator is to be held at a distance, but at the distance of the presentation of material construction, is to be held to that.

Identification is the hold of the image, from the initial assumption of significance, identifying of, to its ultimate confirmation by narrative order, identifying into and with. Certain films refuse the very image itself or reduce it to the very limits of its physical supports – light and screen in *White Field Duration* – but in general, 'structural/materialist films' are engaged with images, assume the fact of their production, often attempt to move in the time of that production – an effect of *Condition of Illusion* where camera focus and pace seem frequently to be hesitating just on the boundary of stability and recognition. Which is to say that they begin at least, like any other type of film, from the primary identification that Metz sees as constitutive in the cinematic apparatus itself: 'the spectator identifies with him/herself, with him/herself as a pure act of perception (as wakefulness, alertness): as condition of possibility of the perceived and hence as a kind of transcendental subject... as he/she identifies with him/herself as look, the spectator can do no other than identify with the camera too, which has looked before at what is now being looked at...'.[5] They begin from but end against the solicitation of the unity of the look that the apparatus offers for exploitation (is developed to exploit): the all-perceiving subject free in the instrumentality of the camera that serves to relay and reproduce at every moment the power of that central vision. 'Structural/materialist film' has no *place* for the look, ceaselessly displaced, outphased, a problem of seeing; it is anti-voyeuristic.

What is thus at stake is a practice towards 'a deliberate exterior reflexiveness of the audience': 'the viewer is forming an equal and possibly more or less opposite 'film' in her/his head, constantly anticipating, correcting, re-correcting – constantly intervening in the arena of confrontation with the given reality, i.e. the isolated chosen area of each film's work, of each film's production'.

If the figure of memory is metaphor (one signifier for another which, absent, repressed, is consequently retained nevertheless in a certain effect of signification), then the project of 'structural/materialist film' is non-metaphorical: a film must not substitute for its process (and reproduce the spectator in the image of that substitution); must not substitute narrative, the predominant metaphor in cinema, onto the order of which the process of filmic production is transferred (the Greek *metaphora* means transference), this narrativization containing the heterogeneous elements and fixing a memory of the film, making it coherently available as a sure progress of meaning. Without narrative, the memory of a film fails. Simple test: after a viewing of *Condition of Illusion,* the account given will be extremely 'subjective' (particular traces of desiring relation: liking-remembering this or that moment, wanting it in the repetition) or extremely 'objective' (towards a description of the film's construction, its use of repetition, camera mobility, and so on), the two, exactly at their extreme, joining up with one another; what is missing is the habitual common ground, the narrative metaphor or transference or model of the film, its memory for the spectator placed as its subject, bound and centred on its terms of meaning. Or rather, the spectator as subject-ego (the ego is the place of the imaginary identifications of the subject), the maintained illusion of coherence (derived in film from the maintained coherence of the illusion); but the subject is always more than the ego, the 'more' that 'structural/materialist film' seeks to open out in its demonstration of process: the subject circulation in the symbolic with its chains of signifying elements, unity overturned in the other memory of repetition.

'There can be no radical narrative film.' This basic tenet of 'structural/materialist film' (narrative is the culminating order of illusionism, identification, subject unity, etc.) is at the same time a continual point of debate and doubt. Le Grice can find himself 'not convinced that illusion and narrative are excluded as elements of the 'structural/materialist' problematic'; Gidal even can talk of 'the narrative of a black labourer building a window frame and pane' in his *C/O/N/S/T/R/U/C/T* (1974, a film that depends on multiple superimposition of almost identical images). The difficulty is the very term 'narrative' which tends to be used with an absolute imprecision: what is the historical force of the statement that there can be no radical narrative film? Arguments the other way, however, are often equally imprecise, themselves avoiding effective historical questions and appealing to a kind of inevitable presence-of-narrative schema, narrative as inescapable in film construction.

Take *Condition of Illusion:* no agents of action are given in the film; agency is with the camera, its movement over and focusing of the room's surfaces, which agency itself is tensed into (taken up in the tension and the time of) the structural functioning of the film's duration with its pattern of repetition. It is sometimes said that the film is the narrative of the progress round the room, a notion that transfers the identification of surfaces and objects in a temporal succession to the agency of the camera as narrating source, as narrator, the seen film thus held together as the narrative product of that agency narrator. What is interesting here is to grasp the extent to which narration is in our imaginary of film as important as, and, in fact, more important than, narrative: film, that imaginary has it (supported by the conventional systems of address in narrative cinema), must be representation for, in order, directed towards something for someone (narrative as the common ground of film and spectator. Thus with *Condition of Illusion*, the power of the response against the film to find an order of narration, a direction; 'against the film', since what such a response has to ignore, impossible in the experience of the film, is, once again, the repetition, the disturbing return of the signifier across the signs of any narration (where 'a sign represents something for someone', 'a signifier represents a subject for another signifier'[6]).

In the expression 'structural/materialist film', 'structural' stands in some sense as the term of the eviction of narrative which it thus also serves to replace, taking over the problem of relations in film, referring to aspects such as the use of repetition. At the same time, however, it can be seen as covering over questions of history, of the history of the subject.

Three instances can be distinguished in the relation of the spectator as subject in a film: *preconstruction*, *construction* (or *reconstruction*) and *passage*. Preconstruction involves the ready-made positions of meaning that a film may adopt, not simply large categories of definition, political arguments, thematic boundaries, and so on, but equally, for example, the codes and orders of language itself, the existing social conventions of colour, the available ideas of film (genre is a major factor of preconstruction). Construction is the totalizing of a more or less coherent subject position in the film as its end, its purpose, the overall fiction of the subject related. Passage is the performance of the film, the movement of the spectator making the film, taken up as subject in its process. The ideological achievement of any film is not merely in one or the other of these instances, it is first and foremost in its hold of the three: the appropriation of preconstruction in reconstruction (the film's construction effectively reconstructs from its different materials) and the process of that appropriation. As has been said, the operation of that hold in the classic narrative film is exactly the narrativization, the constant conversion of process to narrative, catching up the spectator as subject in the image of the narrative, the narrative images, and in the film as its/their narration.

'Structural/materialist film' is posed entirely in terms of the instance of passage, its area of work the presentation of the process of film (so that 'passage' becomes a misleading term: there is no simple movement 'through' the film); which is to say that it minimizes construction-reconstruction, by the eviction of narrative, and preconstruction, by the reduction as far as possible of given signifieds. The latter strategy is theorized by recourse to a conception of relative potency: there are potent and less potent signifiers, representations: 'the image of a pregnant woman, for example, is locked into a signification so ideologically overdetermining that no kind of other operation affecting the editing, zooming, focusing, camera work, subject position behind the camera, off-screen space or sound, can subvert, attack or deny its meaning; it remains culturally enclosed'; other images are less enclosed, objects in a hall, say, or a room; the minimal level of potency allows for the attention to the *film's* process, *its* construction. Yet, in fact, not merely is minimalization not meaninglessness, so that the objects continue to bring significations into play in the film (Gidal later finds it necessary to dissociate himself from *Hall* inasmuch as 'utilizing potent – signifying, overloaded – representations'), but the minimalization itself begins to create a veritable intensity of meaning (the statuette in *Condition of Illusion,* for example, becomes charged with a focus and importance and beauty and force).

The idea of minimal potency 'forgets' preconstruction and construction-reconstruction, the historical problem of meaning and subject position, in the interests of stressing the experience of the process of film in the viewing situation which is then given a sufficiency and, in the end, an existence outside contradiction, the concern with 'materiality' becoming a defined and limited project with its confirmed audience – and its own cultural trap. 'Structural' is again the symptomatic term of this, as though it could *simply* be a question of opposing 'non-narrative' to 'narrative', 'signifier' to 'signified'.

Generally, avant-garde independent film-making has suffered from being provided with a history of its own (Le Grice's *Abstract Film and Beyond is* not really any advance in this respect). What we need most is a quite different history, radically theoretical, something like *Towards a Political Economy of Film Meaning-Production and Use.* 'Structural/materialist film' would have its urgency in such a history, a history that the films, and this is their radical, political actuality, ceaselessly suggest in the scope – and from the limits – of their practice.

NOTES

Published in *Wide Angle* vol. 2 no. 3 (1978) pp. 411. Further consideration of Gidal's theory of 'structural/materialist' practice can be found in my 'Afterword' to his essay 'The Anti-narrative': *Screen* vol. 20 no. 2 (1979) pp. 93-9.

1. See Peter Gidal (ed.) *Structural Film Anthology* (London: British Film Institute, 1976) and Malcolm Le Grice, *Abstract Film and Beyond* (London: Studio Vista, 1977); unattributed quotations in the present text are either from those sources or from various unpublished pieces of writing by Gidal and are taken as representative of emphases constantly made. 'Structural/materialist film' is an indication of a certain practice and a rough grouping accordingly, not 'a movement'; it would include works by the following (amongst others): Gidal, Le Grice, Michael Snow, Peter Kubelka, Kurt Kren, William Raban, Gill Eatherley, David Crosswaite, Fred Drummond.

2. Roland Barthes, *Le Plaisir du texte* (Paris: Seuil, 1973) p. 43; translation, *The Pleasure of the Text* (London: Cape, 1976) p. 26.

3. Jacques Lacan, *Le Sèminaire livre XI* (Paris: Seuil, 1973) p. 60; translation, *The Four Fundamental Concepts of Psycho-Analysis* (London: Hogarth Press, 1977) p. 61.

4. Ibid.

5. Christian Metz, 'Le signifiant imaginaire', *Communications* no. 23 (1975) *pp.* 34–5; translation, 'The imaginary signifier', *Screen* vol. 16 no. 2 (Summer 1975) p. 51–2.

6. Jacques Lacan, *Écrits* (Paris: Seuil, 1966) p. 840.

Emily - Third Party Speculation – Malcolm Le Grice (1979)

MALCOLM LE GRICE

The History
We Need

First published in *Film as Film*, Exhibition
Catalogue, Hayward Gallery, London, 1979

The underlying thesis of a historical construction not only affects the ordering of facts but also the articulation of what constitutes the facts themselves. In addition a historical formulation has a different function for the involved practitioner in a field than for the less involved 'general public'. For that nebulous 'general public' (in whose name so many decisions are made) a historical exhibition like 'Film as Film', as well as drawing attention to a particular field of past activity also validates those current practices which derive from them – providing them with historical credentials. In effect, whilst a current practice is evidently determined by its historical relationship, definition of a structure for this causality is a constructive production very much parallel to the practice itself. It is only when the historical enterprise becomes an aspect of defining and analysing the determinants of current practice that it begins to have a real function for the involved practitioner. Unfortunately, the basic level of public awareness in the area covered by 'Film as Film' is such that the didactic intention has played the major part in defining the direction of the exhibition. That this may be seen as inevitable does not remove the need for a critique and this article affords me the luxury of making one from the standpoint of the involved practitioner. Bearing in mind that the 'we' of the title may be no more that a conceit which disguises an 'I', it symbolizes an attempt to be more than idiosyncratic. The 'we' addressed is broadly the involved practitioner, film-maker or theorist so committed as to be illiberal about films or their presentation. 'The History We Need' implies a recognition that a neutral and inclusive history is broadly impossible and that the historical enterprise should be aimed at aiding the development of contemporary practice. Whilst clearly given a didactic framework, the involved' practitioner will polemicize inclusions or exclusions, recognising how this serves promotion and suppression. On the other hand, even outside the polemical motive, selection and suppression is inevitable, implying no question of falsification but one of evaluation and priorities.

One of the problems with the current exhibition is the difficulty of defining its underlying thesis. This difficulty has increased with the expansion of the exhibition through a committee structure for the London presentation. In its original form, being largely conceived by Birgit Heins and Wulf Herzogenrath and aimed at a particular situation in Germany, some of its underlying principles were more readily discerned. Even then, expediences, like limited availability and the presentability of works in the art gallery affected the selection, tending to obscure some principles. Other inclusions, particularly the extent of attention to the American West Coast abstract films, signalled unresolved and, in the context of the exhibition, seemingly unproblematic contradictions.

Before attempting to unravel some of the fundamental assumptions which underlie 'Film as Film', I should point out that the critique is simultaneously a self-critique. This exhibition was initiated as one stage in a series of publications and exhibitions which have developed and refined the concepts it embodies. My own writing, in particular *Abstract Film and Beyond,* has formed a part of that development. Its historical view is very similar to that which underlies 'Film as Film'. My own book is based on many of the same fundamental assumptions, makes the same suppressions for similar reasons and fails to resolve similar contradictions.

Two fundamentals for the cultural enterprise represented by this exhibition can be defined by tracing a negative and positive expression. Negatively, it is contained in the rejection of what constitutes the mainstream of commercial narrative cinema. Positively it is the progressive exploration of the potentialities of the medium in-it-own-terms. The consistency of the positive expression with the basis of modernism is evident – 'Painting as Painting', 'Sculpture as Sculpture', 'Art for Art' – a general set of notions designating special and particular qualities to the medium in question. Thus the consistent tendency in this framework to talk of 'Film', the material, rather than 'Cinema' which has come to mean the form of the dominant commercial film institution. The negative and positive expressions are in a sense axes which have simultaneously motivated the actual practice. In general it would be tempting to argue that the negative expression has been primarily a feature of theoretical pronouncements and critical writing supporting the practice, which, on the other hand, has attempted to seek a non-narrative rather than anti-narrative cinematic form. But already some caution must be introduced on the degree to which negation functions as a constructive principle within art work. More at issue is the problem of defining what is being rejected in the general opposition to narrative cinema.

'At first look the cinema, born only a few years ago, may seem to be Futurist already, lacking a past and free from traditions. Actually, by appearing in the guise of a theatre without words, it has inherited all the most traditional sweepings of the literary theatre. Consequently, everything we have said and done about the stage applies to cinema. Our action is legitimate and necessary in so far as the cinema up to now has been and tends to remain profoundly passéist.... '1916 Futurist manifesto.

'Filmdrama is the opium of the masses'.
1920 Dziga Vertov.

'All current cinema is romantic, literary, historical, expressionist, etc.'
1926 Fernand Léger.

'Narrative is an illusionistic procedure, manipulatory, mystificatory, repressive.'
1971 Peter Gidal.

These few quotations briefly illustrate what has been a continuing, consistent and explicit rejection of the dominant narrative cinema. On the one hand, this rejection is, of the commercial cinema institution with its constriction of independent experiment and radical concept by the strangle-hold high finance has on production, publicity and the presentation system – a deep cultural control. On the other hand, and unclearly differentiated from it, it is the rejection of the forms and devices of narrative – identification with characters, story structure extending to a more general rejection of work whose images are broadly 'expressionist' or 'symbolic'. That the dominant cinema has grown up on the basis of the forms of identificatory narrative indicates a correspondence between them and the social effects desired (consciously or otherwise), by that sector of society controlling its finance.

Within the history represented by 'Film as Film' and *Abstract Film and Beyond,* the most obvious first level of exclusion is based on the rejection of works made within the dominant cinema framework. It has been seen as confusing to discuss work like *The Cabinet of Doctor Caligari* or Gance's *Napoleon* for example even though aspects of certain films from this context might relate to the motives of 'Film as Film'. But much more problematic has been the definition of the borderline of exclusion of films within the experimental area whose makers also reject the commercial cinema institution. (Some film-makers who are otherwise considered as central to the history even have works excluded if in some way they suggest a return to 'narrativity'.) For example, whilst Man Ray's first two films, *Retour a la raison* and *Emak Bakia* are both clearly 'in', I have not been alone in the impulse to reject his subsequent films as a retrogression. Man Ray's case illustrates this borderline which represents the basis of the major and most contentious exclusion made by this version of experimental film history. Though some of these works are included in the film programme of the London show, whose selection has been on more liberal and inclusive lines, the surrealist, mythic and broadly symbolist work from the Bunuel-Dali collaborations on *Un chien andalou* and *L'age d'or,* Dulac's *Coquille et le clergyman,* through much of the mainstream of the American Underground film, like Maya Deren, Ron Rice, Jack Smith, Gregory Markopoulos, Kenneth Anger and so on has been placed outside this historical concept. Most of the work in this direction rejects the dominant cinema institution but for the concept of this history does not sufficiently reject its forms. Whilst in my book I explained this exclusion primarily on the basis of scope, it now demands fuller consideration, resting on the need for a better articulation of the distinctions within the broad category of 'narrativity' .

If this history is seen as the history of a certain contemporary practice, loosely designated the 'formal' or 'structural' film (in other words assuming the validity of a certain state of current work and tracing its precursors, the history of its ideas), then the loosely defined surrealist, symbolist axis is difficult to integrate. But its oversimplified exclusion on the basis of narrativity masks many issues within the work which is included. As well as the issues of spectator 'identification' to which I shall return, the broadly symbolic work initiates consideration of the mechanisms of psychological association as it functions in the representational image. A very large proportion of so called 'formal' and 'structural' film makes use of representational imagery. The psychological signification in these films needs attention and in this respect the critical tradition which has emerged along the symbolist axis is a necessary reference. Invariably, the issues of signification within the image of much 'formal' work is masked by attention to the formal manoeuvres. Whether reference to the surrealist, symbolist tradition would function to refine further exclusions, rather than include films from this axis is not to be pre-judged, but if there is a distinction in kind to be made between the image signification in the 'formal' film and the surrealist/symbolist work then it needs clarification.

Image signification is not a problem confined to films which make use of representational imagery. Even in extreme non-representational art, the production of the image and its subsequent 'received' meaning is affected by the mechanisms of psychological association. The image, however abstract, is read associatively and signifies, produces and takes on meaning. Furthermore, and most important in 'formal' cinema, it must be understood that association and signification are not processes of meaning confined to the constituent images, representational or abstract, but belong also to the formal manoeuvres themselves.

What is designated form or structure in film is primarily related to the pattern of its temporal construction. Each work is a particular instance of temporal pattern, having likenesses to, and differences from, other instances of form. It, like the image, is subject to the mechanisms of association and, by its instances of difference, signifies. Rejection of symbolist/surrealist practice does not eliminate the issues of signification from 'formal' cinema but may encourage a false assumption in the practice that it does.

Through attention to the temporal manoeuvres (form) in cinema we may clarify some of the issues in the rejection of narrative. Rejection of the commercial cinema institution as repressive through vicarious satisfaction has carried over to a general rejection of the narrative forms through which it functions. In the film culture represented by 'Film as Film' the rejection of narrative structure might be simply interpreted as the basis of a search for 'new' form, but I think it is more properly understood as primarily motivated by rejection of the social function associated with it. A number of recent works by film-makers who come clearly out of the culture represented by 'Film as Film', have to one degree or another worked in areas which have related to the mechanisms associated with narrative. That *Rameau's Nephew* by Michael Snow, or my own *Blackbird Descending (Tense Alignment),* for example, might be seen as some 'return to narrative' is, in general, false. At the same time these films and works by Hammond like *Some Friends* or Gidal's *Condition of Illusion* tend to problematize, rather than simply oppose, some of the mechanisms to be found in narrative film. Work in this direction demands a more refined definition of narrative because implicit is the question 'are all aspects of narrative irrevocably embroiled with the repressive social function it has come to serve?' This development in the practice has been accompanied by an emerging theoretical concern focusing on the psychological formations in the activity of the film's spectator rather than on the intentions or psychology of the maker. This is particularly true of the film-makers like Hammond, Gidal, Dunford and myself who, more or less from the outset of our film work, have couched the issues of structure primarily in terms of the spectator's act of structuring. Recent theoretical work from another direction, stemming mainly from Christian Metz's 'Imaginary Signifier' article, indicates that some awareness of this problem exists outside the limits of 'structural/materialist' film theory. This theoretical direction is concerned to focus on fundamental psychological strategies involved in the process of identification. Many questions are raised by this radical change of focus from the issues of film structure embedded in the concerns of film-making to that of film viewing. For example, if, by implication, certain processes of structuring meaning or unconscious reaction are either fundamental or very deeply embedded by the culture in the psyche, how can the posture of diametric opposition dialecticise these processes? A continued discussion of these particular problems is outside the scope of this article, but it indicates some possibility of distinguishing between the processes of identification with portrayed characters, identification with the film's view-point on the scene via the camera on one hand, and the consequential structures of narrative on the other.

In the simplest sense, narrative is the story, it is the story told in the act of narration. A narrative represents a temporal chain of occurrences, a thread of causality. The narrative is not the events themselves, but a representation of events. It is a method of representing consequential temporality by way of a temporal presentation – the narration. A sophisticated narration may present the narrative in a sequence which does not represent the events in a simple sequential correspondence (making use of conventions like flash-back for instance), but whatever the complexity, one temporality is used to represent another. A narrative may represent a series of events which have taken place (in the world) or it may represent, from fragments of the possible, events which never have, nor will take place – a fiction. The former, based on 'fact', is not strictly a fiction, though as a narrative, with its inevitable linear ordering, its selected representation of causality is not simply factual. The narrative form within 'documentary' cinema raises its own particular questions of veracity and the relationship between document and documentary is of particular importance to film, based as it is in the mechanical recording of photography. In a practical sense, the culture represented by this exhibition raises the general question of the relationship of a presentation's sequence to the implications of meaning brought about by that sequence.

Though various experiments have been made in presenting films without sequential projection, it is none the less basic in general to film that, through projection, film controls presentation sequence – one section inevitably precedes another. In the history of the search for non-narrative structure, the notion of simultaneity represents the earliest alternative to developmental narrative. As in aspects of Dziga Vertov's *Man with a Movie Camera,* for example some of the sequential presentation does not imply that the events depicted took place sequentially as a consequence of each other, they are rather to be read as continuing independently at-the-same-time, related by some thematic similarity. The dissolution of consequential relationship in the narrative sense makes possible various systems of connective relationships between film images or sequences, analogous in a sense to collage as opposed to conventional story montage. These concepts attempt to establish a kind of a-temporality within the temporal presentation of the film. Many of the formal developments which have occurred with this history, including Brakhage's *Dog Star Man* and Kren's development of editing systems on mathematical principles stem from the concept of a-temporal montage.

Another direction which has initiated alternatives to narrative form comes from stress on the presentation sequence itself, mainly by way of repetition devices. This work, traceable back to Léger's *Ballet Mécanique,* subverts temporal representation by containing the consequentiality of image/shot transformations within the film itself. Or, if there are no transformations within the film then the transformations in perception or response in the spectator become central.

An allied direction, but leading to other conceptual problems, is that of extremely minimal change, not necessarily involving repetition. This direction mainly emerges from Andy Warhol's early films, like *Empire* and *Sleep,* drawing attention to the material passage of time in the presentation. Though there are works which follow Warhol which concentrate on duration without use of a camera, when based in photographic representation the material durational aspect becomes linked to those problems surrounding the notion of document.

Within the specific limits of the mechanism, the photograph as a mechanical trace of particular aspects of reality has veracity as a document – evidence within definable limits. With particular conditions of unbroken durational recording, cinephotography carries similar implications and problematics. This has little to do with 'documentary', which by manipulations at the level of sequential reconstruction breaks any possibility of durational veracity. Work which is an extreme of photographic, durational representation in fact subverts temporal representation by a change in terms. This involves the need to distinguish between representation and recording. When the cinephotographic makes its specificity evident within the work the record is no longer read in its secondary sense as narrative representation but as temporal document. It is outside the present scope to pursue the implications of this difference and the conditions necessary within a film's structure to resist the reading of 'record' as 'representation'. My further reference to cinematic representation carries the implication that this terminology is inadequately resolved.

It is evidently possible to pursue a film practice which is not based in photographic 'representation' (recording) but the historical development of the machinery is largely predicated on this function. The photocinematic recording is clearly a primary level of representation in cinema, though through the practice of editing this level of representation is not its primary *narrative* means. Literature shows that a narrative representation is possible without the facsimile representation afforded by cinephotography – words bear no resemblance to those objects to which they refer. As we have seen it is possible for films which are representational at the level of their images to be non-narrative at the level of their temporal structure. Conversely a film which is non-representational at the level of image may be quite justifiably interpreted as narrative at the level of temporal representation if its structure is readable anthropomorphically.

The resistance to anthropomorphism, which may be seen as a more general expression, and includes within it the resistance to narrative, is similarly a problematic enterprise again raising issues of psychological mechanisms of interpretation and the function of resistance to them. Gidal has pronounced the need to resist and frustrate anthropomorphic interpretation in general; considering the fact that his films are representational in the special sense of photographic recording, this can be interpreted as a tactic to dialecticize what would otherwise be assumed as inevitable (that the human spectator integrates all experience in human terms). Clearly the dominant cinema brings up no problem of this kind, it is anthropomorphic with no resistance at any level – its pictorial representation matching the identificatory desire of the spectator within the narrative – there is no conflict of interpretation, no dialecticization. Whatever the adequacy of theorization of this issue, in one form or another, the opposition to representation in painting, the resistance in music to classical (and because of the physics of the ear it can be argued, natural) harmony, can be seen as a thread of opposition to anthropomorphic interpretation in modern art.

From the positive axis of the fundamentals underlying 'Film as Film', the exploration of the medium in-its-own-terms, the exhibition demonstrates how the earliest approaches to this concept came through the application of the abstract developments in painting to film. I have argued that this early direction, rather than setting the terms for film as an autonomous art practice tended to replace the dominance of literature and theatre over cinematic form by that of painting and music. I have further argued that a more appropriate basis can be found in work which relates itself to the photocinematic aspect of the medium rather than its suppression (thus the emphasis given to Léger and Man Ray's first two works and the photographic contribution of Moholy-Nagy). Paradoxically, the concept of appropriateness in film reintroduces issues of representation that in painting it served to resist.

Whilst my general rejection of the abstract film tradition from Fischinger to the American West Coast is primarily based on the dominance of these painterly concepts in film, it does not invalidate the possibility of a cinematic form with no basis in photography. Unless an argument can be made in general against the temporal, aural abstraction – music, then no argument can be made against the possibility of its visual equivalent.

At a more fundamental level, the underlying assumption that a practice would seek autonomy is problematic. This assumption implicit in 'Film as Film', inevitably draws all those arguments which can be brought against modernism. In an historical sense, there is no doubt that tendencies which were at work in other arts are reflected in the attempts to define an art practice intrinsically cinematic. As in painting this process has concerned itself progressively with an exploration based on the materials and properties which can be defined as 'belonging to the medium'. Unfortunately the rhetoric of this enterprise has tended to reflect an essentialism – pure painting, pure film – to encourage tautologies like painting is painting, film is film and to become attached to phenomenalism in a way which assumes a kind of unmediated direct response leading to expressions like: 'the work is just itself, an object'. However, this is more an issue of faulty theorization than faulty practice. In effect, the attempt to determine the intrinsics of a medium is always in one sense or another a relativist and historically placed activity. Any assumption that absolute irreducible essences can be uncovered in the enterprise is not borne out by its practice, the very definition of seeming fundamentals is always open to historical re-definition. The possibility that an autonomous film practice can be postulated already rests on certain historical conditions. The technological development of the materials and machinery is a prerequisite, but the form which this technology takes is already enmeshed with historical pre-conditions of its social function and psychological determinants. It is impossible to separate the materials and the practice to which it is attached. It is in this sense that any engagement with the medium becomes a signifying practice within the historical framework. At the same time, if seen in a relativist sense, aesthetic strategies which suppress, in one form or another, current significations make possible manipulations leading to new meaning (so called 'work on the signifier').

Instead of treating the attention to the photocinematic basis of film or any other definable aspects of its machinery or materials in the terms of fundamentals or essences of cinema, they should be considered instead as predominant problematics of the medium in its historical placement and signification. The terms in which this issue is theorized is important not only for an understanding of the practice which has taken place, but also as the basis for a critique. The critique affects the developing practice. For example certain concerns on the one hand with the cinematic materials and machinery and with exploration of a variety of non-narrative structures, by becoming critically dissociated from their historical signification, can become simply recuperable formalist exercises. However, a formalist critique of some developments within the 'Film as Film' direction should not be made without consideration of the critical institution within which it is made. It must be in productive rather than destructive terms lest it merely assists the dominance of dominant cinema by weakening the only real cultural alternative.

Though still fragile and largely unrecognized, the cinematic development represented by 'Film as Film' is a substantial history. It has already begun some definition within its own terms, but the didactic necessity in its presentation inhibits this definition as it is veered towards polemics. This tendency of the committed to polemicise is in its turn counteracted by a tendency of liberal inclusiveness, a classical balancing of viewpoints. The major historical problem for the involved practitioner is the definition of the issues. Without stressing my own formulation of the most demanding current problems, in the course of this brief outline, I have indicated where I think some might be taken up.

So the 'history we need' is more a question of the manner and function of the enterprise than a polemical assertion of its constituents. To function as it should towards the critical development of current practice it needs to begin from a more limited theoretical definition of the problems and be designed as an operation to elucidate them rather than as an exhibition to present a particular construction.

Neither the current institution surrounding cinema nor that related to the presentation of the plastic arts has forms which suit such a concept of presentation.

Meshes of the Afternoon – Maya Deren (1943)

LIS RHODES

Whose History?

First published in *Film as Film*, Exhibition
Catalogue, Hayward Gallery, London, 1979

Feeling unwilling to write – an inability to manipulate ideas into a theory and facts into a convincing argument, an apprehension at intervening in the hierarchy of film history; an alienation from its underlying thesis of development – I began to reflect.

I stopped writing. I read a sentence written by Gertrude Stein, 'Define what you do by what you see never by what you know because you do not know that this is so'.[1]

I knew that 'Film as Film' represented a particular history: 'facts' fragments of film, arranged in sequence; an illustration of a theory; film history re-surfaced, the underlying method unchanged. What was blindingly apparent was the lack of women both represented in, and involved with the selection and structuring of, the exhibition.

I began making notes. The first word of every heading I made was 'problem'; the 'problem' of history and historical method; the 'problem' of researching women who apparently don't exist; the 'problem' of whether to present material in an overtly alienating context. Who was to be represented, how and why?

I put these questions to a group of women involved in various aspects of filmmaking and creative practice. It is the thoughts and experiences of this group that lead to this different presentation of history; history made by women about women.

Remembering a few hours that my sister and I had spent, over last Christmas, looking through a drawer full of old photographs and postcards, I began to think about my own history; images, moments of emotion, fragments of an event. A sentence re-heard, the sound of... the sounds most of all crept back into my mind surrounding the crumpled snapshots. A remembered face, a forgotten figure, my sister and I remember differently. Moments of remembrance for her were nothing to me. Others were shared. We talked and laughed together. Traces of this and that remembered and forgotten centred around a photograph. Is this history? It is certainly my history, her history, our history.

The present is the centre of focus. The image moves moment by moment. The image is history. The view through the lens may be blurred or defined – focused or unfocused – depending on what you think you know; what you imagine you see; what you learn to look for, what you are told is visible.

There is another history. A history that I have been taught; that I am told I am part of: a reconstruction of events, that I had no part in, causes that I didn't cause and effects that testify to my sense of exclusion. This is the history that defines the present, the pattern that confirms and restricts our position and activities.

History is not an isolated academic concern but the determining factor in making 'sense' – 'nonsense' – of now. Yesterday defines today, today tomorrow. The value placed upon truth, changes viewed from different orientations, different moments flicker with recognition others fade into oblivion.

The reason for this discussion of other histories is not necessarily to prove or disprove the validity of the historical thesis presented by 'Film as Film', but rather to consider its relevance and question its authority. Such authority is implied by the didactic and impersonal approach, and reinforced by the circumstances and context of its presentation; therefore a history not only acceptable to an institution, but fundamentally determined by it. The focuses, permissions, controls, histories are all male oriented. Our problem was not to find an alternative thesis from that of 'formalism' or 'structuralism', or attempt to exclude women's work from this thesis, but to consider our own history. How do women need to look at the work they do, the lives they lead? Can we be satisfied with token representation, a reference here and there in support of a theory of film history, which is not our own?

PROBLEMS OF HISTORY

In a patriarchial class-based society a man's position is determined by social and economic factors, but women are further defined as secondary within that class system, the values of their activities and their contributions to that society are considered secondary. This difference in experience, difference in opportunities, must produce difference in history; a history of secondary value and largely neglected and unwritten.

Film history defined by men necessarily positions women outside its concerns. Women appear, but on whose terms? Within whose definitions? Apparently historical accuracy is based upon acceptable 'facts', that is those facts that are the concern of men. Unacceptable 'facts' are forgotten or rearranged. If they are remembered they are contained within the existing fabric. Alice Guy made some 200 films between 1896 and 1907. Why has she been forgotten? Her films attributed to Jasset and Feuillard?

At the present time we need to show in a polemical but positive way the destructive and creative aspects of working as women in film, and examine these phenomena as products of our society, and the particular society of film art. Women filmmakers may or may not have made 'formalist' films, but is the term itself valid as a means of reconstructing history? Is there a commonly accepted and understood approach? Historians cannot avoid value judgments. They select and value certain works. When women are not selected their work plays no further part in film theory, or in historical exhibitions such as this one. A system of theory and criticism uses authorship and uniqueness to create the value of a work; then through publication and exhibition it publicises the authors and perpetuates the values they are said to represent. The construction of 'new' theories or re-evaluation still relates to the established authors and their works. The purpose of 'Film as Film' is to establish relations between and attribute influences upon, assign importance to... etc., both of film to film, and film to other works of art, irrespective of author. This establishes a system of recognition but does not necessarily reflect the ideas or sensibilities of the author. Historians take possession of a film or painting as something to be used or restated. Traditionally scholarship is not concerned with persons but works and it is therefore, assumed that such discussions/writings are impersonal and unbiased. Any work can be included provided that analysis can reveal such elements of style as the theory entails.

As a method of reconstructing film history the thesis of 'Film as Film' is useful only in so far as it satisfies an apparent need to classify, organise and contain. This imposition of a fixed point of view on film history is dubious and contradicts the idea that films can be evaluated on their own presuppositions and not manipulated to fit those of the historian. If we are to reconsider this method of reconstruction then we must appeal to our own experience, the experience of women filmmakers, not to theoretical generalisations that either exclude our work or force it into an alien impersonal system of explanation.

The history represented here is the illustration of a philosophical ideal, the meshing of moments to prove a theoretical connection. It is as though a line could be drawn between past and present, and pieces of a person's life and work pegged on it; no exceptions, no change – theory looks nice – the similarity of item to item reassuring – shirt to shirt –

shoulder to shoulder – an inflexible chain, each part in place. The pattern is defined. Cut the line and chronology falls in a crumpled heap. I prefer a crumpled heap, history at my feet, not stretched above my head.

There is the obvious and enormous difference of experience (between women and men) in the first place; but the essential difference lies in the fact not that men describe battles and women the birth of children, but that each sex described itself[2]. It is the case, perhaps, that men have described both. If this 'difference' is unmistakable then the concept of equality is neither useful nor relevant. Such a concept presupposes 'sameness'. It disguises 'difference'. Similarity, not difference, expresses the containment of female within the dominant masculine modes of creativity. Any attempt to express 'difference' must cause opposition and therefore appear as the expression of a minority; as is visibly demonstrated in this catalogue and exhibition.

It is neither a question of defining a feminine mode of filmmaking, nor of persuading any women to a feminist point of view, but simply suggesting that seeing 'difference' is more important than accepting 'sameness'; realising our own histories and understanding their many, possibly divergent, forms. It seemed, therefore, more vital to present a separate approach to history than to argue for an equal part in the selection and presentation of 'Film as Film'.

The historical approach that surveys works either published or collected must reinforce the society/film system that leads to their publication or protection in the first place. Ideology, therefore, predetermines information and its availability. The source material valued, written about and conserved reflects a male-dominated society. Had Alice Guy not written about herself would she be accessible now, as a woman, as a filmmaker?

Women have already realised the need to research and write their own histories; to describe themselves rather than accept descriptions, images and fragments of 'historical evidence' of themselves; and to reject a history that perpetuates a mythological female occasionally glimpsed but never heard. Women are researching and conserving their own histories, creating their own sources of information. Perhaps we can change, are changing, must change the history as represented by 'Film as Film'.

PROBLEMS OF PRESENTATION

The group discussions we had during the autumn of 1978 centred on how to present a history that was our own. We visited film archives and libraries. This was revealing in two ways; first the dicovery of a category called 'women', pleasant perhaps, as an indication of a demand for information, but distressing in its confirmation of history presumed to be male unless otherwise defined.

Without a particularly detailed search our discoveries were encouraging. We found numerous women engaged in filmmaking prior to 1975. How could we select a few from amongst them?

It was the last question that focused our attention on the problem of *who* makes history for *whom*?

The space at the Hayward Gallery should surely be about women making their own history; to show history being re-described, re-thought, re-evaluated. If there *are* differences in approach to filmmaking between women and men this will become explicit without theoretical pre-determination. The work presented should not be seen as illustrating a particular concept of either feminine or feminist filmmaking. The presentation is as much concerned with the women researchers and their attitudes as it is with the subjects of their research, women looking at their own history.

We were still faced with the problem; was there any sense in trying to intervene in the context of 'Film as Film'? Would any representation of women's work be seen as merely token in a predominantly masculine exhibition, a ghetto in a male environment? However, had no intervention been made then the 'Film as Film' exhibition would publicly confirm the apparent lack of women filmmakers and the authority of a particular history.

Even if the presentation was to be token in dimension and context, it could provide a public space for information and discussion, not only of what women have done, but how we understand ourselves and our history. Hopefully, it may encourage women who are engaged in research, writing or filmmaking to discuss and describe our histories, in our own ways, on our own terms. A different *history*.

NOTES

1   Gertrude Stein, *The geographical history of America.*
2   Virginia Woolf reviewing R B Johnston's book *The Women Novelist.*

Riddles of the Sphinx – Laura Mulvey & Peter Wollen (1977)

LAURA MULVEY

Film, Feminism and the Avant-Garde

Written as a lecture for the series 'Women and Literature' organised by the Oxford Women's Studies Committee in 1978 and published in the anthology of the series Mary Jacobus (ed.), Women Writing and Writing about Women.

It is not until recently that any conjuncture has been possible between feminism and film. Women's political consciousness, under the impetus of the Women's Movement, has now turned critically towards cinema and, in spite of its brief time span, cinema now has a history that can be analysed from a feminist point of view. For the first time, the consciousness is there, and the body of work is sufficient. The heterogeneity of the cinema as an institution is reflected in its first encounter with feminism. There have been campaigns against sexism within the industry, analyses of sexism in representation, use of film for propaganda purposes and debates about culture politics. 'Woman and film' and 'woman in film' have only existed as critical concepts for roughly a decade. A first phase of thought has, it seems, been achieved. It is now possible to make some tentative assessments of feminist film criticism, find some perspective on the past and discuss directions for the future.

The collision between feminism and film is part of a wider explosive meeting between feminism and patriarchal culture. From early on, the Women's Movement called attention to the political significance of culture: to women's absence from the creation of dominant art and literature as an integral aspect of oppression. Out of this insight, other debates on politics and aesthetics acquired new life. It was (not exclusively, but to an important extent) feminism that gave a new urgency to the politics of culture and focused attention on connections between oppression and command of language. Largely excluded from creative traditions, subjected to patriarchal ideology within literature, popular arts and visual representation, women had to formulate an opposition to cultural sexism and discover a means of expression that broke with an art that had depended, for its existence, on an exclusively masculine concept of creativity.

What would women's cultural practice be like? What would art and literature within an ideology that did not oppress women be like? Debate has swirled and spiralled around these questions. On the one hand, there is a desire to explore the suppressed meaning of femininity, to assert a women's language as a slap in the face for patriarchy, a polemic and pleasure in self-discovery combined. On the other hand, there is a drive to forge an aesthetic that attacks language and representation, not as something naturally linked with the male, but rather as something that soaks up dominant ideology, as a sponge soaks up water.

It is at this point that a crucial problem has to be faced. Can the new be discovered, like a gold-mine in a garden? Or does the new grow only out of the work of confrontation that is done? Does the very act of opposing traditional aesthetics and questioning male-dominated language generate a new language and carry an aesthetic with it? It is at this point that feminists have recently come to see the modernist avant-garde as relevant to their own struggle to develop a radical approach to art. At the moment this is still a wary approach, given the hesitations feminists necessarily feel towards any aspect of male dominated culture. But the avant-garde poses certain questions which consciously confront traditional practice, often with a political motivation, working on ways to alter modes of representation and expectations in consumption. These questions arise similarly for women, motivated by a history of oppression and longing for change. However, the path leading even to this point of view is twisted. In this essay I want to trace the turning-points, moments of reassessment and outside influences, to show how feminist film practice has come to be interested in – and have almost an objective alliance with – the radical avant-garde.

As a preamble, before dealing specifically with cinema, I want to outline the main arguments about women's place in past culture. Behind all the arguments lies a fascination with the unspoken history of women that has become mysterious because unrecorded by male chroniclers and overlooked by male historians. And there is a corresponding need to fantasise a tradition, a line of work, a feminine cultural context, however tenuous, as a homage to the trivialisation endured by women in the past.

First of all, particularly in the early days of the Women's Movement, but still present, there is a hope that women have, in fact, produced more in mainstream culture than has even been recognised. Research discovered at least some handfuls of women artists and writers whose work had been overlooked and undervalued. Secondly, in contrast to this rediscovered presence is the emphasis on absence, the insistence on the part of some feminists that a few outstanding, exceptional women do not properly alleviate the overall picture of discrimination. Thirdly, in proportion to women's exclusion from cultural participation, their image has been stolen and their bodies exploited. Finally, there has been an important revival of interest in minor arts and crafts, where, allocated their place in the division of labour, women 'embroider' their daily work, also drawing attention to the way that women have worked together, without claims to authorship or genius. A clash arises here between a celebration of the past and a guideline for the future. There is a difference between an interest in women's traditions – the individual or group achievements which women have to their credit, despite a hostile environment – and a belief in a feminine sensibility, tied to the domestic and then freed only into a similar orientation in art.

These general issues have found their place in debates between women about film. I want to trace the way in which these debates developed and how each line of argument both advanced and blocked the growth of feminist film culture. Feminists then had to become more ambitious, more demanding. It is these developments that I will discuss in the second part of my essay as 'The Search for a Theory' and 'The Search for a Practice', describing the alliances and influences which have worked together to produce an aesthetic that is still only in its infancy.

In 1972 *Women and Film,* the first journal of feminist film criticism, came out in California, and the first two women's film festivals were organised (in New York and in Edinburgh). These events were a response in film terms to the early attention paid by the Women's Movement to the politics of representation. A rough history of women in the cinema soon started to emerge.

RESEARCHING THE PAST

These early days of research into women's place in film history quickly established the fact that women had been excluded from the production and making of films, possibly in proportion to their notorious exploitation as sexual objects on the screen. The women's film festivals showed the results of painstaking research: surprise finds and lost women directors could be counted on the fingers of very few hands. Overall, the history of the cinema presented a particularly depressing picture of discrimination and marginalisation of women. In the very early days of one-reelers, before the film industry attracted big money, some women did direct films in Hollywood. The coming of the studio system, and, even more so, economic reorganisation with the introduction of sound, involved large-scale investment from banks and the electronics industry. Money and studio hierarchy closed the ranks so completely that Dorothy Arzner and Ida Lupino were literally the only women to direct films regularly in Hollywood until the 1970s. Both found their way up through acceptable women's jobs: Arzner was an editor, Lupino an actress. They are the exceptions that prove the rule. The work of women directors in the pioneering days has been largely lost. There is little left of the films of Lois Weber and Alice Guy, the outstanding women directors of the pre-First World War period. Leni Riefenstahl, the maker of Fascist documentaries in the 1930s, is ironically the only woman director whose name is a household word. Leontine Sagan, the brilliant director of *Madchen in Uniform* (Germany, 1931) is still forgotten, in spite of the interest her film aroused in the women's festivals. In Europe in the 1950s, in film industries impoverished and disorganised by the war and overshadowed by American imports, a few women began to make films: Mai Zetterling, once again actress turned director; Agnes Varda, photographer; and, in Eastern Europe, Marta Meszaros and Vera Chytilova. And then there was the avant-garde tradition. Here, outside the distrust of women endemic in commercial cinema, marginalised within a marginal sphere of cinema, women had more impact. At least they were recorded and remembered. Germaine Dulac appears in the history books, if only through Artaud's denunciation of *The Seashell and the Clergyman.* Maya Deren's pioneering work in the United States during the 1940s had earned her the title 'Mother of the Avant-garde'. But both directors' intermingling of cinematic movement and interior consciousness interested feminists and avant-gardistes alike. And it was this tradition that appeared to feed most dynamically into women's contemporary work.

Behind the work of research that went into these festivals, there lay a hope that, once rediscovered, films made by women would reveal a coherent aesthetic. The experience of oppression, awareness of women's exploitation in image, would act as a unifying element for women directors, however different their origins. Careful analysis would show how the struggles associated with being female under male domination found an expression that unified across diversity of all kinds. Certainly, the films made by women were predominantly about women, whether through choice or as another aspect or marginalisation. But it began to look increasingly doubtful whether a unified tradition could be traced, except on the superficial level of women as content. Claire Johnston and Pam Cook in their study of

Reel Time – Annabel Nicolson (1973)

Dorothy Arzner took the question further, arguing that Arzner managed to throw the male assumptions and codes dominant in Hollywood into crisis, subverting them and opening up their contradictions.

> In general the woman in Arzner's films determines her own identity through
> transgression and desire. Unlike most other Hollywood directors... in Arzner's
> work the discourse of the woman... is what gives the system of the text its structural
> coherence while at the same time rendering the discourse of the male fragmented
> and incoherent. The central female protagonists react against and thus transgress the
> male discourse which entraps them. These women do not sweep aside the existing
> order and found a new female order of language. Rather, they assert their own
> discourse in the face of the male one, by breaking it up, subverting it, and in a sense,
> re-writing it.[1]

This argument took the debate beyond a simple hope for a unified tradition into a careful, detailed analysis of the language and codes used by a woman director alone in an otherwise exclusively male world. Such work became a crucial advance in feminist film criticism, the first bricks towards building a theory. Claire Johnston continues: 'The need for oppressed people to write their own history cannot be overstressed. Memory, an understanding of struggles of the past and a sense of one's own history constitute a vital dynamic in any struggle.'

THE ATTACK ON SEXISM

Certain stylistic conventions have grown up hand in hand with narrative cinema. The language of form should not intrude or overshadow the free flow of the story and must allow content to come to the fore. The first steps of feminist film criticism accepted these conventions, concentrating on the sexist *content* of cinematic narrative and exploitation of women as *images*. This was indeed a necessary polemic (similar politically to campaigns against sexism in advertising or role-indoctrination in children's books), exposing and protesting against the way in which active and passive roles in film narrative are divided along sex lines. At this point (the early issues of *Woman and Film,* the special women's issues of *The Velvet Light Trap* (Fall 1972) and *Take One* (February 1972)) the main demand was to replace one female role-model by another, stronger and more independent. Or to find images of women that were realistic and relevant to women's real-life experience. Both these demands assume that identification is the fundamental problem for cinema, and that feminist films would offer alternatives – the optimistic in fantasy, or the pessimistic in reality – lived out through the protagonists on the screen.

The importance of denouncing sexism is undoubted. But, as these demands are directed primarily at commercial and popular cinema, they also involve a confrontation with the sexist nature of the industry itself and its discrimination against women. Hollywood's immediate response to the Women's Movement was a retreat into what Molly Haskell in *From Reverence to Rape* describes as 'the buddy movie', showing how far these campaigns would still need to travel from the late 1960s and early 1970s.[2] The commercial cinema was not going to change overnight in either of its fundamental attitudes to women. Furthermore, a change in content alone, based on reversal of sex-roles, could do no more than reproduce the conventions established by male-dominated exploitative production with a new twist, and this twist could itself easily degenerate into a fetishistic male fantasy about fascinating, phallic women. However, the tradition of the melodrama, the old Hollywood genre of women's problems and family traumas, has re-emerged, providing vehicles for the women stars - always a necessary precondition for a Hollywood film concerned with women to become a bankable commodity.

FIRST FEMINIST FILMS

The conditions in which it was first possible for women to make films arose through economic and technical changes that allowed a cinema to develop with an alternative economic base to the 35mm commercial product. So far as women were affected, these changes allowed them to enter the world of cinema in considerably greater numbers than the previous drop in the ocean. Looking at the production side of the cinema industry, there seems to be a negative correlation between the size of the investment and the participation of women. The larger the amount, the less likely was a woman to be trusted with it. Shirley Clarke describes her experience in Hollywood in an interview in *Take One:*

> I didn't have any means of getting any money. It may have to do with the fact that people with money do not talk about money to women. That's one of the things that showed up in my Hollywood dealings. Everyone said 'Fantastic. Do something for us. But don't expect much. Being a woman it's going to be difficult'. So when I got out there they had a man who was going to be my producer. And he was going to tell me how to make my film. Men just don't like to talk to women about money – that's all.[3]

The first glimmer of an alternative world came, hardly noticed, in the 1940s. Maya Deren made *Meshes of the Afternoon* in 1941 with 16mm equipment and no sound. After the war, 16mm equipment that had been used for wartime newsreels came onto the second-hand market in the United States and provided the basis for what came to be called the Underground Cinema. These developments opened up film-making to people outside the industry, and allowed not one but several new cinemas to be born. The equipment is smaller, cheaper in itself, in stock and laboratory costs. But it was not until the early 1960s, with the invention of Coutant's Eclair camera in France and the Nagra tape recorder in Switzerland that synchronised sound could be recorded with ease. In cultural terms these developments produced two distinct cross-fertilisations. Film became available as a medium for artists, both in the visual arts and dance. In the 1960s film could be used by political activists for propaganda and campaign films. The particular association of 16mm with *cinéma-vérité* gave it the appearance of an instrument of truth itself, grasping the real, unmediated by ideology. Film seemed to be freed from its historic enslavement to the commercial product.

Looking back at feminist film criticism and festivals in the early 1970s, it is obvious that the first unified wave of films produced by women came directly out of the Woman's Movement, a mixture of consciousness raising and propaganda. Film was used to record women talking and then to direct discussion, so that the women on film could interact with the experiences and ideas of women at a meeting. There was a particular heady excitement to these films. For the first time ever, films were being made exclusively by women, about women and feminist politics, for other women. Susan Rice in the first issue of *Women and Film* comments on Kate Millett's film *Three Lives*:

> *Three Lives is* a Women's Liberation Cinema Production, and it is the only feature
> film I know of that not only takes women as its subject-matter, but was produced,
> directed, shot, recorded, lit, and edited by women. What makes this more than a
> stunt is the intimacy that this female crew seems to have elicited from its subjects.
> The element I find most compelling about the film is that it captures the tone and
> quality of relationships and significant conversation between women. If the film
> were to fail on every other level, this would stand as a note-worthy achievement.[4]

Or Dora Kaplan in the next issue writes of 'This new movement of women making political films politically' that:

> This commitment to educate, change consciousness, and sensibility showed itself to

be unalienated; that is, carried over to the process of film making itself; a film crew working collectively without hierarchy and specialization; a film crew working on an equal basis with the 'subject' in decision-making and production; and a film crew recognizing the distribution of the product to be an integral part of the process.[5]

Although it is hard to overestimate the vigour and immediacy of some of these films, they are closely tied to the ideology of consciousness raising and agitation around particular feminist issues. This is their strength; their weakness lies in limitations of the *cinéma-vérité* tradition. While as documents they can have an immediate political use, their aesthetics are bound by a concept of film as a transparent medium, reproducing rather than questioning, a project which reduces the camera to a magical instrument. There lies behind this a further assumption, that the camera, by its very nature and the good intentions of its operator, can grasp essential truths and by registering typical shared experiences can create political unity through the process of identification. The politics are thus restricted to emotion and the cinema stays trapped in the old endless search for the other self on the screen.

SUMMARY

Up to this point, I have used feminist film criticism around 1972 to mark a particular stage of conscious development and to show a need for a theoretical leap forward. But no leap forward could be conceived without this first spring-board: awareness of sexist exploitation and cultural oppression, and the resurrection of women who had struggled to make movies in the past. However, the way forward seemed blocked. The answers offered in this period did not match the needs of a feminist film culture. Demands for identification, for women's films that played on identification processes, still stayed subservient both to pre-existing cinematic formal traditions redolent of sexual exploitation and to the cinema of male domination. Any changes within the industry could only result from long-term agitation and activity on the part of women wanting to work within it, and from outside, gradual erosion through shifts in ideology. As a 16mm cinema took off and discrimination still prevailed in the industry, it became obvious that the independent sector would see the birth of a specifically feminist film-making practice. What would this cinema be like?

Desire to break with the past is rational and passionate. It is both an instinctual retreat from forms associated with oppression and a conscious drive to find uncontaminated ground on which to build a feminist aesthetics. Aesthetic and theoretical questions posed by mapping this new ground then widen the gap with the past. Is it then enough to break with sexist content alone? The dominant cinema has privileged content, whether in fiction or documentary, to subordinate the formal cinematic process itself. Identification between spectator and screen protagonist closes up remaining or necessary gaps between form and content. (For instance, Hitchcock reconciles his extravagant and unusual use of cinema with the demands of convention, involving the spectator through suspense.) In order to construct a new language of cinema, therefore, a break in this all-pervasive artistic unity appeared to be a priority. At the same time a pre-digested, fully grown, alternative cinematic language could not be expected to fall neatly from the sky at the moment of need. Such an expectation assumes that women's cinema had a developed tradition winding through the overt history of cinema like an unseen thread, or that the very fact of being a feminist and making a film would in itself be an answer. Neither proposition could hold up. The first ignores the extent of past oppression, the second asserts that individual intention transcends the language and aesthetics of cinema. A language must have a collective existence, otherwise pervasive forms of expression return willy-nilly, penetrating any intuitive rapport between spectator and creator, at best a matter of hit and miss.

Thus the first constructive steps towards feminist film culture have begun to turn in the direction of the matter of film language itself, probing dislocation between cinematic form and represented material, and investigating various means of splitting open the closed space between screen and spectator. As woman's place in past cinematic representation has been mystified, at once a linchpin of visual pleasure and an affirmation of male dominance, so feminists now have become fascinated with the mysteries of cinematic representation itself, hidden by means of the sexualised female fantasy form: a tearing of the veil, but no ready-made answers lie behind it. The absence of answers, combined with fascination with the cinematic process, point towards the development of a feminist formalism. Politically, a feminist formalism is based on rejection of the past and on giving priority to challenging the spectator's place in cinema. From an aesthetic point of view the space and time of realist or illusionist aesthetics have immense limitations: they cannot satisfy the complex shifts feminist imagery desires. Splits in the cinematic sign allow ideas to interact with fiction and thought with fantasy. At the same time there is a pleasure in *tabula rasa.* Structures become visible and the bare bones of the cinematic process force themselves forward. Finally, from a theoretical point of view, it is essential to analyse and understand the working of cinematic language, before claims can be made for a new language of cinema.

At the end of May 1978, three women from the collective of the only English-language journal of feminist film theory – *Camera Obscura* (published in Berkeley, California) – presented their work at the London Film-makers' Co-op, for discussion with English film-makers (men and women) and feminists interested in the cinema. The three had been associate editors of *Women and Film,* the pioneering magazine of feminist film criticism. They broke with *Women and Film* on the grounds that feminism had to move beyond the first spring-board – the basic critique of sexism and the affirmation of women's lost tradition – and search for new images. The new journal, *Camera Obscura,* is conceived on two linked fronts. First, to investigate the mechanisms by which meaning is produced in film:

> It is important to know where to locate ideology and patriarchy within the mode of representation in order to intervene and transform society, to define a praxis for change. Crucial to the feminist struggle is an awareness that any theory of how to change consciousness requires a notion of how consciousness is formed, of what change is and how it occurs.

And then the journal takes particular texts, so far only films made by women, as 'contributing to the development of a feminist counter-cinema, both by having as their central concern a feminist problematic, and by operating specific challenges to cinematic codes and narrative conventions of illusionist cinema'.[6]

A new theory and a new practice. I was struck at the Co-op weekend by the similarity between the *Camera Obscura* analysis and the thoughts I was developing for this essay. I was also struck by the historic conjuncture between feminist film theory, the *Camera Obscura* presentation, and the Co-op, home of avant-gardist film practice. This was a meeting, I felt, that could not until recently have taken place. It seemed to be a concrete indication, or mutual recognition, of a growing two-way traffic. On the part of feminist theorists, there is growing awareness of the avant-garde tradition; and on the part of the avant-garde, among both men and women film-makers, a sense of the relevance of the feminist challenge.

THE SEARCH FOR A THEORY

Both film theory and feminism, united by a common interest in the politics of images and problems of aesthetic language, have been influenced by recent intellectual debates around the split nature of the sign (semiotics) and the eruption of the unconscious in representation (psychoanalysis). There has also been a definite influence from Louis Althusser's Marxist philosophy, especially his essay 'Ideology and Ideological State Apparatuses'.[7]

The importance for the workings of bourgeois ideology which Althusser attributes to identification processes, imaginary representation of the subject and the illusion of reality, gave a new sense of political seriousness to aesthetic debates among avant-garde film-makers and film theorists. The realist aesthetics used means to entrap the spectator similar to those of bourgeois ideology itself. One could not, therefore, confront the other. Pam Cook (in her essay on Dorothy Arzner) makes the point that the system of representations generated by the classic Hollywood cinema fixes the spectator in a specific closed relationship to it, obliterating the possibility of experiencing contradiction.[8] This kind of argument fed into a reinforced anti-realism, providing the ground for theoretical links between avant-gardists opposing illusionism and political film-makers opposing bourgeois ideology. Furthermore the debate continued around the nature of the cinematic apparatus: how to liberate the destiny of the photographic process from simply recording, in keeping with the natural perspective vision of the human eye. Formalism provided an answer: foregrounding the cinematic process privileging the signifier, disrupts aesthetic unity and forces the spectator's attention on the means of production of meaning. *Camera Obscura* (in the first editorial) pointed out that

> Like the Camera Obscura, the cinematic apparatus is not ideologically neutral,
> but reproduces specific ideological predispositions: codes of movement, of
> iconic representation and perspective. The notion that 'reality' can be reflected in
> film negates any awareness of the intervention, the mediation of the cinematic
> apparatus. The impression of reality in the cinema is not due to its capacity for
> verisimilitude, its ability to reproduce faithfully a copy of an object, but rather to the
> complex process of the basic cinematic apparatus itself, which in its totality includes
> the spectator.[9]

From a feminist point of view, one crucial area of struggle is with or in ideology. Patriarchal ideology is made up of assumptions, 'truths' about the meaning of sexual difference, women's place in society, the mystery of femininity and so on. From this political point of view, feminist film theory has followed the aesthetic debate. However, ideology – whether bourgeois or patriarchal – is not a blanket-like or eternal totality and it is crucial for feminists to be aware of contradictions within it.

The twentieth century has seen the growth of oppositional aesthetics, under various avant-garde banners and movements. Although here too women have played only a marginal part, a search for theory cannot overlook the kind of questioning and confrontations that underlie other radical aesthetic movements.

I want to mention only one aspect of relations between semiotics and the avant-garde that affects women. Julia Kristeva, in her work on modernist poetics, has linked the crisis that produced the language of modernism with 'the feminine'.[10] She sees femininity as the repressed in the patriarchal order and as standing in a problematic relation to it. Tradition is transgressed by an eruption of linguistic excess, involving pleasure and 'the feminine' directly opposed to the logical language and repression endemic to patriarchy. A problem remains: woman, in these terms, only stands for what has been repressed, and it is the male poet's relation to femininity that erupts in his use of poetic language. The next step would, from a feminist point of view, have to move beyond *woman* unspeaking, a signifier of the 'other' of patriarchy, to a point where *women* can speak themselves, beyond a definition of 'femininity' assigned by patriarchy, to a poetic language made also by women and their understanding. But Kristeva's important point is this: transgression is played out through language itself. The break with the past has to work through the means of meaning-making itself, subverting its norms and refusing its otherwise imperturbable totality. Here, by extension, the importance of the independent film-making sector for feminism appears fully: it is outside the constraints of commercial cinema, in debate with the language of counter-cinema, that feminist experimentation can take place. Semiotics foregrounds language and emphasises both the crucial importance of the signifier (for a long time overlooked and subordinated to the signified) and the dual nature of the sign, thus suggesting the aesthetic mileage that can be gained by play on separation between its two aspects. For feminists this split has a triple attraction: aesthetic fascination with discontinuities; pleasure from disrupting the traditional unity of the sign; and theoretical advance from investigating language and the production of meaning.

One crucial contribution made by Freudian psychoanalysis is to pinpoint femininity as problematic for a society ordered by masculine dominance. Female sexuality, and also the feminine in male sexuality, hover as difficult and potentially uncontainable elements, repressed or erupting into neurotic symptoms. Here again there is a split, insisted on by Freud, between an appearance (whether a symptom, a habit or a slip) and the meaning behind it. In positing an unconscious the workings of which could not find direct conscious expression, Freud showed how, psychoanalytically, things can seldom be what they seem. Thus the image of woman in patriarchal representation refers primarily to connotations within the male unconscious, to its fears and fantasies. As Claire Johnston says in her study of women in the films of Raoul Walsh:

> For the male hero the female protagonist becomes an agent within the text of the
> film whereby his hidden secret can be brought to light, for it is in woman that his
> lack is located. She represents at one and the same time, the distant memory of

maternal plenitude and the fetishized object of his fantasy of castration - a phallic replacement and thus a threat.[11]

I have argued elsewhere ('Visual Pleasure and Narrative Cinema') that psychoanalysis can be used to reveal the way in which conventions of narrative cinema are tailored to dominant masculine desire – that voyeuristic pleasure is built into the way a spectator reads film.

> The place of the look defines cinema, the possibility of varying it and exposing it. This is what makes cinema quite different from, say, strip-tease, theatre, shows, and so on. Going far beyond highlighting a woman's to-be-looked-at-ness, the cinema builds the way she is to be looked at into the spectacle itself.[12]

Polemically, this proposition leads on to the necessity, for counter-cinema, of exposing the force of pleasure inherent in the cinematic experience in so far as it is organised around male erotic privilege and built on an imbalance between male/female, active/passive.

THE SEARCH FOR A PRACTICE

The disparate elements which I have drawn together under the heading 'The Search for a Theory' do not add up to a coherent whole. I have concentrated, furthermore, on those influences on feminist film theory that have implications for film-making practice, influences which all point towards both a desire and a need for rupture with closed, homogeneous forms of representation. Psychoanalysis dissolves the veneer of surface meanings: semiotics focuses on the split nature of the sign and on language itself as a site for change; confrontation with ideology brings up the issue of identification, of how a text 'places' a spectator. Now I want to outline influences from the avant-garde tradition and the ways in which feminist film-making practice has taken a position in relation to them.

Throughout this essay, I have referred to the persistent difficulty of articulating the means by which an aesthetic break can find formal expression. How does an independent aesthetic evolve out of confrontation with a dominant one? An important aspect of avant-garde aesthetics is negation: a work is formed, or driven to find a position, by the very code of the dominant tradition that is being opposed. These works have then to be read, and achieve meaning, in the reflected light of the aesthetics they negate. One aspect of the problems implicit in formulating a new aesthetics from scratch is thus circumvented. Traditional forms are known and recognised, and the spectator can recognise and read their negation. In cinematic terms traditional illusionist aesthetics have privileged the signified, organising a text so that its mechanics would attract minimal notice. A crucial and influential response within avant-garde aesthetics has been pioneered by the New American Cinema of the 1960s, which stresses the place of the signifier, illuminating the complexity of the cinematic process (as Annette Michelson puts it in the introduction to *New Forms in Film,* 'the assertion of the still photographic frame composing the strip, the assertion through the flicker of the medium as projection of light, the assertion of the nature of projection through the use of sound...').[13]

This emphasis on the importance of the signifier has thrown the place of the signified into crisis. For instance, Peter Gidal, a leading avant-garde film-maker in England, has rejected all content and narrative, both in his own work and as an aesthetic principle. In the introduction to *Structural Film Anthology,* he writes: 'The Structuralist/Materialist film must minimize the content in its overpowering, imagistically seductive sense, in an attempt to get through this miasmic area of "experience" and proceed with film as film'.[14]

For feminist film-makers, the way these arguments elevate the signifier is important. There is a link with those aspects of feminist film theory that demand a return to *tabula rasa* and question how meaning is made. But women cannot be satisfied with an aesthetics that restricts counter-cinema to work on form alone. Feminism is bound to its politics; its experimentation cannot exclude work on content. Peter Wollen (in his article 'The Two Avant-Gardes') traces a line of development where the demand for a new politics inseparably links problems of form and content. Going back to Eisenstein and Vertov, influenced by Brecht, re- emerging with the late work of Godard, this tradition has broken down rigid demarcations between fact and fiction and laid a foundation for experimentation with narrative.[15]

It is hard, as yet, to speak of a feminist film-making practice. Women film-makers are still few and far between, and influences on them are not necessarily coherent. Rather than generalising, it is preferable to exemplify tendencies and movements among women film-makers. For instance Annabel Nicolson (a long-standing member of the London Co-op) has used the old tradition of women's applied arts to experiment with film as material. In her expanded piece *Reel Time (1973),* she brings out the relationship between the projector and a sewing machine, running loops of film depicting herself sewing film through the sewing machine, then runs it through the projector until the film tears and starts to slip. Joyce Wieland in her first film *Handtinting* (made in New York in the 1960s) carried over her previous experiments with quilting into film, puncturing the strip with needles and dyeing the celluloid. There is also an aspect of her work which is miniature, home-movie scale: she describes *Rat Life and Diet in North America* as 'a film made at my kitchen table' and, using her pet gerbils as characters, she creates a narrative version of a domestic still life.[16]

Yvonne Rainer turned to film-making from dance (Maya Deren and Shirley Clarke also started their careers as dancers – one role in the arts where women are less likely to suffer discrimination and oppression). Rainer has done crucially important work with narrative, exploring its radical possibilities. She describes her way of working:

> A novelist might well laugh at my makeshift dallying with story-telling. For me the story is an empty frame on which to hang images and thoughts which need support. I feel no obligation to flesh out this armature with credible details of time and place... I was much more concerned with interweaving psychological and formal content, i.e., with images being filled up or emptied by readings or their absence, with text and image being illustrated to various degrees...

> This made for a situation where the story came and went, sometimes disappearing altogether as the extreme prolongation of certain soundless images... I accumulate stuff from my own writing, paragraphs, sentences, scraps of paper, stills from previous films, photos. Ultimately the process of sorting out forces me to organise it and make the parts cohere in some kind of fashion.[17]

Rainer shifts her story-telling and gives an ironic commentary on its development by means of written titles, interrupting the flow of images, using cliché in words and in situations, dwelling on emotion and performance and women's relation to them as traditional modes of expression. As a logical conclusion, perhaps, to this combination of interests, melodrama is invoked, but also, other forms of communication considered special to women (diaries, letters, intimate conversations and confidences), all distanced by an ironic handling of familiar self-doubts and self-questioning.

In my own films (co-directed with Peter Wollen), *Penthesilea* (1974) and *Riddles of the Sphinx* (1977), and also in Chantal Akerman's films, there is a meeting between the melodramatic tradition and psychoanalysis. Akerman's *Jeanne Dielman,* for example, shows the life of a woman over three days, dwelling minutely on daily repetition and domestic details. Once her routine is thrown off course, slight slips accumulate, leading almost imperceptibly to a cataclysmic eruption at the end. And then Akerman's *News from Home* uses letters from an anxious mother to her daughter read as sound-track over long static shots of New York on the image-track, separating sound and image to create action. *Riddles of the Sphinx* deals with dilemmas of motherhood lived within patriarchal society; the story of a woman (first married, in the home, then separated and working) with a two-year-old daughter is embedded in the centre of other approaches to the subject, direct or visual or poetic. What recurs overall is a constant return to woman, not indeed as a visual image, but as a subject of inquiry, a content which cannot be considered within the aesthetic lines laid down by traditional cinematic practice. Pleasure and involvement are not the result of identification, narrative tension or eroticised femininity, but arise from surprising and excessive use of the camera, unfamiliar framing of scenes and the human body, the demands made on the spectator to put together disparate elements. The story, the visual themes and the ideas are not in coherent conjunction with one another, and ask to be read in terms of developing relations between feminism and experimental film and psychoanalysis.

I began by pointing out how, in the brief history of film, feminism has only recently had any impact at all. Even now, the sphere in which the impact has been felt is extremely restricted. Recent technological developments allow the growth of film outside the industry, but without solid economic foundations. The future directions of 16mm and of experimental film are uncertain, but the conjunction between their growth and the historic eruption of feminist politics is unprecedented in the history of the arts. Here, at last, the demands of women can have a determining effect on aesthetics, as the work of feminist film theorists and film-makers gains strength and influence within the experimental sphere.

NOTES

1   Pam Cook and Claire Johnston, 'Dorothy Arzner: Critical Strategies', in Claire Johnston (ed.), *Dorothy Arzner, Towards a Feminist Cinema* (London: British Film Institute, 1975).

2   Molly Haskell, *From Reverence to Rape: The Treatment of Women in the Movies* (Chicago: University of Chicago Press, 1987) p. 362.

3   Shirley Clarke, 'Image and Images', *Take One,* III, 2 (1972).

4   Susan Rice, 'Three Lives', *Women and Film,* I, 1(1972).

5   Dora Kaplan, 'Selected Short Subjects', *Women and Film,* I, 2 (1972).

6   'Feminism and Film; Critical Approaches', *Camera Obscura,* 1(1976).

7   Louis Althusser, 'Ideology and Ideological State Apparatuses', *Lenin and Philosophy and Other Essays* (London: New Left Books, 1971).

8   Claire Johnston paraphrasing Pam Cook, 'Approaching the Work of Dorothy Arzner', Johnston, *Dorothy Arzner,* p. 2.

9   'Feminism and Film; Critical Approaches', *Camera Obscura,* 1(1976).

10 Julia Kristeva, 'Signifying Practice and Means of Production', *Edinburgh '76 Magazine; Psychoanalysis, Cinema and Avant-Garde* (1976).

11 Claire Johnston, 'The Place of Women in the Cinema of Raoul Walsh', in P. Hardy (ed.), *Raoul Walsh* (Edinburgh, 1974) p. 45.

12 Laura Mulvey, 'Visual Pleasure and Narrative Cinema', *Screen, xvi,* 3 (1975).

13 Annette Michelson, 'Film and the Radical Aspiration', *New Forms in Film* (Montreux,1974), p. 15.

14 Peter Gidal, 'Theory and Definition of the Structural/Materialist Film', *Structural Film Anthology* (London: British Film Institute, 1976).

15 Peter Wollen, 'The Two Avant-Gardes', *Studio International,* 190, 1978 (November/December 1975).

16 'Kay Armatage Interviews Joyce Wieland', *Take One,* XIII, 2 (1972).

17 'Yvonne Rainer: Interview', *Camera Obscura,* 1(1976).

1980s and 1990s

Vertical – David Hall (1968)

NICKY HAMLYN

Structuralist
Traces

At a recent screening of his work at the National Film Theatre in London[1] the American film-maker Stan Brakhage declared that he thought that Structuralism was the worst thing that ever happened to artists' film-making. He then went on, however, to say how much he admired the work of the eminent Structuralist film-makers Michael Snow, Ernie Gehr and Malcolm Le Grice. The aim of Brakhage's remarks seem to have been to separate the films of Snow and others from the label by which they came to be known, and under which they were subsequently discussed. The American critic P. Adams Sitney (for whom Brakhage's own work was an essential precursor of Structural film) gave the following brief characterisation of the work:

> The Structural film insists on its shape, and what content it has is minimal and
> subsidiary to the outline. Four characteristics of the Structural film are its fixed
> camera position (fixed from the viewer's perspective), the flicker effect, loop printing
> and re-photography off the screen.[2]

Naturally, not all Structural films contain all four elements. Some, for example Michael Snow's *Central Region* (1971) have none. Conversely, there are films which display some of Sitney's characteristics, but which do not fall within the Structuralist period. Notable in this respect is Fernand Leger and Murphy's *Le Ballet Mécanique* (1924) which famously employs loop printing. In fact, *Le Ballet Mécanique* conforms more closely to Sitney's notion of 'formal film' which he distinguishes from Structural film as follows:

> ...the formal film is a tight nexus of content, a shape designed to explore the facets

of the material... Recurrences, prolepses, antitheses and overall rhythms are the rhetoric of the 'formal'.[3]

Whereas in Structural film "the shape of the whole film is predetermined and simplified, and it is that shape which is the primal impression of the film'.[4]

The difference between Sitney's position and that of Peter Gidal, the British based American theorist and practitioner of Structural-Materialist film (of which more later) was not so much aesthetic as political.[5] Indeed, the addition of the term 'Materialist' to 'Structural' flags the Marxist dimension to Gidal's project, distinguishing it from Sitney's more aesthetic characterisation. For Gidal, Structural-Materialist film was not simply an artistic style or movement, but a socio-cultural struggle in which all forms of representation, and hence reproduction, were challenged: 'My arguments have been directed all along against reproduction in any form'.[6] This meant prevailing forms of economic, ideological, social and sexual reproduction, as well as visual. Needless to say, Gidal is particularly opposed to the cinema wherein audiences passively consume seamless amalgams of these reproductions.

Again, beyond the similarities between Sitney's and Gidal's formulations at a formal level, the latter's are, crucially, represented as strategies designed to overcome audience passivity:

> In Structural/Materialist film, the in/film (not in/frame) and film/viewer
> material relations, and the relations of the film's structure, are primary to any
> representational content. The structuring aspects and the attempt to decipher
> the structure and anticipate/correct it, to clarify and analyse the production
> processes of the specific image at any moment, are the root concern of the
> Structural/Materialist film.[7]

In other words, the film creates a dialectical relationship with the viewer, who must actively work at apprehending the film. In this sense the film is not an autonomous artefact. Rather, the viewing itself becomes a politicising experience because the viewer is prised out of his/her usual state of passive spectatorship and forced into a continually questioning and revising interaction with the film.

Malcolm Le Grice, the other major British theorist and film-maker, has stated that 'my predominant concern has been with the spectator'.[8] Both Gidal and Le Grice define their work in terms of opposition to what we call mainstream cinema.[9] But unlike Gidal, Le Grice is still exercised by questions which imply the possibility of a return to narrative. 'Are all aspects of narrative irrevocably embroiled with the repressive social function it has to come to serve?'[10] This is where the two part company, because for Gidal there can be no entertaining the possibility of narrative whether it be experimental, deconstructed or whatever:

> I take issue with the notion of deconstruction for the very reason that it reinvigorates narrativity, within whatever 'more perfect' definition of diegesis is come up with.[11]

Brakhage's recent remarks at the National Film Theatre, coming from a perspective which both precedes and to some extent stands outside the Structuralist period, point to the desirability of alternative readings. This is not in order to dilute the radical force of the work but to create more possibilities that can perhaps be developed. Some of these possibilities began to be explored by those near-contemporaries of Gidal and Le Grice who congregated at the London Film-makers' Co-operative (LMFC) from the late 1960s to the mid 1970s.

Closest to the two in aesthetic and political terms were Mike Dunford, John Du Cane, Roger Hammond, Gill Eatherley, David Parsons and David Crosswaite. But just outside this smaller group lay a diverse range of artists whose particular backgrounds and disciplines inflected their work in different ways. Steve Dwoskin made films like *Girl* (1974) which controversially involved filming a naked woman who returns the camera's gaze, disturbing the spectator's usually voyeuristic position. Ron Haselden, a sculptor by training, made a number of installations and films like *Tracking Cycles* (1975) which extended his concerns into the time-based domain. Annabel Nicolson performed live events incorporating, for example, projected film of a sewing machine in operation, which was simultaneously sewn into a real sewing-machine and re-projected. This is a neat linking of film to the technology which inspired the claw mechanism by which film is passed through both camera and projector. William Raban and Chris Welsby, both working in the landscape, used mechanical (e.g. time-lapse) and natural systems (e.g. the sun's movement in the sky) to structure such films as their collaborative twin-screen *River Yar* (1971-2). In his film *Monkey's Birthday* (1975) David Larcher used diaristic footage as a basis for a long, highly romantic meditation on light and colour that was substantially structured through re-photography (optical-printing). Besides being based around the LFMC, most of these artists shared a common preoccupation with the material qualities of film and with the nature of illusion, duration and the structuring of experience. To this extent they could be said to constitute a movement.[12]

David Hall must also be mentioned here. Although he moved rapidly from film-making into video in which area his pioneering work has been crucial in establishing a modernist video practice. In his uncompromising tapes and multi-screen installations he has engaged critically with broadcast television unlike the film-makers, most of whom have avoided a corresponding engagement with mainstream cinema.

Following the first phase of activity based around the LFMC, which reached a peak in the mid to late 70s, a new generation of film-maker's emerged who also had specific things in common. They were, principally: Steve Farrer, Penny Webb, Michael Maziere, Lucy Panteli, Rob Gawthrop, Joanna Millett, Will Milne and myself. Before discussing these people as a group two things have to be said. Firstly, there are many other film-makers of the same generation who were not film-makers at the time, or whose work falls outside the area under consideration. Secondly, the group itself is by no means homogenous. Farrer moved from a concern with material processes to poetic eroticism, Panteli from structural minimalism to ethnography. Penny Webb moved into experimental narrative, before giving up film to study philosophy. Milne, the most talented of the group and who never considered himself a Structuralist, abandoned film-making altogether in 1987.

However, all emerged in the late 1970s and were all taught by Gidal, Le Grice or both. Most importantly, all tried consciously to develop the formal possibilities suggested by the work made at the LFMC in the 60s and 70s. But Structural film and theory were by no means the only influence on these artists. All were at art school at a time when figurative painting had become almost unthinkable. Minimalist or anti-form sculpture, post-painterly abstraction, earthworks, body art, performance and conceptualism were the order of the day. Gidal's own work too, despite his anti-aestheticism, can be seen as a filmic counterpart to the use of repetitive and non-hierarchical structures which characterise much minimal sculpture to which he would have been exposed during his time in New York in the 1960s.[13] There was a turning away from the making of objects.[14] and a rejection of the gallery system which represented market values and the commodification of art. Many artists became interested in systems and process, and this came to be more important than any end-product, even among painters and sculptors.

This climate gave rise to a number of film performances which drew inspiration from works like Robert Morris's emblematic *Box with the sound of its own making* (1961); a wooden box containing a tape recorder which played a tape of the sound of the box being constructed.[15] At the Festival of Expanded Cinema, held at the Institute of Contemporary Arts (ICA) London, in 1976, Steve Farrer presented a performance called *Exposed* (1975). In a darkened auditorium he stapled sheets of photographic paper to a large board using a staple gun with a small torch attached. The paper was then processed in situ and the light turned on to reveal the results. Farrer went on to make cameraless films, notably *Ten Drawings* (1976) in which the imagery was produced by painting or drawing patterns onto large areas of film made up of strips of 16mm film laid out in rows. The strips were then joined together to form the film.

At the same festival, Rob Gawthrop presented a projection event *Eye of the Projector* (1975-6) which involved running a single strip of found-footage simultaneously through three projectors. During the event Gawthrop manipulated the imagery by removing a lens and holding it in different positions in front of the light beam. He also pulled the film off the projector claw so that the images became a distorted stream of coloured light. Lis Rhodes and Ian Kerr presented an ongoing process event called *C/CU/CUT OFF/FF/F.* This consisted of two one-hundred foot long hoops of film, one clear, the other black. The loops were projected side by side and allowed to drag along the floor. As the clear loop accumulated dirt and the black one scratches, they were periodically photocopied and the photocopies exhibited as part of the work.[16]

In addition to the various influences of the younger generation described above, politics was also an important factor in the cultural climate at this time. Gidal's writings continually stressed the political nature of representation, hence his absolutist position on the representation, finally, of anything, but especially women.

> Recent valorising of certain representations of women: ones which are again and again so close to the mystery, the secret, the unknown, 'yet' at the same time motherhood, the feminine, and the emotional as to make one wince at the representations and even more at the lack of superego amongst those producing and feeding on them. As no concrete historical materialist analysis or practice has existed for those who play with these images, we find ourselves confronted with profoundly reactionary archetypes covered by verbiage ostensibly denying this fact but in fact revelling in it. Examples could be found in different ways in the films of the Berwick Street Collective, The London Womens' Film Group, Oshima, Comolli, Akerman, Mulvey/Wollen, Le Grice etc.[17]

Gidal sees his work above all as political work on the signifier. Images never resolve themselves into firm representations, a strategy designed to force the viewer to confront his or her own easy and unselfconscious relationship to representation. All representation is by definition conservative in that it re-presents, that is, shows again, that which is already familiar, thus reinforcing prevailing attitudes and ideologies. For Gidal, a progressive film should present the viewer with new and hence difficult structures which force them to think about what they are looking at and their own role in that viewing process. Thus a self-reflexive viewer is engendered who cannot also then be a voyeur. Again this idea is not so far from Robert Morris's dictum that: 'the disorientating in Art is the as yet unperceived new structure'.[18] Morris and Gidal share an anti-aesthetic stance, in that neither is interested in questions of beauty, balance, composition and so on. They are concerned with form, perception and cognition, and with developing a rationalistic debate around these notions. But whereas Gidal couches his polemic in political terms, Morris has no explicit political programme. For all his anti-aestheticism, however, Gidal's films cannot but be experienced as aesthetic since, ironically, their very distance from mainstream cinema assures them an autonomy which permits them to be viewed as modernist art-works. For example, *Room Film 1973* (1973) was received and understood in England as a defiantly ascetic and an uncompromisingly difficult film. Yet the process of grasping the structural procedure employed in the film is as enriching as discerning the structural operations in a piece of music. The green cast and sensuous movement of the grain even moved some viewers to compare his work to that of Brakhage to whose romantic position Gidal was fiercely opposed.

The combative and puritanical tone of Gidal's and Le Grice's writings[19] found a ready audience and were enormously effective in determining the way in which their work was received. For a less combative later generation, though, it is their films, at least as much as the theories, which suggests a way of making cultural artefacts. These later films also share the seriousness of intent of much contemporary minimalist paintings and sculpture, and continue to owe as little to the banalities of the orthodox cinema as the work of the earlier generation. Conversely Gidal's own work has often contained attenuated references to cinema. His recent work, shot in Vienna, Prague and Egypt, displays an increasing fascination with locations, giving his work a certain emotional tone.[20]

In the late 1970s numerous women's groups and Troskyist parties were active, as were various political film-making groups. Collectives like Cinema Action and the Poster/Film Collective made grass-roots campaign films around specific issues and strikes like that at the Grunwick photo-processing plant in North London in 1978. At the other end of the spectrum was the work of the Berwick Street Collective and Peter Wollen and Laura Mulvey. The former's *Nightcleaners* (1975) began as a straight documentary about the pay and conditions of night-time office cleaners, but later various formal devices were introduced to try to break the conventional relationship between film and spectator. Mulvey

Silent Film – Michael Maziere (1982)

and Wollen's *Riddles of the Sphinx* (1976) started with a narrative about a woman's separation from her husband, her search for work, a nursery place for her son and her ensuing politicisation. The film has a pyramidal overall structure with a central section of thirteen circular pans. It was a self-proclaimed 'film of theory' which attempted to construct a feminist discourse out of a theoretical position compounded from marxism, semiology and psychoanalysis.[21]

In his earlier writings, Peter Wollen had argued for a 'polysemous' cinema in which different types of signs – spoken, written, drawn and photographic – would combine to render meanings that could do justice to the complexities of modern life. Jean-Luc Godard's film *Le Gai Savoir* (1968) was regarded as exemplary in this respect, while Structural film was held, by contrast, to be reductive and implicitly essentialist as for example in its eschewal of sound supposedly in a quest for visual purity.[22] Yet would one really want to argue that painting and music, basically 'mono-semous' art forms, are inferior to film? Or that Brakhage's films are impoverished by their not having soundtracks?

Despite a stifling atmosphere of political correctness occasioned by these debates in the late 1970s, the later generation of film-makers seem not to have been seriously deflected. Indeed, some of the most determinedly formal yet varied work was produced around this period, and will be discussed below.

The emergence of the quarterly magazine *Undercut* which was published by the London Film-makers' Co-operative from 1981 to 1990, helped to consolidate the role of the Co-op and its associated film-making. *Undercut* was primarily dedicated to film and video art, unlike *Screen*, hitherto a journal of high theory, or *Framework* which was concerned with identifying and discussing forms of cinema which were both popular and politically progressive. Lucy Panteli, Michael Maziere and Will Milne wrote reviews and manifestos for *Undercut* as did many other film-makers including Le Grice and Gidal.

Maziere, Panteli and Milne, along with Rob Gawthrop, were all students at the Royal College of Art in the late 1970s, where besides Gidal, the staff included Laura Mulvey, Steve Dwoskin and Ray Durgnat. They could be said to constitute a core grouping of later Structuralists, even if, like Milne, they could not be said to be wholehearted Gidalians. Gawthrop, however, undoubtedly was. In his prolific output – twelve films completed between 1979 and 1982 – he consistently treated the pro-filmic as a pretext for various kinds of temporal and structural operations, and the degeneration of the image, including the physical manipulation of the film-strip. Perhaps his most interesting film is

Distancing (1979) which in its complexity moves beyond much of his other work. The camera points at a rain-spattered window through which can be seen a plant, a head, houses, the sea and the horizon. Gawthrop pulls focus and aperture continuously throughout the fifteen minute film, so that the picture plane and its contents are shifted and transformed, with the objects appearing and disappearing out of the flux. The imagery is also superimposed on itself, slightly out of register, thickening the textures, yet at the same time, creating a sense of immateriality. Gawthrop erodes the transcendental place of the cardinal viewpoint whilst yet shooting from just such a fixed position.[23]

In most of her early films, Lucy Panteli uses simple pro-filmic events which are then subjected to various re-animation processes to foreground the material constructedness of the image, indeed any image. But the presence of women in a number of her works is clearly designed to bring the representation of women onto the agenda in a particularly acute form: can an ascetic, highly formal kind of film-making accommodate such representations, without simply perpetuating the ideological conditions within which such representations are embedded and understood? In *Photoplay* (1984) Panteli raises the stakes by portraying women in a variety of feminine pursuits: applying make-up, knitting etc. The film was shot by taking single-frame time exposures of about one second every second over very long periods. Thus there was temporal continuity in the shooting, but a resulting film that compresses time by a factor of about twenty-four. *Photoplay* is a beautiful and extraordinary film, not least in the Herculean task of shooting it, and it shows how far a formalist approach can be pushed. But whether it can be said to be feminist work is open to question. One has to ask whether what is represented can adequately be analysed through the use of a formal procedure that is uniformly indifferent to the particular imagery in each section. What is really required is an analysis at the level of content, and this is what the film shies away from, since that could lead back into conventional modes of film-making, and a restoration of precisely the passive spectator that the film sets out to challenge.

Perhaps Panteli recognised this paradox herself, because *Photoplay* was the last of its kind made by her. Her most recent *Time Over Again* (1991) is concerned with cultural identity – Panteli is Maltese but was born and raised in London – and her return to 'the collective identity of our motherline'.

Michael Maziere[24] produced two of his strongest films while at the Royal College of Art: *Untitled* (1980) and *Colourwork* (1981). The black and white *Untitled* explores two adjacent spaces; a room and the street outside as seen from the room. Through an exhaustive use of focus-pulls, pans, tilts and superimposed zooms, Maziere draws out the innumerable ways of seeing these two spaces and their interpenetration. Sometimes the room is an interior world illuminated with light from the single window. At other times it is a blackened void and the window a screen. At other moments the window permits a view out. The restless camera movements successively redefine the exterior space, reminding us that seeing is relative. Since each sweep of the camera displaces its predecessor the stability of the cardinal viewpoint is undermined. From a process/systems perspective the film sets in interactive motion a number of elements – room, window, exterior, camera, light and darkness. In Structuralist terms, the continual redrawing and effective destabilising of the spaces causes the viewer to reassess constantly their perception of what is being depicted. Hence the viewer is drawn into an active engagement with the film.

In contrast, *Colourwork* is sumptuous and architectonic. Whereas the camera movements in *Untitled* are often loose, in *Colourwork* they are taut and geometric. The relationship between camera moves and edit points is central. The film is composed of domestic interiors in London and Provence. Most of the shots have some degree of precise circular movement, and each shot is repeated twice, a device which creates rhythm and stresses the particular form of a shot over its content. Repetition also invites us to see the shot as a shot, and not primarily as a representation, an effect first explored by Léger and Murphy in *Le Ballet Mécanique.* In addition to these ternary rhythmic units, larger rhythmic sequences occur when the camera movement in the second-repeat of one sequence is picked up and continued by the motion of the incoming shot. Sometimes these shots are spatially contiguous as well, but often the contiguity is produced by the camera movements alone. With these two options Maziere works through a number of variations in which different combinations of full and partial spatial contiguity and/or full or partial contiguity of speed and direction of camera movement are possible.

The way in which the second-repeat sometimes continues to form the subject of the next shot, is reminiscent of the system of staggered repeats used by Gidal in his *Room Film 1973.* But although *Colourwork* draws on this and other aspects of the avant-garde tradition it has distinct qualities of its own. Not least it contributes to the genre of 'room films' which were a feature of much younger generation Structuralist-influenced work of the early 1980s which I'll discuss later. Many of Gidal's films were shot in rooms, but he was careful to neutralise them, removing any objects which had obvious connotations. The room then became a dimly lit arena of which low-powered signifieds could not flood the working of the signifiers. Despite the strong Structural character of *Colourwork* the room is very much a personal space, and Maziere takes obvious pleasure in colour and the qualities of light. Although the work is not autobiographical the room is much more than a mere pretext, a convenient uninhabited space in which to manipulate forms.

Le Grice also set his later experimental narrative films in domestic spaces, but has only ever discussed them in terms of their theoretical ambitions.[25] *Emily – Third Party Speculation* (1979) is set in a dark, exotic interior and features the film-maker, his wife and various small domestic events: a table being laid, a record put on etc. But for Le Grice 'the film revolves around a primary cinematic problem of the psychological space moved through in the spectator's attempt to construct the film's relations'.[26] The process of identification and the 'fugitive moment' when attention shifts from one event to another in a narrative. The specificity of the events and the moods the film creates through its use of location and music are secondary for Le Grice. His silence on these aspects of his work is remarkable, especially since four of his most substantial films were made in his own home; *After Lumiere – l'arroseur arrose* (1974), *Blackbird Descending – tense alignment* (1977), *Emily* and *Finnegans Chin* (1981). For Gidal, Le Grice's later works are nothing other than a return to cinema, to illusionism.[27] But for other film-makers who felt hampered by Gidal's absolutist position, the evolving scope of Le Grice's aesthetic opened up new possibilities for working with representation and narrative yet retaining a critical attitude to it.

Two such film-makers who consciously owed more to Le Grice's project were Tim Bruce and Penny Webb. At the same time as Structural film-making dominated activities at the Co-op, a number of film-makers based loosely around the Royal College of Art were making so-called deconstructed narrative films inspired by the work of Jean-Marie Straub and Daniele Huillet.[28] Bruce and Webb's work straddled the two camps. The former's *Corrigan, having recovered* (1979) had characters, a rudimentary storyline and music. But the work was not realised as a conventional film. Instead these elements were distributed among several screens to form a large installation. Webb's *The Young Girl in Blue* (1979) was a more conventional single-screen work. A cryptic and desultory story is told in a minimalist style characterised by long-takes, with many scenes devoid of the human activity which usually drives a narrative.

Despite the growing interest in work of this nature, Le Grice himself shied away from developing the area. Or perhaps he would say that he had completed the programme of work that he began in 1966. It was not his intention to make self-sufficient artworks, but to create a viewing experience in which the spectator became aware of his/her role in that experience. To that extent the films themselves were simply a means to an end, if not expendable. He saw this as a philosophical endeavour, discussing it in terms of how knowledge is possible and in terms of the viewer's immediate experience of audio visual phenomena. Thus Le Grice was not particularly amenable to 'personal' or expressionistic film-making, although he was not against representation as long as those representations

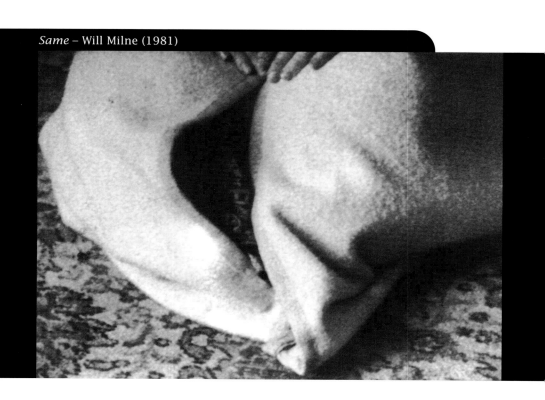

Same – Will Milne (1981)

occurred within a critical context. *Finnegans Chin* brings full circle an abiding concern with the role of the spectator that began with *Castle One* in 1966. This was a found-footage film that was shown with a powerful light-bulb hanging by the screen which periodically flashed on, obliterating the screen's image and illuminating the audience. After 1982 he made nothing until 1990, when he returned with a programme of abstract, computer generated, moving image work.

The challenge to develop the formal possibilities suggested by Le Grice's pioneering work has not been really taken up by later generations[29] who have in any case been exposed to new and different influences.

The problem is how to make cinematography expressive (technology emotional); it wasn't invented for that purpose. In theatrical movies the actors carry the can while the technology underscores the performance; we watch the past rather than the present of the actual film. How to draw attention to the image and time as themselves, make them desirable, draw you in, fascinate you, get under your retina.[30]

These remarks by Will Milne perfectly express his artistic position, both in relation to Structural film and to mainstream cinema, and seem to owe as much to Robert Bresson as they do to Structuralist thinking. Like Maziere and Gawthrop, Milne also studied at the RCA in the late 1970s. But whereas the former embraced wholeheartedly the teaching and example of Gidal, Milne kept a critical distance. As his remarks indicate, he shared with his contemporaries a desire for self-reflexivity in the viewer and a foregrounding of the forms and materials of film. He was unhappy, however, with the relentlessly intellectualised approach of Gidal and Le Grice, whose tendency was always to dismiss or rationalise away any talk of beauty or poetry in their work.

Nevertheless, Milne certainly produced his most structural and ascetic work whilst at the RCA. *Parts* (1975) consists of two black and white shots of five minutes each. The first is an extreme close-up of a finger tip hovering over and sometimes touching a flat surface. The second is a quadruple exposure of a figure seated in a room. Both shots are virtually abstract – the finger tip and surface in silhouette, the figure obscure and shimmering – so that interpreting the image becomes a central task for the viewer.

Mesopotamian Background (1977) takes as its text the Encyclopaedia Britannia's entry on Mesopotamia. The text is spoken by female actors and non-actors in various locations. But although it has these seemingly conventional ingredients, the work as a whole is rigorously organised.

Short Film Series – Guy Sherwin (1976-)

length of shot, actress, height of camera, distance of camera, number of words per shot all permutated against each other, and each take bracketed by a ritual of dissolve, focus-up, frame up/frame off, focus-off, dissolve. The idea was to void the text, acting, montage etc. of drama, to emphasise the drama of decision and technology meeting the given of objects, bodies, spaces.[31]

The first shot in the film is thirty seconds long, and each successive shot is a second shorter than its predecessor until the last, which is ten seconds. Milne describes the film partly as an experiment to see what gets notices of all this structuring. Also: 'It was an attempt to allow the film to make itself, to keep the author's taste out of it, to show the way the system works'.[32] These remarks, as much as they are obviously Cageian, are consistent with the prevailing systems in sculpture and painting, understood as a way of bypassing decisions made on the basis of taste. For Milne though, the film was an experiment, and is untypical of his work as a whole.

Two other films – *Christ of Feathers* (1976) and *Same* (1981) contributed to the emerging sub-genre of 'room films' in which, increasingly, the room becomes the setting for small human actions, domestic scenes and oblique depictions of nudity. The genre was consolidated by Milne's screening of a selection of such films at the LFMC in 1980 when he showed his work along with Brakhage's *Anticipation of the Night* (1959), Deborah Lowensberg's *What Just For Me?* (1979), my own *Guesswork* (1979) and New York based Canadian Vincent Grenier's *Closer Outside* (1979-81).[33] As I've already mentioned, the 'room film' arises, to some degree, out of Gidal's use of interior spaces.[34] However in 'room films' the rooms are often personal spaces.

Gidal's negative aesthetic is given a positive turn. Grain, colour, the play of light on objects and near-abstractions created by extreme close-ups – all regular elements in Gidal's films – are highlighted and explored as ends in themselves.

The decline of the Structural film can be attributed to a number of causes. By the mid-80s the New Romantic film-makers such as John Maybury and Cerith Wyn Evans dominated the area. Their emergence as purveyors of an aestheticism owing much to figures like Cocteau, Kenneth Anger and Derek Jarman, also coincided with the general return to surrealism and the image in the fine arts with the arrival of the Italian 'Trans Avant-Garde' painters Sandro Chia, Francesco Clemente and Mimmo Palladino. The LFMC's acquisition of an optical printer, allowing film-makers to slow-down, colour and process their imagery, led to gratuitous image manipulation and concomitant conceptual weakness in films of the period.

Beyond Le Grice's schematic later films, a handful of film-makers have continued to make valuable work which if not itself Structuralist, shares common aesthetic roots. Guy Sherwin's *Short Film Series* (1976-79) is an exquisite exploration of the visual phenomena generated from the interaction of light, seemingly solid objects and the mechanical and optical peculiarities of the film camera. John Smith's films *The Girl Chewing Gum* (1979), *The Black Tower* (1987) and *Slow Glass* (1991) reveal the ephemeral and paradoxical nature of the visual world and the way language structures our understanding of what we see. Both Smith and Sherwin had their roots in Structural film as colleagues of David Parsons at the then North East London Polytechnic. Their work retains a formal and conceptual rigour that is very much a product of the English avant-garde film culture of the 1970s.

In retrospect, it can be seen that Gidal's and Le Grice's anti-cinema polemics could not by themselves constitute a self-sufficient artistic theory, and this partly explains the decline of Structural film. However, their theories can usefully serve as a set of background beliefs to sustain a film-making which reinstates to its programme the investing of perception, exploring the peculiarities of the human eye, the experience of time and movement and their complex relationship to film technology.

NOTES

1   On the 18th June 1994 when Brakhage was part of a two-day symposium 'Art into Cinema' National Film Theatre, London.

2   P. Adams Sitney *Visionary Film: The American Avant-Garde 1943-1978* 2nd ed, Oxford University Press, 1970 p370

3   Ibid p369

4   Ibid p369

5   For a discussion of the differences between American and English formulations of Structural film theory and practice see Michael O'Pray 'Framing Snow' *Afterimage* no 11, 1982-3, pp51-65

6   Peter Gidal 'The Anti-Narrative' *Screen* vol 20 no 2 Summer 1979 p73.

7   Peter Gidal 'Theory and Definition of Structural/Materialist Film' in *Structural Film Anthology* ed Peter Gidal, 2nd ed, British Film Institute, London, 1978 p1.

8   Malcolm Le Grice 'Towards a Temporal Economy' *Screen* vol 20 nos 3/4 Winter 1979 p62

9   See especially Gidal op cit and Le Grice ibid.

10 Le Grice ibid p59

11 Gidal (1979) op cit p75

12 For writings by and about this generation see Gidal (1978) op cit and Le Grice's *Abstract Film and Beyond.*

13 See Peter Gidal *Andy Warhol: Films and Paintings*, Studio Vista, 1970 for a discussion of repetition and duration in relation to Warhol.

14 On the move away from object-making see Lucy Lippard *Six Years: The Dematerialisation of the Art Object*, Praeger, New York, 1973

15 Robert Morris also made a number of films at this time, *Gas Station* (1969) and *Mirror Displacement* (1970) are notable for the manner in which they engage with questions of cinematic space and perceptual processes.

16 Interestingly two artists virtually unknown as film-makers, Derek Jarman and Peter Logan, showed work of a very different character from the dominating aesthetic. Jarman showed a three-screen Super 8 film *The Art of Mirrors* (a later extended version of which became *In the Shadow of the Sun* (1981)). Logan projected Super 8 footage of the television sports programme Match of the Day onto a three dimensional arrangement of gauze screens.

17 Gidal (1979) op cit p77

18 Robert Morris *Continuous Project Altered Daily*, MIT Press, 1995, p82

19 Besides writings already cited see Le Grice 'Kurt Kren' in *Studio International* vol 190 no 978 Nov/Dec 1975 pp183-188; *Abstract Film and Beyond* Studio Vista, 1977; Problematizing the Spectator Placement in Film *Undercut* no 1 1981 pp13-18 and Gidal *Materialist Film*, Macmillan, 1989

20 For a brief discussion of Gidal's engagement with cinematic devices see my 'Peter Gidal's Influence in the 1980s *Undercut* no 19 Autumn 1990

21 For a critique of the film's portrayal of women see Judith Williamson *Consuming Passions*, Marion Boyars, 1986 p83

22 See Peter Wollen *Signs and Meanings in the Cinema*, Secker & Warburg, 1972 p154 and his 'The Two Avant-Gardes' in this volume.

23 A similar strategy is found in my own film *Only at First* (1991).

24 Maziere originally studied at what was then Trent Polytechnic where he made *A Sentimental Journey* (1978) and *Clear Cut* (1979).

25 See Le Grice 'Problematising the Spectator Placement in Film' op cit

26 Le Grice in *London Film-makers' Co-op Catalogue*, 1993, p84

27 Gidal 'On Finnegans Chin' *Undercut* no 5 1983 p21

28 On Straub/Huillet see Richard Roud *Straub*, Viking, New York, 1972.

29 William Raban and Marilyn Halford's film *Black and Silver*, made about the same time as *Finnegans Chin*, was another kind of attempt by formalist artists to break into experimental narrative.

30 Will Milne 'My film work and theoreticals' *Undercut* no 6 Winter 1982 p17

31 Will Milne *London Film-makers' Catalogue* op cit p84

32 Milne *Undercut* op cit p19

33 See Michael O'Pray 'Movies, Mania and Masculinity' *Screen* vol 23 no 5 November-December 1982 for a discussion of the body and space in relation to Milne's, Lowensberg's and my own films.

34 In 1983 Michael Maziere also curated at the LFMC a similar programme of films which by now were explicitly presented as 'room films'.

Imagining October – Derek Jarman, 1985

PETER WOLLEN

The Last New Wave

MODERNISM IN THE BRITISH FILMS
OF THE THATCHER ERA

First published in *British Cinema and Thatcherism,* UCL Press, London, 1973

Independent filmmakers of the eighties reacted strongly against the effects of Thatcherism. They responded to the imposition of market criteria in every sector of society, to political authoritarianism, to the 'two nations' project of Thatcherism, and to the leading role of the City, in films as various as Peter Greenaway's *The Cook, the Thief, His Wife, and Her Lover* (1989), Derek Jarman's *The Last of England* (1987), Terry Gilliam's *Brazil* (1985), Stephen Frears's and Hanif Kureishi's *Sammy and Rosie Get Laid* (1988), Mike Leigh's *High Hopes* (1988), Laura Mulvey's and Peter Wollen's *Crystal Gazing* (1980), and Reece Auguiste's *Twilight City* (1989). Paradoxically, these are all London films, precisely because of the success of Thatcher's polarization of the country between North and South – a polarization that, as shown in the films, is doubled within the metropolis itself. Their roots can be traced back to the sixties – to the art world, the satire boom, experimental theater, and the post-1968 avant-garde. It was in these areas that a modernist impulse had finally made itself felt in British culture and had eventually combined with an emphasis on the visual dimension of television, theater, and film. Together, these films provide a definitive picture of the Thatcherization of London.

Negatively, Thatcherism has aimed to destroy the postwar Keynesian settlement, dismantle the public services provided by the state, and eliminate obtrusive foci of political opposition. Positively, Thatcherism combines three elements: (1) an economic 'unregulated market' neoliberalism, (2) a politically neoconservative authoritarianism, and (3) a social 'two nations' project, dividing the country geographically, between North and South, and socially, in terms of the labor market, between a de-unionized 'peripheral' sector and a 'core' company union sector. The 'two nations' project, of course, hits ethnic minorities especially hard and encourages a sharp division between 'inner city' and suburb. Thatcherism is a modernizing movement in a very specific sense. It aims to modernize the finance, service, communications, and international sectors of the economy, but not domestic manufacturing industry or civil society. New 'core' industries, largely dependent on international capital, are consolidated in the South, while the North of the country is left as a peripheral, decaying hinterland. The South, organized around the City of London, traditionally the hegemonic pole of the economy, is increasingly decoupled from domestic manufacturing industry. Thus Thatcherism, terrified that the City will lose even more of its world role, given the continuing relative decline of the British economy, has an Atlantic rather than a European outlook in its international policy and aims to provide the point of entry into Europe for American and Japanese capital. Money rather than goods are paramount. Socially and visually, the citadels of international capital are abruptly juxtaposed with the decay of London's old industries and docklands.[1]

The Thatcher years provoked a long-delayed efflorescence of British film, still largely unrecognized in Britain itself. It can be seen, I believe, as a 'British New Wave', coming long after the idea of a New Wave had crumbled away in most other European countries. The first New Wave, of course, exploded on the world from France in the 'Miraculous Year' of 1959, which launched Truffaut's *Les Quatre Cents Coups,* Resnais's *Hiroshima Mon Amour,* and Chabrol's *Les Cousins.* Godard's *A Bout de Souffle* followed in 1960, also the year of *L'Avventura,* the first film of Antonioni's trilogy. This, in turn, drew attention to the work of Pasolini and, soon, Bertolucci. A few years later, Fassbinder, Syberberg, and Wenders were grouped together as the core of a somewhat belated 'German New Wave'. Since then critics gathered at festivals around the world have sought out 'New Waves' wherever they could, broadening their net to include the Third World and hailing the Brazilian, African, and Chinese 'New Waves". No one thought of looking again at Britain, which, having missed the bus in the sixties, could hardly expect a second chance. Besides, the British were notoriously unvisual, unartistic, and uncinematic. What was it Truffaut had said? 'Aren't the words "Britain" and "Cinema" incompatible?'.[2]

It has been argued that the 'Angry Young Men' films of 1959-63 were the 'British New Wave,' rather than the 'Jeune Cinéma Anglais', as the French, who certainly ought to have known, dubbed it at the time.[3] Yet surely to call these films New Wave is both inappropriate and misleading. First, the idea of a New Wave was intimately linked to the project of directorial 'authorship.' A good case can be made for Lindsay Anderson as a bilious but authentic 'auteur' (something he himself might well deny in a fume of irascibility), but nobody has made a serious claim for the auteurist credentials of Reisz, Richardson, Schlesinger, and others. In fact, it would be much more plausible to argue for the producer-director duo of Relph and Dearden as auteurs, filmmakers whose 'social problem' cycle, beginning with the *Blue Lamp* in 1950 and continuing through, via *Sapphire* (1959) and *Victim* (1961), to *A Place to Go* in 1963, preceded and paralleled the work of the Angry Young Men. Moreover, in 'daring' to deal with race and homosexuality, for whatever headline-grabbing reasons, they showed greater courage, prescience, and, indeed, political sense than their more celebrated and supposedly more progressive and innovative younger colleagues.

Second, the idea of a New Wave involved putting film first and not subordinating it to literature or theater, as Truffaut argued in his notorious polemic against adaptation in *Arts* magazine. The Angry Young Men films, however, plainly put film second. Their success was directly derived from the success of the original plays and novels by Osborne, Amis, Braine, and Sillitoe. *Look Back in Anger, Room at the Top, The Entertainer, A Taste of Honey, Saturday Night and Sunday Morning,* and *The Loneliness of the Long Distance Runner* came out in their original forms between May 1956 and September 1959. The film versions, which came out after a three-year interval, between 1959 and 1962, clearly depended on the prepublicity and acclaim already generated by their literary sources for their initial impact. Moreover, Woodfall films, beginning with *Look Back in Anger (1959),* set a pattern by having the original writers first collaborate on the film scripts with professional scriptwriters and then write them entirely. Osborne, Sillitoe, and Delaney all wrote their own scripts for the film adaptations of their work. The same procedure was followed with *This Sporting Life* (1963), written by the author of the novel, David Storey (and directed by Lindsay Anderson), and with John Schlesinger's *Billy Liar* (1963), written by Keith Waterhouse and Willis Hall, based on their own play of Waterhouse's novel! This film of an adaptation of an adaptation is about as far from Truffaut's ideal of auteurism as you can get.[4]

Third, both critics and the directors themselves explicitly justified the Angry Young Men films in terms of 'realism.' Their attitude reflected an old shibboleth and plaint of the British cinema establishment, both in production and reception, best summed up by Michael Balcon's programmatic preference for 'realism' over 'tinsel'.[5] This system of value, though most strongly entrenched on the Left, ran all the way across the political spectrum. For the Right, as with the Left, the aesthetic preference for realism was bound up with nationalism. 'Tinsel,' of course, was identified with Hollywood escapism and, in contrast, realism evoked local pride and sense of community. It meant showing ourselves honestly to ourselves, rather than indulging in other people's alien and deceptive fantasies. British critics praised films they liked in terms of their realism and damned those they did not as escapist trash. The French New Wave, however, aimed to transcend this shallow antinomy. The third term that made this possible was, of course, 'modernism.' The films of Resnais and Godard, even when adaptations, placed themselves clearly in a modernist tradition, as did Truffaut's crucial *Jules et Jim* (1962). Resnais, to take the most obvious example, collaborated with writers like Robbe-Grillet and Duras. The *Cahiers* group followed the path blazed by the Nouveau Roman and recognized Jean Cocteau as their godfather. Yet in Britain filmmakers fetishized the second-rate novels of regionalists, realists, and reactionaries.

The history of modernism in Europe followed a definite geographical pattern, which reflected an underlying historical reality.[6] The more a country felt the ambition to catch up economically and culturally, the more an aggressively avant-garde section of its intelligentsia embraced and radicalized a version of modernism. After the collapse of the old absolutist regimes, avant-garde artists often rejected the search for new modes of personal expression in favor of a depersonalized rationalism or functionalism. They attempted to subordinate the arts to industrial and technological needs and imperatives, and to merge the artist with the masses. Thus in backward Russia, the avant-garde moved rapidly from symbolism to futurism and then, after the impact of the October Revolution, to constructivism. In Italy futurism developed its own technocratic ideology and, in Germany, expressionism gave way to the Bauhaus. In France, where the ancien régime had been toppled more than a century before, cubism was followed by the much weaker current of purism, around Le Corbusier, but also, more significantly, by surrealism. The surrealists, like the constructivists or the later Bauhaus artists, lined up on the left politically, and yet reacted with hostility to the norms of modern industrial development, unlike their counterparts in revolutionary Russia or Germany. In Britain, after the brief flurry of vorticism, modernism never took root in any lasting way.

Britain, of course, was both the homeland of the Industrial Revolution, the pioneer of manufacturing capitalism, and the European country with the most remote and attenuated experience of absolutism. Modernism, in its pure form, appealed to very few in Britain, especially not in England. England's most committed modernists were very often expatriates – Eliot, Pound, H.D., Wyndham Lewis. In the visual arts, vorticism rapidly dissolved and modern currents were smoothly amalgamated into the English landscape tradition, as in the work of Ben Nicholson or Henry Moore. A mild and heavily romanticized anglicization of surrealism surfaced briefly and then sputtered to a halt. In the world of literature and in taste-setting journalism, there was a bloodless transfer of power to the Bloomsbury group, within the traditional intelligentsia itself, and an increasingly emollient modernism was

Vertical Feature Remake – Peter Greenaway (1979)

assimilated into the ongoing high culture with hardly a break. Indeed, the most effective protagonists of modern literature – Eliot and Leavis – argued for modernism in frankly traditionalist terms. Far from wanting a break with the past, they saw modernism as the culmination of a long national literary history. This history now needed only to be reassessed retrospectively, rather than brusquely overthrown. Moreover, modernism was treated as something that had already happened and been absorbed, rather than as an ongoing project.[7]

Modernism first impinged on British film culture during the silent period with the London Film Society and the journal *Close Up*. But the coming of sound quickly wiped out these tender plants, as it did much stronger film avant-gardes elsewhere. The *Close Up* circle, around the writers Bryher and H.D., produced Kenneth MacPherson's *Borderline* (1930), financed by Bryher (then married to MacPherson), and starring H.D., alongside Paul and Eslanda Robeson. It remains the one outstanding British avant-garde film of the period. However, *Close Up* folded shortly thereafter, and its contributors lost heart and dispersed.[8] Meanwhile, after the collapse of the London Film Society, its moving spirit, the irrepressible Iris Barry, left for New York in 1930.[9] In New York she met Philip Johnson at a cocktail party and soon afterward, she was hired by Alfred Barr to run the new Museum of Modern Art's film program. Thus the modernist impulse was transferred from London to America, where the Museum played a crucial role in the survival of avant-garde film through the thirties, enabling it to resurface again in the forties. In Britain, of course, this did not happen.

The Film Society's most significant outcome was its impact on Alfred Hitchcock, a habitual and doubtless punctual attender at screenings. There Hitchcock not only mingled with the cultural elite but also absorbed modernist aesthetic ideas, which he later attempted to nurture within narrative film. Hitchcock experimented with sound in his first talking picture, *Blackmail* (1929), but soon retreated into conformity. Nonetheless, once he felt his career in the industry was secure, both in Britain and subsequently in the United States, he cunningly contrived a place for experimental ideas within commercial genre films – the Salvador Dali dream sequence in *Spellbound* (1945), the ten-minute takes in *Rope* (1948, produced by another Film Society alumnus, Sidney Bernstein), the 'pure cinema' project of *Rear Window* (1954), the montage murder sequence in *Psycho* (1960), and so on. Hitchcock's collaborator, Ivor Montagu, whom he met through the Film Society, also worked with Eisenstein, and many echoes of Eisenstein appear in Hitchcock's own work. But, in general terms, Hitchcock seems to have drawn the conclusion that modernist experiments were best contrived as a kind of illicit contraband, which he could smuggle in and secretly enjoy, while lapping up the praise and the dollars for his success within the mainstream of the industry.

During the thirties, the surviving vestiges of twenties modernism were channelled into the state-sponsored British documentary movement. John Grierson, a Scot, remained more open to modernism than other British producers and hired coworkers (like Alberto Cavalcanti, a Brazilian, and Len Lye, a New Zealander) who had impeccable experimental film credentials: Cavalcanti's *Rien que les Heures* (1926) was a landmark of the French avant-garde and Lye had made his abstract film *Tusalava* for the London Film Society in 1928. Nonetheless, the main drift of Grierson's project was to subordinate modernism (in its Russian form) to realism and to national propaganda. Grierson was impressed by Eisenstein's vision of an epic, silent cinema based on the masses and achieving its dramatic effects through formal means rather than character identification, and he believed it could be transposed to fit British documentary and propaganda film. Grierson's documentaries aimed to represent the society at large rather than particular individuals. They were meant to inform rather than entertain. In this context, he could draw productively from Eisenstein and Pudovkin. Similarly, other modernists could have a role to play within his team. Thus, in this unlikely setting were to be found artists like Lye, W. H. Auden (who wrote the voiceover for *Night Mail*, 1935), and Humphrey Jennings (a chief organizer of the London surrealist exhibition of 1936).[10]

To critics at the time, Grierson's efforts seemed to combine the realism they desired with a prudent preservation of modernist elements in an acceptable, marginal role. Meanwhile, Alexander Korda became the standard bearer for narrative film in Britain, launching a series of costume dramas celebrating the popular high spots of British history and a cycle of extravagant imperialist epics, mainly directed by his brother, Zoltan Korda.[11] Korda's initial success with *The Private Life of Henry VIII* (1933) sprang from a canny combination of grandiose costume spectacle with music-hall comedy, but he was never able to repeat it, and his backers, Prudential Insurance, abruptly withdrew their support in 1937. Korda, however, did succeed in inspiring the British cinema world with the idea that they could and should set their sights on Hollywood as a model to be emulated. He pointed the way toward Rank's brave attempt to take on Hollywood after the war and, more recently, the pathetic false dawn of David Puttnam. Meanwhile, British cinema continued to churn out a series of 'quota quickies': George Formby vehicles and vernacular potboilers for the domestic audience. But when the deadly grip of heritage drama and pierhead comedy finally broke down during the 1939-45 war, it was romanticism, and not realism, that carried the day: whether the operatic Technicolor romanticism of the Archers and Gainsborough or the contorted black-and-white 'man-on-the-run' romanticism of the 'spiv' film and Carol Reed.[12]

The war years saw a revival of English romanticism in response to the need for an idealized reaffirmation of British history and shared values (as perceived within the dominant ideology) and, on the other hand, for release into fantasy and dream to relieve the stress, hardship, and agony of war.[13] During the war, film production was necessarily limited, but nonetheless the national mood is much better conveyed by the visual ambition and expansive romanticism of Olivier's *Henry V* (1944) than by the restrained grittiness of Coward and Lean's *In Which We Serve* (1942), however much the critics may have welcomed the realism they felt that it conveyed. After the war was won, still sheltered from American competition, British cinema blossomed. This period saw not only Powell's and Pressburger's trilogy of *Black Narcissus* (1947), *The Red Shoes* (1948), and *Gone to Earth* (1950), in which a series of intensely desirous women are thwarted and finally plunge over the edge to their death, but also Carol Reed's trilogy of *Odd Man Out* (1947), *The Fallen Idol* (1948), and *The Third Man* (1949), in which appealingly desperate heroes are caught in paranoid labyrinths of pursuit and betrayal.

It is important to stress the strength of this 'new romanticism,' as the parallel movement in painting and poetry is called, because it partly explains the success of the Angry Young Men films in the next decade. In 1945 the top box-office film was *The Seventh Veil,* a sublimely over-the-top drama of female desire, classical music, and psychoanalysis. The same year, Cavalcanti, having left Grierson's documentary unit, made a small masterpiece of the grotesque in *Dead of Night* and followed this up, in 1947, with *They Made Me a Fugitive,* the definitive expressionist 'man-on-the-run' film. Thus even a hero of 'documentary realism' showed himself the master of 'docklands romanticism' (along with Robert Hamer and *It Always Rains on Sundays,* 1947). British films, none of them remotely 'realist,' dominated the domestic box office for four straight years, until American political and economic power became irresistible and the British finally capitulated to Washington arm-twisting and a Hollywood boycott in 1948.[14] Both *The Third Man* and *Gone To Earth* were coproductions with Selznick and, apart from them, the most impressive films from 1949 onward were Hitchcock's transatlantic *Under Capricorn* (1949), Dassin's *Night and the City* (1950), and Huston's series of 'runaway productions' beginning with *The African Queen* (1952). The stage was now set for the critics at last to welcome a truly 'realist' counterblast to Hollywood, one that simultaneously reacted against the romanticism and aestheticism of earlier British film.

However, the Angry Young Men were not the only cultural countercurrent of the fifties. In 1956, the same year that *Look Back in Anger* was produced at the Royal Court Theatre (May 8), the exhibition *This Is Tomorrow* opened at the Whitechapel Gallery (August 8).[15] This was the culmination of the work of the Independent Group of artists, architects, and critics and the emblematic beginning of British pop art. Both the Angry Young Men and the Independent Group, founded in 1952, reacted strongly against the diluted modernism of the traditional intelligentsia, a decaying amalgam of Bloomsbury and Cold War pieties. However, while the Angry Young Men turned back toward a provincial Little Englandism, the Independent Group openly welcomed American consumer culture in their struggle against the English countryside and the villa in Tuscany, celebrating science fiction, Hollywood movies, tailfins, and advertising. The Angry Young Men were resentfully anti-American, although they did energize their English populism with a taste for traditional jazz, uncontaminated either by Tin Pan Alley or by post-bebop modernism. 'Trad' enlivened the sound tracks of Reisz's *Momma Don't Allow* (1955) and Richardson's *Look Back in Anger* (1959). Visitors to *This Is Tomorrow,* on the other hand, were greeted by a giant Robbie the Robot (from the sci-fi movie *Forbidden Planet)* and a wall montage celebrating CinemaScope. A leading proponent of the Independent Group's work, Lawrence Alloway, went on to become a kind of godfather to the auteurist film magazine, *Movie,* in the early sixties.

Pop art was a way to outflank the dominant elite culture by turning simultaneously to popular consumer culture and to the avant-garde tradition. Reyner Banham, for instance, carefully placed pop technophilia in the context of the modern movement, and Richard Hamilton, the pioneer pop artist, turned back to Marcel Duchamp as a revered ancestor. Pop broke through to a wider cultural audience with the 1961 appearance of a new phalanx of artists, the Young Contemporaries, encouraged by Alloway, and then Ken Russell's benchmark television show, *Pop Goes the Easel,* the following year. In retrospect, we see that the nonexistent British 'New Wave' of the time would have been much more closely linked to pop than to the Angry Young Men. Pop prefigured the sixties transformation of British culture. When the transformation came, however, it was expatriates who showed the way, at least as far as the cinema was concerned: Richard Lester, especially with *The Knack* (1965); Joseph Losey, who made *Modest Blaise* (1966); and Antonioni, whose *Blow-Up* (1967) became the archetypal film of the decade. These directors aligned themselves much more closely with their French counterparts. Their scripts derived from absurdism rather than realism – Harold Pinter or the Goon Show. Local directors appeared very late in the decade – Cammell's and Roeg's *Performance* was shot in 1968, but its distributors cravenly delayed its release until 1970. Alongside Roeg, John Boorman and Ken Russell both developed into 'auteurs,' but basically they were neoromantics (low-key and high-key, respectively), clearly anti-Kitchen Sink, but only incidentally modernist.[16]

We can better see the long-term importance of the sixties for British film in the subsequent work of Derek Jarman and Peter Greenaway. Both went to art school in this period, Jarman after getting a literature degree at London University, in deference to his family, and Greenaway in preference to going to university, in defiance of his family. Jarman and Greenaway both set out to make films within the visual arts tradition. The dominant painters in Jarman's world were gay – David Hockney and Patrick Procktor. He was also close to Ossie Clarke on the fashion scene, which interlocked with the art world during the sixties. Hockney's significance, of course, sprang not only from his success as a painter, but also from his public declaration of homosexuality and its increasingly crucial presence in his art. Jarman himself, however, was not a pop painter, but a landscapist who moved toward abstraction. His early paintings show monoliths on English 'west country' hills – descendants of Paul Nash or Henry Moore. Jarman is deeply attached to the landscape around Swanage in Dorset (which appears many times in his films), where he spent many childhood holidays and whose unique features Paul Nash also celebrated in his surrealist paintings. Jarman's own landscape tour de force at Prospect Cottage on Dungeness, a garden of Elizabethan flowers, stones, and driftwood, over which looms a massive nuclear power station, recreates the surrealist world of Chirico, with the respect for the 'genius loci' always felt by Nash. There is a lasting tension in his work between a delirious neoromantic Englishness and a pop modernism, always in touch with 'street culture.' His two influential teachers at university were Eric Mottram, who introduced him to William Burroughs's *Naked Lunch,* and Niklaus Pevsner, who directed him to Gothic cathedrals, Lincoln, Canterbury, or Ely. The eerie elegiac tone of his recent films has its roots in this metaphysical historicism and in his deeply ambivalent nostalgia for childhood, fed by an intransigent anger and a will-to-resist rooted in gay culture.[17]

In his films, rather than his paintings, Derek Jarman first articulated the gay world in which he lived, its tastes, routines, extravagances, and crises. Filmmaking began for him as a personal art of home movies, strongly contrasted with his professional work as a set designer for Ken Russell. The crucial turning point came when he turned down Russell's invitation to design *Tommy* (1975) and determined instead to make his own first feature, *Sebastiane* (1976). What strikes me now about *Sebastiane* is no longer its place as a pioneering transposition into film of age-old visual motifs aestheticizing beautiful, tormented boys in Mediterranean settings, but its 'high camp' silver Latin dialogue track. To me, this makes the film like an opera, whose libretto is in a foreign language, foregrounding the role of performance and visual composition. Dialogue has always seemed an awkward necessity for Jarman, and he has increasingly been happiest with preexisting literary texts – *The Tempest* (1979) or *The Angelic Conversation* (1985) – or, as with *War Requiem* (1989), musical texts. (Here he carries out Michael Powell's old ambition of the 'composed film,' in which the music preceded the filming, as in episodes of *Black Narcissus* or, of course, *The Red Shoes.)*[18] Greenaway, on the other hand, is fascinated by words and over-loads his sound track with dialogue, sometimes as though the characters were mouthpieces for an abstruse disputation taking place outside the film.[19]

Peter Greenaway was much more directly influenced by sixties pop artists, such as R. B. Kitaj (after whom a star is named in *Drowning by Numbers* [1988]) and Tom Phillips, the creator of *A Humument,* with whom he collaborated on his television film *Dante's Inferno* (1989), the pilot project for *Prospero's Books* (1991). In Greenaway's case, the fascination centers on artists who explore the relationship between words and images, between literature and painting. Greenaway discovered Kitaj's paintings at the same Marlborough Gallery show in 1963 that Derek Jarman also visited. Like Greenaway, Kitaj maintains an impenetrably enigmatic relation to his sources. Like Greenaway, too, he is drawn to the arcana of old engravings, incunabula, emblems, or maps. Kitaj has sought to people his paintings with imaginary characters, like those in novels, who appear in a series of works. In the same way, Greenaway too has his caste of imaginary characters, presided over by Tulse Luper, who crop up in film after film, sometimes in central roles, sometimes as fanciful marginalia. At heart, Greenaway, like Kitaj, is a collagist, juxtaposing images drawn from some fantastic archive, tracing erudite coincidental narratives within his material, bringing together Balthus and Borges in a bizarre collocation of bizarre eroticism and trompe l'oeil high modernism. Kitaj also, of course, is a cinephile, through whose painting, *Kenneth Anger and Michael Powell* (1973), we can trace a strange connection between the myth-worlds of Greenaway and Jarman.[20]

At first sight, Derek Jarman and Peter Greenaway have little in common. Indeed, Jarman is notorious for his vitriolic attacks on Greenaway. Yet both were products of sixties art schools, both were trained as painters and still are painters, both developed a strong visual style and dedicated themselves to making personal films marginal to the populist mainstream of the industry, both pay court to narrative while shamelessly revealing that their true interests lie elsewhere. Both can be seen, in a certain sense, as modernists. Both, in another sense, can also be seen as neoromantics, steeped in a personal vision of the English landscape, endlessly revisiting and rejecting the temptations of Victorianism and antiquarianism, returning much more willingly to their memories of childhood, mediated through home movies and family snapshots for Jarman, and through pored-over children's book illustrations for Greenaway. Derek Jarman accuses Greenaway of succumbing to antiquarianism in *The Draughtsman's Contract* (1982), a vice he attributes first to Poussin and thereafter to the Victorians. In contrast, he cites his own *Caravaggio* (1986), with its

Epiphany – Cerith Wyn Evans (1984)

contemporary references on image and sound track, its obvious debt to Pasolini, its inauthentic modernity. But Greenaway does not see *The Draughtsman's Contract* as authentic. On the contrary, he reacts angrily to a comparison with Kubrick's *Barry Lyndon* (1975): 'My film is about excess: excess in the language, excess in the landscape, which is much too green – we used special green filters – there is no historical realism in the costumes, the women's hair-styles are exaggerated in their height, the costumes are extreme. I wanted to make a very artificial film.'[21] In the same interview, he dismisses *Chariots of Fire* (1981, also Derek Jarman's most hated film) as reactionary and lacking any real aesthetic, even that of a *Saturday Night and Sunday Morning* (1960).

The difference between them, of course, lies in their divergent strategies for avoiding antiquarianism. Derek Jarman explicitly modernizes, introduces contemporary references and false touches, interprets Caravaggio's life and art through a filter of topical and personal preoccupations and tastes. Greenaway, on the contrary, exaggerates the archaism, pushing all the elements into an unreal and peculiarly inauthentic realm of caricature and pastiche, trying to turn a Restoration comedy into *Last Year at Marienbad* (1961). *Prospero's Books* (1991) follows in the same tradition by recreating the high Renaissance world of masque, pageant, and emblem in exaggerated splendor, while at the same time placing the play within Prospero's mind and experimenting with video effects and infography. The risks run by the rival strategies are clear. Jarman opens himself to the charge of anachronistic travesty, Greenaway to that of lavish overindulgence. When I saw *The Draughtsman's Contract* at its premiere at the Edinburgh Film Festival, I was nauseated by the excess of Englishness, the hyperbolic heaping of English language on English acting on English landscape on English country-house murder on English preciousness and whimsy, the dilettantish celebration of eccentricity and games-playing. The modernist dimension of Greenaway's work, the side that takes us toward Hollis Frampton's *Zorns Lemma* or toward the Oulipo writers in France,[22] toward an intricate conceptualism or a Nabokovian dandyism, can appear overingenious and willfully bizarre – another rerun of Lewis Carroll, yet with its shadow side made ever more apparent in erotic tableaux and Jacobean cruelty.

Derek Jarman is much more intimately linked to 'New Romanticism'. His most prominent disciples (John Maybury and Cerith Wyn Evans) were part of the 'Blitz crowd' and his own work is related not only to this 'club scene' new romanticism,[23] but to a much deeper, more long-lasting tradition: to the medieval poets, the Elizabethans (not only Marlowe and Shakespeare, but magicians, alchemists, and herbalists), Blake and Shelley, the late Victorians, the Apocalyptics, and, of course, Michael Powell and Emeric Pressburger. Modernism in Britain has prospered precisely in alliance with the underground currents of this broad national-romantic strain in the culture. Neoromanticism fitted intimately with the experience of the war, in poems by Edith Sitwell, Dylan Thomas, or T. S. Eliot, in drawings or paintings by Moore and Piper, in films by Humphrey Jennings and Powell and Pressburger. This wartime mood still runs through Jarman's films, especially in *The Last of England* (1987), with its recurrent imagery of a blitzed and burning London, recalling also the Great Fire of 1666, the burning of the Houses of Parliament painted by Turner, and the burning down of his own studio. 'Fire turned nasty.' It was no longer the comforting glow of childhood hearth and picnic bonfire. The palette of *The Last of England,* too, like that of Jarman's more recent paintings, is all tarry black and fiery red, made to look like cathedral stained glass.

Whereas the mainstream of romanticism has always expressed and consolidated national myths, Jarman's subverts them. Underlying the imagery of the blitz and the wasteland lies a critique of a destructive society and government – in a word, of Thatcherism. The desolate cityscape is contrasted with the imagery of the garden, as the state terrorism of *Jubilee* (1977) was contrasted with the closing masque of *The Tempest* (1979), the two films linked through the role of two Renaissance magicians, John Dee and Prospero. Jarman's political commitment draws on the sense of an alternative tradition, on the great homosexual texts – Plato's *Symposium,* Shakespeare's sonnets, the paintings of Caravaggio. At the same time, it is inseparable from his day-by-day involvement in the gay world, in the struggle against Clause 28 and the solidarity of gay men in the face of AIDS as they confront an authoritarian and homophobic regime whose leader's insistent moral appeal was to 'Victorian values' and against the 'permissive society.'[24] The key turning point, for Jarman, came with the Royal Jubilee of 1977 and its riotously sinister shadow, punk. Jarman's *Jubilee is* a protest against the whole horrendous notion of the 'second Elizabethan age', the backdrop of national grandeur and creativity against which Britain's economic and cultural decline was played out for twenty-five years. After that, of course, Thatcherism came as a movement not of renewal, but of vengefulness against everything she disapproved of that had somehow still managed to survive.

Peter Greenaway emerged from a strangely contradictory background. On the one hand, he worked for the government Central Office of Information, making films meant to express the British way of life, and, on the other hand, he made idiosyncratic 'structural films' in his own free time. His affinities are with 'international' modernism – before making *The Draughtsman's Contract,* he screened films by Fellini, Bertolucci, Rohmer, Straub, and Resnais for the crew, so that they could understand his intentions. At the same time, he secretly remade his own earlier *Vertical Features Remake* (1979), in which a group of film

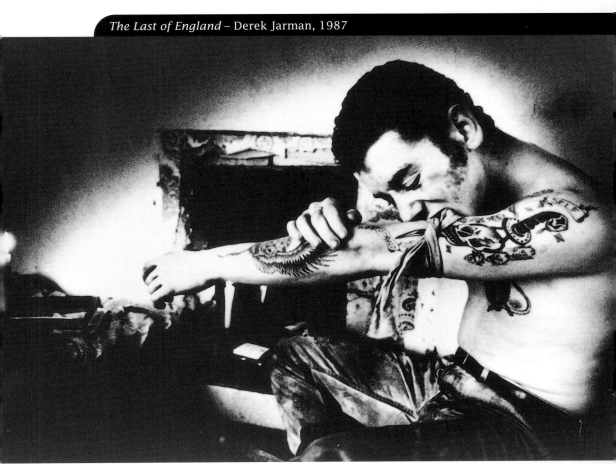

scholars try to reconstruct a lost film from a series of surviving views. Greenaway is also close to movements in modern art and music that employ modular and serial structures. Like many conceptual artists, he is fascinated by lists, grids, catalogs, counting games, and random procedures, which appear in his work as 'coincidences' or 'accidents'. He is also fascinated by mysteries and their concomitant troop of red herrings, deceptive riddles, and false trails, the stock-in-trade of the peculiarly English form of the cerebral detective story. His films are made under the twin signs of the taxonomy and the enigma. Such an aesthetic is perhaps strongest in an intrinsically nonrealist art like music, but even in literature and painting, it subordinates content to formal preoccupations, so that subject matter often seems no more than a pretext. The structure comes first and the content – say, a series of fictions – is then fitted into it, a lesson Greenaway learned from John Cage. This school of modernism, unlike neoromanticism, was historically decoupled from politics, yet, under the pressure of Thatcherism, Greenaway too turned to political invective in *The Cook, the Thief, His Wife, and Her Lover.*

Greenaway's antipathy toward Thatcherism stems from an ethical and aesthetic dislike for the philistinism and vulgarity of her regime, her exaltation of the profit motive, her determination that art and scholarship should only be supported if they served an economic function, her authoritarianism, her social philosophy of frugality and order for the poor combined with greed and license for the rich. Thus an expensive restaurant was a logical setting for his film, a place where Spica's own authoritarianism, greed, and license can be publicly indulged. Moreover, one of Greenaway's recurrent preoccupations is with the food chain, the process of ingestion of the weak by the strong and the dead by the living, in curious configurations of cruelty and death with sex and dinner. At the same time, the restaurant is symbolically a cathedral, a cinema, and an art museum, the chef its officiating priest and artist. As in other Greenaway films, the woman is the controlling character, bent on revenge on the world of men, destroying the figure of the artist en route. The brutalization of an innocent child recalls that of Smut in *Drowning by Numbers* (1988), a grueling moment when a ludic commedia dell'arte is suddenly transformed into a macabre Jacobean drama. Indeed, as Greenaway puts it, 'The Jacobeans were looking over their shoulder at the grand Elizabethan age; Britain still looks over its shoulder at the Great Empire. In Jacobean times, syphilis was the new sexual scourge; we now have AIDS. There's a certain comparison in that sexuality has become complicated, so there's a similar spirit of melancholy. The same sensation of fatalism exists vis-à-vis the sort of cruelty we see every day, especially cruelty in the home, the abuse of children, and so on.'[25] From their very different angles, Greenaway and Jarman unexpectedly converge on a surprisingly similar standpoint.

Both Greenaway and Jarman made key films for the British Film Institute (BFI) Production Board, under Peter Sainsbury: *The Draughtsman's Contract* (1982), suggested by Sainsbury, who asked Greenaway whether he had ever thought of making a dialogue film, and later, Jarman's *Caravaggio* (1986). The board had become completely divorced from its experimental function until Sainsbury, former editor of the avant-garde journal *Aftermage,* was appointed in the mid-seventies. Sainsbury became something like a new, but decisively modernist and antirealist Grierson. Toward the end of the sixties, under the dual impact of New York 'structural film' and the European experiments in narrative of Godard and others, a film avant-garde crystallized for the first time in Britain since *Close Up.* It was built around the BFI, The Other Cinema, the Workshop Movement, and the Independent Film Makers' Association (IFA).[26] Neither Greenaway nor Jarman participated in the avant-garde debates and activities of the time, which they saw, perhaps, as too politically doctrinaire or too potentially time-consuming. In a way, their noninvolvement probably made it easier for them to break out of the earlier pattern of their filmmaking, unencumbered by a baggage of past positions and pronouncements. Also, they did not confront Thatcherism head on, as 'political filmmakers,' but from a less explicit artistic position within which their political anti-Thatcherism emerged.

Nonetheless, films like those of Greenaway and Jarman should be seen as part of a wider and disparate shift in British film, due in part to a decisive shift toward the visual arts as a source for cinema, and in part to the theoretical and practical consolidation of a film avant-garde in the IFA and at the BFI. The emergence of a post-Godardian 'political modernism' at the BFI, although it never achieved even the limited popular success of Greenaway or Jarman, helped to create an alternative pole of attraction within British cinema and thus the space between mainstream and countercinema that they later occupied.[27] Greenaway and Jarman are much closer in background and outlook to other directors emerging from the BFI and the workshops than they are to the upscale TV drama and ad directors who constitute the rump of the 'film industry' left behind in Britain after the more ambitious of them have been called to the Coast. The other important condition, of course, was the fabulous collapse of Puttnamism and the flight of its leader to Hollywood, where his pretensions were ignominiously liquidated. 'The British are coming' indeed.[28]

Thatcherism, by breaking the mold of British politics and carrying through radical right-wing cultural policies, directed, in essence, against the legacy of the sixties, succeeded paradoxically in politicizing filmmakers who had been formed during the comparatively liberal years of Wilson, the decade of sexual liberation, the last hurrah of welfare Keynesianism, and the belated entry of modernism into the general culture. This 'delayed modernism,' however, proved resilient enough to survive into the eighties. It decisively influenced a generation then in a position to make oppositional films first for the BFI, later for Channel Four, and eventually for independent producers within the industry or in Europe. As a result, Britain saw an efflorescence of filmmaking paralleled only in the forties. Britain finally produced the 'Last New Wave,' a series of uncompromising films made by original, oppositional, visually oriented modernist auteurs. It was worth waiting.

NOTES

1   This analysis of Thatcherism emerges from debates carried on by a number of authors. See especially the following: Andrew Gamble, *The Free Economy and the Strong State* (Basingstoke: Macmillan, 1988); Stuart Hall, *The Hard Road to Renewal* (London: Verso, 1988); Bob Jessop, Kevin Bonnett, Simon Bromley, and Tom Ling, *Thatcherism* (London: Polity Press, 1988); Scott Newton and Dilwyn Porter, *Modernisation Frustrated* (London: Unwin Hyman, 1988); and Henk Overbeek, *Global Capitalism and National Decline: The Thatcher Decade in Perspective* (London: Unwin Hyman, 1990). For the general anti-Thatcherite cultural efflorescence under Thatcherism, see Robert Hewison, *Future Tense* (London: Methuen, 1990). Films coming from outside London, it should be noted, like Bill Forsyth's Scottish films or the Liverpudlian *Letter to Brezhnev,* seem strangely less bitter than the London films, although a vein of cynicism underlies the mood of astringent comedy and wry fantasy. Northern Ireland has been marginalized in the cinema, as in the political arena, although Alan Clarke's extraordinary television work there represented the most startling and successful convergence of political with formal preoccupations in any of the media.

2   These words are quoted without citation by Roy Armes, in *A Critical History of the British Cinema* (London: Secker and Warburg, 1979). They are requoted parodically in Peter Greenaway's *The Draughtsman's Contract,* with painting substituted for cinema. For another version, see also Truffaut's remark that there is 'something about England that's anti-cinematic,' in François Truffaut, *Hitchcock* (London: Panther, 1969).

3   Jacques Belmains, *Jeune Cinéma Anglais* (Lyon: *Premier Plan,* no. 44, May 1967).

4   On the Angry Young Men and their impact on the cinema, see Harry Ritchie, *Success Stories: Literature and the Media in England 1950-1959* (London: Faber and Faber, 1988); and Robert Hewison, *In Anger* (London: Weidenfeld and Nicolson, 1981). John Hill, *Sex, Class and Realism: British Cinema, 1956-63* (London: British Film Institute, 1986) provides a comprehensive survey of the movement in film.

5 See Robert Murphy, *Realism and Tinsel* (London: Routledge, 1989), which takes its title from Michael Balcon's pamphlet *Realism and Tinsel,* based on a talk given to the Film Workers Association in Brighton in 1943. This is available in *Michael Balcon's 25 Years in Films,* ed. Monja Danischewsky (London: World Film Publications, 1947). In his talk, Balcon especially stressed the contribution Grierson's unit had made as 'the men who kept realism going on the screen' and the potential for a new type of film bringing a realistic treatment to 'story elements' within the industry.

6 See Peter Wollen, 'Scenes from the Future: Komar and Melamid,' in *Between Spring and Summer* (Tacoma, Wash.: Tacoma Art Museum, and Boston: Institute of Contemporary Art, 1990).

7 For the postwar history of modernism in Britain, see Alan Sinfield, *Literature, Politics and Culture in Postwar Britain* (Oxford: Basil Blackwell, 1989). He is also very illuminating on the sexual and class politics of the Angry Young Men.

8 For *Close Up* and *Borderline,* see Roland Cosandey, 'Reassessment of 'Lost' Film,'*Afterimage* (London), no. 12 (Autumn 1985), which contains a full bibliography. See also Anne Friedberg, 'The Film Journal *Close Up,*' (Ph.D. diss., New York University, 1983).

9 For the Film Society, see Jen Samson, 'The Film Society, 1925-1939,' in *All Our Yesterdays,* ed. Charles Barr (London: British Film Institute, 1986).

10 For Humphrey Jennings, see Mary-Lou Jennings, *Humphrey Jennings* (London: British Film Institute, 1982).

11 Sir Alexander Korda can be seen as one of the roster of émigré knights described by Perry Anderson in 'Components of the National Culture,' *New Left Review,* no. 50 July-August 1968), along with Sir Isaiah Berlin, Sir Ernst Gombrich, Sir Lewis Namier, and Sir Karl Popper. Yet Korda, it should be noted, worked with the revolutionary Bela Kun regime in Hungary and was a refugee from counterrevolutionary dictator Admiral Horthy. Later, however, he became an intimate and patron of Churchill and his circle.

12 For the music hall, pierhead, and seaside tradition, best exemplified by George Formby, the ukelele-playing hero of the Beatles and Morrissey, see Murphy, *Realism and Tinsel.* Murphy's chapter 'The Spiv Cycle' also provides the best introduction to this riveting British equivalent to film noir. A 'spiv' was a petty racketeer involved in the postwar black economy. He wore flash ties, suits with wide lapels, and a sneer or grin.

13 For wartime and postwar romanticism, see especially David Mellor, *A Paradise Lost* (London: Lund Humphries, 1987); and Robert Hewison, *Under Siege* (London: Weidenfeld and Nicolson, 1977).

14 The best brief treatment of the British struggle against the economic power of Hollywood, led by Harold Wilson, is in Murphy, *Realism and Tinsel.*

15 See *This Is Tomorrow Today* (New York: P.S. 1, Institute for Art and Urban Resources, 1987); and, for the subsequent shift in British popular culture, Dick Hebdige, *Hiding in the Light* (London: Comedia, 1988).

16 For a general treatment of the 1960s, see Robert Hewison, *Too Much* (London: Methuen, 1986).

17 The indispensable sources for Derek Jarman are his two books of journals, Derek Jarman, *Dancing Ledge* (London: Quartet, 1984), and *Modern Nature* (London: Century, 1991). See also the special number of *Afterimage,* 'Derek Jarman... of Angels and Apocalypse,' *Afterimage* (London), no. 12 (Autumn 1985). I have also drawn from Derek Jarman, *Derek Jarman's Caravaggio* (London: Thames and Hudson, 1986), *The Last of England* (London: Constable, 1987), and *War Requiem* (London: Faber and Faber, 1989).

18 Michael Powell was inspired by Friedrich Feher's film *The Robber Symphony,* which is described by Graham Greene in his review in the *Spectator,* May 24,1936, reprinted in Graham Greene, *The Pleasure-Dome* (Oxford: Oxford University Press, 1980).

19 For Greenaway, I have drawn mainly from Peter Greenaway, *Papers* (Paris: Dis Voir, 1990), which contains a selection of his artwork with his own commentary, and Greenaway, *Fear of Drowning by Numbers* (Pans: Dis Voir, 1988). A number of Greenaway's scripts are also published.

20 For Kitaj, see Marco Livingstone, *R. B. Kitaj* (Oxford: Phaidon Press, 1985). Kitaj did actually introduce Kenneth Anger and Michael Powell to each other: 'I brought Anger and Powell together because they admired each other. They're both quite mysterious and since I introduced them, I painted them together in their disjunction.'

21 See Peter Greenaway, 'Meurtre dans un jardin anglais," *L'avant-scène cinema* (Paris), no. 333 (October 1984). The translation of Greenaway's remarks is my own.

22 For the Oulipo group of writers, see *Oulipo,* ed. Warren F. Motte, Jr. (Lincoln: University of Nebraska Press, 1986).

23 For new romanticism and Blitz culture, see Caroline Evans and Minna Thornton, *Women and Fashion: A New Look* (London: Quartet, 1989).

24 Derek Jarman is one of a number of gay filmmakers who made films in Britain during the Thatcher years, including Terence Davies, Isaac Julien, John Maybury, Ron Peck, and Cerith Wyn Evans.

25 See Gary Indiana's interview with Peter Greenaway, in *Interview* 20 (March 1990),120-21, on the occasion of the New York release of *The Cook, the Thief, His Wife, and Her Lover.*

26 Reliable sources are few for this period in British cinema. For the black workshops, see especially *Blackframes,* ed. Mbye B. Cham and Claire Andrade-Watkins (London: Celebration of Black Cinema and MIT Press, 1988); and Coco Fusco, *Young, British and Black: The Work of Sankofa and Black Audio Film Collective* (Buffalo, N.Y.: Hallwalls/Contemporary Arts Center, 1988).

27 See D. N. Rodowick, *The Crisis of Political Modernism* (Urbana: University of Illinois Press, 1988).

28 'The British are coming!' was the media slogan propagated after *Chariots of Fire* won an Oscar. It is strange that the next British Oscar sweep, for *The Last Emperor,* had no discernible impact whatever in Britain, presumably because its director was an Italian. Conversely, a director like Ridley Scott, even though he has retained his personal and working ties with Britain, has been systematically neglected. Yet Scott's vision of the city in *Blade Runner* (1982) has much in common with its British counterparts.

Handsworth Songs – Black Audio Film Collective (1986)

REECE AUGUISTE, MARTINA ATTILLE, ISAAC JULIEN, PETER GIDAL

Aesthetics
& Politics

WORKING ON TWO FRONTS?

First published in *Undercut*,
no 17 Spring 1988

INTRODUCTION BY REECE AUGUISTE

An interrogation of cultural identities through the parameters of politics and aesthetics
presents a set of theoretical difficulties. Problems to do with how questions of politics and
aesthetic sensibilities relate to audio visual culture. Politics and aesthetics have been the
subject of much debate in the writings of theoreticians as diverse as Benjamin and Lukács;
Tarkovsky and Glauber Rocha. Artists who are passionate about the development of audio
visual culture must take into account the histories of left radicalism and artistic production
but also, more importantly, the contributions that can be made towards these debates by
these writers and theoreticians

There are other problems inherent in the ideologies of interpretation; paradoxes of *langue*
and *parole,* of being caught between the metaphoric in speech and the symbolic in political
thought. The texts presented by Martina Attille, Peter Gidal, Isaac Julien and Reece Auguiste
constitute modalities of difference(s) and a plurality of strategic interests. These political
positions in film culture are themselves articulations of different moments in the history of
independent film culture. Moments that attempt to address critically, issues of sexuality.
gender, race, power and the broader issues of representation and cinema.

In this debate we are presented with Peter Gidal's materialist film practice and non-
representational cinema, with Isaac Julien's critique of European master discourse and
Western Europe's avant-garde cinema. Martina Attille considers the construction of multiple
identities in cinema and the position of black film practitioners in the institutional matrix of
the cultural industries. Reece Auguiste speaks on black independent film poetics and the
possibilities of developing an aesthetic of terror based on the convergence of cinema and

New World poetics.

Of equal importance is the subsequent debate, which centres largely on questions of desire and pleasure in cinema and which gives rise to some questions on the supposed oppositional/confrontational politics between Black Audio Film Collective and Sankofa. It could be said that in this debate there seems to be a refusal to recognise parallel developments in black independent film culture and the possibility of black film-makers having a space to develop and experiment in film art, of finding the appropriate methodological tools for visual production. Essentially, we are struggling to construct and articulate a politics that can begin to address, in cinema, the complexities of post colonial existence in the already troubled terrain of post-modernism. At the time of the debate I remember thinking, 'When did I last note white workshop groups being pitched in opposition to each other?'

Peter Gidal's concerns with epistemological issues of the split between knowledge, production and optical projection was another point of issue in this debate. His non-representational and anti-narrative stance denies the possibility of truth and pleasure in cinema. It is a position that belongs to various debates as encountered in the pages of *Screen* and previous issues of *Undercut*. 'If I hear the word desire one more time, I am going to throw up', was Gidal's response to the introduction of desire on the agenda. I am still forced to maintain that desire and pleasure are imperative criteria in the development of independent film culture.

Finally, two points: cinema is a relatively new artistic movement in comparison to painting and sculpture, so the possibilities for innovation and experimentation are immense and allow for a plurality of forms and expressions. Secondly, the presence of black film-makers in Britain is also relatively new. With new arrivants we must have new departures. You must now draw your own conclusions from this debate around politics and aesthetics.

It is amusing to note that these discussions were hosted by the Commonwealth Institute, where in its exhibition space, colonial and post-colonial fantasies around national identities are frozen and fixed for public consumption. Nicos Mendoza[i] would also have been bemused by this paradox.

MARTINA ATTILLE

Industrial countries in the First World are undergoing a political crisis, which is both economic and cultural. People on the Left and the Right are trying to find some direction, trying to identify some of the problems. There's also a plurality of identities, articulated by specific interests coming from different social groupings. It's no longer adequate just to group people in terms such as black women or the working class, because within those categories there are constituencies that are making claims and giving voice to their own particular interests and needs. There is also a realisation that identities are not actually fixed, that they can be constituted towards forming and consolidating political allegiances, and it becomes increasingly difficult to talk about a monolithic Left. It's probably more accurate to talk about the constituencies within the Left. Politics and aesthetics; it is difficult to divide them, especially when aesthetics can be aligned with politics. One instance when aesthetics becomes very self-conscious is in the work of film production; when you talk about the audience that you want to address and when you want to make the best use of cultural forms available to you. Aesthetics in a film collective like Sankofa inevitably means talking about desires, what sort of films you want to produce, what sort of images you want to see. Not talking so much about positive images, or a purity of representation, but about a diversity which allows us far more space than is allowed by present images of black people. Our work in Sankofa is to broaden the vocabulary of production on our own terms, contributing to a cinema that affirms our existence and our politics, and also to have a certain amount of autonomy in that practice. This doesn't necessarily mean looking for some authenticity, but that we should recognise the economic and cultural processes of change and inevitable repositioning of interests, not only in production, but also in film forms, in theory and the economics of production. It means being aware of the 'interests' of funding institutions, like Channel 4 and the BFI, and also the need to make international links with other film-makers in the black diaspora. We're very aware that there are forces which want to define what black film practitioners should be engaged in. People find it very difficult when we do draw on wide sources in our productions. They think maybe we should be concentrating on ethnic problems or positive images. We as a group recognise that working in this culture we do have access to a wide range of languages. A film like *Territories* has been regarded by the BFI and others to be very much like Jean-Luc Godard's work, when in fact it draws on far wider sources, going beyond Eurocentric theory. In Sankofa we recognise that in a time of economic and political reaction, each intervention in film theory and in film practice tends to pull people into line, rather than to encourage a pluralism of approaches to production, or even to theory. Intervention makes it possible to clear the way to finding out where political allegiances can be made. Allegiances are probably far more important than specific identities.

A film like *Territories* is usually held up as typical of what we do, but our practice is far wider and our other film, *Passion of Remembrance,* shows another aspect of our work and interests. *Passion of Remembrance* comes at a time when it's important to address and become interested in the audiences we want to reach, not by using methods that might be seen as alienating, but by an approach that will actually engage people in dialogue. If anything, our practice is about encouraging dialogue rather than indoctrination.

REECE AUGUISTE

Black Cinema, Poetics and New World Aesthetics

The histories of black independent film practice in Britain has hemmed black film-makers into a set of social relations which demand that the inventories of cinema be addressed anew. An analytical reading of this cultural field reveals two distinct, yet interrelated historical antecedents which inform our filmic practices: the early period of British black independent film production from Lionel Ngakane's allegorical *Jemima and Johnny* (1974), to the 1970s, with the films of Henry Martin, Horace Ove, Imruh Bakari (Caesar) and Menelik Shabazz, and the political and aesthetic interventions of Third Cinema, as a counter movement in film, which is critical of its own position, as it is of European cinema.

Our point of departure is that each generation re-writes its own history. Black independent film practice is at a critical conjuncture where it must make a radical departure from other film practices. Our presence in independent cinema, as it is currently structured and mediated by the institutional and the political is, I believe, engaged in a struggle for its epistemological terrain through modes of visual articulation and narrative concerns which do not desire to emulate or mimic other cinemas. It is a cinema critical of its own discourse as it is of other cinemas.

There are two distinct traditions from which black independent film-makers can extrapolate materials towards the development of their own film aesthetic; one is the literary traditions of the diaspora, rich and diverse in myth, parables and orature and its diverse practices in the diaspora, the second is Teshome Gabriel's theoretical work on Third Cinema; *Third Cinema in the Third World – The Aesthetics of Liberation.* It is these interrelated fields that are capable of producing the desired inflections, new forms and new narrative structures in cinema. Black British independent film-makers are the product of the New World, also of Africa and India, and whether born in the Third World or in the spectacle of declining British inner cities, they have a generic connection with the perils, pleasures, passions and contradictions, the cultural landscapes of the New World.

I want to turn my attention to Derek Walcott, who in my view, is the Caribbean's greatest poet. Assuming that Derek Walcott's maxim; 'Each generation re-writes its own history',[2] is correct – as I believe it is – it therefore becomes possible to locate the manner in which black independent film articulates a series of incisions and inscriptions into the history of British independent film culture. A combination of the system of racial representations and the inventories of cinema have structured our engagements with the histories and practices of cinema, with narrative forms and structures, and with political/economic questions upon which independence is based.

I shall make reference to Brazilian cinema – *Cinema Novo* – a cinema of extreme solitude, reflection and revelation. Historical, geographical and economic differences aside, I am compelled to reiterate Glauber Rocha's insights on oppositional film practice: 'When film-makers organise themselves to start from zero, to create a cinema with new types of plot lines, of performance of rhythm, and with a different poetry, they throw themselves into the dangerous revolutionary adventure of learning while you produce, of placing side by side theory and practice, of reformulating every theory through every practice, of conducting themselves according to the apt dictum coined by Nelson Pereira dos Santos from some Portuguese poet: "I don't know where I'm going, but I'm not going over there"'.[3] I'm not arguing for an uncritical reproduction of the filmic practices of Third Cinema; I make reference to Glauber Rocha so as to demonstrate an affinity with the desire to rupture and embark on new beginnings. Black film-makers are constituted by diverse histories of exclusion and emigration; by cultural experiences emanating from the historical conditions of the New World, Asia and Africa. The cultural terrain upon which we work is invested and structured by pluralism, which indicates the immense problems involved in attempting to affirm a unitary definition of cultural identity and social experience(s) through the apparatus of cinema. Cultural diversity disavows the singular and monolithic in cultural production. It is precisely this diversity of experiences that must inform aesthetic production and the problematisation of representation.

Derek Walcott has painted in words a visual representation of the Caribbean archipelago, finding the source of his vision in its human tragedies, its terrors and triumphs. It is revealing that Walcott once remarked that: 'The truly tough aesthetics of the New World neither explains nor forgives history'.[4] Given that in this forum we're talking around the binary of politics and aesthetics in cultural production, it is appropriate that I enunciate the invaluable contribution that New World literary discourses and aesthetics can make in the development of black cinema in Britain. It is here that memory must assume the position of privileged informer. The extrapolation of memory from literary forms and contexts crystallises the intersection between literary concerns and cinema. New World poets such as Pablo Neruda of Chile and the Martiniquan, Aimé Césaire, for example, have made memory the substance of their work. The desire to grapple with the tropes of memory, with the intersection of myth and history must not be understood as being exclusive to literary productions although these constitute a body of archival material which can inform our film practice.

Although history continues to weigh heavily on the present, there exists a paradox in that it is not the unbearable forays of past history which continue to traumatise New World consciousness, but the ambivalence and tragedies of the modern; a contemporary vision which struggles with tragedy. Here the myth of the 'noble savage' collapses under its own metaphysical contradictions. Walcott reminds us of this when he says: '...that myth never emanated from the savage but has always been the nostalgia of the Old World – its longing for innocence'[5]. Our vision is not naïve, unlike the great monumental poetry of the Old World; we do not pretend such innocence. Memory as it is conceptualised by New World poets is salted with the bitter memory of migration and fragmentation. It is this acidic taste of memory that has to be brought to the service of the struggle of black independent film practitioners.

New departures in film culture also necessitate a struggle for radical forms, reference points, for a filmic vitality in narrativity and audio visual style. Film practitioners cannot continue to re-articulate the discourses which structure positive/negative representations of race. Film-makers who want to develop a cinema of relevance must jettison the discursive concerns of multi-culturalism and the positive/negative image to the cultural wasteland. Our presence in the '80s demands an interrogation of the rhetoric of race in relation to cinema. It also necessitates a re-politicisation of the technological apparatus of cinema. Politicisation can occur in the production process itself; a testing of possibilities and limitations. Thus the successes of the black independent sector rests on an astute reading of the political economy of independence, institutional practices and a radical reconvergence of cultural identities and filmic representation/production. If Walcott's notion of an aesthetics which 'neither explains nor forgives history' is to supersede the dominant discourses of the European avant-garde and other cinema traditions, then film-makers have to interrogate and evaluate the genealogy of those traditions. Again, it is a question of testing limitations. Engagement with cinema thus assumes a set of multiple practices, which is why I believe that the title of the forum is both inadequate and deceptive. The struggle for new life and vibrancy in cinema must occur on multiple fronts.

Diasporic Discourse and Inventories of Tradition

The Ethiopian film-maker, Haile Gerima, has signified the importance of literary subjects in the formation of oppositional cinema: 'Because of the rich history of black literature and our renewed oral tradition, the independent cinematographer must, out of necessity, incorporate and fully use this astounding body of resource material'[6]. Gerima's insights put into sharp focus the organic connection between New World poetics and the possibility of forging new aesthetic presences in black cinema. The poets of the New World have had to address memories of terror, its historical antecedents and the manner in which the present is mediated by it. These themes of terror and exploitation are indicative of the breadth and vision of New World imagination, as in for example, the poetics of the Guyanese poet Martin Carter, in his beautiful poem *The Terror and the Time,* which is the title of a film from the same country by the Victor Jara Collective about the formation of the Guyanese working class.

Notes Towards an Aesthetics of Terror

It is possible, I believe, to develop an aesthetic of terror in cinema akin to Walcott's 'tough new aesthetic', which is ultimately transgressive, capable of producing mutations and incisions, which can ensure that the Western gaze can never regain its privileged position as the ultimate arbiter of symbolic meaning and representation. A black independent cinema which attempts to register an aesthetic of terror is concerned with possibilities, critical of its genealogy and trajectory. When we allow memory to assume the seat of privileged informer, of having a transgressive function, then the process of re-naming begins. As Walcott says: 'We were blest with a virginal, unpainted world, with Adam's task of giving things their names'[7]. The act of naming things anew is a fundamental prerequisite of a cinema with new voices and visions.

Finally, I shall address the issue of audience accessibility and questions of language. My reference point is Black Audio Film Collective's slide/tape production *Expeditions: Signs of Empire* and *Images of Nationality.* The collective has often been asked the question, 'Who is your audience?'. The question is always premised by the understanding that the language in which we have chosen to articulate colonial exigencies is thought of as rather abstract, difficult and ultimately inaccessible. I must deploy a Shakespearian subject so as to affirm the importance of the use of this language. The subject? Caliban.[8] A subject whose historical existence is characterised by a psychic split: the language of Caliban's unconscious is as much to do with exclusion and accommodation, as with fear. The paradox is that Caliban's presence reveals to us the psychic turmoil of his master Prospero. Through Caliban's action, Prospero's soul is revealed. Listen to Walcott on this dilemma: 'Your view of Caliban is of the enraged pupil. You cannot separate the rage of Caliban from the beauty of his speech, when the speeches of Caliban are equal in their elemental power to those of this tutor, the language of the torturer has been mastered by the victim.' Now the terrain upon which we work is such that the critical deployment of that language is towards the production of new meanings. This is viewed as collaboration with dominant language, but for us it is victory.

PETER GIDAL

In Representation or Out? Some Condensed Notes on Aesthetics and Politics

To endlessly denounce questions of form as irrelevant at best and elitist at worst, is to play straight into the hands of dominant representation, i.e. dominant forms. By 1986 this ought no longer to have to be stated. It certainly ought not to be arguable, as the alternatives are to pander to various realisms, or to pander to carefully watered-down formal changes which are already co-opted, and do not inculcate resistance to anything. Academicism thrives precisely on such co-options, which is why, in the end, literary analysis takes over, as it did in the appalling libertarian voice of reaction of Gayatri Spivak in the debate on *Sexual Identities.* Spivak's thrice-repeated denials – and I quote: 'I don't dislike these British films' – is a slick marginalisation of British work, the better to dispense with its force. 'Didactic' is her condescending code word for this work. Spivak's denials also betrayed a notion of pleasure which denied the political question of the ideology of pleasure. This digestible post-modernism is in power in academia, especially in the United States, France and here.

Clare Joseph's carefully precise elucidation in *Culture and Representation* leaves me with one problem, namely, the notion of 'political identification'. I fear that the concept is not the same as solidarity, because identification destroys the objects one is ostensibly identifying with. To identify the 'other' is not the same as 'identification with'. 'Identification with' structurally excludes a political solidarity because it substitutes the self and the ego for, and in the place of, any other political identification. I think that this is important to realise, so that we don't end up with another realism as a decoy for the realism we're supposedly doing battle with, although we need realism of another kind.

What worries me is the illusion that one individual's identifications could equal solidarity, and by individual I'm referring to the viewer. That is why taking a position is a political act, but it is not based on nature, ethnicity or biology. Otherwise, being black would be *the problem,* or being a woman would be *the problem,* rather than oppression being the problem. All positions are arbitrary; this doesn't mean that they are irrelevant, but simply that they have nothing to do with a natural order or essence.

First of all I try to make films, secondly I try to make films where each image, each object, is never given the hold of any recognition. To not reproduce the given as given, to see each image, each object, each imaginary space-time narrative as imaginary projection, so that nothing takes on the status of truth. The lack of recognition, and I'm not saying that it always does, can force the construction of all representational motives as constructions, as artifice, as unnatural, as ideology, so that representation is always impossible.

There is always a split between knowledge and perception, between what we know and what we see. In other words, what we think we *know* must not be thought to be the same as what we think we *see*. That split produces a process of film which simultaneously produces a spectator and a spectating that constantly problematises representation. I see no other way to practice film – there must be other ways, but, judging from the response in *Sexual Identities* to Lis Rhodes' film *Light Reading,* perhaps understandably, some ways of film-making find less solidarity than others. The radicality of Lis Rhodes' film is not easy. This is the difficulty we have as film-makers and theoreticians. Voyeuristic pleasure is a structure of power in certain sex interests, or, as Christine Delphy would say, sex-class interests. One can hardly expect an easy relinquishing of such power, and spectators collude, to say the least. The endless reproduction of dominant forms of 'unproblematic' voyeurism is what dominant representation is all about, that is its narrative. All I can add is that irony doesn't change a damn thing and if I hear the word desire one more time I'm going to throw up.

Materialist film, a materialist avant-garde has to get rid of difference, not fetishise it, but that can only be said to an audience that accepts avant-garde and experimental film-making as a valid process. And obliterating difference must be simultaneous to understanding its historical construction and existence. The material of film, for example acetate, and the material of ideology, produce representations which are part of the contradictions within the varying historical materialities of the act of viewing. If you reject experimental film it is of no issue to argue pro or con this concept or that. But I assume that there is some sympathy with avant-garde film here.

The concept of difference assumes a dominant male norm against which the 'other' is 'other', so it must, by definition, be obliterated for a radical process to find its expression; but without such a polemical, political position, the illusion of the 'possible' becomes, unfortunately, broader rather than reduced.

ISAAC JULIEN

Notes on Black British Independent Cinema, the Avant-Garde and Post-Modernism

A few black film-makers were in the front line of the formation of a black British cinema. Among these were Menelick Shabazz and Horace Ove. These black filmmakers attempted to document the struggles of black, Third World people on British soil who formed or still form, the underclass of British society. These films were anchored in a realist documentary mode, dealing specifically with race as a problematic. In oppositional film-making circles, this should not be seen as 'ethnic' or 'other' or anti-racist work, but has to be recognised in the light of the creation of a British identity which is a plurality of multiple identities.[9] It is the white British who have to learn that being British isn't what it was. Now it is more complex, involving new elements consequently there must be a fresh way of seeing cinema and a new way of seeing *per se.*

Experimental film as a left-wing political film practice seems to contain a number of discourses collapsing into each other; the interrelation of race and gender and the primary positioning of 'difference'. On the left of avant-gardism is pleasure, which the avant-garde self denies, clinging to the purism of its constructed ethics, measuring itself against a refusal to indulge in narrative or emotions and indeed, in some cases, refusing representation itself, because all these systems of signs are fixed, entrenched in the 'sin or evil' of representation.[10] The high moral tone of this discourse is based on a kind of masochistic self-censorship which relies on the indulgences of a colonial history and a post-colonial history of cinema of white representations based on our black absence. The problematic that surfaces when black film-makers experiment with the idea of black film text and the subjective camera, is that subjectivity implies contradiction. But this is not, in itself, fixed. Black political film-making works to unfix the 'other' fragmented self in order to construct a new filmic language, to reconstruct black representations in British cinema, be that in narrative, abstract film, documentary or film essay.

The dominant master discourse demands: 'Let me know your culture, tell me your story', even though we are trying to tell the stories to ourselves first. Critics are only here in typical, First World, master discourse fashion to analyse and criticise, to slot black film into identifiable, legitimised categories. So our work gets compared to, say, Godard's work. An attempt has been made in this debate to keep discussion within a dominant discourse, within its own paradigms. We are aware of this and also critical. To do this is an attempt at containment, a marginalisation of our work in relation both to films made by Third World film-makers and Third World to First World black film-makers born on British soil. It also has to be noted why we are here, the struggles of black communities which have taken to the street to express their frustration, are continued and mirrored in other spaces, ie. cinema.[11]

A simplistic and unproblematic polarity has been forged here between black film practices and the practices of avant-gardism. Structuralism in film has replaced old orthodoxies with new ones. To challenge the Eurocentric master discourse is not only to be seen in binary terms of opposition but also as an intervention which revitalises different film practices with black British identities and black film culture, shifting the definitions of cultural identity itself. More importantly, it reveals the pleasures of our existence, as does black music.

Territories and ideas have to be explored politically through construction and reconstruction then thrown away, if we are to change and master narratives and conventions, and to invest in cinema a wholeness. So that when one enters in on a black subject, it is not seen as 'ethnic', 'other' or 'different', but whole, thus changing the terms of definition for blackness and what it means to us. This does not imply that we enter into romantic ideas of black nationalism. I accept that there exist multiple identities which constitute national identity, which should challenge with passion and beauty the previously static order. Black cinema is part of post-modernism, it needs a space to grow rather than spaces that attempt to fix it.

FOOTNOTES

1 In the oral traditions of the diaspora, it is said that Nicos Mendoza was a Brazilian artist and bohemian who, on hearing from travellers that the Lumière brothers were in India with an instrument that could record movement, left his canvas and paint box for India. In some sections of the New World he is now a deity: The god of light.

2 Derek Walcott 'The Muse of History' in *Carifest Forum - An Anthology of Twenty Caribbean Voices*, ed. John Hearne, Institute of Jamaica.

3 Glauber Rocha 'History of Cinema Novo' *Framework*, issue no 12, 1980.

4 Walcott op cit.

5 ibid.

6 Interview with Haile Gerima in *Frontline*, 1984.

7 Walcott op cit.

8 For a re-reading of Shakespeare's *The Tempest,* in which Caliban and Prospero appear as metonyms of New and Old Worlds respectively, see for example, George Lamming, *Water with Berries,* Longman, 1971. The form and content of this novel are inspired by Lamming's interpretation of *The Tempest* as a political allegory, linking past history with the conflicts of the present. See also George Lamming, *The Pleasures of Exile,* Michael Joseph, 1960, for Lamming's account of the political impact of Africa on his awareness.

9 As outlined in Hanif Kureishi's essay, 'The Rainbow Sign', in *The Rainbow Sign* and *My Beautiful Laundrette,* Faber and Faber, 1986.

10 See Paul Willemen, 'An Avant-Garde for the Eighties', *Framework* 24, Spring 1984. 'This "avant-garde" would, in fact, correspond to modernism. The other one is described as reacting against purism; rejects ontological presuppositions or investigations and is concerned with semiotic expansion (use of mixed media; montage of different codes, signs and semiotic registers; heterogeneity of signifiers and signifieds is activated, etc.). This would correspond to the avant-garde approach. The tendency towards semiotic reductionism clearly

corresponds to the "conservative" impulse, explicitly articulated by Greenberg, towards maintaining the autonomy and institutionalisation of "high art"'. P.60.

11 Robert Crusz, 'Black Cinema, Film Theory and Dependent Knowledge', *Screen*, Vol.26, No.3/4, 1985. (Robert Crusz is a member of Sankofa Film and Video Collective.)

Shadow of a Journey – Tina Keane (1980)
Photo: Rose Finn Kelcey

CATHERINE LACEY

The Poetry of Fact

BEYOND DOCUMENTARY IN THREE NARRATIVE WORKS

First published in *The Elusive Sign: British
Avant-Garde Film and Video 1977-1987*, Arts
Council of Great Britain/British Council,
London, 1987

> The appropriation of a (real) place in the service of a fiction is a political act, as
> the relation of private experience to public space is a political relation.[1]
> Patrick Keiller

It is probably too soon to anticipate what may eventually be seen as the prescriptive
orthodoxies of the decade covered by this selection but in painting and sculpture, as well as
in film and photography, image (as subject or content) seems to have been a central
concern. A return to image, both emblematic and narrative, characterised the paintings in
the influential 'New Spirit' exhibition of 1981[2] but the importance of image was already
evident in, for example, the work of British artists like Tony Cragg and Bill Woodrow, where
the discredited junk status of their materials operated in strong contrast to the pictorial
transformations they effected upon them. However, the *content* of these early sculptures
did not rest solely within their formal configurations, once the materials had been recycled
or transformed. The host materials remained highly visible, offering another associative or
narrative layer. During the same period, artists working outside painting and sculpture but
within the collage traditions of Constructivism or Surrealism have concentrated on
mimicking styles and borrowing images, using the techniques and presentation of, for
example, advertising or science as a means of commenting ironically on the dominant
culture. Pure image appropriation has been taken to extreme pictorial limits by artists like
the American, Sherrie Levine who has simply made reproductions of reproductions of well-
known works of art and added her own name to the titles, without further intervention;[3]
and, most recently, (in a tradition which goes back procedurally and even conceptually to
Duchamp but which in type of object and manner of presentation is nearer to Pop Art), to
extreme material limits in the work of a number of young sculptors in Europe and America.

For example, the much publicised young New York artist Jeff Koons (whose work mimics by means of precise replication the art historical precedent of putting forward non-art artefacts as art), challenging the authority of the model by perfect acts of simulation (or dissimulation[4,5]). It is arguable whether these works' eventual absorption as consumer durables has differed or will differ in any way from the general commodification of works of art within the art market, whatever their physical constituents. Comparisons are suggested with film or video, with the way model and artwork-as-replica might exist in the context of broadcast television, but when the status of a work beyond its existence as image-copy, or equal, remains elusive, as for example in scratch video, how and where it is presented becomes an extension of media, of the work itself.

It has been usual in the twentieth century for artists to make inter-disciplinary forays and many now move easily between media, a number having expanded their work with film or video into performance or installation in the past ten years. However, in so far as the works here are concerned, context, in the sense of physical space, is not a given, it is the separate potential or independence of film as art that is under review.

The fine art background of many of its practitioners has ensured that works from the independent film and video sector mirror the more general artistic concerns of the period. For example, a number of works in this exhibition engage with their subjects through stylistic imitation or homage to earlier models. (The Quay's animated fantasies stand in similar relation to surrealist cinema history, as the 'new expressionist' painters of the early 80s to German Expressionism); feminist politics, expressed in film, and particularly videotape, via what is personal, poetic, and autobiographical have also found expression in installation, performance, painting and sculpture. The appropriation of existing film footage in scratch video finds its equivalents in the work of those artists who re-cycle existing material; the documentary collage of films like *Handsworth Songs* suggest the political documentation or revelation through juxtaposition, of artists such as Hans Haacke.

However, across a range of practice, much of the most interesting work with moving images appears to me to be predicated on those aspects or characteristics which most obviously separate film from most other media – its linear or revelatory narrative potential, its operation in and potential for repetition in time. Film like other art forms may represent by means of mirror or metaphor but its ability to *replicate* is obviously dimensionally, or materially limited. The value of the moving image is less linked to its materiality. As an unmediated object, an unscreened reel of film might have potential in the conceptual sense but this is a minor consideration in relation to its full potential.[6]

In an effort to understand film and video as construction rather than primarily as

The End – Patrick Keiller (1986)

reproduction, I briefly mention three works (all discussed more fully elsewhere in this catalogue) built on 'real' data but which rely on filmic, (in the sense of pictorial or narrative) fictions that extend beyond the usual suppressions or censorship that take place in editing. That each work is transparent in the sense of demonstrating the fictions of its making, ensures its artistic independence, a life beyond documentary. *The End, Almost Out* and *Shadow of a Journey* have a number of characteristics in common.[7] Each imitates or mimics in some way, the documentary form but in a manner which does not conceal that each is more construct than record. Each contains autobiography, narrative, and the hiatuses or correlations which may be established between word and image.

Patrick Keiller has described his method of working as 'a matter of common-or-garden photographic loitering' and on one level *The End*, which is a recent work, might be characterised as 'animated' (in the sense of enlivened) documentary.

It suggests, rather than describing, aspects of a society in decline as its 'narrator', a 'poor creature burdened with neo-classical conceits'[8] appears to insulate or isolate himself from the mundanity of his surroundings, with grandiose pseudo-philosophical ruminations which respond metaphorically to, but do not explain, the landscape through which he appears to be travelling. While the landscape, (views from a car driving through Europe – we appear to travel from Dover via the French channel ports to Brussels, Cologne, Zurich and through the St Gotthard Pass into Italy) is low-key, the script is associative, romantic and theatrical in substance and delivery; for example, the Brussels Atomium seen in long shot and then in section (bottom, lower middle, upper etc) signals a torrent of word images, 'a Disease, a Project, an Obligation, a Threat, a Superstition, a Helmet.' As has already been noted in this catalogue, Keiller, shoots and edits before scripting his films and in *The End* his wandering observer (he has described him as a 'flaneur') delivers a subjective or reactive (reactionary) commentary to existing footage. This animation by means of a superimposed script draws a narrative out of mute place, establishes a running link between discrete images but also emphasises film as potentially manipulative assemblage.[8]

Like *The End* (where non-sequiturs are anticipated in the titles: 'presented by *L'Ufficio d'Inversione,* The Department of Inversion') Tina Keane's title, *Shadow of a Journey* précis the contents of her film, which is layered in an almost sculptural way. As in Keiller's film, image and narrative are super-imposed but in Keane's work, the narrative is explicit while the image, a loop of sunlit water which registers the shadows of the film-maker, her camera and her helper, is vestigal.

The film effectively combines two biographies, a 'visual' auto-biography of the film-maker and her travelling companions, reflected as shadows on the water and a sound biography of the Harris crofters of a hundred years ago, whose history is related by a descendent and contemporary resident of the island, Peggy Morrison. This narrative is the structural core of the work. Like actors in a shadow-play, the figures reflected in the water (a loop) can also be projected onto the past and 'represent' the exiled crofters who, having been cleared from their land, eventually emigrated to Canada. It is possible to relate the loop tape to the circularity of memory (echoed in the repetitive Gaelic songs of the soundtrack). Keane presents us with an unofficial, hence vulnerable, history, which, like the surface of the water could be fragmented or dispersed. In fact the narrative, (a history passed on by word of mouth in Gaelic but translated and scripted for an English audience) is not chronological. The account is genuine 'heard from my mother, as she heard it from her own mother' but at one stage the story appears to shift from the account of the forcible evictions made by a particular 19th century land-owner to a more general history of earlier hardships. The redcoats who burned the Harris houses could be seen to represent the whole history of the Highland clearances.

In an article on the film, Tam Giles pointed out that the idea of juxtaposing a continuum (here image) with a specific focus (the narration) was not new in Keane's work.

> In *Shadow Woman* (now titled *Hopscotch*) a recitation of the events of life for the imminent female was juxtaposed with a small girl who played through the sequences of hopscotch as we watched. This game is as old as recorded history, so as many generations of girls have played this game as women have passed through the shadowy life of the recital. Gradually the real child lost her identity and was transformed from an individual at the beginning of her life-adventures to an anonymous unit of repetitive history.[9]

Tam Giles also draws comparisons with the novels of Virginia Woolf:

> Woolf also typically sets minute fragments of real lives against the continuum eg *The Waves*, *To the Lighthouse*.

(The idea of linking, of continuity has found sculptural expression in the bunching, stacking and coiling configurations of Keane's more recent video installations, for example in the rope ladder and stacked monitors of *Demolition/Escape*, or the monitors organised in a large coil of *Media Snake*.)

Shortly after the completion of *Almost Out*, Jayne Parker wrote of her passive (filmed, rather than filming) part in it!

I Dish – Jayne Parker (1982)

When I see my image on the screen I don't associate my image with myself. I don't feel like that image. I see myself talking, taking on a pose, displaying an attitude. I become a spectator of my image. The image is fixed, I change.[10]

Unlike *Shadow of a Journey* and *The End*, *Almost Out* is only partly scripted but like them, what is said, and what we see, carry rival meanings and the video operates between a series of relationships and ruptures, especially as the editing process is sometimes concealed and at others, revealed. At first it is not apparent that Parker's mother's replies to her daughter's questions were edited although Parker, who at one stage speaks from a prepared script, openly 'edits' herself, referring to her lines on camera. The treatment of the filming of both women (mother and daughter) differs. The daughter is presented more as a performer in a play, while the mother, who in relation to the daughter's questioning represents – and at one stage assumes – the role of an authority figure, is presented visually in a way that challenges the intact and decisive qualities of her replies: her body is chiefly seen in fragmented sections, although she herself can control this on the studio monitor. All filming takes place in the studio (the hard studio equipment is particularly at odds with the two soft unclothed bodies.) This work location frames the contents of the tape as *verité* but also simplifies or stylises. There is a strong element of performance. One critic commented

This enactment itself remained sealed within its own internal structure, the relationships about which it sought to speak protected the exterior.[11]

However it could be that it is this dissembling which rescues the audience from voyeurism, from a sense of complicity.

In contrast to her co-opted cameraman's use of 'intrusive' camera in *Almost Out*, Parker wielded a consciously 'responsible' camera in an earlier work, *I Dish* which similarly concerned what she has described as her 'inner' and 'outer' landscapes and where the actors were naked also – 'Through the camera: I didn't have to go back very far for her to look quite small... It isn't she who is being made small, it is the camera'. (According to Chambers Dictionary 'to Dish' is to outwit, circumvent or ruin but 'dished' also means having concavity: or being completely frustrated.) In this scenario, the woman becomes vulnerable inside a closed landscape 'she is contained, restricted, fettered'. This is the man's domain which in Parker's words 'He occupies completely. Her movements are confined to the edges of his space'.[12] The woman, marginal on the edge of the frame but less vulnerable in the open landscape – there is the implication that she is looking for something *outside* the frame of the film – can only escape inwards but her inner landscape possesses her. It is 'littered with hooks by which she is caught... you cannot detach yourself from your sexuality'. On one level *I Dish* is about the catching, preparing and 'dishing-up' of a fish, but its poetic construction sets up powerful and disturbing resonances which Parker extends in *Almost Out*. For example, in Parker's questioning of her mother's experience of male penetration and the cameraman's reference to the intrusive potential of the camera, *Almost Out* is verbally aggressive, where *I Dish* addresses 'aggressive' imagery visually – (the phallic image of the fish and the man washing himself) but in both works there is a quality that is oblique in a poetic or metaphoric sense.

Both films tackle ideas about power, possession, control, sexuality, 'To be seen, to be desired and to remain untouchable is to have power'.[13] *Almost Out* ends with a surreal reverie which includes a description by Parker of an eel, straight-jacketed. There is an almost palpable feeling of weightiness, of having to take or accept unwillingly, but also of place.

I suggest that, for the art consumer, art as video or film outside what may be seen as both the material (and perceptual) extensions but also the material limitations of full-scale installation, is still difficult to identify as 'art' although we may ask less questions of a vacuum cleaner presented in an art gallery than of a video tape presented in the same space. Nothing today is accompanied by the precipitative shock-into-art which we imagine must have attended the first presentation of, say, a Duchamp readymade. Despite a growing British audience and a degree of public support for film and video by artists, most museums and galleries here have tended to see the newer media primarily as a teaching aid, or documentary back-up. Film and video are also particularly vulnerable in relation to the private collector's market because they are potentially ubiquitous (though costly and labour intensive to produce) and consequently devalued in the market place. An obvious outlet, television, is in the process of being fully explored but art-as-film is easy to miss and it would be a pity if invisibility was to become the price of independence.

However, it seems as though it may be the points at which the works in this exhibition are less easily accommodated within a broader art language which ensure their independence as art. Painted self-portraits may be described as autobiographical art but filmed self-portraits are generally classified as documentary, not art at all.

In 1984 Patrick Keiller described his film as setting out:

> ...to fulfil a desire, to transcend the *disgust* with which so much can so easily (and I suppose rightly) be viewed, and find rather some kind of love, or, if you prefer, to transcend the individualism in subjectivity and effect a collective bridge between imagination and reality, a *realism*.[14]

Despite discrepancies, in dates and styles, *The End*, *Shadow of a Journey* and *Almost Out* bind and represent word and image, the 'real' and the metaphoric, the public and the private, through memory, sequence, duration, fragmentation. Their homogeneity must be read in time but their status as works of art is not easy to challenge.

NOTES

1 In 'Crosscurrents, ten years of mixed media – a Royal College of Art Perspective'. *Catalogue* for exhibition, October 1984, p. 34.
2 'A New Spirit in Painting', *Royal Academy* Jan-Mar 1981.
3 eg See Jeanne Siegel 'After Sherri Levine', *Arts Magazine* Vol 59, Summer 1985, pp. 141-144.
4 eg The material and materialist impact of a Jeff Koons' bronze aqualung or cast stainless steel travel bar is very similar to that of Jasper Johns' metal-plated and cast objects of the 50s and 60s and particularly to the British artist Clive Barker's chrome-plated objects of 1968.
5 The American critic Craig Owens has used 'dissimulation' to describe these 'strategies of mimetic rivalry' see Craig Owens 'Posing' in 'Difference, On Representation and Sexuality', Catalogue for exhibition at The New Museum of Contemporary Art, New York, Dec 84-Feb 85, p. 7.
6 The potential of the unscreened film could be compared to Bruce Nauman's *Concrete Tape Recorder Piece* of 1968 where a tape recording of a scream (playable) (and apparently just audible) was buried in concrete.
7 Patrick Keiller in *leaflet* for film programme, 'Heroic Times' Arts Council, Film and Video Umbrella 1986.
8 In an article in *Undercut* 3 & 4, 1982, pp.42-48 Keiller links his filmic evocations of time, mood and place to the tradition in literature of the wandering day-dreamers: he cites Poe, Baudelaire and Louis Aragon among others. In 'Crosscurrents', ibid, he quotes Lawrence Sterne's 'Tristram Shandy' on the subjective estimation of existence in time, the mental computation of duration 'if in time to come, the succession of our ideas be of any use or service to us at all... in every man's head there is a regular succession of ideas of one sort of another, which follow each other in train just like that...' Keiller's tramp echoes the fallacies of this linear approach 'and, as in any train of thought, the end of one is followed by the beginning of the next' making a subjective leap to a discussion of actual trains, 'the movement of goods across such frontiers' etc.
9 Tam Giles, Peter Wollen on Tina Keane's 'Shadow of a Journey', *Undercut* 2, 1981, pp. 1-3.
10 Jayne Parker in *Undercut* 14/15, p. 56.
11 Nina Danino, ibid, p. 57
12 Jayne Parker 'Landscape in "I Dish"', *Undercut* 7/8, p. 102.
13 *Undercut* 14/15, p. 56.
14 In *Crosscurrents* (see Note 1), p. 34.

E ETC – David Larcher (1969-87)

ROD STONEMAN

Incursions and Inclusions

THE AVANT-GARDE ON CHANNEL FOUR 1983-93

CATEGORIES

The meanings and functions of the term 'avant-garde' have shifted widely as they have been applied to film and video over the last decades. Indeed recently there has been a direct questioning and contestation of the concept itself. But the deployment of experimental and innovative forms to address difficult, marginal or shocking subject matter has been a consistent thread in the developing dynamic of modernism itself.[1]

'Experimental' is a complex term, at once intense and inexact, and it is accompanied by a penumbra of negative connotations, such as 'difficult' and 'boring', in the discourses which circulate British television at the end of the twentieth century. Channel Four's profoundly ambiguous relation with 'experimental' programme making is in contrast with its reiterated commitment to the 'innovative' – the other key term in the statutory imperative for the new Channel to 'encourage innovation and experiment in the form and content of programmes' from the outset in 1982. Significantly it is 'innovation' that retains a positive connotation throughout Channel Four as the cardinal expression in its founding remit.

Avant-garde practices may be difficult to anchor or define in a fixed way as they aim precisely to be consistently inconsistent and exceptional, but they continue to occupy a specific and relative position on the spectrum of audio visual production. They can be defined by their difference (in any direction) from the dominant modes of representation. Their departure from familiar representational strategies may take any form but it is often visually-based and rejects the linear, causal narrative structures of most mainstream forms.

In all their differences, films like Derek Jarman's *The Garden* (1990), Malcolm Le Grice's *Sketches for a Sensual Philosophy* (1988), offer constant exquisite visual pleasure in exchange for the partial loss of narrative. This has been characteristic of experimental work internationally and historically – from Maya Deren to Chantal Akerman, from Kenneth Anger to Jean-Luc Godard. In different ways the genre of creative documentary, from Dziga Vertov's *The Man with the Movie Camera* (1929) to Chris Marker's wide-ranging imaginative and reflective essay *Sans Soleil* (1983) also combines something of the same visual 'compensation'.

The incursion of the filmic avant garde into television is relatively recent. It has speeded up the process whereby those sections of televisual production that constantly search for perceptible novelty, (advertisements, pop promos, the presentational grammar of trails, logos and title sequences) rapidly replicate styles and techniques in order to utilise them for more anodyne and often directly commercial ends. Thus the objective market demand to transform artistic product into a marketable commodity is fulfilled. With BBC 2's witty logo variants, elaborate trailing strategies on Channel Four and the superficially inventive 'idents' on MTV perhaps it is unsurprising that the boundaries are blurred.

Thus it has recent been argued that, in 1995, after the first decade of a relationship with broadcasting, 'there is no independent film avant-garde, no independent video art production...'[2] Of course categories like 'independent' are relative and specific to the conjuncture they operate within; at any given point one would have to think through the implications of making, maintaining or dissolving such categories – the 'imaginary' of the avant garde. The filmic avant garde is a tenuous network, itself a constituent part of what has always been a dispersed and disparate independent sector, but it continues separately – using television funding opportunistically without a committed long-term engagement. For better or worse avant garde practitioners continue to view and experience television as peripheral to their vision, not fully engaging with its problems or possibilities as a site of production or reception. At this particular time in whose interest, and from what perspective is it possible to dissolve the crucial differences between a sector that does not produce primarily for television and one that does?

In some strange way avant garde practices, which reproduce themselves through constant transformation, have the capacity to continue despite recuperation, ingestion and assimilation. Springing from a mentality of play and provocation based on the desire to challenge existent boundaries, inertia or stasis is not possible. From gentle metamorphosis to dramatic counterposition, avant garde styles and preoccupations continue to change and move on. For the vanguard, dialectical re-formation is the underlying dynamic of development.

The avant garde asserts itself through both its formal difference and through its stance as an im- or ex- plicit critique of 'the way things are'. It makes its intervention from a cultural space characterised by a lack of commercial, institutional and audience pressure on the creative process. It enjoys the free assertion of difference and dissidence to build a culture of the imagination. Working within the contradictions of ultra low budgets imposes considerable and constant production constraints but it also liberates the film-maker from the formidable pressures of fully funded 'industrial' production.[3]

In an adjacent domain even a apparatchik can be caught in a version of the contradictions between desire and possibility. My experience of the limitations of the structures has been through a specific singular trajectory inside television; the case of the original incorporation of someone like myself from the London Filmmakers' Co-op end of the Independent Filmmakers' Association into the Channel Four Trojan horse is unusual in television terms. Carrying the unwieldy framework of Seventies *Screen* theory into the practice of British broadcasting has involved a curious journey leading to some strange connections and mixed emotions.

The ultra-rationalism of Structural theory that would seek to build an analytical model of institutional functioning inevitably falls short in that it cannot account for one's own contingent orientation and desires – that perversity for diversity, the search for the Other and the different. Rather than fabricating the laudable factors of conscious cultural policy perhaps one need only see the mischievous motivation of an Oedipal relationship with the institution?[4]

RECEPTION

Through the specific conjuncture of Channel Four, the avant garde, as part of the diverse spectrum of independent film, was 'invited' into British television for the first time in a sustained way[5]. The new channel was bright, small and integrated, naive in its newness but underpinned by its apparently incongruous commercial sources of funding. Experiment existed at the edge of the edge, as part of the channel's singular mix which aimed to 'extend and complement what was available on the other British television channels', perhaps it was understood as a marginal manifestation of the modern, the novel, the fashionable.

This initial inclusion was part of a fragile pluralist instinct, a genuine intellectual curiosity to explore the *terra incognita*. The senior executives who controlled budgets and schedules liked the *notion* of experiment, if not the actual practice of it. Amongst the command structures of television, as amongst other social groups, the avant garde is finally a refined taste that is only of sustained interest to a very small proportion of the potential audience. However the obvious difference from other areas of arcane or minority taste (say esoteric sports or unfamiliar forms of music) is that the filmic avant garde leads to a much higher and more energetic level of rejection from those that decide that they are 'not interested' in it. To a far greater degree it is perceived as an aggressive challenge and assault to settled, complacent personal taste and an affront to precarious notions of professionalism. It often seems to create a visceral over-reaction from those who might merely be expected to pass it by. There is a special English sensitivity to 'self-indulgence'; it is a *criticism* which can often be conjoined with the strangely pejorative use of the term 'masturbatory' in connection with difficult art practice. The result perhaps of a self-denying culture of strict behaviour where it is better to discipline or abstain than to gratify or luxuriate.

The scandal that erupted around Buñuel and Dali's *L'Age d'Or* in Paris in December 1930, or Jack Smith's *Flaming Creatures* (1963) thirty years later in New York, remind one of the many examples in the history of experimental film that have attracted extreme reactions. Perhaps the original, violent critical response to Jean-Luc Godard's *Pierrot Le Fou* when it was first shown in 1965 indicated the aggression provoked by even moderate excursions from narrative economy. In addition to reaction arising from the obvious transgression of sexual and political mores in experimental work, there is a zealous and deep-seated resistance to ambiguity and open meanings in our cultures. Anger seems to erupt in response to the merest threat of polysemy. When some powerful television 'professional' rejected a piece of experimental work with undue force and uninhibited ignorance, I used to find consolation in the words of Mao Zedong, 'to be attacked by the enemy is a good thing and not a bad thing'...

Perhaps part of this overdetermined hostility results from the challenge which avant garde work poses to the conservative and ingrained nature of television language which is ideologically sustained as invisible, neutral, transparent. By insisting on the relative, the cultural and historical provenance of film form, experimentation has a political role. It may be understood as part of the project to understand what Roland Barthes described as the way in which 'society produces stereotypes, i.e. triumphs of artifice, which it them consumes as innate meanings, i.e. triumphs of nature.'[6] It is this reintroduction of difference, unmaking subject identities to produce a critical knowledge, indicating the possible space of other orders, which renders modernism so difficult for the institution of television.[7]

Formal experimentation also invokes the politics of representation to some extent. Even the non-figurative ludic forms of abstract films offer a fierce intensity of sound and image, they implicitly propose another way of seeing, interrupting and disturbing settled expectations and complacencies. Such work is distinguished by its rigour, intelligence and structure from the decorative promos and surface distractions of MTV.

Experiment was specifically included as part of the work of the Independent Film and Video Department[8] at Channel Four. This reflected the arguments made by the casual but sustained alliance of interests represented in the Independent Filmmakers' Association that had lobbied the nascent Channel to fund and transmit a wide spectrum of work. An Independent Film and Video departmental booklet published in 1983 indicated the intention:

> ...with a range of commissions and acquisitions from experimental film and
> programme makers we intend to remain at the interface between the 'difficult' and
> obscure elements of visual experiment and the interests of sizable and significant
> 'minority' audiences.

Although none of the regional workshops that were franchised and funded were committed to experimental work, some capital and revenue funding was provided for access organisations like London Video Arts and Luton 33.[9]

But the initial exposure of the avant garde was limited – not too much was needed in order to function as an additional peripheral attribute to the pluralist self-image of the new station and it did not need to appear on screen too often. The Channel operated within Jeremy Isaacs' judicious founding phrase 'different but not that different'[10]. Even more than other areas of the Independent Film and Video's output (political documentary – 'Critical Eye', community access programmes – 'People to People', gay and lesbian work – 'Out', third world film-makers – 'Cinema from Three Continents' and 'South') the Channel's hierarchy was guided by the unstated assumption that 'a little goes a long way'... The same alibi, which allows self-justification with reference to the more adventurous edges of the remit in public debates and the Annual Report, can be achieved just as well by rare excursions of experimentation as by a sustained on-screen presence.

The drastic limits on the proportion of such work shown were also exacerbated by its placement in the schedule. For the first few years of Channel Four the avant garde was a very occasional part of the *Eleventh Hour* which was established in the tundra of the schedule at 11pm on a Monday night... Even when, in the late eighties, a higher proportion of the Department's output moved to more accessible locations in the evening, the avant garde remained at that remote and unattractive site, or even later. Shocking language and explicit sexuality tended to confine much of the work to way after the 'family viewing threshold' at 9pm but the consistent positioning near midnight was a result of a deeper institutional reluctance.

Experiment was also marginalised and undermined by a lack of concerted promotion and by the invisible inverted commas that were often placed around the work by its on-air presentation. The connotations and nuances of presentation announcements often seemed sceptical, incredulous and occasionally even overtly sarcastic. Unconsciously, innocently but nevertheless ideologically, presenters seemed to be saying 'you will find this very difficult and probably won't like it, I certainly didn't...'.[11]

The question of packaging, presentation and contextualisation became a focal issue for film-makers too. The Department's strategy evolved gradually with different variants from the starting point of the four *Profiles* (1983) made in a traditional television format about Malcolm Le Grice, Margaret Tait, Jeff Keen and a programme about four women film-makers associated with the distributor Circles[12]. Each of the programmes was followed by examples of the film-maker's work. Framed as a 'portrait of the artist', each of the programmes approached experimental works through the presentation of the individual creator as punctual source of their meaning. The presence of a particular personality behind the work reassures the viewer that the position from which diverse, non-linear materials can be seen to cohere is that of the organising and intentional author. Confirming the film as the unproblematic product of the transcendental subject reinforces the dominant notion that a film is 'about' its maker and leads to the production of centred, closed readings. But this was the logic of compromise involved in bringing such work to a vastly greater audience than had ever encountered it before.

The Le Grice programme went some way to counter this through the introduction of theoretical concerns; however, there was difficulty in explaining those concerns accessibly from the audience's point of view. A familiarity with the terms and ideas was too easily assumed and some exchanges betrayed a certain awkward self-consciousness which sounded like fragments from arcane and off-putting discourses. Subjects which were provoking lively debate amongst, say, 2000 students in colleges of art needed careful re-presentation in order to avoid appearing to be the solipsistic preoccupations of an enclosed, distant coterie to a television audience of a quarter of a million people.

Arguably the most successful of the *Profiles* was the programme on Jeff Keen where his fast, colourful, high-impact short films had a striking power when shown on television. Al Rees' accessible questions also fleshed out the idiosyncratic culture of the creator. This leads to the leading question of what 'works' well on television? Is it the context of domestic viewing, a space of interruption and intermittent distraction, which makes some forms (that combine colour/speed/energy) operate more successfully than other forms (say minimalist or duration-based strategies)? It is important to stress that this is not an absolute judgement but a relative, relevant awareness concerning the effectiveness of certain formal strategies in the specific context of television.

Across the decade there were other occasional documentaries on artists – notably Keith Griffiths' *The Five and Dime Animator* (1985) on the American Avant-Garde animator Robert Breer and *Doodlin'* (1987) on Len Lye, which exemplified the way in which the creative exploration of frame by frame difference in the field of animation can connect with avant garde work[13]. The same film-maker made *Abstract Cinema* (1992) which examined non-figurative films from 1930 until the present, from popular examples like Fischinger's *Toccata and Fuque* sequence of Disney's *Fantasia* (1940) and contemporary pop promos to the more rigorous constructions of Le Grice and the German avant garde film-makers Birgit and Wilhelm Hein.

There was minimal packaging of the five compilations that made for the first series of *Dazzling Image* programmes when they were shown in 1990. The short films and tapes were mostly linked together without presentation in a graphic magazine format, clipping the individual films' end credits. This series was well received critically in the press and seen as successful inside Channel Four; it led to a 'best of' programme being assembled for a mid-evening slot during the following Christmas and New Year schedule. A more conventional style was chosen for the second series of seven *Dazzling Image* programmes in 1992 – it was introduced by a range of well known people from other fields such as Spike Milligan, Anthony Clare and Ken Livingstone who offered some overall thematic connections between the films and provided a context for the uninitiated viewer. Often it was almost a matter of saying 'relax, leave your preconceptions behind, don't worry if you don't know the background or immediately understand the foreground, pleasure can be had here...'.

Although these explicit combinations of short films and tapes were only temporary and provisional there was some resistance from film-makers who were used to retaining total control of the presentation of their own work in the context of the fragmentary audiences encountered in the closed environments of colleges and galleries. As a result of this very specific, self-selecting domain of operation, the British avant garde had not been led to consider the question of its audience or its reception in any thorough fashion. Perhaps this is a traditional characteristic of avant garde movements internationally but it becomes a particular limitation when there is an opportunity to encounter wider audiences through television.

For transmission there was a calculation that, whilst the more explanatory presentation style would hopefully not completely alienate denizens of the avant garde for whom these introductions might be stating the obvious, they would certainly make the work more accessible for the vast majority of an audience less familiar with where it came from. This seemed more important than the dangers of presenting a frame of reference which might have a potentially limiting effect on open meanings.

Some series were constructed and linked merely via technological format: *Video 1, 2. 3* in 1985 was transmitted just before John Wyver's selection of American video art in the series *Ghost in the Machine* for the Arts commissioning department in Channel Four. *Video 4. 5.* and *Super Eight* followed in 1986. Although they were constructed around particular technical formats there was a strong sense of the sub-cultural movements that had grown around the motivated use of particular gauges of film and video. Influenced by the work of Derek Jarman, Super 8mm film was used by several film-makers, dubbed 'New Romantics'; their espousal of a looser, richer, camp style was seen as a reaction to a decade of austere minimalism and rationalism from the London Film-makers' Coop. In the video there was a parallel confluence of currents of performance, scratch and conceptual work.

The four editions of *Timecode*, a compilation programme of short commissioned videos from around the world, were completed in six years. The most successful editions of this international experimental television magazine, co-ordinated by Carl-Ludwig Rettinger of ZDF's 'Das Kleine Fernsehspiel', combined short non-verbal pieces around the focused themes of love and music; it provided an opportunity for British video (and eventually film-) makers to produce a short on a sizable budget and led to the creative interaction of pieces made in very different cultures which attracted some attention abroad[14] .

In 1993 the eight programmes of *Midnight Underground* were almost entirely assembled from a more international selection of acquired films; their very late night slot adopted and adapted well to the work of Kenneth Anger and Ken Jacobs but also Derek Jarman and Steve Dwoskin. Introduced by Ben Wooley, the programmes were clustered in poetic thematic groups: Objects in Motion, Little Stabs at Happiness, The Sleep of Reason.

With the exception of the 'experimental classics' that were bought for transmission in *Midnight Underground*, the emphasis of the Department's transmissions shifted over the decade from international purchases to the production of new avant garde work in Britain. The resultant films and tapes were still screened in anthology presentation formats and compilations which included a small proportion of bought-in material. Although support for indigenous production was crucial to the health of the sector, in some sense it was always less relevant to the viewer whether a particular piece was specially produced with television finance or purchased after it had been completed.

The motor for the exponential increase in the production of experimental work for television were the schemes initiated in partnership with the Arts Council. Some forty new British short films and tapes were produced, and of these, only three films were never transmitted. The schemes had the advantage of an arm's length commissioning structure, an armature which usefully separated the individualistic and artisanal mode of avant garde production from the cumbersome legal and financial machinery of industrial television. The film and television technicians' union ACTT[15] was consulted in advance and reassured that these schemes did not pose any kind of dangerous precedent for their employment guidelines. They tended to take a relaxed view as the huge differences of scale and mode of production clearly made standard crewing requirements incompatible and irrelevant for most of the productions. The Eleventh Hour/Arts Council Awards initiated in 1988 evolved into 'Experimenta' in 1992, both schemes offered individual production budgets of up to £25,000, which included modest payments and fees; film-makers retained copyright and Channel Four took the rights for two television transmissions. The economy of these parsimonious budgets follows the assumption that experiment should be cheap. However the opposite could be argued – that standard production methods are straight forward and economical but experiment precisely involves more testing and trial and error, and therefore cost. But that would be to invert the logic of the market…

The British Film Institute's Production Department's equivalent 'New Directors' also included some avant garde work, like *Granny's is* (1990) by David Larcher, and provided a good proportion of the short films which were included in the *Dazzling Image* series. Co-funding with outside institutions meant that a high degree of risk could be openly acknowledged. The broadcaster could co-finance the making of several pieces but might only choose to show a small proportion of them. The fact that nearly everything that was produced through these schemes was eventually transmitted inevitably helped strengthen internal commitment to the partnership.

In its last year 'Experimenta' expanded to include 'Experimenta Longform' (£50,000 for longer pieces)... but the Channel's Independent Film and Video Department had made substantial single pieces en route: David Larcher's EETC (1986), Malcolm Le Grice's *Sketches for a Sensual Philosophy* (1988) and *Blue*[16] (1993) by Derek Jarman.

CONTEXTS

The impact of the visually based and non-narrative practices supported and transmitted by Channel Four had some resonance and limited take-up by other broadcasters. BBC 2 collaborated with the Arts Council on the excellent 'One Minute Television', a series of sixty second pieces shown on *The Late Show* for several years in succession, and commissioned the anthology format *White Noise* series. Carlton television co-funded experimental work with the London Film and Video Agency and Harlech Television with South West Arts.

But television's limited engagement with experiment must be seen in a wider context – the avant garde is blurred and dissolved at the edge, less with other television forms than with some parts of (what is generally characterised as) European art cinema. It shares the same visual emphasis, occasionally extending the boundaries of form, complicating and undercutting narrative structures...

Jean-Luc Godard, who in the latter stages of his wide-ranging creative exploration can certainly be situated as a leading European experimental film-maker, had a season of his most challenging work in the Eleventh Hour in 1985 – including films like *Le Gai Savoir* (1968), *Numero Deux* (1975) and *Passion* (1982), a strange semi-documentary like *Pravda* (1969), radical television work such as *France Tour Detour Deux Enfants* (1977-78), and a new commission, specially made for Channel Four, *Soft and Hard* (1986). The first two episodes of his seminal *Histoire(s) du Cinema* followed in 1992. Alexander Kluge's *The Patriot* (1979) was included in a season of European art cinema, and Dusan Makavejev's *WR the Mysteries of the Organism* (1971) was incorporated in the 'Banned' season. Closer to home the Independent Film and Video Department commissioned low budget British fiction, amounting to perhaps thirty feature films with directors such as Ken McMullen, Derek Jarman and Stuart McKinnon. Channel Four supported work by film-makers like Peter

Greenaway, Sally Potter and Terence Davies, though its commitment to the British Film Institute's Production Department, together this adds up to a concerted attempt to strengthen an indigenous version of art house production.

Against this background, those who habitually wish to mourn the successive sorrows of the avant garde could assert that a decade of this work had marginal impact and little effect on British film and television culture in the Eighties. A transmission is sent out through the ether with little sense of audience or reception, no real way of assessing its impact or its influence. The locomotive power of television, as part of the image spectacle, obliterates such small scale individual incursions. Persistent pessimism about the role of experimental practice may be the result of an unrealistic overestimation of the aspiration at the outset. The avant garde is a demonstration of an oblique, necessarily idealistic challenge – 'A map of the world that does not include Utopia is not worth even glancing at.' Oscar Wilde.

Perhaps the intervention of the avant garde in television and cinema as a whole aspires to what Alexander Kluge designated[17] a 'homeopathic' approach to culture – microscopic amounts and low levels of input aspire to effect the whole body politic. Despite the enclosed nature of the activity, artistic coteries and marginal movements can have a powerful influence on the culture at large.

The first decade of Channel Four constitutes a considerable experiment with experiment – the largest body of avant garde work shown on network television, encountering its widest audiences, anywhere, ever.

NOTES

1 A critique of the alleged paradigm change achieved by post-modernism is outlined in 'Love, music, compromise: the pop promo', Rod Stoneman, *Vertigo* Spring 1993.
2 John Wyver, *What You See is What You Get*, The Third ICA Biennial of Independent Film and Video, 1995.
3 There is a tenuous transition of those serious experimental film-makers who have tried to transpose their concerns from an unfunded space to the possibilities of finance by advertising: Oskar Fischinger's Muratti cigarette advertisements, Len Lye's work for the GPO, Godard's Nike ads... But these marriages of convenience have rarely sustained the film-makers' best work.
4 These attenuated biographical questions are sketched in the context of a general appraisal of the work of the Independent Film and Video department at Channel Four in my article 'Sins of Commission', *Screen* Vol. 33 no.2, Summer 1992.

5　This invitation was preceded by numerous allergic reactions such as the BBC's Aubrey Singer infamous quip, before the Bristol Festival of Independent Film in 1975, that independent work would never be shown – 'not on *my* television'.

6　Roland Barthes, 'Lecture', *Oxford Literary Review*, Vol 4, no 1, 1978/79.

7　Paul Abbott, 'Authority', *Screen* Vol 20, no 2, Summer 1979.

8　The department comprised; Alan Fountain 1981-94; Rod Stoneman 1982-93 and Caroline Spry 1985-95.

9　*Sins of Commission* op cit p 135.

10　Delivered at the *Edinburgh Television Festival* in August 1982.

11　Explicitly by Tracy McLeod on BBC2's *The Late Show* when introducing the Arts Council's One Minute films in 1992.

12　The series was co-funded with the Arts Council of Great Britain, subsequently becoming the Arts Council of England in 1993.

13　A great deal of creative animation was commissioned and brought by Paul Madden in the early years of Channel Four, Clare Kitson eventually took over responsibility for this area.

14　In *Timecode II* there were pieces from eight different countries and Mozambican television transmitted them as interludes to the 1986 World Cup matches.

15　Which later became BECTU.

16　Funded by the Arts Council of Great Britain and transmitted simultaneously in stereo by BBC Radio 4 (exceptionally this hour long programme did not contain any advertising breaks).

17　At a seminar at the Institute of the Contemporary Arts in London, December 1993.

This Unnamable Little Broom – Quay Brothers (1985)

SIMON PUMMELL

Will the Monster Eat the Film?

OR THE REDEFINITION OF ANIMATION 1980-94

In the Hollywood blockbuster *Alien III* (1993 the last film in the *Alien* trilogy), the monster eats all the characters the viewer can identify with or be interested in (excepting the heroine Ripley) in the first third of the film. Especially disappointing was the consumption of Charles Dance as the love interest, before he even made it to a proper first kiss. This could be seen as the film's great claim to be an archetypal post-modern film.[1] In *Alien III*, the real thriller is whether the monster will eat the narrative before it resolves itself in a classical narrative fashion. It represents cinema teetering between the narrative (will the story be resolved at the end?) of classical cinema and the plastic spectacle (the monster) of digital and special fx cinema; in fact the cinema of animation.

The old battle between Méliès and the Lumière brothers has reached another turning point. The massive explosion in 'composite cinema', both in computer animation and the frame-by-frame manipulation of live-action material, creates a possible paradox: animation is eating classical cinema, and possibly at the same time creating conditions for its own ultimate extinction as a distinct category. This has created a quite new context for an examination of the development of what once would have been called 'Independent' of 'Avant-garde' British animation in the last 15 years. The very need to bracket these terms, is another aspect of the inter-penetration of categories that is currently occurring, and cannot be understood without casting an eye on the changing economic and technical context of this work.

'A MYSTERIOUS PENGUIN AND A PAIR OF AUTOMATED TECHNO-TROUSERS' AND OTHER STRANGE PAIRINGS²

The Aardman Studio, has produced a set of popularly successful films in the last decade. After the film *Down and Out* (1978) for the BBC set the style of lip sync to a verité track, the studio produced a string of claymation films, *Conversation pieces* (1989), which matched expressive and detailed animation to highly naturalistic vox-pop interviews. It is a trademark that the voices are hesitant and making real efforts to articulate feelings, and thoughts. Although the films are deceptively light and populist, the formal interplay of sound and animation is reflexive and sophisticated. The conversational soundtracks counter-pointed by underplayed and very 'British' surrealism in the visuals. In later films *Creature Comforts* (1989) and *The Wrong Trousers* (1993) this approach was developed further. A picture postcard/music hall humour combined with their consummate craftsmanship and naturalistic soundtracks has resulted in Oscars for Nick Park the film's director. In particular *Creature Comforts*, which resulted in a series of spin off advertisements, makes the distinction between independent animator, popular television and TV commercials extremely blurred.

The Aardman studio occupies the most viable and popular end of the spectrum of a new area which allows a wide range of film-makers to function and produce work. The interstices of commercials, broadcast television and traditional arts funding have created a new locus where innovative and oppositional work is being created alongside more traditional animated entertainment and advertising. Relationships which once appeared oppositional are now closer to a complex symbiosis.

In the period 1980-94 Britain has become internationally renowned as a prolific centre of excellence for the animated short film. The single event that created much of the context for this growth was the decision by Channel 4 to commission short animated work for adults as part of its programming. This decision has influenced other broadcasters, and has created a new economic context for animation. In particular Channel 4's animation commissioning policy has embraced both mainstream and more formally innovative work, and so film-makers with completely opposed intentions and ideologies have come to work under increasingly similar conditions as independent programme makers for broadcast television.

Another important economic and technical context is London's international reputation as a centre for the production of commercials, and perhaps more specifically the post-production of commercials. British advertising has a high international reputation, and this has allowed a concentration of very high-tech, capital intensive post-production facilities to develop, which attract clients from all around the world. The only comparable concentration of facilities is in Los Angeles, and so London is the obvious choice for Europeans, and also a choice for east coast American advertising agencies, who are equidistant between London and Los Angeles.

Such a concentration of work and facilities has had a profound effect on innovative animators as well as film and television. Within animation, work has been produced by a range of formal and informal relationships between post-production houses and film-makers. Interestingly, the Arts Council of England has increasingly committed to create a range of formal schemes that give frameworks for alliances between commercials post-production houses and individual artist/film-makers. This can be seen as part of an overall shift from a policy of creation of a parallel independent film culture to an explicit policy of intervention in the arena of broadcast television.

And so this period has seen a new hybrid of artist and animator, working within an oppositional and innovative aesthetic but within the context of broadcast television and advertising.

'IMAGINEZ AUTRE CHOSE'[3]

Keith Griffiths and the Brothers Quay met at the Royal College of Art, and have since collaborated on nearly a dozen films.[4] A printed postcard, for many years propped above Keith Griffith's desk in the Koninck office, admonished the reader to 'Imagine something else', an encouragement to value the marginal, the unexpected, the perverse. In many ways it functions as the unofficial motto for the company, which could be seen as the shadow side of the British animation culture that Aardman represents.

The strategy of obliquity extends to the contextualising or disguising of the animated films as arts documentaries or profiles, and sometimes documentaries directed by Griffiths. *Igor - The Paris Years Chez Pleyel* (1983) is an example of an early Koninck film that combines live action with the intricate and introverted puppet scenario. A celebration of Stravinsky's music as he transcribed it to player piano, the soundtrack is entirely the player piano you see within the film, playing rolls recorded by Stravinsky. Thus the sound track is itelf a complex inter-penetration of human and automata. The Brothers Quay and Keith Griffith staked out territory in this film that they were to mine for the decade. The film is formally self-conscious, foregrounding the miniaturisation of animation and the jerking, disturbing half-life of marionettes. It fetishizes the formal intricacy possible with stop-motion techniques. The relationship between live-action and animation is one of counter-point rather than harmony.

Part of the Quays' project has always been to use cultural pre-texts for their work. It is as if their films are in dialogue with the particular artist or work they have selected. The films act as intimate, claustrophobic conversations through time and space. For example the film *Rehearsals for Extinct Anatomies* (1989), is a response not only to an etching by the painter Fragonard, but also a flayed horse created by his nephew Fragonard, the anatomist. *Street of Crocodiles* (1986) is an evocation of certain passages in the tiny oeuvre of the Polish author Bruno Schulz, and *The Cabinet of Dr Svankmajer* (1984) is a tribute to the Czech animator Jan Svankmajer, which includes glances at films such as *L'Ange* (1984) by the French film-maker Bokanofski. The Quays have remarked:

> [A]nimation is a ghetto itself in a strange way, and it can be explored in that respect.[5]

The Brothers Quay intricate constructions are among the most self-conscious and formally sophisticated animated films ever made. They create a world where the 19th century encounters the shocks of the 20th century: an imaginary ghetto within a world in crisis, a world of dislocation, a world in its death throes. In the ghetto a more organic relation to the past still lives on but is threatened by nameless fears and tensions coming both from within and without. Although the Brothers Quay can make many references to Central and Eastern Europe, and the image of the ghetto must conjure up the rich Jewish culture of early 20th century Europe, their world is more closely linked to Joseph Cornell's evocation of a mythical 'Europe' in his melancholy box constructs than to any factual space or tradition.

Puppet animation involves miniaturization, and the re-animation of dead matter, the cult of the marionette, the compression of months of work into films only minutes long. In the Quays' films this compression of space and time is tangible in the strange transformation of objects (fish bones as forks) and in the claustrophobic choreography of the puppets and camera: 'For us the camera is the third puppet in a sense, the motivator.'[6]

The Quays are exceptionally cinematically literate, and this is reflected in their *mise en scène*. Interestingly, their last animated short *The Comb (1990)* incorporated some live action (previously limited to the prologue to *Street of Crocodiles*), and their first live-action feature film *Institute Benjamenta* was released in Autumn 1995.

Both *The Comb* and *Institute Benjamenta* (1995) are based on the writings of the Swiss author Robert Walser. Shot in luminous black and white *Institute Benjamenta* evokes an earlier cinematic age. The film seamlessly combines live action and animation to tell the story of Jacob, a pupil in an enigmatic institute for servants. The intensely claustrophobic setting is the most direct link to the Quay's animated work.

> We intended The Institute would be one of the major actors, objects would play
> an important role. The important thing was no-one should know there was any
> animation... we realised if we failed it would make a dent in the surface of the
> whole film.[7]

And the film does interleave animation and live action in subtle and invisible ways. To such an extent that some of the practices have a ritualistic rather than a functional role in the making of the film.

> Take building the model for the inner sanctum... and animating the light in that,
> which was real sunlight as opposed to studio light. We just pre-lit the scene in the
> most minimal fashion and waited for five o'clock, for the sun to come around the
> building here; and literally it just crept up the walls like liquid, and it was sort of a
> revelation. We did three days, three takes, always at five o'clock. One we clicked off a
> frame every three seconds, one every five, one every seven.[8]

The sense of directness and materiality which the Quays prize so highly transferred to their attitude to the special effects compositing at The Mill, a state of the art digital post-production house. In the Quay's descriptions of the process we begin to see how direct digital manipulation re-introduces metaphors of painting and manual creation of images back into film-making (cutting, pasting, pulling, stretching, painting).

> The Flame artist said you know I can make the glass bow, because it was a separate
> shot which got pasted into the goldfish bowl, and we said I know... I bet... and
> thought it would be a chemical effect... cheap... but it wasn't it was fantastic. He just
> touched the front of the image and literally pulled it towards him, saying is that
> enough or we can make it warp a little bit more.[9]

Such processes are a further blurring of the categories of animation and live action.

Koninck has also produced other animated films such as *Secret Joy of Falling Angels* (Simon Pummel 1992) a film using drawn animation, shadows, and direct painting onto film to create an expressionist reading of The Annunciation, and *Within/without* (Benita Raphan 1994), a photo film, which animates black and white stills and lies in a tradition that runs from Chris Marker's *La Jetée* and early Borowczyk. It is worth noting that Griffiths has also produced a wide ranging set of documentaries about important animators and abstract film-makers, and also brought the work of Svankmajer to Britain.

Koninck's work is heavily based on broadcast television for funding, but also the Quays have made a number of commercials. In many ways the company epitomises the new models of independent animation film.

THE EXTENSION OF THE DISCIPLINE OF DRAWING...

Perhaps the other most original and consistent school of work produced in the period was indirectly created by Ray Fields, a painter, who was influenced by the St Ives School of British Modernism; an informal grouping of artists, which included Naum Gabo, Ben Nicholson, Barbara Hepworth, and Patrick Heron. The St Ives School functioned as a centre of the Modernist tradition in Britain. They looked to European art and Abstract art as an antidote to British representational and more domestic traditions. Fields had also spent time working in advertising, and at Liverpool Polytechnic he combined these experiences by creating an aggressively fine art based animation course. Dealing only with drawn animation, Fields articulated unusually clearly a possible relation between the act of drawing and the practice of animation.

Drawing always offers a problem for the theorising of animation, yet it has always formed a key, almost defining strand of animation. As a form of representation it clearly pre-dates cinema by a millennia. In animation it is possible to identify two opposed strands of approach to drawing; drawing as illusion and drawing as a more self-conscious practice. So a lineage runs through Winsor McCay's *Gertie The Dinosaur* (1914) to the late Disney studio's elaborate multiplane set-ups and carefully timed and weighted realistic characters to the illusionist 3D models that dominate much high-end computer animation. For example, the dinosaurs created for Spielberg's *Jurassic Park* are in a direct line of descent from Gertie. There is also an opposed tradition that highlights the drawing as a set of marks, a representational language, a material practice. This tradition could be seen to run from Fleischer's *Out of The Inkwell* (1922-4) series in the twenties through the more formally reflexive Warner cartoons such as *Duck Amuck* (1953) to Robert Breer's file card films such as *A Man and His Dog Out for Air* (1957). It is a tradition which can be seen as related to the modernist impulse to be reflexive and anti-illusionist. It is the latter tradition that fields engaged with when he started to formulate the Liverpool course.

Starting from the sketchbook, with emphasis on the *practice* of drawing; Field stated animation should simply be 'The extension of the discipline of drawing into the further dimension of time and space."[10] Both his clarity and also his overtly fine art terms of reference attracted many students who otherwise might have attended the painting or printmaking schools. The result was a crop of short films which were semi-documentary, observational; in many ways "moving sketchbooks". In films such as Susan Young's *Thin Blue Lines* (1982) and Jonathan Hodgson's *Dogs* (1981) the forms remain representations, signs and never become characters. What made the work from Liverpool stand out was the freshness and coherence of the draughtsmanship. They were vividly drawn, and in a way that integrated the fact that the marks were animated. The students were encouraged not to think of a sequence of drawings, but rather a single drawing moving through time. And central to the Liverpool aesthetic is the avoidance of traditional anthropomorphism; the drawings remained drawings.

Perhaps the most developed examples of this school are *Carnival* (Susan Young 1985) and Stuart Hiltons films *Save Me* (1994) and *Argument in a Superstore* (1992). Young's film is a free flowing description of the NottingHill Carnival, and is an extension of *Thin Blue Lines* (which was a description of the Toxteth riots). Both depict anarchic public spectacle, and use the open ended episodic form to display fluid and ambiguous figure drawing. *Carnival* uses direct animation with thick Chinese brushes and ink, and directly animated pastel to create figures and crowds that hover between calligraphy and representation. At one point in the film the vibrant colours flood away to leave black, linear figures dancing. The limbs and faces start to decompose into their constituent marks. The figuration is held on the very edge of disintegration, yet the figures still dance. Hilton's *Save Me* takes such disintegration to its logical conclusion. A tumbling play of figurative and abstract marks, as well as letters and scrawled words all struggle to signify but are swept away. We are deluged by fragments of picture and sound: numerical calculations and hand written notes, cartoon drawings (a dog lifted up by its lead in a parody of cartoon violence), rubber stamps, typography and live action. At times the film resembles an animated Cy Twombly drawing; free floating gestural marks that hover uncertainly between drawing and writing. The insertion of live-action is interesting in its variety of methods. Short clips of treated and tinted live-action film are cut in, often with elements that mirror the animation. For example, a close-up of a mug with a slogan on it rotates too fast for us to read the slogan easily; exactly the effect created by the animation with typography and scrawled notes tripping through it. Elsewhere the live-action acts as a picture within a picture, as animated video prints and photographs are stuck down as just another element of collage in the frame.

As an interesting potential crossover, Hilton has recently expressed interest in using a digital Paintbox and Quantel Harry[11] to create elements in a new abstract film. He sees it as an extension of the graphic languages he collects, and has specifically stated that what interests him is the rough mattes and scribbled frame numbering that is normally erased and hidden in the process of compositing film levels. It is interesting that he is incorporating material 'hidden' in his commercial work into his own films, and also that he is extending the Liverpool interest in the *practice* of drawing into the hidden processes of digital compositing, a new cast on the opposition of drawing strands outlined above.

A feature of the Liverpool work is its avoidance of narrative. It is an animation form that is highly developed in graphic drawing terms but as yet unable or unwilling to develop a narrative film language of its own. It is significant that Young has made commercials since leaving a post-graduate course at the Royal College of Art, and Hilton's films have been funded as abstract films by the Arts Council of England.

An isolated but extremely interesting film in this area is Tim Webb's *A is for Autism* (1992). Using the drawings of several autistic children it presents the experience of autism through the precocious draughtsmanship and eyes of the autistic. In doing so it raises issues of form and its relationship to our most fundamental ways of being in the world in an extremely powerful way. It is that strangest of films – a formalist documentary'; the subject is almost entirely communicated through form. It is not what the children draw it is how they draw, and so by inference how they perceive the world.

WANTING TO WORK IN CONDITIONS OF EXAGGERATED PRIVACY...[12]

Women have had a powerful presence in British animation of the last ten years. An early Channel 4 commission was Alison de Verre's *Silas Marner* (1984). The film is representative of a traditional and artisanal way of making animated films, fetishizing the individual, and so personal nature of the film. A subtext of such films is often that a film made by one person is more profoundly expressive than a film made in a more industrial way. This is perhaps a gender issue, as there is a great concentration of women making films in this way. Rather than a fantasy of technical omnipotence, such films use animation as a space where women choose to make films which avoid the complex power hierarchies and industrial techniques of live action film.

In Vera Neubauer's *The World of Children* (1984) such a view is consciously proposed with its use of defiantly crude and limited technique; often so crude as to almost loose the thread of visual fascination that strings the film together. It uses these techniques to present viewpoints outside the dominant discourse, viewpoints of women and children. But this approach is made more complex by the intercutting of live-action into the animation. The live action is also extremely, defiantly, technically crude. However, the composite language the films speak is sophisticated, and has clear references to the tradition of collage artists as well as such film-makers as Stan Brakhage.

Certainly there is a strand of work where women directors' films work with confrontational material and are complex grammatically, but rudimentary technically. Kayla Parker's *A Cage of Flame* (1993) presents a de-sanitised view of women's menstruation; a tumult of mixed media animation including pixillated crimson berries spiralling on a woman's belly, seeds coated in viscous blood-like juice, dancing calligraphic hand-drawn animation, a pixillated woman bursting up through the root structures of a tree and imploding vulva-shaped calligraphy. The film is an assertion of a subjective and mythic view of women which the film-maker states is 'a counter to the sanitised, pastel pretty version we are conditioned to accept.'[13]

Animator Ruth Lingford has commented 'women animators seemed more concerned with the content of their work than with form or technical experimentation'.[14] Although ironically, her own films have experimented with a range of techniques both traditional and low-tech digital on an Amiga home computer. Ruth Lingford's *What She*

Within/Without – Benita Raphan (1994)

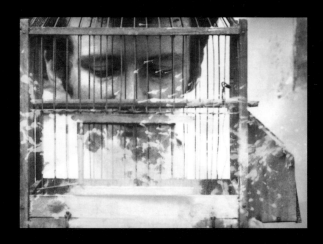

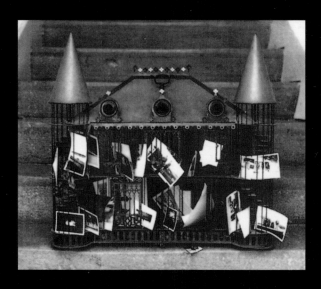

Wants (1994) is a film that asserts women's subjectivity in relation to the received media images. The sexual fantasies of the female protagonist inter-penetrate (literally) images of consumer desire. The woman travels on the tube, staring into her vulva-shaped purse. Subsequent scenes of sex manage to combine references to Goya, food, blow-jobs, birth and shopping to create a sequence of hungry sexuality and violent neediness. On a journey surrounded by advertising hoardings, shoppers and beggars who constantly swell and distend like blood flushed genitals, the 'heroine's' erogenous zone swells grotesquely. She quite literally shops till she drops, or at least detumesces. The consequence of the mode of production of these films is that they confront intimate issues including the film-maker's private anxieties and fantasies in an unusually direct way. They are films that are close to home in a number of ways...

PURE VISUAL TECHNOLOGY[15]

> These images of landscapes 'beyond imagination' do not seem to exhibit the poetry that we have come to associate with the traditional oeuvre of poetic form like abstract painting for instance. The mathematical objects coaxed out of their remote worlds of ideality by electronic visualisation make no appeal to us through any aesthetic language of pictorial forms... they bypass the poetic and become pure visual technology.[16]

Abstract animation, previously the most artisan and low-tech of forms, (often marks painted, scratched and cut into film direct) also has fallen under the digital spell. Work such as *Biogenesis* (William Latham 1993), and *The Arcana of the Primordial Numerological Flux* (Sean Fitzgerald) create abstract forms that derive directly from complex algorithmic programmes and chaos maths. This has had the effect of transforming the grammar of abstract animation away from references to painting and the cinematic apparatus towards something quite new.

The steady leakage of the work of such animators into advertising, special effects and fiction films, shows there is an increasing drive to contextualise and create meaning for such imagery with narrative. Digital imaging has increased the drive in visual media towards bricolage, which started with modernist and cubist painting and arguably with the invention of the film cut itself. And its acceleration constitutes a significant move in film culture towards the previously marginal 'Tradition of Méliès'.

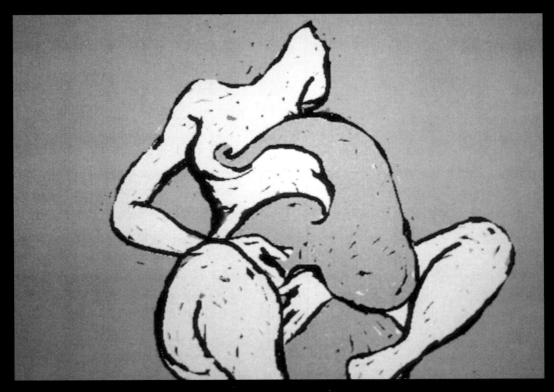

A SELECTION ON AN IMAGE CAN BE CUT, COPIED, PASTED OR DELETED, AS WELL AS TRANSFORMED BY SKEWING, DISTORTING, STRETCHING, ROTATING AND FLIPPING.[17]

Increasingly sophisticated computers such as the Quantel Harry and the Flame are used to layer disparate elements in a single film frame. And animators have been quick to take up the new tools in ways that confound any clear distinction between animation and live action. It is also significant that almost all the film-makers active in this area have directed or produced commercials, thus gaining technical experience, and developing a visual grammar with the new media, plus personal contact with the powerful post-production houses.

David Anderson is such an animator, who primarily makes commercials. In his films *Deadtime Stories for Big Folk* (1989) and *Door* (1990) he has relentlessly collaged images derived from entirely different techniques. Using a range of techniques that almost constitutes a catalogue of possibilities of animation both films are driven by acerbic monologues written by Russell Hoban. The voice acts to bind models, pixilation, photographs and graphic elements together. His recent film *In the Time of Angels* (1994) exercises this magpie aesthetic with a smooth illusionistic narrative space created by careful digital matting of disparate events and elements. A gothic tale of a young woman struggling to turn back time and undo a fatal mistake, it takes certain traditional elements of animation narrative grammar and replays them within a live action special effects film. In contrast, Mario Cavelli's *Soho Square* (1992) uses new technology to create a simulacra of hand-drawn animated film. Observational footage shot on *Soho Square* was re-enacted in a studio with elaborately costumed actors. The resulting footage was then traced and re-coloured by hand on a Quantel Harry and Paintbox. The result is a digital version of the traditional strategy of Rotoscope and hand-drawn animation. The resultant film possibly re-invents the wheel, but its colour and graphic appeal has resulted in the technique being used for a number of commercials and a TV Opera production.

VIDEO BECOMES VISCERAL[18]

Work such as Daniel Reeves' *Obsessive Becoming* (1995), my own *The Temptation of*

Sainthood (1993), and work by John Maybury such as *Remembrance of Things Fast* (1993) integrates animation and digital montage within work that is not primarily driven by the concerns of animation. Within this strand are film-makers who are using animation techniques to disrupt the stable characters and narratives of classical cinema, and express that part of human experience which is in excess of the discourses of rationality, 'character' and fixable identity. What makes the work new is that the balance is radically different to a traditional model of special effects. The distorted and grotesque, the artificial and animated is not an eruption into a primarily ordered world, it is the dominant discourse in the films. For example, *Obsessive Becoming* traces an autobiography of secrecy, bigamy and child abuse through a voice-over set against clips of family home-movies and snapshots that constantly morph and distort into each other. The familiar smiles of a family album decompose into a fluid, twisting mesh of faces which express powerfully the sense of a family whose taboos and boundaries are constantly violated.

Such work points to the traces of animation as they disappear into a film culture where the boundaries between live action and animation is increasingly unclear. What is clear is that as the boundaries shift, a new breed of Paintbox and Harry operators are acquiring a significant cluster of animation skills, slowly displacing the traditional picture of the animator hunched over a lightbox and pegbar. Traditional demarcations and definitions of animation increasingly fail in the face of a continuum of moving image techniques that range from relatively unmediated recording of the real world to the highly artificial creation of worlds that exist only in the human imagination, or the previously unseen world of complex chaos maths.

We are at a point where classical narrative cinema is already being discussed as a specifically twentieth century art form, and an explosion in the creation and distribution of images of all kinds is creating a culture of bricolage. At the same time, philosophically and psychologically, the notion of the stable measured subject has been increasingly eroded. We are left with a hyper-subjectivity, amid a plethora of discourses of fragmentation. Consequently the forms traditionally used to describe the monstrous (plasticity of special effects and stop motion of horror films), the magic (Méliès), the marginal, childish and grotesque (animation as a genre within film), are being used more and more to describe our experience as Post-Modern subjects. We find ourselves surveying the possibility that indeed the monster may eat the film.

NOTES

1 A suggestion made by the science fiction novelist Simon Ings in conversation.

2 Programme note *São Paulo International Short Film Festival* 1994.

3 'Imaginez Autre Chose'. (Ben Vautier. Belgian Surrealist, 1935).

4 See *Afterimage* no 13 Autumn 1987.

5 Brothers Quay interview. *City Limits*. Jonathan Romney.

6 Ibid.

7 Quay interview with Simon Pummell. 21.6.95 Unpublished.

8 Ibid.

9 Ibid.

10 Susan Young in an interview with Simon Pummell, May 1995. Unpublished.

11 Graphics computers for manipulating and layering video images.

12 Ruth Lingford describing her feelings when she animates personal or transgressive passages of her work. *Under the Radar - A Study of Transgression in Animation*. M.A. Thesis. Royal College of Art, 1991.

13 Kayla Parker's synopsis of film in publicity material.

14 *Under the Radar* op cit.

15 'Visual Technology and the Poetics of Knowledge' Richard Wright, paper presented at Animation Studies Conference, West Surrey College of Art and Design. November 1993.

16 Ibid.

17 Adobe Photoshop Manual. 1985

18 Description of Cronenburg's *Videodrome* in 'Who Programs You? The Science Fiction of Spectacle' Scott Bukatman in *Alien Zone* ed. Annette Kuhn, 1990.

Selected
Bibliography

A bibliography including writings on individual artists can be found in Curtis (ed) *A Dictionary of British Film and Video Artists* cited below.

Afterimage English Independent Cinema, no 6, Summer, 1976

Afterimage Of Angels and Apocalypse..... Special Issue on Derek Jarman, no 12, Autumn, 1985

Akomfrah, John, Auguiste, Reece, Gilroy, Paul, Pines, Jim *'Handsworth Songs*: Some Background Notes - Audiences/Aesthetics/Independence' *Framework* no 35 2,1988

Blanchard, Simon and Harvey, Sylvia 'The Post-War Independent Cinema - Structure and Organisation' in *British Cinema History* eds James Curran & Vincent Porter, Weidenfeld & Nicolson, London, 1983

Cavalcanti, Alberto 'Presenting Len Lye' *Sight and Sound* vol 16 no 64 1947

Christie, Ian '"Has the Cinema a career?" Pictures and prejudice: the origins of British resistance to film' *Times Literary Supplement* no 4833, November 17 1995.

Christie, Ian 'The Odd Couple' in *Spellbound: Art and Film* Hayward Gallery/British Film Institute, London, 1996.

Cottringer, Anne 'On Peter Gidal's Theory and Definition of Structural/Materialist Film' *Afterimage* no 6 Summer 1976

Curtis, David *Experimental Cinema*, Studio Vista, London, 1971

Curtis, David 'Where does one put Norman McLaren?' *Norman McLaren* ed Lindsay Gordon, Scottish Arts Council Catalogue, 1977.

Curtis, David 'The Artists Film/Avant Garde Film' in *Art inglesi oggi 1960-1976*, Catalogue. British Council/Commune di Milano, Milan, 1976.

Curtis, David & Dusinberre, Deke eds *A Perspective on English Avant-Garde Film*, Catalogue, Arts Council of Great Britain/British Council, London, 1978

Curtis, David 'The Economics of the Independent Film' *Cinema* (UK) no 2 March 1979

Curtis. David, *Len Lye* Catalogue, Watershed, Bristol, 1987

Curtis, David (ed) *A Directory of British Film and Video Artists*, Arts Council of England/John Libbey Media, London, 1996.

Drummond, Phillip 'Notions of Avant-garde Cinema' *Film as Film* Catalogue, Hayward Gallery Catalogue, London, 1979

Dunford, Mike 'Experimental/Avant-Garde/Revolutionary/Film/Practice *Afterimage* no 6 Summer 1976

Dusinberre, Deke 'The Other Avant-gardes' *Film as Film* Catalogue, Hayward Gallery Catalogue, London, 1979

Dusinberre, Deke 'On Expanding Cinema' *Studio International* vol 190 no 978 November/December 1975

Dusinberre, Deke 'See Real Images!' *Afterimage* nos 8/9 Spring 1981

Dusinberre, Deke 'St George in the Forest: the English Avant-Garde' *Afterimage* no 6 Summer 1976

Dusinberre, Deke 'Consistent Oxymoron - Peter Gidal's Rhetorical Strategy' *Screen* vol 18 no 2 Summer 1977

Dusinberre, Deke 'On British Avant-Garde Landscape Film' *Undercut* nos 7/8 Special Landscape Issue, Spring 1983

Dwoskin, Steve *Film Is* Peter Owen, London, 1975.

Eaton, Mick 'The Avant-Garde and Narrative' *Screen* vol 19 no 2 Summer 1978

Field, Simon 'Comment' [to Greenaway's The Falls] *The New Social Function of Cinema, Catalogue British Film Institute Productions* 79/80, eds Rod Stoneman & Hilary Thompson, London, 1981

Field, Simon 'Editorial; The Troublesome Case' *Afterimage* no 12 Autumn 1885.

Field, Simon and O'Pray, Michael 'On Imaging October, Dr Dee and Other Matters: An interview with Derek Jarman' *Afterimage* no 12 Autumn 1985.

Gidal, Peter *Andy Warhol: Films and Paintings The Factory Years* (with new introduction) Da Capo Press 1991 (originally published Studio Vista, 1971).

Gidal, Peter 'Theory and Definition of Structural/Materialist Film' *Studio International* vol 190 no 978 November/December 1975

Gidal, Peter *Structural Film Anthology*, British Film Institute, London 1976

Gidal, Peter 'The Anti-Narrative 1978' *Screen* vol 20 no 2 Summer, 1979

Gidal, Peter 'Technology and Ideology in/through/and Avant-Garde Film: An Instance' in *The Cinematic Apparatus* eds Teresa de Lauretis & Stephen Heath London: Macmillan 1980

Gidal, Peter '13 Most Beautiful Women and Kitchen' *Undercut* no 1 Spring 1981

Gidal, Peter 'The Current British Avant-Garde Film: Some Problems in Context' *Undercut* no 2 Summer 1981

Gidal, Peter *'On Finnegan's Chin'* *Undercut* no 5 Summer 1982

Gidal, Peter 'Against Sexual Representation in Film' *Screen* vol 25 no 6 Nov-Dec 1984

Gidal, Peter *Materialist Film*, Methuen, London 199

Hamlyn Nicky 'Recent English Super 8 at B2 Gallery' *Undercut* nos 10/11 Winter/Spring 1983/4

Harvey, Sylvia 'The 'Other Cinema' in Britain: Unfinished business in oppositional and independent film 1929-1984' *All Our Yesterdays: 90 Years of British Cinema* ed Charles Barr, BFI, London, 1986.

Hartney, Mick 'The Cinema We Need? Some Notes on *Finnegan's Chin*' *Undercut* no 5 Summer 1982

Heath, Stephen 'Afterword' *Screen* vol 20 no 2 Summer, 1979

Higson, Andrew 'A Celebration of Cinema: The Leicester International Super 8 Festival' [Review] *Screen* vol 25 no 6 Nov-Dec 1984

Hodgkinson, Anthony W & Sheratsky, Rodney E. *Humphrey Jenning: More than a Maker of Films,* University Press of New England, 1982

Jarman, Derek *The Last of England* Constable, London, 1987

Keiller, Patrick 'The Poetic Experience of Townscape and Landscape and Some Ways of Depicting It' *Undercut* nos 3/4 Winter/Spring 1981/2

Kiernan, Joanna 'Reading *Light Reading*' *Undercut* nos 10/11 Winter/Spring 1983/4

Krikorian, Tamara *'On the Mountain* and *Land Makar:* Townscape and Landscape in Margaret Tait' *Undercut* Special Landscape Issue nos 7/8 Spring 1983

Le Grice, Malcolm 'Problematizing the Spectator Placement in Film' *Undercut* no 1 Spring 1981

Le Grice, Malcolm 'Towards temporal economy' *Screen* vol 20 nos 3/4 Winter 1979/80

Le Grice, Malcolm *Abstract Film and Beyond* Studio Vista, London 1977

Macpherson, Don ed *Tradition of Independence: British Cinema in the Thirties,* Brtish Film Institute, London, 1980

Manvell, Roger ed *Experiment in the Film,* Grey Walls Press, London, 1949

Mathee, Jean, 'On Wounds, Artificial Flowers, Orifices and the Infinite: A Response to the Films of Nina Danino' *Undercut* no 19 1990.

Maziere, Michael 'Lucy Panteli's *Motion Picture*' *Undercut* no 5 Summer 1982

Maziere, Michael 'John Smith's Films: Reading the Visible' *Undercut* nos 10/11 Winter/Spring 1983/4

Maziere, Michael 'Towards a Specific Practice' *Undercut* no 12 Summer 1984

Mellor, David, 'Sketch for an Historical Portrait of Humphrey Jennings' in *Humphrey Jennings: Film-Maker/Painter/Poet* ed Mary-Lou Jennings, British Film Institute/Riverside Studios, London, 1982

Mercer, Kobena 'Recoding Narratives of Race and Nation' *Black Film British Cinema* ed Kobena Mercer, ICA Documents 7, 1988

Mercer, Kobena 'Diaspora Culture and the Dialogic Imagination: The Aesthetics of Black independent Film in Britain' *Welcome to the Jungle: New Positions in Black Cultural Studies* Kobena Mercer, Routledge, London, 1994

Milne, Will 'My Film Work and Theoreticals' *Undercut* no 6 Winter 1982

Milner, Peter 'The London Film-Makers' Co-op: the Politics of Licence' *Undercut* nos 10/11 Winter/Spring 1983/4.

Mulvey, Laura (interviewed by Nina Danino & Lucy Moy-Thomas) *Undercut* no 6 Winter 1982

Mulvey, Laura and Wollen, Peter 'Written Discussion' *Afterimage* no 6 Summer 1976.

Neubauer, Vera (interviewed by Claire Barwell) *Undercut* no 6 Winter 1982

Nicolson, Annabel 'Filmy Tales' *Studio International* vol 190 no 978 November/December 1975

Nicolson, Annabel 'The London Film-Makers' Co-operative' *Framework* no 9 Winter 1978/79

Norris, Tim 'Notes on Modernism, Aesthetics and Psychoanalysis' *Undercut* nos 3/4 Winter/Spring 1981/2

O'Pray, Michael 'Authorship and Independent Cinema Exhibition' *Screen* vol 21 no 2 Summer 1980

O'Pray, Michael 'Modernism, Phantasy and Avant-Garde Film' *Undercut* nos 3/4 Winter/Spring 1981/2

O'Pray, Michael 'William and Marilyn Raban's Black and Silver' *Undercut* no 5 Summer 1982

O'Pray, Michael 'Movies, Mania and Masculinity' *Screen* vol 23 no 5, Nov-Dec 1982

O'Pray, Michael 'William Raban's Landscape Films: The Formalist Imagination' *Undercut* Special Landscape Issue nos 7/8 Spring 1983

O'Pray, Michael and Raban, William 'Interview with Chris Welsby' *Undercut* nos 7/8 Spring 1983

O'Pray, Michael 'In the Trenches' *Undercut* nos 10/11 Winter 1983-4

O'Pray, Michael 'Introduction' *British Film and Video 1980-1985: The New Pluralism Catalogue,* Tate Gallery, London, 1985.

O'Pray, Michael. Essay on Judith Goddard and Holly Warburton *Sound and Vision,* Exhibition Catalogue, Plymouth Arts Centre/Spacex Gallery 1985

O'Pray, Michael 'Tina Keane: Profile' *Performance* magazine, April/May 1988

O'Pray, Michael 'Borderline' *Art Monthly* May 1988

O'Pray, Michael 'The Elusive Sign: From Asceticism to Aestheticism' *The Elusive Sign: British Avant-Garde Film and Video 1977-1987* Catalogue, Arts Council of Great Britain/British Council, London, 1987

O'Pray, Michael 'The Aesthetic Impact of Film Printing Processes on British Avant-Garde Film Since 1966' *Issues* vol 2 no 1 Winter 1991-2.

O'Pray, Michael 'The British Avant-Garde and Art Cinema from the 1970s to the 1990s' in *Dissolving Views: Key Issues in British Cinema* ed Andrew Higson, Cassell, London, 1996.

Rayns, Tony 'Born to Kill: Mr Soft Eliminator' [on Jeff Keen] *Afterimage* no 6 Summer 1976

Rees, AL 'Conditions of Illusionism' *Screen* vol 18 no 3 Autumn 1977

Rees, A.L. 'Warhol Waves: The Influence of Andy Warhol on the British Avant-Garde Film' in *Andy Warhol: Film Factory* ed Michael O'Pray, British Film Institute, London, 1989.

Sheridan, Alan 'David Dye; Artist/Film-maker' *Studio International* vol 190 no 978 November/December 1975

Stoneman, Rod 'Film-related practice and the avant-garde' *Screen* vol 20 nos 3/4 Winter 1979/80

Undercut Special Landscape Issue nos 7/8 Spring 1983

Undercut Special Isssue: Cultural Identities no 17 Spring 1988

Undercut A Decade of British Experimental Film and Video Art no 19 Autumn 1990

Welsby, Chris (interviewed by Michael O'Pray and William Raban) *Undercut* Special Landscape Issue nos 7/8 Spring 1983

Willemen, Paul 'An Avant-Garde for the 80s' *Framework* no 24 Spring 1984

Willemen, Paul 'Voyeurism, the Look and Dwoskin' *Afterimage* no 6 Summer 1976

Williamson, Judith 'Two Kinds of Otherness: Black Film and the Avant-Garde' *Black Film British Cinema* ed Kobena Mercer, ICA Documents 7, 1988

Wollen, Peter 'The Two Avant-Gardes' *Studio International* vol 190 no 978 November/December 1975 reprinted in Peter Wollen *Readings and Writings,* Verso, 1982.

Wollen, Peter '"Ontology" and "Materialism" in Film' *Screen* vol 17 no 1 Spring 1976

Wollen, Peter 'Introduction' *Chris Welsby Films/Photographs/Writings,* Arts Council of Great Britain [undated 1980?]

Wollen, Peter 'Arrows of Desire' *Arrows of Desire: Second ICA Biennial of Independent Film & Video,* Catalogue, ICA, London, 1992.

Wyver, John '*What You See is What You Get I: Third ICA Biennial of Independent Film and Video,* Catalogue, ICA, London 1995.

Relevant Journals

Afterimage 1-13 (1971-1987)

Undercut 1-19 (1981- 1990)

Coil (1995-)

Pix (1993-)

Film stills acknowledgements to British Film Institute Stills Library for pp.36, 43, 44, 50, 64, 86, 91, 97, 132, 200, 247; Arts Council of England, Keith Griffiths (Koninck Films) and the film-makers.

Contributors Notes

Lindsay Anderson was a film-maker whose work included *This Sporting Life, If, Britannia Hospital.* He was a leading member of the Free Cinema in the 1950s. He died in 1994.

Martine Attille is a London-based film-maker and lecturer. A founding member of Sankofa film/video collective 1984-88. Her film include *Dreaming Rivers* (1988) and *Urban Loving* (1996)

Reece Auguiste is a member of the Black Audio Film Collective. His films include *Twilight City* (1989), *Mysteries of July* (1991), *Moment of Sacrifice* (1992). He has taught film theory in England, Canada, Switzerland and USA and published in Undercut, Framework and Cineaction among other journals.

Roland Cosandey teaches at the Ecole cantonale d'art de Lausanne. He is a specialist in early film history and Swiss cinema history. He contributes regularly to many European film journals and is the author of *Welcome Home Joye! Film um 1910 - Aus der Sammlung Joseph Joye* (1993) and co-editor of *An Invention of the Devil? Religion and Early Cinema* (1992) and also of *Cinema sans frontieres 1896-1918 Images Across Borders: Internationality in World Cinema* (1995)

David Curtis is Film and Video Officer at the Arts Council of England. He is the author of *Experimental Cinema* (1971) and has published widely on avant-garde cinema. He has organised many film exhibitions including Film as Film, Robert Breer, Len Lye and Brothers Quay. He has been advisor/contributor on many television programmes including Doodlin' Impressions of Len Lye; New York Framed and Midnight Underground. He has contributed chapters to books on Jonas Mekas and Anthony Gross.

Deke Dusinberre was an influential critic and curator of British avant-garde film of the 1970s. He is now a translator and lives in Paris.

Steve Dwoskin was born in New York and moved to Britain in 1964 where he still lives and works. He has taught at the London College of Printing and Royal College of Art, London. He has always combined teaching with his work as a film maker, painter and photographer. He has made many films including *Behindert* (1974), *Silent Cry* (1977), *Outside In* (1981), *Further and Particular* (1988), *Face of Our Fear* (1992), *Trying to Kiss the Moon* (1995)

Robert Fairthorne made $X+X=0$ (with Brian Salt) in 1936 and was a writer and activist in the pre-War film avant-garde.

Peter Gidal's latest films include *Denials* (1986), *Guilt* (1988) and *Flare Out* (1992). He is the author of *Andy Warhol: Films and Paintings* (1971), *Structural Film Anthology* (1977), *Understanding Beckett: Monologue and Gesture* (1986), *Materialist Film* (1989). He has published in *Studio International, Artforum, Undercut, Screen* and *Parkett* among other journals. His most recent essay '*The Polemics of Paint*' was published by d'Offay Publications (1995).

Nicky Hamlyn is a film-maker and lecturer in Time Based Media at the Kent Institute of Art Design. He was a founding member of the *Undercut* editorial collective and has published widely on avant-garde cinema.

Stephen Heath was a member of the *Screen* editorial board in the 1970s; a number of his essays on film for *Screen* and other journals are collected in *Questions of Cinema* (1981).

Isaac Julien was a co-founder of Sankofa in 1983. His films include *Young Soul Rebels* (1991) *The Attendant* (1992)and *Black and White in Colour* (1992) He edited (with Kobena Mercer) 'The Last Special Issue on Race?' *Screen* 1988 and has published widely on cinema.

Catherine Kinley (Lacey) studied fine art at St Martins School of Art 1963-7 and at the Royal College of Art. Since 1978 she has been a curator with special responsibility for British art in the Modern Collection of the Tate Gallery, London. She was a member of the Arts Council Artists Film and Video Committee 1984-7.

Malcolm Le Grice is Professor of Video and Digital Media at the University of Westminster. An originator of the British experimental film movement in the 1960s, he has made many films. In 1990, his film *Sketches for a Sensual Philosophy* was broadcast on Channel 4. He is the author of *Abstract Film and Beyond* (1977) and has published widely on avant-garde cinema.

Laura Mulvey is the author of *Visual and Other Pleasures* (1989), *Citizen Kane* (1992)) and *Fetishism and Curiosity* (1996). She has also directed films in collaboration with Peter Wollen. Having taught film practice and theory in Universities both sides of the Atlantic, she is now Post-graduate Studies Co-Ordinator at the British Film Institute.

Simon Pummell makes films combining animation with live-action which include *Surface Tension* (1986), *Secret Joy* (1991), *Stain* (1992), *Temptation of Sainthood* (1993) and *Rose Red and Butchers Hook* (1994). His films have won numerous awards and have been broadcast internationally. His is currently developing his first feature film.

Lis Rhodes lives and works in London. Artist, writer, film and video maker since the 70s, she has also done performances and installations. Her works are in several permanent collections and have been exhibited and screened widely. She teaches at the Slade School of Fine Art, University College, London.

Rod Stoneman has been the Chief Executive of Bord Scannan na hEireann (the Irish Film Board) since 1993. Before that he worked as Deputy Commissioning Editor in the Independent Film and Video Department at Channel Four, London. He has made a number of documentaries and written on film and television in *Screen*, *Afterimage, Sight and Sound* and *Film Ireland*.

Peter Wollen has written *Signs and Meaning in the Cinema*, *Raiding the Icebox* and *Singing in the Rain*. He co-directed a series of films with Laura Mulvey including *Penthesilea, Riddles of Sphinx* and co-wrote the script for Antonioni's *The Passenger*. He also directed his own film *Friendship's Death*.

Virginia Woolf (1882-1941) is one of the most influential writers of the twentieth century. A prominent member of the Bloomsbury group, her novels include *To the Lighthouse, Orlando* and *The Waves*.

Name Index